CLASSICAL PRESENCES

## CLASSICAL PRESENCES

The texts, ideas, images, and material culture of ancient Greece and Rome have always been crucial to attempts to appropriate the past in order to authenticate the present. They underlie the mapping of change and the assertion and challenging of values and identities, old and new. Classical Presences brings the latest scholarship to bear on the contexts, theory, and practice of such use, and abuse, of the classical past.

# Conversing with Antiquity

*English Poets and the Classics, from Shakespeare to Pope*

DAVID HOPKINS

OXFORD
UNIVERSITY PRESS

OXFORD
UNIVERSITY PRESS

Great Clarendon Street, Oxford OX2 6DP

Oxford University Press is a department of the University of Oxford.
It furthers the University's objective of excellence in research, scholarship,
and education by publishing worldwide in

Oxford New York

Auckland Cape Town Dar es Salaam Hong Kong Karachi
Kuala Lumpur Madrid Melbourne Mexico City Nairobi
New Delhi Shanghai Taipei Toronto

With offices in

Argentina Austria Brazil Chile Czech Republic France Greece
Guatemala Hungary Italy Japan Poland Portugal Singapore
South Korea Switzerland Thailand Turkey Ukraine Vietnam



Published in the United States
by Oxford University Press Inc., New York



First published 2010



British Library Cataloguing in Publication Data
Data available

Library of Congress Cataloging in Publication Data
Library of Congress Control Number: 2009935902

Typeset by SPI Publisher Services, Pondicherry, India
Printed in Great Britain
on acid-free paper by
MPG Books Group, Bodmin & King's Lynn

ISBN 978–0–19–956034–9

# Contents

*Preface* vi

Introduction: Reception as Conversation 1

1. 'The English Homer': Shakespeare, Longinus, and English 'Neoclassicism' 37
2. Cowley's Horatian Mice 55
3. The English Voices of Lucretius, from Lucy Hutchinson to John Mason Good 88
4. 'If He Were Living, and an *Englishman*': Translation Theory in the Age of Dryden 113
5. Dryden and the Tenth Satire of Juvenal 130
6. Dryden's 'Baucis and Philemon' 163
7. Nature's Laws and Man's: Dryden's 'Cinyras and Myrrha' 177
8. Dryden and Ovid's 'Wit out of Season': 'The Twelfth Book of Ovid his *Metamorphoses*' and 'Ceyx and Alcyone' 202
9. Translation, Metempsychosis, and the Flux of Nature: Dryden's 'Of the Pythagorean Philosophy' 238
10. Some Varieties of Pope's Classicism 250
11. Pope's Trojan Geography 270
12. Colonization, Closure, or Creative Dialogue? The Case of Pope's *Iliad* 293

*Bibliography* 311
*Acknowledgements* 333
*Index* 335

# *Preface*

This book collects, in a substantially corrected, revised, and updated form, and with an entirely new Introduction, studies published over a number of years, all of which are concerned with seventeenth- and eighteenth-century English poets' relations with their classical predecessors. Most of the studies concern translation, and a central focus of the volume is the translated work of John Dryden, with which I have also been engaged elsewhere as critic and editor. The chapters were originally written on a variety of occasions and to a variety of commissions, but – or so friends and colleagues have been kind enough to suggest – form parts of a coherent intellectual enterprise which justifies revising and presenting them as a single sequence. The volume is unified by a commitment to a view of English poets' dealings with the classical past as a process of dialogue or conversation between past and present – a notion which I attempt to describe, with reference to some recent scholarly debates, in the Introduction, and to which I return explicitly in the final chapter.

Work of the interdisciplinary nature represented by this volume is necessarily indebted to the work of many other scholars in both English and classics. Specific debts are registered in my text in the normal way, but I would like to take this opportunity to acknowledge the more general assistance I have received in the course of my work. For various kinds of support, encouragement, friendship, and advice, I am indebted to John Barnard, Richard Bates, Colin Burrow, Greg Clingham, Robert Cummings, Paul Davis, Howard Erskine-Hill, Edward Forman, Robert Fowler, Christine Gerard, Philip Hardie, James Hopkins, Derek Hughes, Ronald Hutton, Emrys Jones, Duncan Kennedy, Alexander Lindsay, John Mason, the late J. C. Maxwell, the late D. F. McKenzie, David Norbrook, Fred Parker, Jan Parker, Lois Potter, Claude Rawson, Pat Rogers, Felicity Rosslyn, Christopher Rowe, Niall Rudd, Cedric D. Reverand II, Philip Smallwood, Robin Sowerby, Garth Tissol, Charles Tomlinson, Tim Webb, Judith Williams, James Anderson Winn, and David Womersley. The University of Bristol Institute of Greece, Rome, and the Classical

Tradition, of whose Executive Board I am a member, has provided a supportive and enriching environment in which to pursue my kind of work. I have greatly benefited from my collaboration with Stuart Gillespie on Volume III of *The Oxford History of Literary Translation in English* (2005) and on our edition of *The Dryden–Tonson Miscellanies, 1684–1709* (2008). Paul Hammond, to whose scholarship and counsel I am deeply indebted, has been a friend and collaborator over many years. Tom Mason has long shared my literary enthusiasms, and has constantly afforded me the benefit of his learning, wisdom, and fellowship. I am extremely fortunate to have been able to exchange ideas on an almost daily basis with Charles Martindale. My wife Sandra has scrutinized my work with sharp intelligence, and has helped me to clarify my thought (and prose) in countless ways. I am grateful to Hilary O'Shea for her interest in the project, and to Lorna Hardwick and Jim Porter for paying me the compliment of including my book in their series. My longest standing debt is to the late H. A. Mason, whose teaching first stimulated my interest in English / classical literary relations, and whose work, published and unpublished, has remained a constant source of inspiration.

## A NOTE ON TEXTS AND ABBREVIATIONS

Quotations from classical authors are taken from the Loeb Classical Library editions. Prose translations are also from these editions, modified where necessary. Significant discrepancies between the Loeb texts and those used by seventeenth- and eighteenth-century English writers are noted *ad loc.*

The following abbreviations are regularly used throughout the book:

***Poems***: *The Poems of John Dryden*, ed. Paul Hammond and David Hopkins, Longman Annotated English Poets, 5 vols. (London, 1995–2005).

***TE***: *The Twickenham Edition of the Poems of Alexander Pope*, ed. John Butt et al., 11 vols. (London, 1939–69).

***Works***: *The California Edition of the Works of John Dryden*, ed. E. N. Hooker, H. T. Swedenberg Jr. et al., 20 vols. (Berkeley, Los Angeles CA, London, 1956–2000).

# Introduction: Reception as Conversation

The classical past is a pervasive presence in English poetry from the early Middle Ages to the present day, and particularly in the centuries which are the main concern of the present volume. Many of the most prominent English poetic forms – epic, verse-tragedy, ode, formal satire, elegy, pastoral, verse-epistle – derive from classical precedent. English writers have regularly invoked what they took to be the assumptions and criteria of ancient literary criticism. And a long line of English poets has devoted substantial energy and practised artistry to the direct translation of Greek and Latin verse, a topic which will be a central concern of this book. Thus, when the late Philip Larkin remarked that 'to me the whole of classical and biblical mythology means very little, and I think that using them today not only fills poems full of dead spots but dodges the writer's duty to be original',[1] he was giving voice, in a deliberately provocative manner, to sentiments that he knew to be unrepresentative even of such well-known contemporaries as W. H. Auden and Louis MacNeice, let alone of the great poets of the past. English writers, to be sure, had often noted the dangers of excessive or injudicious use of classical material, or expressed more open hostility to classical influences. Thomas Carew, for example, had lamented the imminent return, of 'the goodly exil'd traine / Of gods and goddesses' which had been 'banish'd' during the 'just' poetic 'raigne' of John Donne. After Donne's death, Carew feared, 'The silenc'd tales o'th'Metamorphoses' would return to 'stuff' the lines of English poetry, and 'swell the windy Page' of English poets' work: English poets would, alas, be

[1] Philip Larkin, *Further Requirements: Interviews, Broadcasts, Statements, and Book Reviews, 1952–85* (London, 2001), p. 20.

once again 'Possest, or with Anacreons Extasie / Or Pindars, not their owne', and would indulge in

> The subtle cheat
> Of slie Exchanges, and the jugling feat
> Of two-edg'd words, or whatsoever wrong
> By ours was done the Greeke, or Latine tongue.[2]

In the following century, Samuel Johnson commented on the 'puerilities of obsolete mythology', noted that 'the heathen deities can no longer gain attention', and famously deplored what he thought to be Milton's academic and clichéd deployment of the conventions of ancient pastoral in *Lycidas*: 'Among the flocks and copses and flowers appear the heathen deities, Jove and Phoebus, Neptune and Aeolus, with a long train of mythological imagery, such as a College easily supplies.'[3] Later, William Blake inveighed against the classics after his own fashion: 'We do not want either Greek or Roman Models if we are but just & true to our own Imaginations, those Worlds of Eternity in which we shall live for ever in Jesus our Lord.'[4] But such objections coexisted with a larger agreement among English poets that the inclusion of classical material, if handled skilfully, in no way compromised the liveliness of their work. Nor did it compromise its originality, since the matter of the ancient poets could be creatively reworked and reinvented in an infinite number of ways.

Larkin's sub-romantic ideal of 'originality' – *sub*-romantic, because it does not fairly represent the views of the Romantic poets themselves (Shelley, it might be remembered, was a translator of Plato, Euripides, and the Homeric hymns)[5] – does, however, seem to be shared by some modern undergraduate students of English literature. Such students regularly become suspicious when con-

[2] Thomas Carew, 'An Elegie upon the Death of the Deane of Pauls, Dr. Iohn Donne', in *Poems*, ed. Rhodes Dunlap (Oxford, 1949), pp. 72–3.

[3] Samuel Johnson, *The Lives of the Most Eminent English Poets*, ed. Roger Lonsdale, 4 vols. (Oxford, 2006), 4. 138, 71; 1. 278–9. For further examples see Joseph Epes Brown, ed., *The Critical Opinions of Samuel Johnson* (Princeton NJ, 1926), s.v. 'Mythology'.

[4] William Blake, 'Preface' to *Milton: A Poem in 2 Books*, in *Complete Writings*, ed. Geoffrey Keynes (London, 1957), p. 480.

[5] For a detailed study, see Timothy Webb, *The Violet and the Crucible: Shelley and Translation* (Oxford, 1976).

fronted with the tradition of translated verse that once formed such a central part of the English poetic canon. How, they ask, can such works as Dryden's *Aeneid*, Pope's *Iliad*, or Ted Hughes's *Tales from Ovid* be thought of as great English poems when they are merely translations of *other* poets' work? And modern readers who have no familiarity with classical myth and history sometimes find the density of classical reference in older English poetry a serious obstacle to comprehension and pleasure. Some, to be sure, rise to the challenge and set about acquiring the requisite classical knowledge. ('Experience' is probably a better term than 'knowledge', since what is usually required is the memory of particular classical characters and stories rather than handbook information *about* the classical world.) Others take a less generous view, rejecting what they do not immediately comprehend. In this they are sometimes supported by teachers who themselves regard displays of classical knowledge as little more than the shared snobberies of a privileged elite whose heyday is mercifully over. With regard to translation, the situation described by Ezra Pound in the 1920s remains substantially the case today:

> Histories of English literature always slide over translation – I suppose it is inferiority complex – yet some of the best books in English are translations.[6]

Classically-grounded English verse, and particularly the translated verse which forms a central focus of the present volume, tends also to be neglected at the undergraduate level by students of classics. The decline in the teaching of classical languages has meant that many school and university classics courses are now taught entirely in translation. Students on such programmes are often inexperienced in earlier forms and styles of English, and thus find such texts as Dryden's *Aeneid* and Pope's *Iliad* difficult to read. Since, moreover, the translations which form the basis of their course are being offered as substitutes for the originals, teachers tend to prefer modern academic versions, which appear to stick more closely to the paraphrasable content of those originals, to freer or more creative renderings. And since many students cannot read classical texts in the original languages, the study of the afterlife of the classical world, a

[6] Ezra Pound, 'How to Read', in *Literary Essays*, ed. T. S. Eliot (London, 1954), p. 34 (essay first published, 1927–28).

growing area in classics courses, tends to concentrate on broad cultural trends rather than the detailed interconnections between texts. For all these reasons, classical students rarely encounter the body of English poetry which engages most closely with the culture and writing of Greece and Rome.

At the scholarly level, of course, there have been more detailed and energetic attempts to explore the area in which classical and English literatures intersect. In times past such study was customarily categorized under such headings as 'The Classical Tradition', 'Classical Heritage', 'Classical Background', or 'Classical Influence'. These terms have increasingly come to seem unsatisfactory, since they suggest an inertia and passivity in the way that classical elements are assimilated by later cultures. They also evoke a cosily reverential attitude to the past, in which the art and thought of the classical world are seen as legacies to be preserved intact and in trust, rather than a body of material which might provoke more creative engagement – perhaps, indeed, being actively resisted, or radically re-oriented. Nowadays, the preferred term for the relation between later periods and the classical past is 'Reception' (a term which, incidentally, itself does not entirely escape the suggestions of passivity and inertia associated with those it has displaced), and it seems appropriate in this Introduction to locate the concerns of the present book within the areas of enquiry currently being pursued under that head, particularly with regard to the reception of classical poetry.[7]

Recent debates about the reception of classical poetry have tended to polarize into two camps which, though their representatives sometimes differ widely on particulars, might be broadly categorized as 'historicism' and 'reception aesthetics'. In 1993 Charles Martindale launched a forthright attack on what he characterized as the 'positivist, empiricist, referential, and realist' assumptions which, in his view, have underpinned much traditional study of the classical past.

[7] For larger surveys of the field of classical reception, see particularly Mary Beard and John Henderson, *Classics: A Very Short Introduction* (Oxford, 1995); Lorna Hardwick, *Reception Studies*, Greece and Rome New Surveys in the Classics, No. 33 (Oxford, 2003); Charles Martindale and Richard F. Thomas, eds., *Classics and the Uses of Reception* (Oxford, 2006); Craig W. Kallendorf, ed., *A Companion to the Classical Tradition* (Oxford, 2007); Lorna Harwick and Christopher Stray, eds., *A Companion to Classical Receptions* (Oxford, 2008).

Traditional classicists' attempts to describe the past 'as it really was', Martindale argued, have led them to dismiss the later reception of ancient literature as a sequence of misunderstandings and irrelevances which have stood in the way of proper appreciation, and which it is the scholar's duty to correct.[8] A recent document produced by a group of distinguished classicists has, for example, declared its authors' belief 'that... ancient texts can only ever be truly understood in the social and cultural contexts which originally produced them if the layers of meaning which have become attached to them over the intervening centuries are systematically excavated and brought to consciousness'. The scholar's duty, the same authors continue, is to 'return' classical texts 'to their original producers, now separated... from the anachronistic meanings imposed upon them'.[9]

Such an approach has seemed, to Martindale and others, to be open to a number of obvious objections. Since great writers – it may reasonably be supposed – were capable of interrogating and extending rather than simply reflecting the stock assumptions and cliché wisdom of their 'age', why should it be assumed that their work can only properly be appreciated within frameworks of understanding familiar to their contemporaries? Shelley, after all, was not alone in believing that poets 'were called in the earlier epochs of the world legislators or prophets', because a poet 'not only beholds intensely the present as it is and discovers those laws according to which present things ought to be ordered but he beholds the future in the present, and his thoughts are the germs of the flower and the fruit of latest time'.[10] Matthew Arnold, similarly, spoke of the way in which some thinkers, by taking a 'stand against the inadequate ideals dominant in their time' have 'kept open their communications with the future, lived with the future'.[11]

[8] See Charles Martindale, *Redeeming the Text: Latin Poetry and the Hermeneutics of Reception* (Cambridge, 1993) (quotation on p. 4.).

[9] C. J. Rowe and others, AHRB Doctoral Awards proposal, quoted in Martindale and Thomas, *Classics and the Uses of Reception*, p. 12.

[10] 'A Defence of Poetry' in *Shelley's Prose*, ed. David Lee Clark (Albuquerque NM, 1954), p. 279.

[11] Matthew Arnold, 'Falkland', in *Complete Prose Works*, ed. R. H. Super, 11 vols. (Ann Arbor MI, 1960–77), 8. 204.

Similar problems with traditional literary historicism occur when one considers the responses of readers. A recurrent element in literary historiography has been the attribution of common assumptions to historically-delimited 'interpretive communities'.[12] The appeal (quoted above) to 'the social and cultural contexts which originally produced' ancient texts makes an implicit attribution of this kind. And literary historians regularly invoke such categories as 'the Enlightenment response to Homer' or 'the Victorian attitude to Greek tragedy'. But such homogenizing moves collapse under close scrutiny. As William Empson once quipped, 'the idea that everyone held the same opinion at a given date, "the opinion of the time", is disproved as soon as you open a history book and find a lot of them killing each other because they disagreed'.[13] The point is developed by Charles Martindale:

> What we call 'our' time is always something made up of fragments of 'the past'. Similarly the boundaries we select for historical definition are always, from some other perspectives, tendentious, or arbitrary, or hegemonic. We privilege a 'period', or a 'culture', which we then define, and characterize, on the basis of our selection, eliding innumerable possible differences of place, life-style and discourse. Periodization – like the division into Antiquity and the Middle Ages, or Republic and Empire – is so engrained that we take it for granted (we can call this 'the ideology of periodization'). Similarly, since the 'present' is not one thing, the difference between the past and present need not be seen as *necessarily* greater than the difference which exists today within a single 'culture'; thus 'understanding' some Romans may not be more difficult than understanding some of our fellow citizens.[14]

If there are such radical discontinuities as is sometimes implied between the mentality of past writers and readers and those of later times, by what means can past mentalities be understood at all? How can we be sure that 'our' responses to the past are any less anachronistic and appropriative than those of our predecessors? Will future ages treat us any less kindly in this respect than we treat our forebears?

[12] The phrase is Stanley Fish's in *Is There a Text in this Class? The Authority of Interpretive Communities* (Cambridge MA, 1980).

[13] William Empson, 'Mine Eyes Dazzle', *Essays in Criticism*, 14 (1964), 80–6 (p. 85).

[14] Martindale, *Redeeming the Text*, p. 10.

*We* think our *Fathers* Fools, so *wise* we grow;
Our *wiser Sons*, no doubt, will think *us* so.[15]

But, it has been suggested, the gap between 'our' thought and that of the past might not be as unbridgeable as such despairing rhetorical questions might suggest. In an important study, the philosopher Bernard Williams has reminded us of the degree to which we are, more than we customarily acknowledge, *products* of the very classical culture that is the object of our study:

The ancient Greeks . . . are among our cultural ancestors, and our view of them is intimately connected with our view of ourselves. That has always been the particular point of studying their world. It is not just a matter, as it may be in studying other societies, of our getting to know about human diversity, other social or cultural achievements, or, again, what has been spoiled or set aside by the history of European domination. To learn those things is an important aid to self-understanding, but to learn about the Greeks is more immediately part of self-understanding. It will continue to be so even though the modern world stretches round the earth and draws into itself other traditions as well. Those other traditions will give it new and different configurations, but they will not cancel the fact that the Greek past is specially the past of modernity.[16]

Engaging with Greek thought, therefore, Williams argues,

is not a question of *reviving* anything. What is dead is dead, and in many important respects we would not want to revive it even if we knew what that would mean. What is alive from the Greek world is already alive and is helping (often in hidden ways) to keep us alive.[17]

In the course of his plea for a more adequate conception of classical literary reception, Charles Martindale suggested that the positivist agenda of earlier scholarship should be replaced by one inspired by the hermeneutic theories of Hans Georg Gadamer, Hans Robert Jauss, and Wolfgang Iser, theories which figure reception not as 'the handing down of material from the past to the present' but as an enterprise which involves 'the *active* participation of readers (including readers

[15] Alexander Pope, *An Essay on Criticism*, 438–9 (*TE*, 1. 288).
[16] Bernard Williams, *Shame and Necessity* (Berkeley, Los Angeles CA, London, 1993), p. 3.
[17] Ibid., p. 7.

who are themselves creative artists) in a two-way process, backward as well as forward, in which the present and past are in dialogue with each other'.[18] Such views have some affinities with T. S. Eliot's belief that a proper appreciation of the operations of literary tradition, which involves an awareness 'not only of the pastness of the past, but of its presence', should cause one to 'not find it preposterous that the past should be altered by the present as much as the present is directed by the past'.[19] Such conceptions would suggest that literary reception – whether in the form of discursive commentary or artistic recreation – is to be seen not as an optional (and perhaps undesirable) appendage to the examination of the past 'as it really was' but as an essential part of any fully self-conscious investigation of the significance and interest of older literary works.

Over the last two decades, the historicist study of classical literary reception has taken a more explicitly political and ideological turn. Where earlier historicists had ascribed later interpreters' misunderstandings of the classical past, unsympathetically but unperturbedly, to the quaint delusions of their respective 'periods', more recent scholars have taken a sterner moral line, castigating their predecessors for the ideological blinkers (political, religious, sexual, racial) which, they think, have compromised their responses to classical antiquity (as well as some aspects of antiquity itself). In response to this trend towards 'ideology critique', there have been calls for a return to the aesthetics of Immanuel Kant, and particularly to the famous account of 'the judgement of taste' in Kant's Third Critique (1790).[20]

Modern Kantians have been particularly attracted by the philosopher's stress on the direct, unpredictable, and disinterested – though not dispassionate – encounter of readers (or viewers, or listeners) with the object of their attention. Kant's stress on the role of the receiving mind in any act of aesthetic judgement, they believe, usefully dissolves 'the sharp distinction between antiquity

[18] Charles Martindale, 'Reception' in Kallendorf, *A Companion to the Classical Tradition*, p. 298.

[19] T. S. Eliot, 'Tradition and the Individual Talent', in *Selected Essays* (2nd edition, London, 1934), pp. 14–15.

[20] See, particularly, Charles Martindale, *Latin Poetry and the Judgement of Taste: An Essay in Aesthetics* (Oxford, 2005).

itself and its reception over the centuries',[21] according to which reception was thought to 'tell us only about the receiving culture, little or nothing about the work received', and where *what* it told us about the receiving culture was all too often merely a catalogue of 'quaint practices' or 'errors we have outgrown',[22] – or, in the more recent historicisms, of outmoded assumptions about race, class, or gender.[23]

Unrepentant advocates of 'ideology critique' have retorted that Kantian aesthetics offers an unsatisfactory model of reception as an encounter between lone original and lone receiver, which underplays the ways in which a receiver's response to his or her source is influenced by other texts, by the contingent circumstances (cultural, social, political, religious) surrounding both source and receiver, and by influences or circumstances – such as the historically-determined elements in the very language which poets deploy – beyond the contributing parties' ken or control. The Kantian emphasis on the 'disinterested' nature of aesthetic response, they have argued, demands a separation of artistic from moral and political elements which, given the verbal nature of literary artefacts, is never possible, even if it were desirable. The universalizing claims of Kantian aesthetics, moreover, they have insisted, obscure the self-conscious awareness of past and present contingencies that is essential to any proper response to older artworks.[24]

The insistence of advocates of 'ideology critique' on the need for modern readers to register the 'otherness' of the past has been particularly prominent in recent work on translation. In a widely-discussed book, Lawrence Venuti has attempted to combine translation and post-colonial theory, suggesting that the most acceptable kind of renderings are those in the 'foreignizing' tradition, in which

[21] Martindale and Thomas, *Classics and the Uses of Reception*, p. 4.

[22] Martindale, in Kallendorf, ed., *A Companion to the Classical Tradition*, p. 303.

[23] Charles Martindale, 'Dryden's Ovid: Aesthetic Translation', in *Translation and the Classic: Identity as Change in the History of Culture*, ed. Alexandra Lianeri and Vanda Zajko (Oxford, 2008), pp. 83–109 (p. 85).

[24] See particularly Simon Goldhill, 'Cultural History and Aesthetics: Why Kant is No Place to Start Reception Studies'. This essay is a reply to Charles Martindale's 'Performance, Reception, Aesthetics'; both are included in *Theorizing Performance: Greek Drama, Cultural History, and Critical Practice*, ed. Edith Hall and Stephe Harrop (London, forthcoming, 2010).

the translator deliberately emphasizes differences of idiom and assumption between source and rendering, thereby clearly signalling the 'alterity' of the source-text to native speakers of the receptor-language.[25] The more familiar 'domesticating' tradition (practised by the translators discussed in the present book), in which the original is fluently 'accommodated' to the linguistic and literary traditions of the receiving culture, and in which the translation thus 'reads naturally' to speakers of the host language, is stigmatized as an act of 'appropriation' or 'ethnocentric violence', in which the translator exercises an 'imperializing' or 'colonizing' control over his source. The 'domesticating' tendency of seventeenth- and eighteenth-century English verse translation, it is suggested, is a 'discursive sleight of hand' that 'masks the political interests' of the 'hegemonic classes' which it 'serves'.[26]

Where does the present book stand in relation to the debates briefly described above? A casual perusal of its contents will show that most of the essays which it contains concern the translation and reception of individual classical authors (Homer, Horace, Juvenal, Lucretius, Ovid) by individual English poets (particularly, but not exclusively, Abraham Cowley, John Dryden, and Alexander Pope). The book argues that the English poets' responses to the classics are not merely the expression of anachronistic misunderstandings or appropriative ideologies but have important things to tell and show us about classical poetry itself. It proceeds in the manner of much mainstream literary criticism, by offering detailed analyses of specific examples, and appealing to the reader's assent that the critic's conclusions, though necessarily personal, are neither merely idiosyncratic nor merely the predictable (though perhaps unacknowledged) by-products of some *a priori* ideological commitment or bias.[27] It questions, sometimes explicitly, sometimes more obliquely, a number of long-held assumptions both about particular authors and

[25] Lawrence Venuti, *The Translator's Invisibility: A History of Translation* (London, 1995; 2nd edition, 2008).

[26] Venuti, *The Translator's Invisibility* (1995 edition), p. 65.

[27] The view that all literary judgements are necessarily ideological in basis seems vulnerable, like all 'false consciousness' arguments, to an obvious objection: if it is true, then how has the unmasker of ideological bias himself escaped the ideological prison in which all others are trapped?

about the literary 'period' which it covers. It supports the conception of reading as an enterprise which involves 'the *active* participation of readers . . . in a two-way process, backward as well as forward'.[28] In all these respects, the book might seem to stand at some distance from historicism – of both the old-style positivist and new-style ideological forms – and to position itself firmly within the tradition of 'reception aesthetics'.

The book, however, is not unmindful of some of the important considerations insisted upon by both the positivist and culturalist traditions. It stresses repeatedly that, though acts of reception are necessarily made in and by individual minds, those minds are themselves already full of the imaginings, intuitions, and emotions of *other* human minds.[29] Thus, in Chapter 6, for example, I attempt to show how Dryden's response to an episode in Ovid's *Metamorphoses* was profoundly affected by Milton's response to the same episode, and by Christian allegorizations of Ovid's pagan tale. In Chapter 12, I draw attention to the way in which Pope's recreation of a speech in Homer's *Iliad* was significantly coloured by Dryden's rendering of a passage in Lucretius which had been, in its turn, indebted to Homer's speech. Reception and translation, the book suggests – and I return to this topic below – is never a lone encounter between two parties.

This book, moreover, regularly touches on historical, religious, political, biographical, or commercial factors in its discussions of particular literary texts. Philosophical matters, for example, necessarily come to the fore in the book's treatment of Cowley's Epicureanism (Chapter 2), and political factors in its discussions of Dryden's renderings of 'On the Pythagorean Philosophy' (from Book 15 of Ovid's *Metamorphoses*) and of Juvenal's Tenth Satire (Chapters 9 and 5). And Chapters 6 and 7 consider the specific challenges of rendering pagan texts in the very different moral and ethical climate of Christendom.

[28] Martindale, 'Reception', in Kallendorf, *A Companion to the Classical Tradition*, p. 298.

[29] This point, it should be emphasized, is also made by Martindale, in 'Performance, in Reception, Aesthetics', who notes that 'a reader is . . . never alone in the room with a book; there are always numerous other readers there with her, even if she is unconscious of them, all those other receivers who have left their traces in the text and helped to determine how it is read'.

Kantian aesthetics insists – indispensably in my view – on the necessary part played by considerations of beauty in discussions of art. But while the disinterested 'judgement of taste' in its pure form might seem appropriate to certain kinds of musical or visual art (a string quartet, for example, or an abstract painting), it is surely the case that, since the aesthetic appreciation of a poem's beauty can never be separated from an understanding of the poem's semantic content, it can never be entirely divorced from moral, philosophical, or political considerations.[30] Conversely, it is difficult to square the unashamedly affective language deployed by some ideological critics with their insistence that ideological and contextualizing considerations must take precedence over individual judgement in the contemplation of artworks from the past.[31]

Reception aesthetics has insisted repeatedly that 'meaning is always realized at the point of reception',[32] an emphasis that has been strengthened by the Kantian belief that the perception of beauty exists 'not in terms of knowledge of any quality inherent in the object but as a feeling of pleasure and displeasure in the perceiving subject'.[33] But literary response might perhaps be more usefully described as a complex *interaction* between perceiver and perceived. In this connection, F. R. Leavis's famous description of the literary-critical process offers a model of literary reading which seems to chime with the assumptions implicit in the work of the translator-critics discussed in this book, and which might also serve as a useful basis for students of their work:

You cannot point to [a] poem; it is 'there' only in the re-creative response of individual minds to the black marks on the page. But – a necessary faith – it

[30] The point is made by Goldhill in 'Cultural History and Aesthetics'.

[31] In his discussion, for example, of the 1910 London production of Richard Strauss's *Elektra* (used to illustrate the variety of agencies involved in the production and reception of a work of performance art), Goldhill describes Strauss's music as 'wonderful, fiercely modern, precisely violent and perversely sexual, searing, and thrilling'. Elsewhere he has written of the 'sublime' quality of Greek tragedy, and has noted its 'uncanny ability to transcend the specific', to 'resonate across the generations', and to 'speak intensely to modern audiences'. See Simon Goldhill, 'Cultural History and Aesthetics'; *Love, Sex, and Tragedy: How the Ancient World Shapes our Lives* (London, 2004), pp. 220, 215.

[32] Martindale, *Redeeming the Text*, p. 3.

[33] Martindale, *Latin Poetry and the Judgement of Taste*, p. 17.

> is something in which minds can meet... The implicit form of a [critical] judgment is: This is so, isn't it? The question is an appeal for confirmation that the thing *is* so; implicitly that, though expecting, characteristically, an answer in the form, 'yes, but' – the 'but' standing for qualifications, reserves, corrections. Here we have a diagram of the collaborative-creative process in which the poem comes to be established as something 'out there', of common access in what is in some sense a public world.[34]

Leavis, while recognizing that the qualities of a work of art can only be registered by a receiving mind, simultaneously acknowledges that there must be *something* 'in' the work being received, to which that receiving mind responds. He suggests that, as Tim Whitmarsh has recently put it, 'meaning is... not determined *solely* at the point of reception; it is the product of a complex dialogue between producer and receiver'.[35] The critic, like the translator, is answerable to 'something out there' – the artistic qualities of which can be described, as well as its formal properties – without there being any supposition that that 'something' is – as old-style positivist historicism believed – fixed, absolute, or 'objectively' knowable.

The model of literary reception offered by this book, as its title suggests, is one of conversation and dialogue, a model which, I hope, might go some way towards mending the rift between 'reception aesthetics' and 'historicism'. The conversation in question is conducted across time, and across large cultural divides. Though it might seem at first sight like a conversation between individuals, there are always more than two parties involved. Human beings never come to any conversation without a vast array of existing concepts, experiences, and reading. Conversations always involve the recollection, invocation, and questioning of *other* conversations. They occur at particular historical moments, but are not necessarily limited to the immediate concerns of those moments. The notion of conversation implies both difference and continuity between the parties involved. For conversations to be more than exercises in extended solipsism, participants must register the 'otherness' of their interlocutors, and proceed on the assumption that, while they may never

[34] F. R. Leavis, *Nor Shall My Sword: Discourses on Pluralism, Compassion, and Social Hope* (London, 1972), p. 62.

[35] Tim Whitmarsh, 'True Histories', in Martindale and Thomas, eds., *Classics and the Uses of Reception*, pp. 104–15 (p. 106).

fully grasp their 'essence' (if such an entity can, indeed, be said to exist), they can move towards them to some degree, momentarily escaping, or at least taking a momentary glimpse beyond, the prison-house of their own head and their own environment. But conversation also depends on some sense of continuity, some faith that, however alien their interlocutors' premises and findings might at first sight seem, some sense can be made of their utterances – a sense that does not merely involve rewriting those utterances so that they accord with the conversationalists' own. It might, indeed, involve re-writing the conversationalists' utterances so that they accord more closely with those of their interlocutors. One can be changed by a conversation, either by having one's existing ideas or assumptions overturned, or by being alerted to possibilities that one might have dimly registered, but would not have been able properly to focus without one's interlocutors' help. To conceive of translation, in particular, as conversation is to admit the possibility that a translation might transform one's appreciation of an original rather than simply confirm (or fail to confirm) an impression already derived from direct contact with the original or from secondary authorities. On such an assumption, translation can be seen, as it was by Ezra Pound and Dante Gabriel Rossetti,[36] as a form of literary criticism, which, like more discursive forms of criticism but with an embodied directness that offers a particular intimacy of access, might illuminate its subject in new and fruitful ways. The fact, moreover, that, as with discursive criticism, the critical insight offered by translation is dependent on intuitive sympathy as much as (or more than) mere head-knowledge might lead one to question Matthew Arnold's assertion that the only adequate judges of a translator are scholars, 'because scholars alone have the means of really judging him'.[37] For, just as scholars regularly derive illumination from discursive critics less learned but more sympathetically in tune with their subject than themselves, so might they benefit from the recreative insights of a

[36] See Ezra Pound, *Literary Essays*, p. 74; Dante Gabriel Rossetti, 'Preface' to *The Early Italian Poets from Ciullo D'Alcamo to Dante Alighieri* (London, 1861), p. viii: 'a translation (involving, as it does, the necessity of settling many points without discussion), remains perhaps the most direct form of commentary'.

[37] Matthew Arnold, 'On Translating Homer', in *Complete Prose Works*, ed. R. H. Super, 11 vols. (Ann Arbor MI, 1960–77), 1. 117.

translator-critic. Dryden may thus have been displaying more than merely a poet's arrogance in suggesting that he had 'discover'd' in his translations, 'some beauty yet undiscover'd by those Pedants [the '*Dutch* Commentators'], which none but a Poet cou'd have found' (*Works*, 3. 4). Similarly, Pope may have been indulging in more than professional self-aggrandizement when he described himself as 'one, who values the Authority of one true Poet above that of twenty Critics or Commentators'. For, it should be noted, he immediately qualified his comment by adding the following rider: 'But tho' I speak thus of Commentators, I will continue to read carefully all I can procure, to make up, that way, for my own want of a Critical understanding in the original Beauties of Homer'.[38] Pope, this shows, was not the victim of 'the popular belief that the scholar's effort to understand a text actually causes his imagination to atrophy', whereas 'a professional poet, no matter how many errors of detail he may make in translating another poet, must necessarily achieve "fidelity to the spirit of the original"'.[39] Scholarly knowledge, in Pope's view, was necessary but not sufficient for the understanding of a great poet's meaning and beauty.

Various common assumptions may seem to compromise the notion of reception and translation as conversation, particularly when applied to the period of literary history considered in this volume. It is often supposed that, for much of this period, English writers had such a strong sense of the continuity of human nature that they overlooked its differences, complacently assuming that all men and women, under the skin, were essentially inhabitants, like them, of the Age of Reason. Did not John Dryden, after all, famously claim that 'Mankind is ever the same, and nothing lost out of Nature'?[40] It is generally forgotten, however, that Dryden's sentence continues: '... though every thing is alter'd'. To consider Dryden's whole statement is to become aware that, rather than asserting a bland essentialism, it encompasses a bold paradox: Nature is constant; Nature changes over time *in every minute specific*. The remark is made,

[38] Alexander Pope, *Correspondence*, ed. George Sherburn, 5 vols. (Oxford, 1956), 1. 44.

[39] K. J. Dover, 'Translation: The Speakable and the Unspeakable', *Essays in Criticism*, 30 (1980), 1–8 (p. 2).

[40] John Dryden, Preface to *Fables Ancient and Modern* (*Works*, 7. 37–8).

significantly, in the context of a discussion of a great poet. It is only an artist with the 'comprehensive Nature' of Chaucer, Dryden suggests, who can reveal continuities in human nature that would otherwise remain hidden. Chapter 9 of the present book considers further how Dryden's thoughts on literary translation and reception are inextricably intertwined with his larger reflections on change and permanence in Nature.

The other great English 'Augustans' were no less aware than Dryden of the vast cultural and circumstantial differences that separated them from the ancients with whom they had such regular discourse. In his Preface to his translation of the *Iliad*, Pope registered in the clearest possible terms his realization of 'the *integral* role of a sense of its historical otherness to an aesthetic appreciation' of Homer's poem:[41]

> When we read *Homer*, we ought to reflect that we are reading the most ancient Author in the Heathen World; and those who consider him in this Light, will double their Pleasure in the Perusal of him. Let them think they are growing acquainted with Nations and People that are now no more; that they are stepping almost three thousand Years back into the remotest Antiquity, and entertaining themselves with a clear and surprizing Vision of Things no where else to be found, the only true mirror of that ancient World. By this means alone their greatest Obstacles will vanish; and what usually creates their Dislike, will become a Satisfaction.
>
> (*TE*, 7. 14)

Samuel Johnson, similarly, was convinced that 'To judge rightly of an author, we must transport ourselves to his time, and examine what were the wants of his contemporaries, and what were his means of supplying them',[42] and remarked tartly that 'Those who have no power to judge of past times but by their own, should always doubt their conclusions'.[43] Johnson's extreme admiration for Pope's *Iliad* ('a performance which no age or nation can pretend to equal') was dependent neither on a belief that Pope had transported Homer's 'essence' unchanged into English nor on the assumption that Pope

[41] Goldhill's phrasing in 'Cultural History and Aesthetics'.

[42] Samuel Johnson, *The Lives of the Most Eminent English Poets*, 2. 119.

[43] Ibid., 1. 270. For further examples, see Joseph Epes Brown, ed. *The Critical Opinions of Samuel Johnson*, s.v. 'Criticism: Historical Method'.

himself thought that he had done any such thing. Translation, Johnson knew – and knew that Pope knew –, depends as much on the resources and capabilities of the host writer and the host language as it does on those of the original. 'Pope,' Johnson affirmed, 'wrote for his own age and his own nation', at a time when – even more than for Virgil, who, though writing 'in an age nearer to Homer's time by eighteen hundred years', faced some of the same problems – 'mere nature would be endured no longer'. Pope's version is thus the result of numerous acts of compromise and negotiation – many of them searchingly discussed in the notes which accompany the translation itself – in which the English poet both adds 'elegances' to meet the demands of readers unwilling to take Homer's 'awful simplicity', 'artless grandeur', and 'unaffected majesty' head on, but also – and equally importantly – makes available to those readers systems of value and states of feeling far different from those current in their own culture. Pope, Johnson knew – and knew that Pope knew –, has added 'many *Ovidian* graces' that have lost Homer 'something of his sublimity'. But enough of what is distinctive has been preserved to ensure that Pope's version is a genuine translation of Homer, not merely a genteel updating like the recent heavily cut and rewritten French version by Houdar de la Motte.[44] The profit-and-loss balance of Pope's version needs to be judged with delicacy. If some qualities have been lost, there may have been some gains in bringing Homer's situations, which Johnson clearly feels he can appreciate to some extent 'in themselves', closer to the pulse of his contemporaries: 'To have added can be no great crime, if nothing be taken away. Elegance is surely to be desired, if it be not gained at the expense of dignity. A hero would wish to be loved, as well as to be reverenced.'[45]

Homer's *Iliad* provides a particularly apt instance of the idea of translation-as-conversation in practice. For Pope's translation of that work had been immediately preceded by a version of Book 1 of Homer's poem by the writer on whom he looked 'with the greatest

[44] On this translation, see Kirsti Simonsuuri, *Homer's Original Genius: Eighteenth-Century Notions of the Early Greek Epic (1688–1798)* (Cambridge, 1979), pp. 48–51, and Richard Morton, *Examining Changes in the Eighteenth-Century French Translations of Homer's* Iliad *by Anne Dacier and Houdar de la Motte* (Lewiston, Queenston, Lampeter, 2003).

[45] Johnson, *The Lives of the Most Eminent English Poets*, 4. 73–4.

veneration', and from whom he had claimed he had 'learned versification wholly'.[46] Such admiration, however, did not mean that Pope looked upon his great predecessor uncritically, or feel obliged to follow his precedent exactly.

John Dryden's translation of 'The First Book of Homer's *Ilias*' appeared in his last volume of verse, *Fables Ancient and Modern*, published in March 1700 when the poet was 68. He designed it, he tells us in the Preface to *Fables*, as 'an Essay to the whole Work'. His 'Intentions are', he says, 'to translate the whole *Ilias*; provided still, that I meet with those Encouragements from the Publick, which may enable me to proceed in my Undertaking with some Chearfulness.' He has, he tells us,

> found by Trial, *Homer* a more pleasing Task than *Virgil*... For the *Grecian* is more according to my Genius, than the *Latin* Poet.... *Virgil* was of a quiet, sedate Temper; *Homer* was violent, impetuous, and full of Fire. The chief Talent of *Virgil* was Propriety of Thoughts, and Ornament of Words: *Homer* was rapid in his Thoughts, and took all the Liberties both of Numbers, and of Expressions, which his Language, and the Age in which he liv'd allow'd him: *Homer*'s Invention was more copious, *Virgil*'s more confin'd.
>
> (*Works*, 7. 24, 28)

In a private letter to his friend, Charles Montagu Dryden repeats his affirmation that Homer is, he now thinks, 'a Poet more according to [his] Genius than Virgil', to whom, if he is 'encouragd' to the task by Montagu's 'favour', he hopes he may 'do... more justice, in his fiery way of writeing; which, as it is liable to more faults, so it is capable of more beauties, than the exactness, & sobriety of Virgil.'[47]

The intensity of Dryden's self-identification with Homer's 'fiery way of writeing' might lead one to expect an idiosyncratically personal rendering of Book 1. Dryden did indeed engage with Homer in fresh and – especially for those coming to the version from his Virgil – surprising ways. But his translation was by no means an unaided effort. Dryden – as scholarship has long since established, and as later chapters in the present book will confirm – 'researched' each of his translations with extraordinary care, ranging around the commentators and his translator-predecessors for hints as how best

[46] Joseph Spence, *Observations, Anecdotes, and Characters of Books and Men*, ed. James M. Osborn, 2 vols. (Oxford, 1966), 1. 25, 24.

[47] John Dryden, *Letters*, ed. Charles E. Ward (Durham NC, 1942), p. 121.

to convey the 'spirit' of his chosen author. But it was not until the appearance of Volume 5 of the Longman edition of his *Poems* in 2005 that the full extent of his use of such materials when preparing 'The First Book of Homer's *Ilias*' was first made public.[48] The Longman edition shows that Dryden drew on the Latin commentary and translation of *Iliad* 1 by Spondanus (Jean de Sponde, 1583), together with a range of other renderings in several languages. These include the *ad verbum* Latin version of Andreas Divus (1537) and the more artistic Latin versions by Lorenzo Valla (1474), V. Obsopoeus (1527), Joachim Camerarius (1538), Helius Eobanus Hessus (1540), and Constantinus Pulcharelius (1619). Among English Homers, Dryden drew on the complete versions of George Chapman (in all three versions: 1598, 1610, and 1611), John Ogilby (1660, revised 1669), and Thomas Hobbes (1676), plus the version of Book 1 by Thomas Grantham (1660), and the burlesque rendering of Books 1 and 2 by James Scudamore (1664). He may also have used the version of the first 412 lines of *Iliad* 1 by Arthur Maynwaring (or Mainwaring), published in Tonson's *Poetical Miscellanies: The Fifth Part* (1704), but perhaps previously seen by Dryden in manuscript. Dryden also consulted French versions of Homer's original by S. Du Souhait (1540), Hughes Salel (1580), Salomon Certon (1615), and the Abbé de la Valterie (1681). He also drew on the Italian versions by Luigi Groto (1570) and (in burlesque) by G. F. Loredano (1654). His version, moreover, shows traces of Ovid, Milton, Shakespeare, and other poems of his own. Dryden's rendering of 'The First Book' is thus the result of a vast, multilingual exchange with those who had attempted to explain or render Homer's text before him, or whose poetic imaginings seemed to him to have some relation to it. But though his predecessors' presence is visible in almost every line of his translation, the version is no mere mechanical compilation. Dryden's genius in collecting, combining, amplifying, and animating[49] his materials is everywhere in evidence, and his rendering, despite its numerous 'sources', achieves an extraordinary overall coherence of tone and purpose.

[48] The edition's substantial debts to previous scholarship are, of course, fully acknowledged *ad loc.*

[49] The phrasing is Samuel Johnson's: see *The Lives of the Most Eminent English Poets*, ed. Roger Lonsdale, 4 vols. (Oxford, 2006), 4. 65.

Some of Dryden's echoes of his predecessors simply draw on commentaries or earlier translations for rhymes, or for idiomatic ways of rendering the sometimes curious or obscure circumstantial details of Homer's text into English – as when, for example (216), he replaces Homer's 'hecatomb' with the word 'sacrifice', drawn from Thomas Grantham and/or Arthur Maynwaring, or describes (279) Achilles' 'hut' as a 'tent', drawing on a noun used by Chapman, itself an adaptation of Spondanus' gloss 'tentorium'. But frequently Dryden's borrowings and personal additions to the literal meaning of Homer's text bring us closer to his sense of the leading conceptions which he seems to have thought had shaped Homer's first book.

One group of such borrowings relates to Dryden's depiction of the Homeric Achilles. In numerous details throughout his rendering, Dryden has emphasized and enhanced Homer's depiction of Achilles as a figure of impulsive passion and intransigent pride – the 'impatient' figure of Horace's celebrated description,[50] which is specifically echoed by Dryden in his version (284) and quoted in the Preface to *Fables* (*Works*, 7. 30). Dryden's Achilles, in terms added by the English poet, smiles 'sourly' (284) as he contemplates drawing his sword on Agamemnon, and responds 'with surly Faith' (328) when Athene prevents him, turning on Agamemnon a torrent of witheringly abusive sarcasm:

At her departure his Disdain return'd:
The Fire she fan'd, with greater Fury burn'd;
Rumbling within till thus it found a vent:
Dastard and Drunkard, Mean and Insolent:
Tongue-valiant Hero, Vaunter of thy Might,
In Threats the foremost, but the lag in Fight;
When did'st thou thrust amid the migled Preace,
Content to bid the War aloof in Peace?
Arms are the Trade of each plebeyan Soul;
'Tis Death to fight; but Kingly to controul.
Lord-like at ease, with arbitrary Pow'r,
To peel the Chiefs, the People to devour:
These, Traitor, are thy Tallents; safer far
Than to contend in Fields, and Toils of War.

(332–45)

[50] *Ars Poetica*, 121.

Homer (223) simply says that Achilles addressed Agamemnon 'with hurtful words'. Dryden has drawn on a recurrent trope in his own poetry[51] to evoke the volcano-like eruption of Achilles' tirade. For Achilles' description of Agamemnon as 'mean and insolent' (not in Homer) he has drawn on de la Valterie ('lâche et insolent'), and for his 'Tongue-valiant' (again an addition) on his own translation of Virgil.[52] Later, Dryden's Achilles, by accusing Agamemnon of exercising 'arbitrary Pow'r', associates him with the absolutist ambitions regularly anathematized in the political discourse of Dryden's own day.[53] And for Achilles' contemptuous remark that Agamemnon's talent is 'To peel the Chiefs, the People to devour', Dryden has combined echoes of de la Valterie – whose Achilles says to his Agamemnon, 'Vous n'estes propre qu'à piller les peuples' (You are only good at plundering people) – and of Spondanus, whose Achilles describes Agamamemon as 'populivorator' (devourer of the people).

Earlier in 'The First Book', Dryden had echoed predecessors in order to emphasize the physical signs of both Agamemnon's and Achilles' proudly impulsive behaviour. Here, for example, is how his Agamemnon responds to Calchas' advice that Chryseis must be returned to her father:

> Thus answer'd then
> Upstarting from his Throne, the King of Men,
> His Breast with Fury fill'd, his Eyes with Fire;
> Which rowling round, he shot in Sparkles on the Sire:
> (151–4)

Homer notes that Agamemnon's eyes were 'like blazing fire', but Dryden's expansion (and half his rhyme) are drawn from Chapman's version of 1610:

> his eyes like burning fire
> Cast sparkles from his bended browes, all blowen out of his Ire.

A little later, Achilles responds to Agamemnon's declaration that he will seize Briseis:

[51] For the relevant passages, see *Poems*, 5. 307 (ll. 332–4*n*).

[52] It is used of Drances in 'The Eleventh Book of the *Aeneis*', 514.

[53] For uses of the term in Dryden's own political poetry, see *Poems*, 5. 308 (l. 342*n*).

> At this, *Achilles* roul'd his furious Eyes,
> Fix't on the King askant; and thus replies.
>
> (223–4)

Here Dryden seems to have expanded Homer's reference (148) to Achilles' 'angry glance' with a memory of Satan's response to Abdiel in Milton's *Paradise Lost*:

> Whom the grand foe with scornful eye askance
> Thus answerd.
>
> (6. 149–50)

And when Achilles, having thrown the golden sceptre to the ground, sits down, 'boiling' with rage, we are told (in phrases with no direct precedent in the Greek) that he 'churn'd' 'Foam betwixt his gnashing Grinders' (360–1) – like Lycaon in Dryden's translation of 'The First Book of Ovid's *Metamorphoses*' (309–10), the boar in his 'Fourth Book of the *Georgics*' (400), Alecto in 'The Seventh Book of the *Aeneis*' (633), and the Calydonian boar in 'Meleager and Atalanta, Out of the Eighth Book of Ovid's *Metamorphoses*' (26–7).

If Dryden draws on a variety of predecessors (including earlier works of his own) to emphasize the impulsive passions of Homer's heroes, so has he deployed the thoughts and phrasing of others to convey the earthy realism of the sacrifice which the Greeks offer to the gods after the return of Chryseis to her father:

> Now when the solemn Rites of Pray'r were past,
> Their salted Cakes on crackling Flames they cast.
> Then, turning back, the Sacrifice they sped:
> The fatted Oxen slew, and flea'd the Dead,
> Chop'd off their nervous Thighs, and next prepar'd
> T' involve the lean in Cauls, and mend with Lard.
> Sweet-breads and Collops, were with Skewers prick'd
> About the Sides; imbibing what they deck'd.
>
> (627–34)

The details of the feast are here described with butcherly accuracy. Dryden draws his 'Sweet-breads' from the 1611 edition of Chapman, and for his 'Cauls' (fatty membranes) and 'Skewers' echoes Scudamore's burlesque version of Book 1, where the sacrificers 'with skew'rs . . . stuck the cawle' ('caul' also appears in Ogilby). Dryden himself adds the final detail that the sweetbreads and collops 'imbibe' (soak up) what they 'deck' (adorn). The sacrifice lasts all day. Then

> At Sun-set to their Ship they make return,
> And snore secure on Decks, till rosy Morn.
>
> (649–50)

Homer merely says that they slept by the stern cables of their ship. Dryden takes 'on Decks' from Ogilby, and takes his cue for the sailors' undignified 'snore' from Scudamore's burlesque, where it is said that they 'snort'.

Dryden also makes use of his dealings with his predecessors in his rendering of the final part of 'The First Book', in which Jove and Juno quarrel about Jove's tête-à-tête with Achilles' mother Thetis, and which ends with the gods feasting on Olympus. Critics had been uneasy about this episode from antiquity, and had cited it as a principal instance of how Homer had brought the Olympian gods into disrepute by depicting them as quarrelsome, irresponsible, and bibulous. In his version, Dryden renders such suggestions of divine ill-temper, irresponsibility, and recklessness with a positive relish, and draws on hints in his predecessors which bring such traits to the fore. His Jove, for example, tells Thetis how his wife Juno 'In Council . . . gives Licence to her Tongue / Loquacious, brawling, ever in the wrong' (699–700), phrasing that associates her with 'Zimri', one of the subversive courtier-villains of Dryden's *Absalom and Achitophel*.[54] Later, Juno repays his description with interest, addressing her husband as 'Author of Ills, and close Contriver *Jove*' (725), thereby linking him with Milton's Satan (described as the 'Author of all ill' in *Paradise Lost*, 2. 381) and Shakespeare's Hecate (described as 'The close contriver of all harms' in *Macbeth*, 3. 5. 8). As their quarrel progresses, Jove rounds on Juno:

> My Household Curse, my lawful Plague, the Spy
> Of *Jove*'s Designs, his other squinting Eye:
> Why this vain prying, and for what avail?
> *Jove* will be Master still and *Juno* fail.
> Shou'd thy suspicious Thoughts divine aright,
> Thou but becom'st more odious to my Sight,

[54] 'Stiff in Opinions, always in the wrong' (547; *Works*, 2. 21).

For this Attempt: uneasy Life to me
Still watch'd, and importun'd, but worse for thee.

(752–9)

Dryden expands Homer considerably here, strengthening Jove's threats if his wife persists in her suspicions, and expanding the suggestion that she is always spying on him. He here draws on Groto's Italian version (where Juno's constant spying is similarly emphasized by Jove),[55] and Spondanus, whose Latin Dryden echoes in his 'suspicious' and 'odious': 'Suspicione tua nihil proficies . . . quin & eo nomine magis odiosa esse mihi incipis' (You will not accomplish anything by your suspicion, . . . no, you will be more odious to me on that account).

Later, Dryden enhances the bibulous jollity of the gods' feast by describing how Hephaestus

crown'd a Bowl, unbid:
The laughing Nectar overlook'd the Lid:

(784–5)

These lines draw on a long-standing tradition of depicting joyfully animated liquor – the Longman edition cites examples from Spenser, Crashaw, and Cotton.[56] A few lines later, Hephaestus' comic antics at the feast are enhanced by Dryden's description of him as a 'rude Skinker' – that is, an ale-house potman or tapster. This term had been used by Chapman in a marginal note to his 1611 text ('Vulcan skinker to the Gods'), and by Thomas Hobbes in his deliberately 'bald' and 'low' version of the *Iliad* of 1676, where we are told that

the Gods laught all at once outright
To see the lame and sooty *Vulcan* skink.

And, pursuing his disreputable characterization of the gods to the last, Dryden embellishes Homer's simple statement that Zeus went to his bed and slept with Juno beside him, and closes his rendering of 'The First Book' thus:

[55] See *Poems*, 5. 329 (ll. 752–3*n*).
[56] See *Poems*, 5. 331 (l. 785*n*).

The thund'ring God
Ev'n he withdrew to rest, and had his Load:
His swimming Head to needful Sleep apply'd;
And *Juno* lay unheeded by his Side.

(812–15)

Homer makes no explicit mention of Jove's drunkenness or his neglect of marital intimacy. Scudamore's burlesque version (from which Dryden seems here to have taken his cue) had described how Jove went to bed 'with a giddy head'. And for the coarse phrasing which he uses to evoke Jove's inebriated state ('had his Load'), Dryden seems to have remembered his own version of Virgil's Sixth Pastoral, where the drunken satyr Silenus is described as 'Dos'd with his fumes, and heavy with his Load' (21; *Works*, 5. 108).

Alexander Pope's version of Book 1 of the *Iliad* was included in the first volume of his complete translation, published in 1715. A full examination of the translation would reveal as full an engagement with and absorption of numerous predecessors' work as is apparent in Dryden's 'First Book'.[57] For my present purposes, however, I want to concentrate on the ways in which Pope's version of Book 1 engages in conversation with one particular predecessor: Dryden. Pope clearly signals his admiration for Dryden's version in his own Preface:

It is a great Loss to the Poetical World that Mr. *Dryden* did not live to translate the *Iliad*. He has left us only the first Book and a small Part of the sixth; in which if he has in some Places not truly interpreted the Sense, or preserved the Antiquities, it ought to be excused on account of the Haste he was obliged to write in. He seems to have had too much regard to *Chapman*, whose Words he sometimes copies, and has unhappily follow'd him in Passages where he wanders from the Original. However had he translated the whole Work, I would no more have attempted *Homer* after him than *Virgil*, his Version of whom (notwithstanding some human Errors) is the most noble and spirited Translation I know in any Language.

(*TE*, 7. 22)

[57] Such an examination of Pope's Book 1 was partly conducted by Gilbert Wakefield in Volume 1 of his edition of Pope's *Iliad* (1st edition, London, 1796). Further information is contained in Appendix F in Vol. 10 of *TE*. By far the fullest examination to date of Pope's use of his sources is to be found in Felicity Rosslyn's 'The Making of Pope's Translation of the *Iliad*' (Unpublished PhD thesis, Cambridge, 1978), which concentrates on Books 21–4.

Pope's association of Dryden with Chapman here has a double interest. In his Preface, Pope criticizes Chapman for his 'Fustian' expression, and for the arrogant 'Negligence' with which he so speedily completed his version. Pope adds, however, an important qualification:

> But that which is to be allowed him, and which very much contributed to cover his Defects, is a daring fiery Spirit that animates his Translation, which is something like what one might imagine *Homer* himself would have writ before he arriv'd to Years of Discretion.
>
> (*TE*, 7. 21)

Homer's 'Fire', we remember, was precisely the quality in Homer with which Dryden had come to feel a temperamental affinity, and it is also the quality which Pope singles out in his Preface as quintessentially Homeric, comparing it with the surging fire to which Homer himself had likened the advancing Greek army in Book 2 of the *Iliad* (*TE*, 7. 4). It is particularly significant in the present context that Homer's 'daring fiery Spirit' was something that Chapman himself seems to have come to appreciate only at a fairly late stage in his engagement with the *Iliad*. His first attempts at translating Homer, published in *Seaven Bookes of the Iliades* (1598) display the ethical bias characteristic of much Renaissance reading of classical epic. Chapman imbues Homer's narrative with Christian and chivalric resonances, and offers an Achilles motivated by gallant affection for Briseis (who is treated as an object of love rather than a chattel won in combat), and by a righteous virtue that shows itself proof against the passions. In 1598 the pagan elements in the poem are downplayed in favour of moral interpretation coloured with Christian associations. But in his revised translation of 1611, Chapman's emphasis shifts significantly towards a more thoroughgoing pagan conception of Homeric heroism, grounded in self-assertive pride, moody bloodthirstiness, and egotistical will – characteristics close to those which, as we have seen, are prominently stressed in Dryden's version of 'The First Book'.[58] They are characteristics which Pope

[58] On Chapman's shift of emphasis, see Robin Sowerby, 'Chapman's Discovery of Homer', *Translation and Literature*, 1 (1992), 26–51.

seems to have been concerned, at least to some degree, to palliate in his own version.

Pope's Achilles is still to a large extent the same passionate figure as Dryden's but, in rounding on Agamemnon after Athene's departure, he expresses himself with a distinctly more measured eloquence than his predecessor. Where Dryden's Achilles insults Agamemnon as 'Dastard and Drunkard, Mean and Insolent' (325), Pope reverts to a more literal rendering of Homer in making his Achilles address him as 'Thou Dog in Forehead, but in Heart a Deer!' (298). Whereas Dryden's Achilles, told that Agamemnon intends to seize Briseis, 'roul'd his furious Eyes', Pope's is depicted as 'frowning stern' (193). Whereas Dryden's Achilles, having thrown down the sceptre, 'Foam betwixt his gnashing Grinders churn'd', Pope's merely 'sternly silent sate' (327). In the sacrifice scene, Pope omits any reference to 'Sweet-breads', 'Collops', and 'Skewers', shifting the emphasis from sacrifice-as-feast to sacrifice-as-ceremony. Dryden tells us (638) that his sacrificers 'turnd' the 'Roast' 'On five sharp Broachers'. Pope makes no mention of 'Broachers' (spits). Dryden derived this specific 'low' term from Scudamore's burlesque Homer. But Chapman refers at this point to 'spits', and Pope specifically criticized Dryden for being misled by Chapman into referring to a practice that was 'not known in *Homer*'s Days' (*TE*, 7. 117). Dryden's summary description of the feast as a 'Holy Debauch' (647) becomes, more decorously, a 'joyous Banquet' (Pope, 618), and Pope (622) does not follow Dryden (650) in making the sleeping sailors 'snore'.

In his notes on the final episode concerning the gods, Pope appeals against Dryden to the French translator, Madame Dacier. Dryden has, he says, translated the quarrel between Jove and Juno 'with the utmost Severity upon the Ladies, and spirited the whole with satyrical Additions of his own'. Madame Dacier, he says, 'seems willing to give the whole Passage a more important Turn, and incline us to think that *Homer* design'd to represent the Folly and Danger of prying into the Secrets of Providence'. ''Tis thrown into that Air in this Translation,' Pope continues, 'not only as it is more noble and instructive in general, but as it is more respectful to the Ladies in particular' (*TE*, 7. 121). Accordingly, where Dryden, as we have seen, depicts Jove and Juno's quarrel as a domestic squabble, Pope conceives it as a reasoned dispute centring on the nature of divine omnipotence. Where Dryden's Jove rounds on Juno as a 'Household Curse' and 'prying' 'Spy', Pope's expounds to his wife, with Miltonic authority,[59] the profound unreasonableness of attempting to fathom the mysteries of eternal providence:

> Then thus the God: Oh restless Fate of Pride,
> That strives to learn what Heav'n resolves to hide;
> Vain is the Search, presumptuous and abhorr'd,
> Anxious to thee, and odious to thy Lord.
> Let this suffice; th' immutable Decree
> No Force can shake: What *is*, that *ought* to be.
> Goddess submit, nor dare our Will withstand,
> But dread the Pow'r of this avenging Hand;
> Th' united Strength of all the Gods above
> In vain resists th' Omnipotence of *Jove*.
>
> (726–35)

In accordance with such a reading, Pope rebukes Dryden for having been, once again, led astray by Chapman into rendering Hephaestus' conduct at the end of the book 'a little barbarously'. Dryden, Pope says, 'makes his Character perfectly comical, he is the Jest of the Board, and the Gods are very merry upon the Imperfections of his Figure'. Dryden has also, Pope says, been misled by Chapman into 'some Indecencies of Expression' (*TE*, 7. 124). Pope's translation, in consequence, is not the 'Limping Smith', 'Clown', and 'rude Skinker' of Dryden's version (768, 801, 803), but merely 'with awkward Grace his Office plies' (770). And there is no mention of drunkenness or neglected marital rites at Pope's close, which sticks much closer to Homer's literal meaning:

> *Jove* on his Couch reclin'd his awful Head,
> And *Juno* slumber'd on the golden Bed.
>
> (780–1)

Pope can thus be seen to register, through his own translation of Book 1 of the *Iliad*, a Leavisian 'Yes, but' to the 'This is so, isn't it?' embodied in Dryden's earlier version. The two translators are, it could be said, engaged in a critical conversation about how Homer's tone and purport might be best conveyed.

[59] Cf. Raphael at *Paradise Lost*, 7. 120–5, 8. 71–5, 167–97.

Both Dryden's and Pope's translations of Book 1 of the *Iliad* have, interestingly, been seen by modern commentators as viable – though very different – responses to tendencies identifiable in the Greek original. In his pioneering account of 1972, H. A. Mason praised Dryden's translation for what he took to be its discerning rendition of the essential dynamics of Homer's action. Homer's Book 1, Mason argues, is structured around the notion of *timē*, the honour on which the position and status of both men and gods, in the Homeric world, depends. Agamemnon's *mēnis* (anger) is the result of the loss of *timē* which he suffers when forced to give up his *geras*, his war prize, Chryseis. Achilles' *timē* is, in its turn, affronted by having to yield up his captive maiden, Briseis, and leads to the *mēnis* that he manifests for much of the rest of the poem. Homer's heroes, Mason notes, often conduct their disputes about *timē* in a distinctly childish way, and their *mēnis* often resembles something closer to 'filthy temper' than 'noble wrath'.[60] The quarrel between Zeus and Hera near the end of the Book is intended to parallel that between Agamemnon and Achilles. Hera, like Achilles, protests at her loss of *timē*. Zeus exercises his *mēnis* towards her. Hera, however, soon forgets her troubles at the party on Olympus, whereas Achilles nurses his grievance, which becomes the source of much suffering. Homer's depiction of the gods involves a 'dual vision' strikingly different from any to which we are usually accustomed. Homer's gods are *simultaneously* comic and awesome, both actors in a domestic comedy, and figures of frightening cosmic power. Homer's Zeus, Mason argues, 'begins like a husband in a comedy and ends like the Old Testament God'.[61]

Dryden, according to Mason's account, is fully responsive to the Homeric drama of conflicting *timē*, and to the distinctively Homeric handling of the gods; whereas Pope has transformed Achilles into a distinctly more reasonable and more elegantly eloquent figure than his Homeric counterpart, and has brought Homer's Olympians closer to the religion of his own readers, assimilating Zeus to Milton's God, and playing down the element of comedy in the Book's final section. Dryden, in contrast, has relished Achilles' turbulent rage, and has responded fully to Homer's depiction of the gods, bringing

[60] H. A. Mason, *To Homer through Pope: An Introduction to Homer's* Iliad *and Pope's Translation* (London, 1972), pp. 48–9.

[61] *To Homer through Pope*, p. 37.

out the comedy of Hephaestus' conduct at the feast, and commanding a 'middle style' which 'preserves [Hephaestus'] dignity while retaining his familiarity'.[62]

Other critics, however, have reacted more positively to the way in which Pope's more consistent epic decorum gives an overall coherence to his version. Pope's investing of Achilles with a greater nobility rationality than his Drydenian predecessor, it has been suggested, is not merely a concession to eighteenth-century notions of aristocratic decorum but shows a responsiveness to a strand in Homer's original in which Achilles' motivation is shown to emanate from magnanimity and a powerful sense of injustice rather than mere ill temper. It is this strand in Achilles that maintains our sense of his humanity, even when his conduct is at its most brutal, and makes his final admission of his destructive madness moving and plausible. And Pope's more dignified treatment of the gods, it has been suggested, is not merely a concession to contemporary taste but is in line with those commentators from antiquity onwards who had found the irresponsibility of Homer's gods in Book 1 incompatible with the majesty they display elsewhere in the *Iliad*.[63] Mason, it should be noted, had, in praising Dryden's version at the expense of Pope's, himself expressed doubts 'whether he could have succeeded so well with the whole poem as he has done with [the last] part of the First Book'. The bullying, drunken Jove of Dryden's Book 1, after all, would have to have been metamorphosed into the compassionate figure who averts his eyes from the destruction of his son Sarpedon in Book 15, while tears of blood fall from the heavens.

The important question at issue here, I suggest, is not whether Dryden or Pope is more 'correct' in his rendering of Homer but in what ways the two poets' conversations with Homer, with their predecessors, with their own culture, and with each other – and, in turn, the conversations of their critics – have helped to sustain and promote interest in the continuing significance of Homeric epic. The translators' differences might, indeed, be considered a

[62] *To Homer through Pope*, pp. 51–60.

[63] See, particularly, Felicity Rosslyn, 'The Making of Pope's Translation of the *Iliad*', pp. 39–51; Robin Sowerby, 'The Decorum of Pope's *Iliad*', *Translation and Literature*, 13 (2004), 49–79, and *The Augustan Art of Poetry: Augustan Translation of the Classics* (Oxford, 2006), pp. 228–310 (esp. pp. 288–93).

positive advantage in this respect. For, as Ezra Pound once observed, 'It's only when a few men who know, get together and *disagree* that any sort of criticism is born'.[64]

How, it might be asked, can readers in the present gain the understanding of earlier cultures that makes possible the kind of interactive dialogue with past minds discussed above, and throughout the remainder of this book? This question is, surprisingly, passed over in silence by many literary historicists of both the old and new persuasions, but is the main subject of an interesting chapter in a recent book by the philosopher, Simon Blackburn.[65] 'Attempts to understand others', say one group of thinkers described by Blackburn as 'pessimists' (roughly equivalent to the more extreme of Charles Martindale's exponents of 'ideology critique' or Lawrence Venuti's 'domesticating' translators), 'are exercises of power. We impose upon Them. By interpreting them in our way, we annex them, colonize them, trample on their difference, and force them into our mould.' Blackburn's 'optimists' (roughly equivalent to some of Martindale's 'reception aestheticians') reply: 'Not so, ... We can join hands, find ourselves in them, obtain a "fusion of horizons", partake of a common humanity.'[66] The 'pessimist' position, Blackburn observes, can easily induce a spiral of despair, for reasons already touched upon in this Introduction:

> If all we can do is to interpret the others from our own particular standpoint in history, we must be aware that earlier historians – whom we no doubt regard as quaintly mistaken and biased by their own concerns and their own times – did just the same. And historians yet to come will do it as well, and in so doing they will consign our own contingent, situated, partial or biased descriptions to the very same rubbish tip on to which we pile the work of previous writers.[67]

Blackburn surveys the work of various writers who have offered possible ways out of this dilemma. His preferred solution is that offered by David Hume. Hume, Blackburn notes, has often been

[64] Ezra Pound, *Selected Letters, 1907–1941*, ed. D. D. Paige (London, 1971), p. 12.

[65] Simon Blackburn, *Truth: A Guide for the Perplexed* (London, 2005), Chapter 8: 'Historians and Others'.

[66] Ibid., p. 199.

[67] Ibid., p. 206.

accused of being the Enlightenment essentialist *par excellence*, and of being simply blind to the vast divergences of culture, sentiment, and belief that exist in human societies. Was it not Hume, after all, who wrote famously that 'Mankind are so much the same, in all times and places, that history informs us of nothing new or strange in this particular'?[68] But it is notable, Blackburn observes, that Hume, far from ignoring or denying human diversity, dwells on it frequently and at length, and is repeatedly concerned to explain how it might be accounted for. Hume's procedure, Blackburn notes,

> is to come to understand the influence of political necessity, culture, and other social causes in generating differences of custom and morality. The picture is that while we are to recognize the *material* on which these causes operate as universal, the upshot... may be differences as great as you please.[69]

Hume's method in such circumstances, Blackburn explains, is to offer

> an account enabling us to 'see' how circumstances would affect agents' conception of themselves and their circumstances, in order to give rise to whichever differences interest us.

Such an account

> is effected by imagination and sympathy, which together enable us to reconstruct the influence of the circumstances that act on the mind as motives or reasons. We can do this only because the 'minds of men are mirrors to one another': insofar as we are not given something that we can mirror we cannot gain a distinctively historical understanding of an epoch or a people. But when we succeed we can be said to have 'lived through' the history we recount.[70]

Hume's views, as Blackburn points out, have many features in common with R. G. Collingwood's idea of historical understanding, as summarized in his *Autobiography*:

> In re-thinking what somebody else thought, [the historian] thinks it himself. In knowing that somebody else thought it, he knows that he is himself able

[68] *An Enquiry Concerning Human Understanding*, ed. Tom L. Beauchamp (Oxford, 1999), p. 150, quoted by Blackburn, *Truth*, p. 208.
[69] Blackburn, *Truth*, p. 209.
[70] Ibid., p. 210.

to think it. And finding out what he is able to do is finding out what kind of man he is. If he is able to understand, by rethinking them, the thoughts of a great many different kinds of people, it follows that he must be a great many kinds of man. He must be, in fact, a microcosm of all the history he can know.[71]

Blackburn notes that Hume's stress on the imaginative sympathy required for historical understanding explains why the comprehension of alien societies and modes of human behaviour is closely related to self-knowledge:

Hume's own confidence in uniformity underlying diversity gives him the confidence that nothing human is alien to him. (He would have been familiar with the saying from . . . Terence: 'Homo sum, humanum nil a me alienum puto': I am a man; nothing human is alien from me . . . ) . . . If we come across diversity, we can bend to understand it, until in the end we share the routes of feeling and thought that initially may have seemed quite alien. We grow into being like-minded with others . . . Here, there is no distinction between the discovery of others and the discovery of oneself.[72]

It is of particular significance for the present book that the passage from Terence quoted by Blackburn was also cited by Dryden, when describing the flexibility of human sympathy which enabled him to be such a successful translator of classical poetry.[73] It is also of great interest that T. S. Eliot, in a key passage quoted several times in the chapters which follow, wrote of translation as a kind of self-discovery and self-knowledge.

Hume and Collingwood (and their commentator, Simon Blackburn) offer suggestive thoughts about the general conditions under which human beings might make sense of distant communities and historical epochs. Their accounts can be usefully complemented and extended, in a specifically literary context, by a little-known but important essay by H. A. Mason on a short poem by Sir Thomas Wyatt, 'Luck, my fair falcon':[74]

71 R. G. Collingwood, *An Autobiography* (Oxford, 1939), pp. 114–15.

72 Blackburn, *Truth*, pp. 217–8.

73 For discussion of the significance of the passage for Dryden (as for Montaigne before him), see my *Writers and their Work: John Dryden* (Tavistock, 2004), pp. 60–1.

74 H. A. Mason, 'Sir Thomas Wyatt and the Birds of Fortune', *Cambridge Quarterly*, 7 (1977), 281–96.

Luck, my fair falcon, and your fellows all,
How well pleasant it were your liberty
Ye not forsake me that fair might ye fall,
But they that sometime liked my company
Like lice away from dead bodies they crawl.
Lo, what a proof in light adversity!
But ye, my birds, I swear by all your bells,
Ye be my friends, and so be but few else.[75]

Wyatt's speaker, who has been deserted by his fickle friends, appeals to his falcons. However pleasing their liberty would be to them, he speculates, *they* would not forsake him, as have his friends, in pursuit of their own interests. The falcons, he declares, are now his only true friends, swearing by the bells which were, in Tudor times, attached by their masters to the legs of hunting birds.

How, Mason asks, can modern readers respond to a poem which turns centrally on a cultural phenomenon – a Tudor nobleman's relation to his falcons – somewhat removed from anything in their own experience? In the course of his answer, Mason invokes various carefully selected pieces of historical and contextual evidence. He documents from contemporary written and pictorial sources the close bond of affection which a Tudor falconer felt for his birds – as evidenced by the decorative as well as a functional purpose served by their bells, and by the affectionate caresses which accompanied the birds' everyday care. Mason speculates that Wyatt's poem may possibly have been composed in 1541, when the poet was imprisoned on the testimony of powerful enemies. He illuminates the sources in Erasmus and Plutarch which seem to lie behind Wyatt's reflections on false friendship, and, in particular, his image of his friends crawling 'Like lice away from dead bodies'. Mason thus associates Wyatt's poem with a number of very specific features of Tudor political, social, and intellectual life, and (possibly) with a specific moment in the poet's life. But, he insists, the poem's interest and value for us do not ultimately reside in these features *per se*. They lie in the fact that Wyatt has made out of such materials a poem whose voice 'is the voice of all men faced with this specially human predicament, and

[75] The poem is given in Mason's modernized text printed in his *Sir Thomas Wyatt: A Literary Portrait* (Bristol, 1986). Mason's notes explain his choice of 'Luck' (rather than the manuscript alternatives 'Lux' or 'Luckes') as the falcon's name.

making a manly protest'. The protest is all the more poignant, since the speaker's appeal is 'to the unpredictable birds which man can never be sure of': 'The birds are not a satisfactory substitute for human friends. The dramatic spirit inside the poem is therefore eternally on the rack'.[76]

At the end of his essay, Mason turns to the more general implications of his discussion of Wyatt's poem, and asks: 'Where is this poem now?' His conclusion deserves to be quoted in full:

> If it does not sound too portentous, I should say that the difficulty of situating a poem is like that in saying that the historic Christ is now in Heaven. Our faith in both cases demands that we believe that there really was an initial situation on earth, that something really happened in the past at a definite date. We can never know too much in the way of surrounding detail about those original events. Yet what we are dealing with, as readers if not as believers, is not what happened then, but what is happening now. The past is perished: what survives it was never of that past though it came to being in the past.
>
> We reach a similar paradox if we start by saying that we must make the poem up for ourselves. It is clearly not reading if we substitute our own thoughts about friendship failing and the loss of freedom, yet there is no poem to be concerned over if we have not had many thoughts of our own on both topics. We must first have been deeply concerned in order to be able to find an interest in what is being brought up in the poem. But it is a fellow-interest the reader finds, not a selfish, totally egoistic, interest. We listen to a voice not our own in our dramatic replay of Wyatt's poem. But Wyatt, too, had to speak outside, beyond his merely historic rôle of *these* walls, *these* birds, *these* particular untrustworthy friends.
>
> It is therefore better to say that the spiritual reality we both meet and create in reading a poem occurs in a no-man's land, neither the present nor the past. It is the only for-ever-land we can know. It will not last beyond our own lives. Each generation of readers must begin again.[77]

This passage, I think, draws eloquent attention to some of the acute paradoxes involved in the processes of literary reception. It allows us to see the important element of truth in the insistence of 'reception aesthetics' that 'meaning is always realized at the point of reception', while avoiding the crudely 'presentist' implications that such an

[76] Mason, 'Sir Thomas Wyatt and the Birds of Fortune', pp. 294–5.
[77] Ibid., pp. 295–6.

insistence might sometimes seem to suggest. It allows us to see the importance of historical contextualization, while alerting us to the fact that context will never fully account either for the acts of creation which bring works of art into being in the first place or for the acts of imaginative response that are involved in their reception and recreation. It suggests the complexity of the processes of self-transcendence, self-discovery, meeting, and mingling, both in and out of time, that are involved in all acts of literary reception. It gives a suggestive *entrée* into the kinds of dialogic, conversational, encounters between classical past and English present explored in the chapters which follow.

# 1

## 'The English Homer': Shakespeare, Longinus, and English 'Neoclassicism'

Discussions of the relations between English writers and the classics have, whatever the precise nature of their larger assumptions or local conclusions, generally focused on the impact of classical literature and culture *on* those English writers' work, whether by considering the broader effects of classical education and scholarship, or the specific responses of English writers to particular classical authors and themes. But the reception of the classics is also a topic which can have important implications when considering the afterlife of certain English writers themselves. In 'Tradition and the Individual Talent', T. S. Eliot famously observed that

> No poet, no artist of any art, has his complete meaning alone. His significance, his appreciation is the appreciation of his relation to the dead poets and artists. You cannot value him alone; you must set him, for contrast and comparison, among the dead. I mean this as a principle of aesthetic, not merely historical, criticism.

Eliot's main concern was the way in which the appearance of a new work of art inevitably affects readers' appreciation of all the works of art which preceded it. 'What happens when a new work of art is created,' he argued,

> is something that happens simultaneously to all the works of art which preceded it. The existing monuments form an ideal order among themselves, which is modified by the introduction of the new (the really new) work of art among them.

A reader sympathetic to such ideas, Eliot believed, would 'not find it preposterous that the past should be altered by the present as much as the present is directed by the past'.[1]

Eliot's thoughts can, I believe, be usefully extended to encompass a further suggestion: that a significant revaluation of an 'older' work or author might substantially affect readers' responses to a 'newer' one. In this chapter, I shall consider the late seventeenth- and early eighteenth-century reception of Shakespeare in the light of that period's preoccupation with classical literature and literary criticism, a preoccupation which is widely believed to have seriously inhibited appreciation of Shakespeare's distinctive genius. It was only, it is commonly supposed, when 'neoclassical' dogma began to lose its authoritative hold that English readers came, for the first time, to value the unique qualities of Shakespeare's art.

I shall argue, against such a view, that, at least in one notable respect, late seventeenth- and early eighteenth-century writers' preoccupation with the classics was a positively *enabling* force in their developing appreciation of Shakespeare's distinctive artistic stature. During the period, I shall suggest, Boileau's translation of Longinus' treatise *On the Sublime* (1674) was a powerfully influential force in shaping a conception of Shakespeare as an inspired, original, and 'fiery' poet of the Sublime, an 'English Homer'. Since such a conception was central to how Shakespeare's work came to be perceived – and in important respects is still perceived today – it can be seen as significant not merely in the limited context of late seventeenth- and early eighteenth-century Shakespeare criticism but in a more wide-reaching consideration of Shakespeare's work itself. Hence the positioning of this chapter in the chronological arrangement of the present book – not (where it might have been expected) with the chapters on Dryden and Pope, but at its very outset.

It is widely believed that responses to Shakespeare from the Restoration to the mid-eighteenth century were seriously vitiated by a body of assumptions which can be collectively characterized as 'neoclassical literary theory'. In the introduction to the first volume of his comprehensive

[1] T. S. Eliot, 'Tradition and the Individual Talent', in *Selected Essays* (2nd edition, London, 1934), p. 15.

collection of early Shakespeare criticism, Brian Vickers refers to the impact after the Restoration of the 'highly developed critical concepts of rules, decorum, propriety, the unities, and so on – that amalgam of Aristotle and Horace borrowed from the French seventeenth century (who had themselves borrowed it from the Italian sixteenth century), which was to determine neoclassical attitudes to Shakespeare for several generations'. And in his second volume Vickers describes the period from the 1690s to the 1730s as 'one in which the theoretical system of Neo-classicism was applied with energy and with few reservations'.[2] Similar sentiments can be found in a number of influential specialist studies, and still persist in summary form in most handbook accounts of post-Restoration literature and Shakespeare criticism.[3]

According to the received account, the tenets of neoclassical theory placed a number of rigid restrictions on a dramatist's activity: the playwright should observe the Unities of time and place; he should observe the laws of decorum, according to which comedy must be strictly segregated from tragedy; he should never confuse his characterizations of the high-born – and the language which they are given to speak – with those of the 'vulgar', or his depictions of the virtuous with those of the vicious; he must constantly remember that the true purpose of his art is 'instruction'. Consequently, his plays should maintain Poetic Justice, according to which virtue is always seen to triumph and vice to fail; he should eschew linguistic excesses, such as puns, complex metaphors, extravagant conceits, and ambiguities; he should avoid, wherever possible, the on-stage presentation of violent action.

On all these counts, it is claimed, Shakespeare's plays were found conspicuously wanting, and badly in need of 'correction'. With only a couple of exceptions, they violated the Unities, sometimes to an extreme degree. Their language frequently seemed obscure or bombastic, and was riddled with indecorum, quibbling, and strained metaphors. Their action was often morally equivocal or ambiguous.

[2] Brian Vickers, ed., *Shakespeare: The Critical Heritage*, 6 vols. (London, 1974–81) (quotations from 1. 4 and 2. 1).

[3] See, for example, T. R. Lounsbury, *Shakespeare as a Dramatic Artist, with an Account of his Reputation at Various Periods* (London and New York, 1902); R. W. Babcock, *The Genesis of Shakespeare Idolatry, 1766–1799* (Chapel Hill NC, 1931); George C. Branam, *Eighteenth-Century Adaptations of Shakespearean Tragedy* (Berkeley and Los Angeles CA, 1956); for popular summary account, see, for example, Oscar James Campbell, ed., *A Shakespeare Encyclopedia* (London, 1966), p. 6.

They included blindings, assassinations, and mutilations, performed in full view of the audience. They manifested a disconcerting blend of comic and tragic action and language. As a consequence, the story goes on, they were regularly travestied in stage rewritings which reduced the nuanced subtleties of their language and the intricate ambiguities of their plot-construction to displays of studied elocution, stiff didacticism, sentimental melodrama, or bawdy farce. Editors of the period felt free to emend and abridge Shakespeare's texts according to their own canons of literary 'taste'. And discursive critics indulged in regular and prolonged litanies of his 'faults'. For many modern commentators, therefore, the period spanned by the writing careers of John Dryden and Alexander Pope constitutes something of a dark age in the history of Shakespeare interpretation.

But such an account is open to a number of serious objections. Chief among them is the awkward fact that it was precisely during the period between the Restoration and the mid-eighteenth century that Shakespeare was first decisively differentiated from Jonson and Fletcher – the contemporaries with whom he had previously been regularly lumped – and came to be clearly recognized as an English classic: 'the greatest English poet, perhaps the greatest poet of all time'.[4] Why, one might ask, should critics of the period have offered such a radically and daringly affirmative evaluation of Shakespeare when their theoretical principles militated so decisively and comprehensively against him? Why should the 'escape clauses' which, according to Brian Vickers, enabled them to offer high praise of Shakespeare while simultaneously castigating his faults, have been needed?[5] Recent scholarship has illuminated the processes whereby Shakespeare's works were 'appropriated' by various political and ideological interests in the period. But it has had considerably less to say about why Shakespeare should have been selected for appropriation in the first place.[6]

[4] Jean I. Marsden, *The Re-Imagined Text: Shakespeare, Adaptation, and Eighteenth-Century Literary Theory* (Lexington KY, 1995), p. 49.

[5] Vickers, *Shakespeare: The Critical Heritage*, 2. 7.

[6] For the 'appropriation' of Shakespeare, see Michael Dobson, *The Making of the National Poet: Shakespeare, Adaptation, and Authorship, 1660–1769* (Oxford, 1992); Gary Taylor, *Re-Inventing Shakespeare: A Cultural History from the Restoration to the Present* (London, 1990).

In exploring these issues, we might first consider the notorious Restoration stage adaptations of Shakespeare's plays. A survey of these versions reveals that, contrary to common belief, they were prompted by far more diverse considerations than slavish obedience to a set of rigid neoclassical rules.[7] In his *Shakespeare Improved* (1927), Hazleton Spencer offered what is still widely regarded as the most scrupulous and detailed comparison of the adaptations with their originals. Very few of the redactions, Spencer's analyses show, are in fact driven by a dogmatic neoclassicism.[8] Despite contemporary disapproval of what Joseph Addison called 'that dreadful butchering of one another, which is so very frequent upon the *English* stage',[9] adaptations such as Nahum Tate's versions of *Coriolanus* and *King Lear* and Sir William Davenant's of *Macbeth* are conspicuous for their *non*-avoidance of on-stage violence. Like most of the original plays of the period, moreover, few of the Restoration adaptations of Shakespeare make any sustained or serious attempt to observe the Unities.[10] As Jean I. Marsden has recently pointed out, only the adaptations of John Dennis make any systematic attempt to 'regularize' their originals. Even then, the modification is not dogmatically effected. Dennis's versions, moreover, were not popular. And the regularizing tendency of his adaptations co-exists with extravagant praise of Shakespeare in his critical writings.[11] The Restoration

[7] See Paulina Kewes, 'Shakespeare and New Drama', in David Womersley, ed., *A Companion to Literature from Milton to Blake* (Oxford, 2000), pp. 575–88 (p. 586).

[8] Hazelton Spencer, *Shakespeare Improved* (Cambridge MA, 1927). Spencer's findings are fully endorsed by a recent commentator on the redactions. See Barbara A. Murray, *Restoration Shakespeare: Viewing the Voice* (Madison WI and London, 2001), p. 19.

[9] *The Spectator*, No. 44 (20 April 1711).

[10] Dryden's *All for Love*, often singled out as the most 'correct' and 'regular' of the Restoration versions, is an original play on a Shakespearian theme rather than an adaptation as such, and might be best thought of as a one-off, experimental attempt to revitalize serious drama in the mid-1670s by combining elements from the native English and French dramatic traditions. Dryden's adaptation of *Troilus and Cressida* certainly shows the influence of French criticism and drama. But his changes seem motivated not by any mechanically-conceived Rules but by a desire to tighten the linguistic and dramatic coherence of a play which even Hazlitt thought 'the most loose and desultory' of Shakespeare's works. For further discussion, see Maximillian E. Novak's judicious commentary in Dryden, *Works*, 13. 497–522.

[11] Mardsen, *Re-Imagined Text*, pp. 49, 55; Branam, *Eighteenth-Century Adaptations*, p. 23; Dennis, *Critical Works*, ed. E. N. Hooker, 2 vols. (Baltimore MD, 1939–43), 2. 4, 168.

redactions, moreover, seldom effect the strict separation of tragic and comic elements demanded by neoclassical theory. Nor do most of them make any serious attempt to preserve Poetic Justice.

If the prime concern of the adapters was not to square Shakespeare with the neoclassical Rules, what, then, were their motives in altering Shakespeare's originals? Their prime intention, the evidence suggests, was to produce performing versions suited to the needs, expectations, and interests of contemporary audiences in a highly competitive, commercial theatre, at a time when, unlike today, there was no state support for, or academic pressure to attend, Shakespearian performances. Such versions clearly needed to be purged of linguistic archaism and obscurity, so that they would be immediately intelligible at the speed of theatrical delivery to audiences unfamiliar with the original texts, and lacking the annotated editions, synopses, and other aids which twenty-first-century readers and theatre-goers take for granted.

Considerations of clarity and intelligibility seem also to have been responsible for many of the adapters' alterations of Shakespeare's plots. Many of these changes seem designed to compensate for what they perceived as a lack of clarity both of moral focus and of psychological motivation in many of Shakespeare's dramatic designs. Nahum Tate, for example, provided an explanation of Cordelia's blunt refusal to indulge her father's request for flattery in the opening scene of *King Lear* by making her secretly in love with Edgar, and thus unwilling to marry Burgundy. Thomas Shadwell accounted for, and softened, Timon of Athens' sudden outburst of misanthropy by making it the result of his rejection by the coquette Melissa.[12] Sir William Davenant, in his *Law Against Lovers*, excused and explained Angelo's pardon at the end of *Measure for Measure* by depicting his intentions as having been always essentially honourable: he had only been pretending to seduce Isabella in order to test her virtue, and had never intended to take Claudio's life.

Some of the readactors' reshapings of Shakespeare can be explained by their desire to exploit the new circumstances and scenic resources of the Restoration theatre: female actors, moveable scenery,

[12] See Marsden, *Re-Imagined Text*, pp. 26–7.

bands of trained musicians.[13] The adaptations also sought to point up the 'relevance' of Shakespeare to the contemporary political situation. The earlier Restoration versions were often specifically tailored to celebrate the restored monarchy.[14] Two decades later, Shakespeare was extensively 'applied' to the modern situation during the period of the Popish Plot and Exclusion Crisis.[15] The majority of the adaptations from this period are firmly royalist in bias, a fact which – as much as any adherence to academic principles of Poetic Justice – explains the emphasis of such plays as John Crowne's versions of *1–2 Henry VI* and Edward Ravenscroft's *Titus Andronicus* on the benignity of providence and the destruction of socially or politically disruptive forces: the triumph of virtue is seen in such dramas as intimately connected with the protection and preservation of civic order.[16] Finally, the adaptations sometimes sought to accommodate Shakespeare to the philosophical debates, generic fashions, and sensibilities of their own day, incorporating, for example, touches of Hobbesian libertinage in the comic episodes of Shakespeare's 'serious' plays,[17] transforming some of Shakespeare's heroines into icons of suffering virtue,[18] and interpolating additional lascivious dialogue and low buffoonery to transform *The Tempest* into typical 1670s 'sex comedy'.

In all these respects, the Restoration and early eighteenth-century adapters can be seen not so much as neoclassical dogmatists but as practical men of the theatre, tailoring their presentations of Shakespeare – in a manner not dissimilar to the practice of modern stage and cinema producers – to the tastes, expectations, and interests of their audiences. This, of course (as with modern producers), often resulted in versions which were reductive, partial, modish, or downright silly. Few would probably wish to see many of the Restoration

[13] On actresses, see Elizabeth Howe, *The First English Actresses: Women and Drama, 1660–1700* (Cambridge, 1992); on theatrical effects, see Jocelyn Powell, *Restoration Theatre Production* (London, 1984); on music and musicians, see Curtis Price, *Music in the Restoration Theatre* (Ann Arbor MI, 1979).

[14] See Dobson, *Making of the National Poet*, Ch. 1.

[15] See Marsden, *Re-Imagined Text*, pp. 40–2; Susan J. Owen, *Restoration Theatre and Crisis* (Oxford, 1996); Dobson, *Making of the National Poet*, pp. 63–90.

[16] See Marsden, *Re-Imagined Text*, pp. 66–7.

[17] See Kewes, 'Shakespeare and New Drama', p. 582.

[18] See Marsden, *Re-Imagined Text*, pp. 30–7.

redactions revived on the modern stage. The discursive criticism of the period, moreover, contains its fair share of mundane, mechanical and clichéd writing, much of it, indeed, deploying conventional neo-Aristotelian vocabulary and rhetoric, or displaying a merely snobbish aversion to the 'low' elements in Shakespeare's texts. But this should not lead us to assume that the impulses behind Restoration and early eighteenth-century responses to Shakespeare can always be confidently dismissed as mere Rules-bound aberrations. For some of them were prompted by features of Shakespeare's texts which have been found equally problematic by critics in very different contexts and from very different intellectual traditions.

Cordelia's rebarbative bluntness and the Duke's final distribution of justice (already mentioned as features of their respective plays which seem to have disturbed the Restoration redactors) have frequently proved stumbling blocks in later accounts of *King Lear* and *Measure for Measure.* Even Hazleton Spencer – generally no admirer of the adaptations – believed that Shadwell's *Timon of Athens* supplies psychological motivation and dramatic unity which are conspicuously lacking in Shakespeare's original.[19] Fred Parker has argued convincingly that the infamous remarks about the 'horrible' and 'unnatural' aspects of *Othello* to be found in Thomas Rymer's *Short View of Tragedy* (1693) – often regarded as the acme of neoclassical obtuseness about Shakespeare – rest, in large part, not on Aristotelian dogma but on an empirically-grounded appeal to common readerly humanity which finds an echo in many later responses to deeply disturbing elements in Shakespeare's play: Iago's arbitrary malignity, the impotence of Cassio, Desdemona and Emilia in countering his villainy, Othello's seeming incapacity to comprehend or acknowledge the evil which is invading him.[20] And A. D. J. Brown has demonstrated that Alexander's Pope's notorious emendations and excisions from Shakespeare's text in his edition of 1725 depend not on narrowly eighteenth-century canons of taste and decorum but on a subtle and discriminating appreciation of Shakespeare's own stylistic

[19] Spencer, *Shakespeare Improved*, pp. 281–7.

[20] Fred Parker, 'Foul Disproportion: Rymer on *Othello*', *Cambridge Quarterly*, 17 (1988), 17–27.

practices, and on a shrewd (albeit incomplete) awareness of the material circumstances in which his texts were produced and transmitted.[21]

Many of the general reservations about Shakespeare voiced by the critics of the period have, significantly, found powerful echoes in the responses of later critics. A. C. Bradley, for example, an Edwardian Hegelian with (on the face of it) little sympathy for neoclassical aesthetics, substantially endorsed earlier critics' findings that Shakespeare's language is often 'obscure, inflated, tasteless, or "pestered with metaphors"', and offered a trenchant account of Shakespeare's inconsistent, hasty, negligent, and morally confused conduct of his plots, which is substantially in accord with that current in the post-Restoration period.[22] More recently, George Steiner has drawn on the notes of the philosopher Wittgenstein to support his own feelings about the 'prolixity and repetitiveness' in many of Shakespeare's plays, 'the intrusion of vulgarity and waste motion into even the major texts (how many of us have ever seen a production of *Othello* which includes the wretched exchanges with the Clown)', and the elements in Shakespeare's comedies which are 'rancid or verbally witty rather than funny in any real sense'.[23]

It is not necessary to agree with such accounts to concede that the conception of Shakespeare as a profoundly flawed artist – both in his linguistic practices and in the coherence and intelligibility of his dramatic designs – is by no means a limitedly neoclassical phenomenon,[24] but forms part of an ongoing (and still unresolved) debate about the nature of Shakespeare's art. And it is equally clear that such descriptions have often been felt – both within and outside the neoclassical period – to be perfectly compatible with the highest general estimate of Shakespeare's genius.

[21] A. D. J. Brown, 'The Little Fellow Has Done Wonders', *Cambridge Quarterly*, 21 (1992), 120–49; see also correspondence in 21 (1992), 260–1 and 22 (1993), 184–6.

[22] A. C. Bradley, *Shakespearean Tragedy* (London, 1904), pp. 73, 76.

[23] George Steiner, 'A Reading Against Shakespeare', in *No Passion Spent* (London, 1996), pp. 108–27 (p. 127).

[24] For a persuasive argument that Samuel Johnson's strictures on Shakespeare are less affected by neoclassical assumptions than is often assumed, see Philip Smallwood, 'Shakespeare: Johnson's Poet of Nature', in Greg Clingham, ed., *The Cambridge Companion to Samuel Johnson* (Cambridge, 1997), pp. 143–60.

Perhaps the most unfortunate consequence of the modern stress on post-Restoration neo-Aristotelianism is that it has distracted attention from another strand of critical thought in the period – one equally deserving of the label 'neoclassical' – which was of crucial importance in promoting a powerfully positive appreciation of Shakespeare's distinctive artistic qualities. I refer to the growing tendency to characterize Shakespeare as 'the English Homer', a tendency closely bound up with the intense revival of interest from the mid 1670s in the ancient treatise generally known as *On the Sublime* and attributed to 'Longinus'.

The names of Shakespeare and Homer had been occasionally linked from earliest times. In 1598 Francis Meres had affirmed that the English tongue had been 'mightilie enriched, and gorgeouslie invested in rare ornaments and resplendent abiliments' by Shakespeare, just as Greek had been 'made famous and eloquent by Homer'. An anonymous writer in 1651 had pronounced Shakespeare the 'Butler' in the realm of 'Eloquentia' where Homer was 'Master of the Wine-Cellars'. And in 1668 Dryden had referred to Shakespeare *en passant* as 'the Homer, or Father of our Dramatick Poets'.[25] But the association between the two writers became invested with an altogether new charge of significance after the appearance and rapid dissemination in England of Boileau's *Traité du sublime ou du merveilleux dans le discours traduit du grec de Longin*, published in Paris in 1674.[26]

Boileau is still often popularly thought of as the archetypal 'neoclassical' Rules critic, a 'Législateur du Parnasse' who laid down tyrannical and Procrustean laws for literary composition. But as Jules Brody showed long ago,[27] such an account gives a quite misleading impression of the French writer's main critical principles and

[25] See J. Munro, ed., *The Shakespeare Allusion Book: A Collection of Allusions to Shakespeare from 1591 to 1700* (1909), with new Preface by E. K. Chambers, 2 vols. (Oxford, 1932), 1. 46; 2. 18; Dryden, *Works*, 17. 58.

[26] The English translations of Longinus' treatise which appeared in the ensuing decades were explicitly indebted to Boileau. John Pulteney's version of 1680 openly declared itself as 'now Translated out of the *French*', though 'Written Originally in *Greek* by *LONGIN*'. The anonymous translator of 1698 declared his version to have been 'Compar'd with the French of the Sieur Despreaux Boileau'. The first English translation of Boileau's collected *Works*, published in 1711–13, incorporated a third English version of the *Traité*, probably by John Ozell.

[27] See Jules Brody, *Boileau and Longinus* (Geneva, 1958). The received image of Boileau is also tellingly scrutinized in E. B. O. Borgerhoff, *The Freedom of French Classicism* (Princeton NJ, 1950).

priorities. Boileau, Brody demonstrates, thought that the central imperative to which all other rules of literary composition should be subordinated was the capacity of literature to produce powerful and intense emotional effects on its readers – a quality found in its most concentrated and irresistible form in the Longinian Sublime. The Sublime, in Boileau's reading, 'charms' and 'transports', producing 'a certain Admiration mingled with Astonishment and Surprize' (p. 13).[28] It is 'an invincible Force which ravishes the Souls of all that hear' it (p. 13). The '*Sublime* and *Pathetick*, by their Violence and Impetuosity, naturally carry away every thing with them' and 'don't give the Hearer time to amuse himself, with cavilling at the Number of Metaphors; but throw him into the same Rapture with the Speaker' (pp. 65–6). The Sublime is not to be confused with 'Pompous and Magnificent' 'Bombast' (p. 15), or with the 'affected' 'Puerility' which 'wou'd continually say something extraordinary and Brillant [*sic*]' (p. 16). Its most intense effects, indeed, often come from extreme simplicity. It is 'a sort of Enthusiasm and Noble Fury, which animates' literary discourse, 'and gives it a Divine Fire and Vigour' (p. 23). The sublimity of the orator Demosthenes, for example, was visible in the 'Violence[,] Rapidity, and Vehemence, with which he bears down all before him' (p. 36). The sublime poet, similarly, 'carries the Reader along with him . . . making him rather see [the things he is describing] than read of 'em' (p. 59). He chooses 'Words, that give a sort of Soul and Life to things' (p. 64). Art reaches its perfection of sublimity when 'it so nearly resembles Nature, as to be taken for it: And on the contrary, Nature never succeeds better, than when the Art is hidden' (p. 54). The work of the sublime writer will inevitably contain faults, since

> in the *Sublime* . . . the Riches of Discourse are Immense, every thing cannot be so Carefully look'd after, as it ought to be; and something, let the Orator or Poet be never so Exact, will be Neglected. On the Contrary, 'tis almost impossible for a mean and midling Genius to commit Faults; because, as he never ventures, never rises, he always, remains in a State of Safety: Whereas, the *Great* is of it self, and by its Character of Greatness, slippery and dangerous.
>
> (pp. 68–9)

[28] Quotations from Boileau's *Longin* are taken from the 1711–12 English translation (see note 26 above), cited in the text by page references.

The 'Fine Strokes and Sublime Thoughts, which are in the Works of... Excellent Writers,' nevertheless, 'over balances [*sic*] all their Faults' (p. 74). And the supreme exemplar of the Sublime was Homer: the writer who, above all others, could, in his dramatic fictions, ravish and transport readers and rivet their attentions with his fiery intensity. Homer's 'Thoughts', according to Boileau's Longinus, were 'all Sublime' (p. 25). The 'whole Body' of his *Iliad* 'is Dramatick and full of Action' (p. 29), in the manner characteristic of the truly sublime poet.

This praise of the Homeric Sublime was quickly taken up and applied to Shakespeare by a number of English writers, including some of the most influential poet-critics of the period. The rapid impact of Boileau's *Longin* can be seen with particular clarity in two critical prefaces of John Dryden from the late 1670s. It is first evident in 'The Authors Apology for Heroique Poetry and Poetique Licence' prefixed to *The State of Innocence* (1677), where Dryden pointedly notes that '*Longinus*, who was undoubtedly, after *Aristotle*, the greatest Critique amongst the *Greeks*... has judiciously preferr'd the sublime Genius that sometimes erres, to the midling or indifferent one which makes few faults, but seldome or never rises to any Excellence'. Homer's faults, Dryden argues, 'are only marks of humane frailty: they are little Mistakes, or rather Negligences, which have escap'd his pen in the fervor of his writing; the sublimity of his spirit carries it with me against his carelessness'. Such thoughts have stylistic implications which cause Dryden to rethink some of his own earlier critical assumptions. 'The hardest Metaphors, and... the strongest *Hyperboles*', Dryden now argues, are justifiable if they contribute to a poet's capacity 'to sound the depth of all the Passions; what they are in themselves, and how they are to be provok'd'. 'Boldness of expression', which might otherwise seem merely bombastic or magniloquent, is to be thought 'graceful' in the depictions of passion where it seems 'Natural' (*Works*, 12. 87–93).

These thoughts are applied specifically to Shakespeare two years later in 'The Grounds of Criticism in Tragedy' prefixed to Dryden's *Troilus and Cressida.* In the closing pages of this essay, Longinian arguments are vigorously deployed in defence of Shakespeare's mastery of the human passions (the unique preserve of 'a lofty Genius'), and his consequent capacity to kindle in his audiences the utmost 'concernment' for his characters. If 'the fury of [Shakespeare's] fancy,' Dryden declares, 'often transported him, beyond the bounds of Judgment, either in coyning of new words and phrases, or racking words which were in use, into the violence of a Catachresis', this should not be taken as an argument for the total elimination of metaphors in the expression of passion, 'for *Longinus* thinks 'em necessary to raise it'. If 'pompous words' and 'Bombast' are sometimes evident in Shakespeare's passionate speeches, he 'does not often thus', and Dryden goes on to offer examples from *Julius Caesar* and *King Richard II* to illustrate Shakespeare's capacity to articulate 'thoughts . . . such as arise from the matter', and which are 'extreamly natural', their 'expression' not being 'viciously figurative' (*Works*, 13. 244–7). The extravagance and obscurity which Dryden and his contemporaries had observed to be a recurrent characteristic of Shakespeare's writing are now seen as the inevitable price which has to be paid for the true Longinian sublimity of the dramatist's best work.[29]

The application to Shakespeare of the Longinian critique of Homer is also clearly evident in early eighteenth-century English translations of Longinus' treatise. In their versions of 1712 and 1739, Leonard Welsted and William Smith offer many 'applications' of Longinus to English literature, and particularly to the works of Shakespeare.[30] Homer's mastery in the depiction of storms (praised by Longinus in 10. 4) is paralleled, for example, by Welsted (pp. 169–70) with the description of the storm in *Julius Caesar* (1. 3. 4–8) and by Smith (pp. 138–40) with that in *King Lear* (3. 1. 4–9; 3. 2. 14–16, 49–59). No-one, says Smith (pp. 146–8) 'can enter into a Parallel with *Shakespeare*' in the 'affecting Horror' evoked by Longinus

[29] On this subject, see, further, Paul Hammond, 'The Janus Poet: Dryden's Critique of Shakespeare', in Claude Rawson and Aaron Santesso, eds., *John Dryden (1631–1700): His Politics, his Plays, and his Poets* (Newark NJ and London, 2004), pp. 158–79.

[30] See Leonard Welsted, *The Works of Dionysius Longinus, On the Sublime; or, a Treatise Concerning the Sovereign Perfection of Writing. Translated from the Greek* (London, 1712); *Dionysius Longinus on the Sublime: Translated from the Greek, with Notes and Observations . . . by William Smith* (London, 1739). Since the divisions of Longinus' text differ both between Welsted's and Smith's translations and between both versions and modern editions, references to Longinus are keyed for convenience to the modern translation by D. A. Russell included in D. A. Russell and M. Winterbottom, eds., *Ancient Literary Criticism: The Principal Texts in New Translations* (Oxford, 1972).

(15. 1–6) when describing the distraction of Euripides' Orestes after the death of Clytemnestra, and he cites in support the 'dagger' scene from *Macbeth* (2. 1), a scene also invoked, along with that depicting Richard III's nightmares before the battle of Bosworth Field (*King Richard III*, 5. 5), by Welsted (pp. 174–5).

Welsted's summing-up conveys vividly his conviction that the Homeric sublimity of Shakespeare's genius is both intimately bound up with, and also amply compensates for, any defects which his work might contain:

> I am struck with Astonishment when I read *Shakespear*. Can one read him without the utmost Emotion? . . . At the same time it must be granted, that those Writers who excel so highly in the Grand and Lofty, are liable to numerous Failings, and those sometimes very gross ones; but how can one expect it should be otherwise. Human Spirit in such Works is wrought to its utmost stretch, and cannot, as our Critick observes, possibly support it self thro' the whole with equal Majesty: Nature asks a Breathing-time: He must trifle with *Homer*, who would rise to *Homer*'s Altitudes.
>
> (pp. 186–7)

Many of the Shakespearian parallels cited by Welsted and Smith significantly overlap with passages marked out for special approval in Alexander Pope's edition of Shakespeare,[31] and one can witness in Pope's writings on Homer and Shakespeare particularly striking evidence of the effects of the Longinian critique of Homer on the developing early eighteenth-century conception of Shakespeare's genius.

The Longinian provenance of Pope's celebration of Homer's poetic 'fire' is well established.[32] Near the beginning the Preface to his *Iliad*, for example, Pope asserts that

> No Man of a true Poetical Spirit is Master of himself while he reads [Homer]. What he writes is of the most animated Nature imaginable; every thing moves,

[31] In Pope's edition 'some of the most shining passages are distinguish'd by comma's in the margin; and where the beauty lay not in particulars but in the whole, a star is prefix'd to the scene' (Norman Ault and Rosemary Cowler, eds., *The Prose Works of Alexander Pope*, 2 vols. (Oxford 1936–86), 2. 25. Quotations from Pope's prose are taken from this edition cited by volume and page.

[32] For a modern analysis, see Kirsti Simonsuuri, *Homer's Original Genius: Eighteenth-Century Notions of the Early Greek Epic (1688–1798)* (Cambridge, 1979), pp. 13, 60–4.

every thing lives, and is put in Action. If a Council be call'd, or a Battel fought, you are not coldly inform'd of what was said or done as from a third Person; the Reader is hurry'd out of himself by the Force of the Poet's Imagination, and turns in one place to a Hearer, and in another to a Spectator.

(*Prose Works*, 1. 224–5)

This passage, as Pope's early editor Gilbert Wakefield pointed out, clearly echoes Longinus' description of the effects of poetic sublimity, 'Wherein by an extraordinary Enthusiasm and Emotion of Soul, it seems as if we saw the things we speak of, and put them before the Eyes of those that hear us' (p. 40), and of the stylistic devices whereby the sublime poet convinces readers that they are 'not then in Narration but Action', and 'makes the Auditory often think themselves in the middle of the Danger' (p. 58).[33] Pope's account of Homer's ability to find out 'Living Words' (*Prose Works*, 1. 233) is similarly pre-echoed in Longinus' comments on Homer's genius for 'Words that give a sort of Soul and Life to things'. And his account of Homer's pre-eminence in 'the Grandeur and Excellence of his Sentiments' is indebted not merely to Longinus but specifically to Boileau's version (p. 25), which at the appropriate place (9. 4–5 in modern editions) fills out a lacuna in the original Greek text.[34]

There are also notable affinities between Pope's praise of Homer, and the general encomium with which Pope begins the Preface to his edition of Shakespeare. Pope's descriptions of the 'Fire' and 'Rapture' whereby Homer 'animates' his subject matter, overpowers criticism, and carries readers and audiences away in spellbound involvement, are closely paralleled in his remarks on Shakespeare's apparently effortless 'power over the passions':

The *Power* over our *Passions* was never possess'd in a more eminent degree, or display'd in so different instances. Yet all along, there is seen no labour, no pains to raise them; no preparation to guide our guess to the effect, or be perceiv'd to lead toward it: We are surpriz'd, the moment we weep; and yet upon reflection find the passion so just, that we shou'd be surpriz'd if we had not wept, and wept at that very moment.

(*Prose Works*, 2. 14)

[33] The second example is noted by Gilbert Wakefield, ed., *The Iliad of Homer, Translated by Alexander Pope: A New Edition*, 4 vols. (London, 1806), 1. vi–vii.

[34] As pointed out by Wakefield, ed., *The Iliad of Homer*, I. xxi–xxii.

In the Preface to his *Iliad*, Pope had written in a similar vein of Shakespeare's 'Poetical Fire' which – just as powerfully as Homer's, albeit not so consistently or sustainedly – 'strikes before we are aware, like an accidental Fire from Heaven' (*Prose Works*, 1. 225). Precisely the same metaphor was, significantly, used by Anthony Blackwall when writing of the Longinian sublime:

> The Sublime is a just grand, and marvellous thought. It strikes like lightning with a conquering and resistless flame... It carries all before it by its own strength; and does not so much raise persuasion in the hearer or reader, as throw him into an ecstacy, and transport him out of himself.[35]

The connections in Pope's mind between Homer and Shakespeare are equally evident when he voices his conviction that the sentiments spoken by Shakespeare's characters seem to flow from dramatically-conceived creations, rather than appearing as general reflections arbitrarily imposed on their speakers:

> [E]very single character is *Shakespear* is as much an Individual, as those in Life itself; it is impossible to find any two alike; and such as from their relation or affinity in any respect appear to be most Twins, will upon comparison be found remarkably distinct. To this life and variety of Character, we must add the wonderful Preservation of it; which is such throughout his plays, that had all the Speeches been printed without the very names of the Persons, I believe one might have apply'd them with certainty to every speaker.
>
> (*Prose Works*, 2. 13–14)

Here we may remember Pope's distinction in the Preface to his *Iliad* between the characterization of Homer and Virgil:

> In *Virgil* the Dramatic Part is less in proportion to the Narrative; and the Speeches often consist of general Reflections or Thoughts, which might be equally just in any Person's Mouth upon the same Occasion... We oftner think of the Author himself when we read *Virgil*, than when we are engag'd in *Homer*. All which are the Effects of a colder Invention, that interests us less in the Action describ'd: *Homer* makes us Hearers, and *Virgil* leaves us Readers.
>
> (*Prose Works*, 1. 231)

[35] *The Sacred Classics Defended and Illustrated* (1737), cited by Andrew Ashfield and Peter de Bolla, eds., *The Sublime: A Reader in British Eighteenth-Century Aesthetic Theory* (Cambridge, 1996), p. 18.

'Invention', for Pope the distinguishing characteristic of Homer's genius, is, as Paul Hammond has reminded us,

a classical rhetorical term (*inventio*) for the first of the elements of composition, and its etymology implies that the writer does not make up but discovers material, which is thus thought to be there waiting to be used. Accordingly, Homer as the greatest poetic inventor is the writer who is closest to Nature.[36]

Pope's praise of Homer's 'Invention' is thus closely related to his celebration of Shakespeare's 'originality':

If any Author deserved the name of an *Original*, it was *Shakespear*. *Homer* himself drew not his art so immediately from the fountains of Nature, it proceeded through *Aegyptian* strainers and channels, and came to him not without some tincture of the learning, or some case of the models, of those before him. The Poetry of *Shakespear* was Inspiration indeed: he is not so much an Imitator, as an Instrument, of Nature; and 'tis not so just to say that he speaks from her, as that she speaks thro' him.

(*Prose Works*, 2. 13)

These sentiments find a significant echo in the most important piece of Shakespeare criticism to appear in the second half of the eighteenth century, Johnson's great Preface of 1765. Johnson, we may recall, judged that

it would not be easy to find any author, except Homer, who invented so much as Shakespeare.[37]

He also echoed the terms of Pope's praise of the distinctively dramatic qualities of Homer and Shakespeare when comparing Shakespeare's *Othello* with a widely admired drama of his own century, Joseph Addison's *Cato*:

We find in *Cato* innumerable beauties which enamour us of its author, but we see nothing that acquaints us with human sentiments or human actions; we place it with the fairest and the noblest progeny which judgment propagates by conjunction with learning; but *Othello* is the vigorous and vivacious offspring of observation impregnated by genius. *Cato* affords a splendid exhibition of artificial and fictitious manners, and delivers just and

[36] Alexander Pope, *Selected Prose*, ed. Paul Hammond (Cambridge, 1987), p. 8.

[37] *Samuel Johnson on Shakespeare*, ed. H. R. Woudhuysen (Harmondsworth, 1989), p. 145. Subsequent quotations are also from this edition.

noble sentiments, in diction easy, elevated, and harmonious, but its hopes and fears communicate no vibration to the heart; the composition refers us only to the writer; we pronounce the name of *Cato*, but we think on *Addison*.

(p. 140)

And Johnson makes the Homeric parallel explicit when, commenting on Shakespeare's plots, he observes that

every man finds his mind more strongly seized by the tragedies of Shakespeare than of any other writer; others please us by particular speeches, but he always makes us anxious for the event, and has perhaps excelled all but Homer in securing the first purpose of a writer, by exciting restless and unquenchable curiosity, and compelling him that reads his work to read it through.

(pp. 139–40)

Here Johnson stands in a direct line from Longinus (as translated by William Smith) who, commenting on a passage in which Homer addresses his readers directly about the deeds of Diomedes, observes:

By this Address you not only strike more upon his Passions, but fill him with a more earnest Attention, and a more anxious Impatience for the Event.

(p. 65)

Shakespearian redaction and criticism of the late seventeenth and early eighteenth centuries, I have argued, is far less homogeneous, and far less pervasively and damagingly influenced by neo-Aristotelian neoclassicism than is usually supposed. Some of its criticisms of Shakespeare's faults are less pedantic and period-specific than might at first sight appear. And some of the most influential writers of the period developed a powerful and influential conception of Shakespeare as an author of 'fire', originality, and spellbinding dramatic power, whose very failings are an inevitable concomitant of his capacity to achieve the Longinian Sublime, and whose finest effects make him fully deserving of the title 'The English Homer'.

# 2

## Cowley's Horatian Mice

*Belinda*: Oh Gad, I have a great passion for *Cowley* – Don't you admire him?
*Sharper*: Oh Madam! He was our *English Horace*.

William Congreve, *The Old Bachelor*

At the large foot of a fair hollow tree,
Close to plow'd ground, seated commodiously,
His ancient and Hereditary House,
There dwelt a good substantial Country-Mouse:
Frugal, and grave, and careful of the main,
Yet, one, who once did nobly entertain
A City-Mouse, well coated, sleek, and gay,
A Mouse of high degree, which lost his way,
Wantonly walking forth to take the Air,
And arriv'd early, and belighted, there,
For a days lodging. The good hearty Hoast,
(The ancient plenty of his hall to boast)
Did all the stores produce that might excite,
With various tasts, the Courtiers appetite.
Fitches and Beans, Peason, and Oats, and Wheat,
And a large Chesnut, the delicious meat
Which *Jove* himself, were he a Mouse, would eat.
And for a *Haut goust* there was mixt with these
The swerd of Bacon and the coat of Cheese.
The precious Reliques, which at Harvest, he
Had gather'd from the Reapers luxury.
Freely (said he) fall on, and never spare,
The bounteous Gods will for to morrow care.
And thus at ease on beds of straw they lay,
And to their Genius sacrific'd the day.

Yet the nice guest's Epicurean mind,
(Though breeding made him civil seem and kind)
Despis'd this Country feast, and still his thought
Upon the Cakes and Pies of *London* wrought.
Your bounty and civility, said he,
Which I'm surpriz'd in these rude parts to see,
Shows that the Gods have given you a mind,
Too noble for the fate which here you find.
Why should a Soul, so virtuous and so great
Lose itself thus in an Obscure retreat?
Let savage Beasts lodg in a Country Den,
You should see Towns, and Manners know, and men:
And taste the generous Lux'ury of the Court,
Where all the Mice of quality resort;
Where thousand beauteous shees about you move,
And by high fare, are plyant made to love.
We all e're long must render up our breath,
No cave or hole can shelter us from death.
Since Life is so uncertain, and so short,
Let's spend it all in feasting and in sport.
Come, worthy Sir, come with me, and partake,
All the great things that mortals happy make.
Alas, what virtue hath sufficient Arms,
T' oppose bright Honour, and soft Pleasures charms?
What wisdom can their magick force repel?
It draws the reverend Hermit from his Cel.
It was the time, when witty Poets tell
*That* Phoebus *into* Thetis *bosom fell:*
*She blusht at first, and then put out the light,*
*And drew the modest Curtains of the night.*
Plainly, the troth to tell, the Sun was set,
When to the Town our wearied Travellers get.
To a Lords house, as Lordly as can be
Made for the use of Pride and Luxury,
They come; the gentle Courtier at the door
Stops, and will hardly enter in before.
But 'tis, Sir, your command, and being so,
I'm sworn t' obedience, and so in they go.
Behind a hanging in a spacious room,
(The richest work of *Mortclakes* noble Loom)
They wait awhile their wearied limbs to rest,

Till silence should invite them to their feast.
*About the hour that* Cynthia's *Silver light*
*Had touch'd the pale Meridies of the night*;
At last the various Supper being done,
It happened that the Company was gone,
Into a room remote, Servants and all,
To please their nobles fancies with a Ball.
Our host leads forth his stranger, and do's find,
All fitted to the bounties of his mind.
Still on the Table half fill'd dishes stood,
And with delicious bits the floor was strow'd.
The courteous mouse presents him with the best,
And both with fat varieties are blest,
Th' industrious Peasant every where does range,
And thanks the gods for his Life's happy change.
Loe, in the midst of a well fraited Pye,
They both at last glutted and wanton lye.
When see the sad Reverse of prosperous fate,
And what fierce storms on mortal glories wait.
With hideous noise, down the rude servants come,
Six dogs before run barking into th' room;
The wretched gluttons fly with wild affright,
And hate the fulness which retards their flight.
Our trembling Peasant wishes now in vain,
That Rocks and Mountains cover'd him again.
Oh how the change of his poor life he curst!
This, of all lives (said he) is sure the worst.
Give me again, *ye gods*, my Cave and wood;
With peace, let tares and acorns be my food.[1]

Abraham Cowley's 'The Country Mouse: a Paraphrase upon Horace, 2. Book, Satire 6' was first published in the poet's *Verses upon Several Occasions* (1663). It was subsequently reprinted, with a translation of the first half of Horace's satire by Cowley's friend Thomas Sprat, in Alexander Brome's *The Poems of Horace* (1666), and, again, as part of the essay 'Of Agriculture' in Cowley's *Several Discourses by way of Essays, in Verse and Prose* (1668). It is not well known today by readers

[1] Cowley's work is cited throughout this chapter, by volume title and page, from the editions of A. R. Waller: *Poems*, and *Essays, Plays and Sundry Verses* (Cambridge, 1905–06).

of either classical or English literature. For most students of English poetry, Cowley has become a virtually forgotten figure. Twentieth-century literary historians have effectively marginalized him by affording him that most unappetizing of all literary labels, 'transitional figure' – characterizing him as a 'decadent metaphysical' who employed Donneian extravagance without Donne's intellectual energy or emotional commitment and/or as a 'precursor of Augustanism', whose later work can be seen to anticipate the 'public' and 'polite' verse-forms and manner of the Age of Reason.[2]

But things have not always been thus. Contrary to common belief, Cowley was no mere seven-days' wonder, whose work enjoyed a short-lived vogue in his own lifetime and then rapidly fell out of favour. His verse and prose were, in fact, frequently reprinted and read long after his death. The *Essays* in particular were continuously available in popular editions until well into the twentieth century.[3] Cowley's work, moreover, was widely felt to possess qualities and virtues which were distinctively its own. From the beginning, to be sure, many of the poet's admirers had tempered their enthusiasm with serious reservations about his habitual excesses and extravagances. But the praise nevertheless persisted, and frequently came from weighty, and sometimes unexpected, sources.

Milton, for example, is even reported to have ranked Cowley with Spenser and Shakespeare as the third great English poet.[4] Dryden affirmed that nothing could 'appear more beautiful' to him than the 'strength' of the imagery in Cowley's Odes.[5] Pope told Joseph Spence that Cowley was 'a fine poet, in spite of all his faults', praised 'the language of his Heart' – he was referring, perhaps, both to the autobiographical writing of the *Essays* and to Cowley's movingly affectionate poems on friends and contemporaries – and drew on the poet's

[2] For statements of such views which have been influential on several generations of students, see G. Walton, *Metaphysical to Augustan: Studies in Tone and Sensibility in the Seventeenth Century* (London, 1955) and Patrick Cruttwell, *The Shakespearean Moment and its Place in the Poetry of the Seventeenth Century* (London, 1954).

[3] For earlier editions of Cowley, see M. R. Perkin, *Abraham Cowley: A Bibliography* (Folkestone, 1977); on the history of Cowley's reputation, see A. H. Nethercot, 'The Reputation of Abraham Cowley', *PMLA*, 38 (1923) 588–641, and Jean Loiseau, *Abraham Cowley's Reputation in England* (Paris, 1931).

[4] The report derives from Milton's widow; see John Milton, *Paradise Lost*, ed. T. Newton, 2 vols. (London, 1749), 1. lvi.

[5] 'The Authors Apology for Heroique Poetry', prefixed to *The State of Innocence* (1677); *Works*, 12. 94.

phrasing and rhythms on many occasions in his own verse.[6] William Cowper paid eloquent testimony to the way in which Cowley, having retired from Court life, found 'rich amends / For a lost world in solitude and verse'.[7] Samuel Johnson, whose 'Life of Cowley' is often thought of as an attack on the poet and on the 'metaphysical' tradition as a whole, in fact praises Cowley's best work in the strongest possible terms, noting with emphatic approval Cowley's 'agility', 'gaiety of fancy', and 'facility of expression' and judging that, when writing at his best, his 'volatility is not the flutter of a light, but the bound of an elastic mind'.[8] Perhaps the most surprising of all Cowley's admirers (given the apparently vast temperamental and aesthetic gulf between the two men) was Wordsworth, who referred to Cowley as an 'able writer and amiable man' and advised a correspondent to 'read all Cowley; he is very valuable to a collector of English sound sense'.[9]

Written between 1660 and 1667, and published posthumously in 1668, Cowley's *Essays* contain the reflections of the poet's final years. Having been disappointed in his hopes of Court preferment at the Restoration, Cowley obtained a favourable lease of some royal lands and went into retirement, first at Barn Elms near Putney and then, from 1665 at Chertsey, where he lived until his death in 1667. The *Essays* reflect, in part, Cowley's personal sense of regret and sadness at having (as he now saw it) squandered so much of his earlier life in his career as a courtier and public servant.[10]

The first piece in the volume, 'Of Liberty', sets the agenda for the collection as a whole. In this essay, Cowley announces that he intends to discourse on 'the Liberty of a private man in being Master of his own Time and Actions, as far as may consist with the laws of God and

[6] Joseph Spence, *Observations, Anecdotes and Characters of Books and Men*, ed. J. Osborn, 2 vols. (Oxford, 1966) 1. 89; 'The First Epistle of the Second Book of Horace, Imitated', 78; *TE*, 4. 210.

[7] William Cowper, *The Task*, 4. 729–30.

[8] See Samuel Johnson, *The Lives of the Most Eminent English Poets*, ed. Roger Lonsdale, 4 vols. (Oxford, 2006), 1. 215.

[9] M. L. Peacock, ed., *The Critical Opinions of William Wordsworth* (Baltimore MD, 1950), pp. 311, 233.

[10] A useful general introduction to the *Essays* is provided by A. H. Nethercot in 'Abraham Cowley's Essays', *Journal of English and Germanic Philology*, 29 (1930), 114–30.

of his Country... and to enquire what estate of Life does best seat us in the possession of it' (*Essays*, p. 377). Liberty, he suggests, consists in the individual's capacity to free himself from the domination of ambition, covetousness, and voluptuousness. The truly happy man, he argues, in this essay and in the collection as a whole, is he who has achieved the ability to put aside vain desires, and to live in full possession of the 'easie plenty' and 'substantial blessedness' (*Essays*, p. 409) which life can offer.

Cowley's *Essays* are frankly eclectic in form and spirit, and, like the *Essais* of Montaigne on which they are in some ways modelled, treat their subject from a variety of perspectives and in a variety of tones, manners, and voices. Verse is mingled with prose, and 'original' writing with translation, paraphrase, and imitation (from Horace, Martial, Seneca, Virgil, and other classical poets), to form a continuing conversation piece about the nature of contentment and the happy life. The happy man is seen, at various points in the volume, as a wise Stoic, fortified by inner calm and self-possession against the buffets of life, as a happy husbandman relishing the simple pleasures and beautiful scenery of the countryside, as a Lucretian philosopher contemplating the causes of things, as a gentleman-farmer participating in good conversation among choice friends in congenial surroundings, and as a pre-lapsarian Adam, enjoying the delights of a Golden Age innocence.[11] Cowley's version of Horace's tale of 'The Country Mouse' was incorporated in this larger pattern, and to see it in its setting in the *Essays* as a whole is to become conscious of both the daring and the surprising aptness of the poet's decision to excerpt Horace's fable from the *Sermo* (conversation piece) of which it was originally an integral part.

The sixth *Sermo* of Horace's second book offers a set of reflections on the farm in the Sabine hills which has been obtained for Horace by his patron, Maecenas. This farm, Horace says, has provided him with all he could ever have desired. It is true that the presence of his beloved Maecenas gives Rome, in theory, advantages over the country. But when in Rome, Horace reflects, he can scarcely enjoy Maecenas' company. Life in the city is a perpetual jostle and bustle.

[11] See Maren-Sophie Røstvig, *The Happy Man: Studies in the Matamorphosis of a Classical Ideal: Vol. 1: 1600–1700* (2nd edition, Oslo, 1962), pp. 41–3.

Others envy the poet's intimacy with his patron, or try to exploit it for their own ends, pestering him with requests, or trying to pry out of him the state secrets which, as Maecenas' confidant, they are sure he must possess. (When he is not forthcoming, they think he is being strategically cagey.) It is not surprising, therefore, that, whenever he is in the city, Horace longs ardently for his farm, where life is, at one and the same time, more relaxed and more serious. The verse translation of this part of the *Sermo* by Francis Fawkes (1720–77) is both close to the prose-sense of the Latin, and also usefully conveys, for the English reader, something of the affectionate warmth of Horace's tone:

> When shall I see my peaceful Country Farm,
> My Fancy when with ancient Authors charm?
> Or, lulled to Sleep, my easy Hours delude
> In sweet Oblivion of Solicitude?
> O for those Beans which my own Fields provide!
> Deem'd by *Pythagoras* to man ally'd;
> The savoury Pulse serv'd up in Platters nice,
> And Herbs high-relish'd with the Bacon Slice!
> O tranquil Nights in pleasing Converse spent,
> Ambrosial Suppers that might Gods content!
> When with my chosen Friends (delicious Treat!)
> Before the Household Deities we eat;
> The Slaves themselves regale on choicest Meat.
> Free from mad Laws we sit reclin'd at Ease,
> And drink as much, or little, as we please.
> Some quaff large Bumpers that expand the Soul,
> And some grow mellow with a moderate Bowl.
> We never talk of this Man's House or Vill,
> Or whether *Lepos* dances well or ill.
> But of those Duties which ourselves we owe,
> And which 'tis quite a Scandal not to know:
> As whether Wealth or Virtue can impart
> The truest Pleasure to the human Heart:
> What should direct us in our Choice of Friends,
> Their own pure Merit, or our private Ends:
> What we may deem, if rightly understood,
> Man's sov'reign Bliss, his chief, his only Good.[12]

[12] *The Works of Horace in English Verse. By Several Hands. Collected and Published by Mr. Duncombe*, 2 vols. (London, 1757–9), 2. 256–7.

After such a passage, the tale of the town and country mouse is clearly intended to come as a surprise. For Horace's *Sermo* is made to culminate not, as one might have expected, in a report of the poet's earnest philosophical conversations with his well-read peers but in a nursery fable told (as a riposte to one of the company who has spoken enviously of a rich miser) by a rustic neighbour who, we are wryly told, 'garrit anilis / ex re fabellas' (rattles off old wives' tales that fit the case). Horace is obviously taking a considerable risk, which will tax his celebrated urbanity and deft mastery of transitions to the full, if the ending of his poem is not to appear the grossest anti-climax.

Cowley, by including his retelling of the country mouse story in the *Essays*, immediately after his renderings of two of the most famous ancient encomia of rural happiness (the 'O fortunatos nimium' passage from Virgil's second *Georgic*, and Horace's second *Epode*[13]) can be seen to be taking a risk which is in some ways analogous to that taken by Horace himself in *Sermones*, 2. 6. The subject of rural content is one in which, as we have seen, Cowley had a considerable personal investment, and on which, throughout the *Essays*, he sees his own thoughts overlapping with the weighty reflections of a number of his favourite writers, ancient and modern. Indeed, it might be argued that the risk taken by Cowley was in some respects even greater than that taken by Horace. For Horace's treatment of his own concerns throughout *Sermo* 6 and, indeed, throughout the *Sermones* as a whole, is, famously, shot through with a playful irony and self-mockery that frequently leave us slightly unsure how seriously we are to take him, and how seriously he is taking himself. (The joke about Pythagorean beans included in the praise of the Sabine farm, quoted above, provides a good example of this effect.) The surprise which is sprung on the reader at the end of the sixth *Sermo* is, therefore, one of a succession of daring shifts and transitions of tone and manner which the attentive reader of the *Sermones* has come to expect, and to see as characteristically Horatian. In contrast, Cowley's treatment of weighty matters in the *Essays* is, for all his occasional lightness of touch, generally several notches higher up the scale of earnestness and solemnity from that of

[13] Horace's *Epode* is made more simply celebratory in the English version, since his ironical conclusion is omitted by Cowley.

Horace. His decision to reprint 'The Country Mouse' without apology among more obviously 'serious' treatments of rural happiness suggests his confidence that the poem was nothing short of a *tour de force* of witty poise.[14]

Cowley's title describes his method of translation in 'The Country Mouse' as 'paraphrase', and Horace's text is, indeed, freely expanded and extensively reworked in the English version. Cowley relocates the Roman fable in an English setting, and discovers in his original a set of oppositions and contrasts which take on a distinctive edge in their new context. For the sentiments and characters of Cowley's mice embody the contrasts not only of country versus town, and of retirement versus the life of business and affairs, but also of traditional English rural life versus that of the post-Restoration Court, and of hearty hospitality in the English shires versus the refinement and social luxury of London. But in relocating Horace's fable in his own seventeenth-century England, Cowley was, as we shall see, at the same time responding to important dimensions of the tale in its original Latin. For the humour and point of Horace's fable, Cowley had evidently decided, turned on the Roman poet's decision to bestow upon the tiniest of mammals a series of susceptibilities, attributes, and virtues which come into play whenever human beings begin to ponder seriously questions of pleasure, friendship, society, and the good life. And there was, Cowley clearly thought, a particular felicity in Horace's location and dramatization of such matters in the setting of a convivial meal.

When Cowley's town mouse visits the country mouse in his rural retreat he is described as having an 'Epicurean mind'. This was a phrase which the poet clearly expected to have immediate resonance for contemporary readers, and it is, indeed, a key phrase in the poem. For, as Cowley realized, the significance of Horace's fable is closely bound up with the fact that it debates questions about the good life and true happiness in terms which derive ultimately from the teachings of a thinker to whom Horace was greatly indebted throughout his work: the Greek philosopher Epicurus (341–270 BC). It is therefore necessary,

[14] In Brome's *Horace*, Horace's self-ironizing effects are rendered more directly: as well as following Cowley's lead by updating his version of the first half of Horace's poem to 1662, Thomas Sprat humorously recasts Cervius as 'C[owley]'. See Harold F. Brooks, 'The "Imitation" in English Poetry, especially in Formal Verse Satire, before the Age of Pope', *Review of English Studies*, 25 (1949), 124–40 (129–30).

before proceeding further, to consider the important 'Epicurean' dimension of both Cowley's poem and its Horatian original.[15]

The doctrines of Epicurus centred on the need for human beings to achieve *ataraxia*, the state of freedom from mental and physical anxiety which alone can guarantee happiness and lasting pleasure – for Epicurus, the true goals of all worthwhile human activity. The study of philosophy, Epicurus taught, can help men to achieve *ataraxia* by removing all those distracting and irrelevant cares which customarily afflict their lives. Human bodies and souls, like everything else in the world, consist of atomic particles in combination. The soul's mortality is certain, and there is, therefore, nothing to be feared in death. The gods live in perfect contentment in a remote realm, and play no part in the operations of our world. There is thus no need for men to live in hope of divine rewards or in dread of divine retribution. Our cosmos came into being by a chance combination of atoms and is merely one of an indefinite number of worlds, past, present, and future. It is therefore vain to seek after any supernatural explanation of change and causation. Ambition and competition afflict men with the agonies of jealousy and failure. Public life should therefore be rejected in favour of an existence of serene retirement, in which, freed from those turmoils of hope and fear which result from the wrong kinds of intense emotional involvement, men can lay hold on life's solid pleasures and relish their existence with complete and untrammelled fullness.

It is easy enough to see how such a philosophy, centring as it does on doctrines of mortalism and hedonism, would be open to misconstruction and vilification. Indeed, from antiquity onwards, Epicureanism became frequently associated in the popular imagination with a particularly mindless form of gluttony and atheism, and Epicurus' Garden (the eponymous headquarters of his school of

[15] On Epicurus himself, see C. Bailey, *The Greek Atomists and Epicurus* (Oxford, 1928); G. Panichas, *Epicurus* (New York, 1967); J. M. Rist, *Epicurus: An Introduction* (Cambridge 1972); on Epicurus' reception, see C. T. Harrison, 'The Ancient Atomists and English Literature in the Seventeenth Century', *Harvard Studies in Classical Philology*, 45 (1934), 1–79; T. F. Mayo, *Epicurus in England (1650–1725)* (Dallas TX, 1934); R. H. Kargon, *Atomism in England from Hariot to Newton* (Oxford, 1966); L. S. Joy, *Gassendi the Atomist* (Cambridge, 1987); Howard Jones, *The Epicurean Tradition* (London, 1989); Fred S. and Emily Michael, 'A Note on Gassendi in England', *Notes and Queries*, 235 (1990), 297–9.

philosophy at Athens) was often thought of merely as a 'front' for profligate debauchery. His philosophy was, consequently, widely misunderstood and substantially neglected for much of the Middle Ages and the early modern era.[16]

Though a few earlier English writers had displayed some first-hand knowledge of Epicurus,[17] it was the substantial revaluation of Epicureanism in the 1640s by the French philosopher and mathematician Pierre Gassendi (1592–1655) that was to prove crucially influential on this side of the Channel. Two books have been recognized as having played a crucial role in mediating Gassendi's reappraisal of the moral and ethical parts of Epicurus' philosophy to the English general reader. The year 1656 saw the publication of *Epicurus' Morals: Collected and Faithfully Englished*, the first popular exposition in any vernacular of Epicurus' moral teaching, prefaced by 'An Apology for Epicurus' by Walter Charleton (1619–1707), a physician who had probably known Cowley in the 1640s.[18] Four years later, in 1660, the poet and classical scholar Thomas Stanley (1625–78) published, in Volume 3 of his encyclopaedic *History of Philosophy*, a comprehensive account, drawing substantially on Gassendi, of both the physical and moral aspects of the Epicurean system.[19]

The English exponents of Epicurus were, like Gassendi, anxious to emphasize those aspects of Epicurean moral teaching which are closest to Christianity, and to palliate those parts of Epicurean doctrine which could not easily be squared with Christian belief. Both *Epicurus' Morals* and Stanley's *History* distinguish clearly between the pleasure which forms the *summum bonum* in the Epicurean system and the less desirable forms of pleasure which were the goal of other groups of hedonistic philosophers with which Epicureanism had, over the centuries, become popularly confused. Stanley makes a particularly sharp distinction in this respect between the Epicureans and the Cyrenaics, the sect founded by

[16] See R. P. Jungkuntz, 'Christian Approval of Epicureanism', *Church History*, 31 (1962), 279–93 and D. C. Allen, 'The Rehabilitation of Epicurus and his Theory of Pleasure in the Early Renaissance', *Studies in Philology*, 41 (1944), 1–15 for partial exceptions to this generalization.

[17] See Harrison, 'The Ancient Atomists', 1–19.

[18] See L. Sharp, 'Walter Charleton's Early Life, 1620–59, and Relationship to Natural Philosophy in Mid-Seventeenth Century England', *Annals of Science*, 30 (1973), 311–40 (317–18).

[19] 4 vols., 1655–62; the section on the Cyrenaic sect first appeared in vol. 2 (1656).

Aristippus of Cyrene, probably in the third century BC. The Cyrenaics, Stanley explains, asserted 'corporeal pleasure to be our ultimate end, ... not catastematick, permanent pleasure, which consisteth in privation of Grief and a quiet, void of all disturbance, which *Epicurus* held'. For them, pleasure was an intrinsic good 'though proceeding from the most sordid dishonest thing'. The only real pleasure, they believed, was to be found 'in motion'. They therefore rejected the Epicurean goal of *ataraxia*, and asserted that 'one Pleasure differeth not from another Pleasure, nor is one Pleasure sweeter than another Pleasure'. Pleasure for the Cyrenaics, moreover, existed only in the immediate present. It was neither to be had from 'the remembrance of past goods, nor expectation of future compleat pleasure, as *Epicurus* thought, for by time and expectation the motion of the Soul is dissolved'. Aristippus' life, says Stanley, was lived in accordance with his teaching, having been 'employed in Luxury, sweet Unguents, rich Garments, Wine and Women'.[20]

The sharp contrast between the undiscriminating abandon of Cyrenaic hedonism and the temperate reasonableness of the Epicurean position is clearly seen in Epicurus' own defence of his doctrine of pleasure, as rendered in *Epicurus' Morals*:

> III. AND, therefore, when we say; that Pleasure in the General is the end of a happy life, or the Chiefest Good; we are very far from understanding those Pleasures, which are so much admired, courted and pursued by men wallowing in Luxury or any other pleasures that are placed in the mere motion or action of Fruition, whereby the sense is pleasantly tickled; as some, either out of Ignorance of the right, or dissent of opinion, or prejudice and Evil will against us, have wrongfully expounded our words: but only this ... Not to be pained in Body, nor perturbed in Mind.
>
> IV. FOR, it is not perpetual Feastings and Drinkings; it is not the love of, and Familiarity with beautiful boys and women; it is not the Delicacies of rare Fishes, sweet meats, rich Wines, nor any other Dainties of the Table, that can make a Happy life: But, it is Reason with sobriety, and consequently a serene Mind; investigating the Causes, why this Object is to be Elected, and that to be Rejected; and chasing away those vain, superstitious and deluding opinions, which would occasion very great disquiet in the mind.[21]

[20] Thomas Stanley, *The History of Philosophy* (3rd edition, London, 1700), pp. 133–5.

[21] Walter Charleton, *Epicurus' Morals, Collected and Faithfully Englished*, ed. F. Manning (London, 1926), p. 15.

The wise man, in Epicurus' conception, is prudent but not avaricious. He should 'proportion his Expences, as still to be laying up somewhat for the Future; yet without Avarice, and the sordid desire of heaping up wealth. For, it is not the part of a Wise man to neglect his household Affairs'. A wise, temperate housekeeping will assist in the creation of the desired tranquillity of mind. Drunkenness and debauchery are to be avoided, because they impair the true pleasures of eating; for

> those who are daily used to more sumptuous entertainments, have their palats so furred and imbued, and their stomachs so oppressed and weakned by the continual use and ingurgitation of them, that they neither relish nor swallow their meats and drinks with pleasure comparable to that, which a sober man receives, whose Gusto is sincere, and Appetite strong.[22]

Epicurus consequently finds the greatest joy in simple, home-produced fare:

> For mine own part, seriously, when I feed upon simple Bread and Water, and sometimes (when I would entertain myself somewhat more splendidly) mend my chear with a little Cheese; I apprehend abundant satisfaction therein, and bid defiance to those pleasures, which the ignorant and sensual Vulgar so much like and cry up in the magnificence of great Entertainments: and hereupon, if I have no more than brown Bread, Decocted Barly, and clean Water; I think my Table so well furnished, as that I dare dispute Felicity even with *Jove* himself.[23]

Several passages in Cowley's *Essays* show clearly that the poet had attended to the recent defence of Epicurus,[24] and that, while he showed little interest in the more technical aspects of Epicurus' teachings, he felt personally drawn to the philosopher's ideals of retirement, abstemiousness, and spiritual tranquillity. Though he uses the term 'Epicure' in the popular, pejorative, sense on a number of occasions, he shows himself, in the substantial Pindaric ode which forms the second half of 'The Garden',[25] to be well aware of the current debates about 'true' and 'false' Epicureanism:

[22] *Epicurus' Morals*, p. 48.

[23] Ibid., pp. 48–9.

[24] Nethercot ('Abraham Cowley's Essays', p. 529) suggests that Cowley may have read Gassendi's work in the original Latin; see also Richard Aldington, 'Cowley and the French Epicureans', *New Statesman*, 5 November 1921, pp. 133–4.

[25] This essay is significantly addressed to John Evelyn, one of the leading figures in the current English Epicurean revival.

When *Epicurus* to the World had taught,
   That Pleasure was the chiefest Good,
(And was perhaps i'th' right, if rightly understood)
   His Life he to his Doctrine brought,
And in a Gardens shade that Sovereign Pleasure sought:
Whoever a true Epicure would be,
May there find cheap and virtuous Luxurie.

(*Essays*, p. 424)

And in the essay 'Of Liberty', Cowley defends Epicurus and his followers specifically against those who had charged them with the indulging in unbridled gluttony:

*Metrodorus* [one of Epicurus' leading disciples] said that he had learnt . . . to give his Belly just thanks for all his pleasures. This by the Calumniators of *Epicurus* his Philosophy was objected as one of the most scandalous of all their sayings; which, according to my Charitable understanding may admit a very virtuous sence, which is, that he thanked his own Belly for that moderation in the customary appetites of it, which can only give a Man Liberty and Happiness in this World.

(*Essays*, p. 385)

The true Epicurean, who 'rationally guides' his pleasures, 'and is not hindered by outward impediments in the conduct and enjoyment of them' is thus, in Cowley's view, to be clearly distinguished from 'he who blindly follows all his pleasures' and is thus 'but a servant' to his own luxuriousness (*Essays*, p. 384).

For Cowley, as for Gassendi and his English popularizers, the main tenets of Epicurus' ethical teaching are compatible with the teachings of Christianity. The Epicurean command to live in the present, for example, can be reconciled without much difficulty with Jesus' exhortation (Matt. 6: 34) to 'take . . . no thought for the morrow; for the morrow shall take thought for the things of itself':

We are all 'Εφήμεροι (as *Pindar* calls us) Creatures of a day, and therefore our Saviour bounds our desires to that little space; as if it were very probable that every day should be our last, we are taught to demand even Bread for no longer a time.

(*Essays*, p. 448)

The speech in which Horace's town mouse attempts to persuade his country host to visit the city reveals that Cowley had seen connections between the contrasting conduct and sentiments of Horace's two mice and the contrast (as much a matter of debate in first-century BC Rome as in seventeenth-century England) between 'true' and 'false' Epicureanism. But these connections are not as simple as they might seem at first sight. For Horace, a close inspection of the Latin original suggests, is not merely using the pretext of his animal fable to propound a straightforward moral distinction between the admirable 'Epicurean' country mouse and his deplorable 'Cyrenaic' visitor.

Commentators have noted the closeness in phrasing and sentiment of some of the town mouse's words to passages elsewhere in Horace's *oeuvre* where the poet is writing *in propria persona.*[26] Several of Horace's *Odes*, they remind us, are cast in the form of an urgent exhortation to surrender to the pleasures of wine and relaxation, since time is passing rapidly by, and the grave will soon claim us all. *Odes*, 1. 11, for example, ends with the famous exhortation to the poem's addressee, Leuconoe: 'carpe diem, quam minimum credula postero' (seize the present day, putting as little trust as may be in the morrow). *Odes*, 2. 3 exhorts the politician Dellius to surrender to the enjoyment of wines, perfumes, and rose-blossom, in full recognition of the frail brevity of life. Another such injunction occupies the central stanzas of *Odes*, 2. 11. Youth and beauty, Horace there asserts, are speeding fast away. Old age will soon put an end to the sports of love, just as spring flowers and moonlight soon pass away. We should therefore drink wine, while we are still able, and recline in careless ease under a lofty plane or pine tree, our locks garlanded with fragrant roses and perfumed with Syrian ointments. And in *Odes*, 4. 12, Horace invites Virgil to join him in a drinking party, and, mindful of death's dark fires, to cast serious thoughts aside, 'dum licet' (while [he] can). The similarity of all these sentiments (and of some of their phrasing) to those voiced by the town mouse in *Sermones*, 2. 6 is clear enough:

[26] See, for example, *Les oeuvres d'Horace: Satires*, ed. P. Lejay (Paris, 1911), p. 536; N. Rudd, *The Satires of Horace* (Cambridge, 1966), p. 250; F. Stack, *Pope and Horace: Studies in Imitation* (Cambridge, 1985), p. 233.

> 'terrestria quando
> mortalis animas vivunt sortita neque ulla est
> aut magno aut parvo leti fuga – quo, bone, circa,
> dum licet, in rebus iucundis vive beatus,
> vive memor quam sis aevi brevis.'
>
> (93–7)

(Since as all creatures that live on earth have mortal souls, and neither great nor small can escape from death, therefore, my friend, while you may, live rich and happy amid delights; live ever mindful of how brief your life is!)

Some commentators, noting the discrepancy between the note of urgent melancholy which informs the hedonistic exhortations in the *Odes* and the true Epicurean *ataraxia* of life on Horace's Sabine farm in *Sermones*, 2. 6, have implied that Horace gave such sentiments to the town mouse merely to guy them and to expose their banality.[27] Such critics might, indeed, point to the mixture of 'high style' phrasing in this passage (the genitive 'aevi' before 'brevis', the pompous epicizing tmesis, whereby the phrase 'quo circa' is interrupted by the vocative 'bone') with the colloquialism of the town mouse's words a few lines earlier – 'vis tu homines urbemque feris proponere silvis?' (wouldn't you put people and the city above these wild woods?) – to support their suggestion that the creature is here being ridiculed. And the phrase 'aut magno aut parvo', they might also point out, is a punning joke, either meaning (metaphorically) 'great or small' or (literally) 'big or little (like a mouse)'.

But there are problems with an argument which suggests that Horace is merely ridiculing the sentiments of the town mouse's speech. First, it implies that Horace was striving for a philosophical consistency in his poetry which many would claim was no part of his purpose.[28] Secondly, it assumes that, when he came to write the passages in the *Odes* cited above, either his heart was not in them, or he had forgotten his own earlier exposure of their inadequacy. Commentators on *Sermones*, 2. 6, moreover, have pointed out that Horace is less single- and simple-minded in his treatment of the

[27] See F. Villeneuve, ed., *Horace: Satires* (Paris 1932), p. 196.

[28] See, for example, W. S. Maguiness, 'The Eclecticism of Horace', *Hermathena*, 27 (1938), 27–46.

theme of rural retirement than such an interpretation would imply. Horace's *Sermo*, they note, with its constant play of implicitly and explicitly self-mocking irony, is as much, or almost as much, concerned to reveal the potential difficulties and absurdities involved in embracing a philosophy of serene Epicurean contentment in the country as it is to celebrate its attainment.

When Horace's town dweller articulates his 'city' philosophy, the poet, to be sure, never lets us forget the comedy latent in having such sentiments come from the lips of a mouse. The 'terrestria' of the mouse's philosophy denote, for the mouse himself, merely all 'creatures who live on earth'. But for Horace and his readers, the word also has a more specific meaning in context: 'mice who scuttle along the ground'.[29] The little creature's speech, however, has been felt by many readers to be invested with a genuinely persuasive appeal; it immediately convinces his country host, and its force and attractiveness are also, it has been plausibly suggested, intended to be felt by the reader.[30] On such a reading, the town mouse's pre-echoes of Horace's *Odes* should be seen not as a simple matter of self-parody-in-advance but rather as Horace using the comic framework of his mouse fable to subject both the hedonistic yearnings expressed later in the *Odes* and the gentler Epicureanism advocated earlier in this very poem to a process of comic testing, which does not involve the simple dismissal or disparagement of either. Horace, on this reading, is embodying in the figures of *both* mice sentiments and philosophical positions to which he is himself strongly drawn. The fable form allows him to present both positions with a sympathetic warmth, while simultaneously exposing the inherent potential for absurdity in each of them. It allows him, that is, a more poised, teasing and inclusive perspective on his own concerns than could easily be achieved by more straightforward means.

Cowley's rendering supports such a reading. For in his version of this section, the English poet, while slyly alerting us to the fact that

[29] See David West, 'Of Mice and Men', in T. Woodman and D. West, eds., *Quality and Pleasure in Latin Poetry* (Cambridge, 1974), pp. 67–80 (75).

[30] See C. O. Brink, *On Reading a Horatian Satire: An Interpretation of Sermones II. 6* (Sydney, 1965); W. S. Anderson, 'The Roman Socrates: Horace and his Satires', in *Critical Essays on Roman Literature: Satire*, ed. J. P. Sullivan (London, 1963), pp. 5–37 (36).

the town mouse is by no means merely prompted by high philosophical motives, invests the city dweller's address to his country host with a genuine warmth and affection. And though there is certainly an element of flattery and patronage in his words, the town mouse's appreciation of the country mouse's virtue and greatness of soul (34–5) and of the 'bounty' and 'civility' which we have seen with our own eyes is expressed in the tone of genuine feeling, and he is made to seem sincerely concerned that his friend's talents should not remain unrecognized (like those of Thomas Gray's 'village Hampden') in rural oblivion. The town mouse, moreover, does not want his friend to remain a social exile in his 'obscure retreat' (where 'obscure', we observe, denotes the darkness of the mouse-hole as much as its remote provinciality) and stresses that the 'luxury' of the Court is potentially 'generous' – that its wealth affords opportunities which are simply not possible in the depths of the country.

Cowley strengthens the town mouse's commendation of the city by deliberately making him recall the ancient hero whose distinctive quality was precisely his questing thirst for knowledge of the diversity of human society. For when the town mouse tells his country host that he 'should see Towns, and Manners know, and men', he recalls the opening of Homer's *Odyssey* (which had been commended and translated by Horace himself in *Epistles*, 1. 2). The appeal of the city, as Cowley's town mouse presents it, is thus not merely the appeal of unbridled Cyrenaic debauchery. It is, we note, the claims of 'bright Honour' as much as 'soft Pleasure' (49) which tempt the country mouse to make his journey, and we thus do not feel, when he leaves his hole, that he does so for reasons that are simply despicable or ignoble. The tone, moreover, in which Cowley's town mouse reminds his friend of human mortality does not so much resemble the haunted melancholy of the foolish Court libertines who, in Dryden's words, 'Disturb their mirth with melancholy fits'[31] as the sprightly, tripping gusto of Cowley's *Anacreontiques* – those delightful 'familiar and festive' poems of 'voluptuous morality'[32] which Cowley clearly

[31] 'Translation of the Latter Part of the Third Book of Lucretius: Against the Fear of Death', l. 98; *Works*, 3. 50.

[32] The phrases are Johnson's (in the 'Life of Cowley'); on the *Anacreontea* and their appeal for Cowley, see Tom Mason, 'Cowley and the Wisdom of Anacreon', *Cambridge Quarterly*, 19 (1990), 103–37.

found so congenial to translate, yet which are so different in spirit from the ascetic austerity recommended in the *Essays.*[33]

The point can be confirmed by comparing the nonchalant shoulder shrug of Cowley's town mouse (42–5) with the distinctly more anxious note of Thomas Creech's version (which nevertheless draws on Cowley's rhymes):

> *Since all must dye, and must resign their Breath,*
> *Nor great, nor little is secure from Death;*
> *Then spend thy days in Pleasure, Mirth and Sport.*
> *And live like One, that Minds his Life is short.*[34]

—or with the melancholy cadence of Fawkes's:

> 'Since all must die that draw this vital Breath,
> 'Nor great not small can shun the Shafts of Death;
> ''Tis ours to sport in Pleasures while we may;
> 'For ever mindful of Life's little Day.'[35]

Though in life Cowley may, from his very earliest years, have always felt the attractions of a life of retirement and contemplative solitude more powerfully than he ever felt the lure of the Court,[36] he was able, in the comic context of 'The Country Mouse', to invest 'the generous Lux'ury of the Court' with a genuine appeal; and to present its social, sexual, and culinary lure in all its multiple, insidious attractiveness. Cowley's wit, like Horace's, brings together and fuses into an effortlessly delightful unity the appeal of the city for both mice and men. For the 'Cakes and Pies of *London*' which are on the city mouse's mind are both the luxury human fare of the Restoration capital[37] and a natural lure for domestic rodents. And the 'thousand beauteous shees' who, the town mouse promises, will 'move' 'about' the country mouse and 'by high fare' be 'plyant made to love' are, at one and the

[33] On the association of Epicureanism and Libertinism after the Restoration, see Mayo, *Epicurus in England, passim*, and Dale Underwood, *Etherege and the Comedy of Manners* (New Haven CT, 1957), pp. 10–40.

[34] *Odes, Satyrs, and Epistles of Horace. Done into English* (London, 1684), p. 477.

[35] *The Works of Horace*, 2. 258.

[36] In the essay 'Of Myself', Cowley quotes from the retirement poem 'A Vote', first included in *Sylva* (1636), a collection published when he was seventeen or eighteen, and which he says was composed when he 'was but thirteen years old'.

[37] See Samuel Pepys, *The Diary*, ed. Robert Latham and William Matthews, 11 vols. (London, 1970–83), 11. 144, 147.

same time, the finely-dressed belles who crowd the ballroom floor in contemporary paintings of the Restoration Court, and little creatures scuttling around and nudging into one another in search of crumbs and scraps which have been dropped by the rooms' human occupants.

The success and delightfulness of Cowley's wit, however, depends crucially on such thoughts being left subtly implicit. When Christopher Smart's town mouse addresses his country host as 'your mouseship', and rests his invitation to the town on the claim that

> mortal lives must have an end,
> And death all earthly things attend,
> Nor is there an escape at all
> For man or mouse, for great or small,[38]

the translator ruins the effect by making the distinction (and thus the analogy) between man and mouse crudely explicit. William Dunkin fares slightly better when he has his town mouse declare:

> "Since Animals but draw their Breath,
> "And have no Being after Death;
> "Since yet the Little, nor the Great,
> "Can shun the Rigour of their Fate;
> "At least be merry while you may,
> "The Life of Mice is but a Day.[39]

But here, despite the attractive last line, it is the contrast between 'Little' and 'Great' that is drawn too overtly to our attention. The distinctive play of Horace's and Cowley's humour depends (as in Virgil's treatment of the bees in Book 4 of the *Georgics*) on the poets' ability to select terms which are equally, and tellingly, apt in worlds of both human beings and tiny creatures. The reminder of the shortness (in human terms) of a mouse's life (for both are 'mortal') serves simultaneously to remind us of our own frailty.

If the 'Epicurean mind' of Cowley's town mouse combines a reasoned relish of urban delights with the voluptuous abandon of the Cowleian Anacreon, the life and sentiments of his country mouse

[38] *The Poetical Works of Christopher Smart, V: The Works of Horace Translated into Verse*, ed. Karina Williamson (Oxford, 1996), p. 257.

[39] *A Poetical Translation of the Works of Horace, By the Revd Mr. Philip Francis*, 2 vols. (3rd edition, London, 1749), 2. 229.

accord closely with the ideals of Epicurus himself, as expounded in English by the popularizers of Gassendi. Like the wise man of *Epicurus' Morals*, Cowley's country mouse is sober, serious-minded, and frugal. He is justly proud to display the carefully variegated delights of his 'noble' banquet, and to share them with his guest. The joyous spontaneity with which he invites the city mouse to the feast, and his willingness to 'sacrifice the day' to his tutelary 'Genius', denote that he is capable of relishing life's present pleasures in a way which is utterly untrammelled by false delicacy, luxuriousness, envy, or ambition. His Epicureanism is manifested not as a consciously held creed or doctrine (as becomes apparent later, he is entirely unaware of the blessedness of his existence) but implicitly, in his very gesture and tone of voice:

> Freely (said he) fall on, and never spare,
> The bounteous Gods will for to morrow care.

The country mouse's second line recalls several passages in Horace's *Odes* (e.g. 1. 9. 9), and Cowley has here penetrated to the very heart of what, for a number of English readers at least, seemed to represent the truly Epicurean freedom of mind. Horace had, at the beginning of his fable, noted the admirable capacity of his normally austere, even stingy, country mouse to 'solvere' (loosen) an 'animum' (soul) that was normally 'artum' (tight reined, narrow) in acts of bounteous hospitality. This phrase of Horace's seems to have epitomized, for some English readers, the 'Feast of Reason and the Flow of Soul'[40] which was both cause and effect of a truly Epicurean contentment. For when, in 1684, John Dryden came to translate the twenty-ninth *Ode* of Horace's Book 3, a poem which he regarded as the quintessence of Horatian Epicureanism and in which, significantly, Horace is inviting Maecenas to share a simple meal with him at his Sabine farm, he remembered, and incorporated, the phrase 'solvere animum' from *Sermones*, 2. 6 where there was no direct justification in the text of the *Ode* itself:

> Leave for a while thy costly Country Seat,
> And, to be Great indeed, forget
> The nauseous pleasures of the Great:

[40] Alexander Pope, 'The First Satire of the Second Book of Horace Imitated', 128; *TE*, 4. 17.

Make haste and come:
Come and forsake thy cloying store;
Thy Turret that surveys, from high,
The smoke, and wealth, and noise of *Rome;*
And all the busie pageantry
That wise men scorn, and fools adore:
Come, *give thy Soul a loose*, and taste the pleasures of the poor.

(12–21; *Works*, 3. 81; my italics in last line)

Dryden's appropriation of the phrase seems, in turn, to have been remembered by later translators of *Sermones*, 2. 6, who re-appropriated it for their version of the poem from which it had been derived in the first instance. Here, for example, is William Dunkin's rendering of Horace's description of the country mouse's frugality (in this version, both mice are female):

Thrifty she was, and full of Cares
To make the most of her Affairs,
Yet in the midst of her Frugality
Would give a Loose to Hospitality.[41]

And Christoper Smart translated the same passage thus:

This mouse was blunt and giv'n to thrift,
But now and then cou'd make a shift
(However rigid or recluse)
With open heart to give a loose.[42]

Though Cowley does not directly translate the Horatian phrase which so impressed Dryden, his country mouse manifests abundantly the freedom and 'loose of soul' which it evokes. Not for this mouse are the artificially cultivated Frenchified delicacies of the Restoration gourmet's table. His bacon and cheese are offered as an '*Haut goust*' – the Anglicized pronunciation of the culinary term (which commonly rhymed in seventeenth-century English with 'August') matching the strong, pungent, 'peasant' flavour of the dish itself. It is the very simplicity of the meal which, the narrator observes, makes it truly worthy of the gods. The cheese and bacon are

41 *A Poetical Translation*, 2. 227.
42 *Poetical Works*, p. 257.

accompanied by the feast's crowning glory, which we are presumably intended to see as towering above the diners:

> And a large Chesnut, the delicious meat
> Which *Jove* himself, were he a Mouse, would eat,

– the perfect murine equivalent of Epicurus' favourite meal, as described in *Epicurus' Morals*:

> ... if I have no more than brown Bread, Decocted Barly, and clean Water; I think my Table so well furnished, as that I dare dispute Felicity even with *Jove* himself.

Cowley's firm identification of the truly Epicurean nature of the country mouse's life enables him, uniquely among the English translators, to invest the country mouse's banquet with a genuine grandeur and attractiveness, while simultaneously extracting the maximum comedy from discovering such philosophically impeccable conduct and such hearty relish among the humblest of creatures.

The effect of the country mouse's exhortation would be much less, of course, without the carefully imagined details with which Cowley, like Horace, has coloured his fable from the very beginning. Cowley expands Horace's local touches considerably, but always keeps his additions within carefully judged bounds. In this respect, his version differs markedly from the rendering of Wye Saltonstall, whose *The Country Mouse, and the City Mouse, or A Merry Moral Fable, Enlarged out of Horace, Serm., Lib. 2, Sat. 6* (2nd edition, London, 1637) expands Horace's thirty-nine lines to make a shapeless poem of nearly fifteen times the length of the original and reminds us that significant economy of means is as crucial a weapon in the Horatian armoury as narrative deftness and accomplished versification.[43] But as well as being economically managed, Cowley's additions allow a greater variety of tones, attitudes, and perspectives to coexist

[43] This poem, nevertheless, seems to have been very popular. The second edition is the first to have survived, and a twelfth edition, dated 1683, is in the Pepys collection at Magdalene College, Cambridge. There appear to be no extant copies of the other ten editions. In *Small Books and Pleasant Histories: Popular Fiction and its Readership in Seventeenth-Century England* (London, 1981), p. 57, Margaret Spufford comments interestingly on the possible appeal for country readers of its extended descriptions of city fare.

simultaneously than the renderings of any of his rivals. For the other translators of *Sermones*, 2. 6 can all be seen to have achieved their effect by one or other kind of selection and simplification (and thus coarsening) of Horace's wit. Cowley is unique in the number of elements in the Horatian original which he has been able to assimilate, mobilize, and combine as integral parts of an English poem.

Commentators on Horace's original have noted how, from the beginning of the fable, the poet's manner both serves as a credible representation of the garrulous over-deliberateness of the tale's ostensible narrator, the rural neighbour Cervius, and simultaneously allows a larger and more diverse play of mind over the situation.[44] The secret of Horace's wit in the opening section of the fable, as in the speeches examined earlier, lies in the poet's selection of terms which bring out both the human and murine dimensions of the situation without ever allowing the reader's mind to dwell too long on one at the expense of the other. In receiving his visitor, Horace's country mouse becomes a 'paterfamilias' and 'hospes' (host), who is made, wittily, to dispense with magnanimity the bounteous hospitality which is expected of the head of a Roman household. The feast which he provides for his guest is not merely an ordinary 'cena' (meal) but a 'daps' – Horace uses the epic word for a religious banquet.[45] The fare is, moreover, amusingly similar in significant respects to the meals which, as we have been shown earlier in the *Sermo*, Horace himself enjoys with his friends at his country retreat.[46]

At the same time, we are reminded that the country mouse brings in the food for the meal in his mouth (85). The bacon which he serves his guest has already been nibbled and discarded by one of the local peasants (85–6). The 'lolium' which he eats, is, in fact, the wild cereal darnel.[47] The 'acinus' which he carries in his mouth might be (as it appears in many translations) a 'raisin', but the term might just as easily denote a humble 'berry', or even a 'pip'. In stressing (84) that the oats which the country mouse provides are long-grained

[44] P. Lejay and David West, for example (see *Satires*, ed. Lejay, p. 525; West, 'Of Mice and Men', p. 70) see the chiasmus and wordplay of Horace's ll. 79–80 as an attempt to imitate Cervius' laboured manner of narration.

[45] See West, 'Of Mice and Men', p. 52.

[46] See Rudd, *Satires of Horace*, p. 250.

[47] See West, *Of Mice and Men*, p. 54.

(in contrast to the round, pea-like, vetches which they accompany) Horace, momentarily, provides us with a recognizably mouse's-eye view of the fare.[48] And when we are told that the town mouse is scarcely prepared to touch the country mouse's food 'dente superbo' (with squeamish tooth), the joke depends on our seeing him curling his lip in a manner which to a mouse is natural habit, but which to a human observer inevitably denotes fastidious disdain.[49]

In his version, Cowley pursues a similar train of anthropomorphic wit, but completely rethinks and recasts Horace's Italian details in English terms, and finds his own, quite different, means of conveying Horace's mock-naive/mock-heroic narrative manner. In the very first line we are alerted to the diminutive size of the story's hero by having our attention immediately drawn to the position of his hole – 'At the *large foot* of a fair hollow tree' (1; my italics). But the residence occupied by this mouse is, from his own point of view at least, an equivalent of Jonson's Penshurst or Carew's Saxham, a 'commodious' (comfortable and convenient) ancestral 'Hall' which, like the manorial 'seat' of a seventeenth-century English aristocrat or gentleman-farmer, leads straight out on to arable land – in this case, the ploughed fields where the mouse forages for scraps when harvest is over. The country mouse is 'substantial': burly and thick-set (and perhaps a little plump), and also moderately wealthy – a respected figure in the neighbourhood, the murine equivalent, perhaps, of a local Justice of the Peace.

The earlier translators, Thomas Drant, Sir John Beaumont, and Sir Richard Fanshawe,[50] treat Horace's opening with a dry literalness that misses the humour of the poet's imaginings almost entirely. John Ogilby, whose verse-paraphrase of the 'Aesopic' version of the fable is, like several of the other versified *Aesops*, fleshed out from Horace, produces a banquet which, however accurately it may or may not reflect a mouse's diet, destroys Horace's anthropomorphic poise,

[48] See *The Works of Horace*, ed. E. C. Wickham, 2 vols. (Oxford, 1891), 2. 185.

[49] See West, 'Of Mice and Men', p. 56.

[50] See Thomas Drant, in *Horace, his Art of Poetry, Pistles and Satyrs Englished* (London, 1567), pp. 261–8; Sir John Beaumont, in *Bosworth-field* (London, 1629), pp. 37–43; Sir Richard Fanshawe, in *Selected Parts of Horace* (London, 1652), pp. 79–82.

since it seems, from the human side of the equation, distinctly unappetizing:

> Yet had she Fruit, and store of Pulse and Grain,
> Ants Eggs, the Bees sweet bag, a Star's fall'n jelly,
> Snails dressed i'th shells, with Cuckow foame and Rain,
> Frog legs, a Lizard's foot, a Neuts py'd belly,
> The Cob, and hard Roe of a pickled Herring
> Got for a Dog,
> As they did prog,
> And a rush Candle purchas'd by pickeering.[51]

The eighteenth-century renderings of the episode tend to adopt a jauntiness and/or archness which just as effectively destroys the delicate balance of Horace's anthropomorphism. So anxious, it seems, are these translators not to be thought naive that they signal their sophisticated superiority in an all too obtrusive fashion, thus achieving their humour, as it were, at the mice's expense. In Dunkin's rendering, for example, the country mouse's presentation of his meal seems desperately haphazard, as if the poor creature has, from the start, effectively abandoned hope of being able to please his guest. His fears turn out to be amply justified. In this version, the country mouse

> goes and freely fetches
> Whole Ears of hoarded Oats, and Vetches
> Dry Grapes and Raisins cross her Chaps,
> And dainty Bacon, but in Scraps,
> If Delicacies could invite
> My squeamish Lady's Appetite,
> Who turn'd her nose at ev'ry Dish,
> And saucy piddled, with a — Pish![52]

Pope's rendering of the same passage also dilutes Horace's wit, this time by adding contemporary allusions – to Swift, of whose version of the first half of Horace's *Sermo* Pope's is a continuation and

[51] *The Fables of Aesop, Paraphras'd in Verse*, 2nd edition (London, 1668), p. 18. For other 'Horatian' versions of the Aesopic fable, see, for example, Edmund Arwaker, *Truth in Fiction: or Morality in Masquerade* (London, 1708), pp. 84–9; Anon., *Aesop's Fables, with Morals and Reflections . . . done into a Variety of English Verse* (4th edition, London, 1720), pp. 21–5.

[52] *A Poetical Translation*, 2. 227.

imitation, and to the low-grade Suffolk skimmed-milk cheese colloquially known as 'bang and thump'.[53] Pope's references to his own world are, to be sure, deftly incorporated, but are perhaps more designed to draw attention to the poet's own ingenuity in discovering modern analogies than to convey the Horatian grandeur-in-absurdity of the murine banquet:

> He brought him Bacon (nothing lean);
> Pudding, that might have pleas'd a Dean;
> Cheese, such as men in Suffolk make,
> But wish'd it Stilton for his sake;
> Yet to his Guest tho' no way sparing,
> He ate himself the Rind and paring.
>
> (165–70; *TE*, 4. 261)

The question of Horatian poise is equally important when considering the touches of mock-heroic style, which colour Horace's fable. Mock-heroic, as usually defined, consists of the deployment of epic sentiment and diction in distinctly non-epic situations. By being forced to register the discrepancy between lofty manner and banal matter, it is said, the reader is brought to a heightened sense of the triviality of the events and the ludicrousness of the personages being depicted. In Horace's description of the mice's journey to the city, we are certainly intended to register an epic dimension to the narrator's style. The poet employs formulae and phrases which momentarily assimilate the two creatures' journey to the nocturnal ventures of epic warriors, such as those of Diomedes and Odysseus in Book 10 of the *Iliad.* We are, at the same time, never allowed to forget that their 'vestigia' (steps) are also mouse foot-marks, and that the country mouse is 'levis' (light) as he 'exsilit' (leaps out of) his hole.[54]

While most of the English translators make little or no consistent attempt to imitate Horace's mock-heroic style, Cowley displays an

[53] In *The Farmer's Boy* (1800), Robert Bloomfield commented on the properties of Suffolk skimmed milk and its conversion to cheese: 'Its name derision and reproach pursue, / And strangers tell of "three times skimm'd sky-blue". / To cheese converted, what can be its boast? / What but the common virtues of a post / If drought o'ertake it faster than the knife, / Most fair it bids for stubborn length of life, / And, like the oaken stuff whereon 'tis laid, / Mocks the weak efforts of the bending blade; / Or in the hog-trough rests in perfect spite, / Too big to swallow and too hard to bite'.

[54] See West, 'Of Mice and Men', p. 76.

ingenious resourcefulness in replacing Horace's touches of epic tone with periphrases reminiscent of the Jacobean and Caroline mythological narratives which were popular in his youth. The Ovidian fancy of the sun going to bed in the arms of the sea-nymph Thetis (52–5) is close, for example, to a passage like the following from Francis Beaumont's *Salmacis and Hermaphroditus* (1602):

> Now was the Sunne inviron'd with the Sea,
> Cooling his water tresses as he lay,
> And in dread Neptunes kingdome while he sleeps,
> Fair Thaetis clips him in the watry deeps.[55]

But it is also difficult not to see an amused self-reference in Cowley's reference to 'witty poets'. The extravagantly fanciful comedy of Thetis drawing '*the modest Curtains of the night*', as in a four-poster bed, is, after all, characteristically Cowleian.

Cowley's resourcefulness is also seen in his discovery of English analogues for the precise touches of Roman detail which mark Horace's description of the city mansion. Instead of, like Horace, noting the play of light on the scarlet draperies which cover the ivory couches in the room, he has his mice dwarfed by the huge and grandly 'noble' Mortlake tapestries on the walls, and notes that, when the room eventually becomes empty, that is because the human beings have gone off to another room, in the customary Restoration manner so often recorded in Pepys's *Diary*, for an after-dinner dance.[56]

In his version, Pope, too, finds English substitutes for Horace's Roman details, this time inserting references to the *à-la-mode* architectural fashions of the 1730s:

> Away they come, thro' thick and thin,
> To a tall house near Lincoln's-Inn;
> ('Twas on the night of a Debate,
> When all their Lordships had sate late.)
> Behold the place, where, if a Poet
> Shin'd in Description, he might show it,
> Tell how the Moon-beam trembling falls

[55] *Elizabethan Minor Epics*, ed. Elizabeth Story Donno (London, 1963), p. 295.

[56] See Pepys's entries for 26 October 1665; 31 October 1665; 14 March 1666; 28 August 1666; 9 November 1666; 26 March 1668; 23 February 1669.

And tips with silver all the walls:
Palladian walls, Venetian doors,
Grotesco roofs, and stucco floors:
But let it (in a word) be said,
The Moon was up, and Men a-bed,
The Napkins white, the Carpet red:
The Guests withdrawn had left the Treat,
And down the Mice sat, *tête à tête.*

(185–99; *TE*, 4. 261–3)

Here Pope also slyly incorporates references to two modern works of literature – to Shakespeare's Romeo's description of the moon 'that tips with silver all these fruit tree tops' (*Romeo and Juliet*, 2. 2. 108), and to the famous description of the moon casting light on the plain of Troy in his own version of Homer's *Iliad*:

Around her Throne the vivid Planets roll,
And Stars unnumber'd gild the glowing Pole,
O'er the dark Trees a yellower Verdure shed,
And tip with Silver ev'ry Mountain's Head.

(8. 691–4; *TE*, 7. 428)

The moment is carried off with considerable verve and spirit. But, as before, there is perhaps an element of self-conscious virtuosity in Pope's treatment which, if his poem is being considered specifically as a rendering of Horace, seems alien to the original. For the mock-heroic style and circumstantial details in Horace's fable appear, in context, to be neither designed merely to expose the ludicrousness of the mice nor to show the poet's own skill at clever literary allusions. So firmly has Horace, by this stage, established a sense of the mice's humanity-in-mouseliness, and so effortlessly are our minds now passing from human concerns to those of mice and back again, that the mock-heroic treatment seems to work more subtly than the simple mockery of the textbook definition. By showing the mice participating in an enterprise which has grand, formidable, mysterious, and beautiful dimensions that are far beyond anything dreamt of in their philosophy, Horace simultaneously alerts us to the precariousness, fragility, and self-delusion of our own enterprises as human beings. The mice are, as it were, simultaneously aggrandized and diminished by being seen as heroic warriors, just as human figures in epic are both ennobled and diminished by being involved with immortal gods whose power far exceeds their own, but who, nevertheless, care about, and participate in, the activities of human beings. The mock-heroic joke, in Horace's hands, works, as it were, simultaneously in both directions. The trivial is made grand and the grand made trivial.

Just as Pope has simplified the mock-heroic dimension of Horace's fable, so has he diminished Horace's description of the urban banquet:

> Our Courtier walks from dish to dish,
> Tastes for his Friend of Fowl and Fish;
> Tells all their names, lays down the law,
> "*Que ça est bon! Ah goutez ça!*
> "That Jelly's rich, this Malmsey healing,
> "Pray dip your Whiskers and your Tail in."
> Was ever such a happy Swain?
> He stuffs and swills, and stuffs again.
> "I'm quite ashamed – 'tis mighty rude
> "To eat so much – but all's so good.
> "I have a thousand thanks to give –
> "My Lord alone knows how to live".
>
> (200–11; *TE*, 4. 263)

Pope's comedy, though, once again, managed with virtuosic gusto, fails to convey the specific function of this scene in Horace's original. For here Horace had momentarily assigned to his city mouse the role of 'praegustator', the slave who, according to the very latest Roman fashion, was employed to taste each item of food being presented to his master to make sure that it was of acceptable quality.[57] Horace's town mouse 'veluti succinctus cursitat hospes' (bustles about, acting the host in waiter-style), offering carefully selected titbits to his guest (who eats reclining, in the Roman manner), and returning with courteous relish the hospitality which he had received in the country. Pope's town mouse, by contrast, is made into a connoisseur of gourmet conversation, who tastes the various dishes so that he can patronize his country companion with his knowledge of courtly cuisine. The country mouse, for his part, is made a glutton, gauchely blurting out his surprise at his new-found good luck, while simultaneously expressing servile gratitude to his 'lordly' host. Our mirth

[57] See West, 'Of Mice and Men', p. 72; Rudd, *Satires of Horace*, p. 246.

is certainly provoked, but, it seems, it is *at* the mice rather than with them that we are encouraged to laugh. Horace's delicate balance of sympathy and amusement has been abandoned in the interests of a more farcically mocking humour.

In sharp contrast, Cowley's version stresses the 'bounties' entertained by the town mouse, and the warm camaraderie and shared pleasure of both the little creatures, and we are allowed to participate in their delights, both by being shown the 'delicious bits' with which the floor is strewn, momentarily, from their point of view, and as we observe (80) that, even in his transformed circumstances, the country mouse's old frugal habits die hard. This amusedly affectionate play of sympathy encouraged here is also apparent in the narrator's mock-portentous intervention a few lines later, when the mice's new-found bliss is interrupted by the servants and dogs.

Here, as before, the shortness and insignificance of a mouse's 'mortal' life is assimilated, by Horace's and Cowley's anthropomorphic wit, to the shortness and insignificance of human ideals and ambitions. Horace, Cowley's rendering suggests, has ended his sixth *Sermo* with a fable which was both intended to reinforce and simultaneously to subject to humorous exposure earnest Epicurean vows of the kind enunciated in the first half of the poem. Sabine farmers, Roman poets, epic heroes, and mice, the fable's comic logic seems to suggest, are, for all their apparent differences, faced with life problems which are essentially the same. Life is uncertain and short for all of them. All have to decide how they will spend the short space of time which is allotted to them. All have an exaggerated sense of their own importance in the larger scheme of things, and for that reason make themselves unhappy by neglecting the true goods of life – even perhaps at those very moments when they are pursuing the quest for happiness with the greatest passion and resolve, and expressing their ideals with the greatest elegance and eloquence. But since this state of affairs is inevitable, the tale implies, it is saner to laugh than to cry.

In his portrayal of the two mice, Horace, I have suggested, involved some of his own most deeply cherished ideals and aspirations. When the country mouse begs, at the very end of the poem, to be allowed to return to his hole in the country, the two key words, 'tutus' (safe) and 'tenuis' (simple, homely) which he employs are terms which Horace regularly used in his own evocations of country happiness.[58] (The latter term is also used by Horace of the style of his writing in praise of simplicity and moderation.) The blend of sympathy and affectionate mockery which characterizes this moment, like the rest of the fable is therefore at one and the same time an act of dramatic imagination and an act of self-knowledge and self-criticism on the poet's part. In embodying his own passionate convictions in the conduct and pronouncements of a pair of mice, Horace is, without cynicism or loss of integrity, hinting at the potential absurdity of his own attempts, of any human being's attempts, to defeat or deny the inevitable conditions of life.

Cowley, too, I have suggested, found himself personally implicated in the conduct and sentiments of his two mice. Whereas elsewhere in the *Essays* he had treated the subject of rural retirement with a uniform commitment and earnestness that can make a reading of the volume as a whole a slightly monotonous experience, he had discovered while composing his imitation of Horace's tale, a means of subjecting his ideals of retirement (as well as the hedonistic zest of his earlier *Anacreontiques*) to a delightful extension by means of the comic scrutiny allowed by the mouse-fable form. For Cowley, as much as for Horace, the fable was a voyage of self-discovery and gentle self-mockery in which his own cherished notions could, by being miniaturized, be put in a larger, more inclusive, perspective. As in Horace's original, the country mouse's final longing for 'peace' – a term, we might note, resonant with significance for a poet who had just lived through a civil war – prefaced by a vow of apocalyptic earnestness to be hidden in the deepest obscurity,[59] is his murine version of the longing for 'liberty' which receives such extensive elaboration in the *Essays*. The poem's warmly attractive geniality of tone and humorous perspective, and the self-knowledge achieved by the poet in its composition, are thus twin sides of the same coin. But Cowley's geniality, like Horace's, is no mere compromise or fence-sitting. Cowley's conclusion is as firm in its 'moral' as any of the 'Aesopic' versions of the story, though more tellingly and convincingly so, because the situation has been imagined so

[58] See West, 'Of Mice and Men', p. 78.
[59] Compare Rev. 6: 15–16.

comprehensively, and in such attentive detail. Without 'peace', the country mouse comes to realize, none of the other goods of life, whatever attractions they might genuinely hold, have any validity or worth whatsoever. The country mouse's fully Epicurean conclusion is the more impressive because it has been tested by experience and seen in the round. It is in this way that, for all his version's apparent infidelity to its original, Cowley was able to offer a more convincing and inclusive creative response to the end of Horace's *Sermones*, 2. 6 than many a more 'accurate' version. For in his free rendering of Horace's fable of the two mice, Cowley was indeed, in T. S. Eliot's phrase, 'giving the original through himself and finding himself through the original'.[60]

[60] T. S. Eliot, 'Introduction: 1928', in *The Selected Poems of Ezra Pound* (London, 1948), p. 13.

# 3

## The English Voices of Lucretius, from Lucy Hutchinson to John Mason Good

This chapter considers the ways in which writers from the mid-seventeenth to the late eighteenth century sought to give the Roman poet Lucretius an English poetic voice. Prominent attention will be paid to translations of the *De Rerum Natura*, in whole or part. But the chapter will also explore the ways in which specific passages from the *De Rerum Natura*, or the poem's larger structures and rhetorics, were more obliquely recreated by English poets. The main focus is thus on specifically literary responses to Lucretius, rather than on the larger role of the *De Rerum Natura* in disseminating Epicurean ideas in England. But a distinction between 'poetic' and 'philosophical' responses to Lucretius can never be absolute. English poets and critics regularly affirmed their admiration for Lucretius' 'poetry', while deploring his 'philosophy'. But is it possible to write convincing Lucretian poetry without displaying, or betraying, *some* sympathy for the Roman poet's ideas? And can English poets, whatever their philosophical sympathies, convey anything of Lucretius' poetic quality without being themselves poets of comparable stature?

One leading translator-poet of the period, John Dryden, was certainly convinced that successful translation depends as much on the translator's own poetic gifts as on his knowledge of his original, and that a translator must feel some affinity with the 'genius' or 'soul' of his source-author. But Dryden simultaneously, and paradoxically, stressed the importance of respecting the alterity of one's original by conveying its 'distinguishing character': the individuating features which crucially differentiate it from the productions of other poets, and which must be preserved if a translation is genuinely to resemble its original.[1] For Dryden, successful translation characteristically occurs when the translator feels simultaneously intimate with and at some distance from his source.

Only three poetic responses to Lucretius in our period, I shall suggest – one (Dryden's rendering of five episodes from the *De Rerum Natura*) a translation in the normally accepted sense of the term, the other two (John Milton's *Paradise Lost* and Alexander Pope's *Essay on Man*) responses of a more oblique or refracted kind, in which admiration for the Roman poet is balanced by a degree of sceptical distance – attain an artistic quality comparable to their original. And while other poetic responses render, or offer insight into, particular aspects of Lucretius' art, it was only in these three works that Lucretius was given a sustainedly convincing English poetic voice – albeit one which was sometimes made to utter sentiments which would have surprised Lucretius himself.

The first near-complete English verse translation of Lucretius – composed in the 1650s, though remaining in manuscript for over four centuries – was that of the puritan poet and biographer, Lucy Hutchinson (1620–81).[2] Some years after completing her translation, Hutchinson firmly dissociated herself from any involvement with Lucretius' 'Atheisms and impieties', and repenting of the 'youthfull curiositie' which had led her to 'amus[e] [her] selfe with such vaine Philosophy'.[3] But by the 1670s Lucretian Epicureanism had become associated with the (to Hutchinson, repellent) libertinism of the Restoration court, and it seems likely that Hutchinson's remarkable pioneering engagement with Lucretius, the

[1] See Preface to *Sylvae* in *Works*, 3. 5–6. For further discussion of this point, see Chapter 4 below.

[2] Hutchinson omitted the treatment of love from Book 4 of *De Rerum Natura*. For the date of her version, see *Lucy Hutchinson's Translation of Lucretius:* De Rerum Natura, ed. Hugh de Quehen (Ann Arbor MI, 1996), pp. 10–11. Quotations from Hutchinson below are taken from this edition. On Hutchinson's translation, see, in addition to material cited below, Reid Barbour, 'Between Atoms and the Spirit: Lucy Hutchinson's Translation of Lucretius', *Renaissance Papers*: 1–16 (1994), and 'Lucy Hutchinson, Atomism, and the Atheist Dog', in Lynette Hunter and Sarah Hutton, eds., *Women, Science, and Medicine, 1500–1700* (Stroud, 1997), pp. 122–37.

[3] *Lucy Hutchinson's Translation*, p. 23. The remarks occur in the dedication of her manuscript to Arthur Annesley, first Earl of Anglesey in 1675.

product of a tradition of learned puritan humanism, had originally been more open-minded than her later remarks suggest.[4] Hutchinson's hostility to Lucretius' theology seems to have been counterbalanced by an attraction to his intellectual radicalism, and particularly his scathing attacks on war-mongering, priestcraft, superstition, and courtly luxury: she was to recycle some of Lucretius' anti-court sentiments in *Order and Disorder*, the Christian epic of her last years.[5] She may also have been motivated by a desire to emulate the neo-Epicurean writing currently fashionable in the royalist Cavendish circle, and had perhaps at one stage conceived of her translation of Lucretius as a tacit rebuke to the royalist writers John Evelyn, who, she thought, had failed to complete the task, and Alexander Brome, who had apparently ignored the challenge to undertake it.[6]

The translation by the diarist Evelyn, of which Book 1, the only one to be printed in his lifetime, appeared in 1656,[7] was clearly inspired by Pierre Gassendi's recent reassessment of Epicureanism (discussed in Chapter 2 above) and by the appearance in 1650 of Michel de Marolles' French translation of the *De Rerum Natura*.[8] But, despite an admiration for Lucretius' descriptive and expository powers, and for some aspects of his moral teaching,[9] Evelyn was from the start openly hostile to Lucretius' religious views. He told

[4] See David Norbrook, 'Margaret Cavendish and Lucy Hutchinson: Identity, Ideology and Politics', *In-Between: Essays and Studies in Literary Criticism*, 9 (2000), 179–203, on which I draw below.

[5] See Lucy Hutchinson, *Order and Disorder*, ed. David Norbrook (Oxford, 2001), pp. xvii–xix.

[6] See Norbrook, 'Margaret Cavendish and Lucy Hutchinson', 191–2; Anna Margaret Battegli, *Margaret Cavendish and the Exiles of the Mind* (Lexington KY, 1998), p. 40; Emma L. E. Rees, '"Sweet Honey of the Muses": Lucretian Resonance in *Poems and Fancies*', *In-Between: Essays and Studies in Literary Criticism*, 9 (2000), 3–16.

[7] The rest remained in manuscript until it was published as *John Evelyn's Translation of Titus Lucretius Carus De Rerum Natura: An Old-Spelling Critical Edition*, ed. Michael M. Repetzki (Frankfurt, 2000). Quotations from Evelyn below are taken from this edition. Book 2 was completed, but is now lost. Like Hutchinson, Evelyn omits the end of Book 4 of *De Rerum Natura*.

[8] See Michael Hunter, 'John Evelyn in the 1650s: A Virtuoso in Quest of a Role', in *Science and the Shape of Orthodoxy: Intellectual Change in Late Seventeenth-Century Britain* (Woodbridge, 1995), pp. 67–98, on which I draw below.

[9] See the notes quoted by Hunter, 'John Evelyn in the 1650s', p. 88 and Repetzki in *John Evelyn's Translation of Titus Lucretius Carus*, pp. l–lii.

Jeremy Taylor that he would use the substantial commentary on his translation to 'provide against all the ill consequences' of Lucretius' opinions,[10] and seems, moreover, to have little personal commitment to Lucretius' atomistic view of nature. Some contemporaries were favourably impressed by the translation, Edmund Waller proclaiming that Evelyn's *Essay on the First Book* presented '*Lucretius* whole... / His Words, his Musick, and his mind',[11] and Sir Richard Fanshawe telling Evelyn in a private letter that his version was '*Lucretius* himself', and that 'though' it 'retaine neither his Voyce, nor yet his Hayvinesse', 'it hath both his Soule and his Lineaments'.[12] But, as his work proceeded, Evelyn appears to have become increasingly anxious about the potentially dangerous effects of an English Lucretius on modern morality. In the first of his manuscript comments on *De Rerum Natura* 3 he expressed his intention of offering 'som Antidote against the Poyson of the Errors, which our Author, here striues to convey vnder all the gildings of Poetry and Arte'.[13] And by 1657–8 he had abandoned any attempt to publish the full version, later telling Meric Casaubon that the manuscript now lay 'in the dust of [his] study, where 'tis likely to be for ever buried'.[14]

The next full-length English Lucretius – and the first to appear in print – was that of the brilliant young Oxford don Thomas Creech (1659–1700), published in 1682. It was an instant success, going through two further editions in the next two years, and becoming the standard full-length English Lucretius throughout the eighteenth century.[15] In the Preface to his first edition Creech forthrightly listed the poetic virtues that make Lucretius 'extream difficult to be follow'd':

> any man... may perceive that he is *elegant* in his kind; curious and exact in his *images*, happy in *disposition*, flowing, even to *satiety*, in *Instances*, of a

[10] Letter of 1657, quoted in Michael Hunter, 'John Evelyn in the 1650s', p. 90.

[11] Evelyn, John, *An Essay on the First Book of T. Lucretius Carus De Rerum Natura, Interpreted and Made English Verse* (London, 1656), p. 4.

[12] Sir Richard Fanshawe, *The Poems and Translations*, ed. Peter Davidson, 2 vols. (Oxford, 1997–9), 1. 333–4.

[13] Quoted in *John Evelyn's Translation of Titus Lucretius Carus*, pp. xl–xli.

[14] Quoted in Michael Hunter, 'John Evelyn in the 1650s', p. 87.

[15] For the bibliographical history, see Cosmo Alexander Gordon, *A Bibliography of Lucretius* (London, 1962), pp. 174–80.

brisk and ready Witt, pointed in Satyrs, severe in taunts, grave in precepts, quick and vivacious in his discourses, and every way fitted for his bold attempt.[16]

But, like Evelyn before him, Creech used his preliminaries and notes to repudiate many of Lucretius' sentiments.[17] His own translation was justified, he argued, since 'the best Method to overthrow the *Epicurean Hypothesis*... is to expose a full System of it to publick view',[18] and Nahum Tate praised Creech precisely for his ability to combine a scrupulous presentation of Lucretius' thought with a salutary correction of his 'Errors', thus providing an effective 'Antidote' 'for his Poyson'.[19] But some commentators thought that Creech sympathized with Lucretius' sentiments of his original to a greater degree than he was prepared to admit. In the Preface to his own Latin edition of the Roman poet (1695), Creech himself admitted to loving Lucretius 'fere plus aequo' (almost more than is right), and, when he committed suicide in 1700, some observers attributed his action, admiringly or contemptuously, to an obsession with Lucretius so intense that it had provoked him to emulate the Latin poet's own fabled end.[20]

Over a century was to pass before the next full verse translation of Lucretius, that by John Mason Good (1764–1827), a professional physician who supplemented his medical salary with scientific and poetic writing. Encouraged by friends, including Lucretius' editor Gilbert Wakefield, Good began his translation in 1797, composing it 'in the streets of London during [his] extensive walks, to visit his

[16] Thomas Creech, *T. Lucretius Carus the Epicurean Philosopher, His Six Books* De Natura Rerum *Done into English Verse, with Notes* (Oxford, 1682) [Gordon, *Bibliography*, No. 331], sig. b4ʳ. The quotation from Creech's translation below is from the third edition (London, 1683) [Gordon, *Bibliography*, No. 331C].

[17] See T. F. Mayo, *Epicurus in England (1650–1725)* (Dallas TX, 1934), pp. 65–71.

[18] Thomas Creech, *T. Lucretius Carus the Epicurean Philosopher*, sig. b2ʳ.

[19] Thomas Creech, *T. Lucretius Carus. The Epicurean Philosopher, His Six Books* De Natura Rerum *Done into English Verse, with Notes. The Second Edition, Corrected and Enlarged* (Oxford, 1683) [Gordon, *Bibliography*, No. 331A], sig. d1ʳ.

[20] See Mayo, *Epicurus in England*, p. 103; Hermann Josef Real, *Untersuchungen zur Lukrez-Übersetzung von Thomas Creech* (Bad Homburg, 1970), p. 29. According to a tradition transmitted by St Jerome, Lucretius was poisoned by a love philtre and took his own life at the age of 44. For an admiring response to Creech's suicide, see William Wycherley, *Posthumous Works* (London, 1718), pp. 210–11; for contempt, see Anon, *The War with Priestcraft* (London, 1732), pp. 23–4.

numerous patients'.[21] It was finished by October 1799, but the preparation of extensive and erudite notes delayed publication until 1805. As a scientist and devoted student of philosophy, Good was clearly attracted by the most celebrated ancient exposition of atomism, a theory which 'at last appears to have obtained an eternal triumph, from its application, by Newton and Huygens, to the department of natural philosophy, and, by Locke and Condillac, to that of metaphysics'.[22] He was, moreover, disposed – in ways that may be coloured by his Unitarian leanings at the time – to see a far greater degree of compatibility than most of his predecessors between Lucretian Epicureanism and Christianity. Though he concedes that 'Epicurus and his disciples disbelieved in a future state', this can, he thinks, 'be no impeachment of [their] wisdom or virtue' since, without the scriptural revelation of Christ's resurrection, they could not have been expected to entertain a belief, for which nature alone affords such 'feeble and inconclusive' evidence.[23] Lucretius, moreover, Good argues, is by no means the outright atheist of tradition, since beyond his own serene, detached deities lurks the presence of an '*unseen, incomprehensible*, or *mysterious* POWER',[24] the *vis abdita* of *De Rerum Natura* 5. 1233, which underpins and informs the laws of material nature.

In addition to the four full-length versions, a number of translations or adaptations of shorter Lucretian episodes appeared during our period. One of the most popular, Thomas Sprat's *The Plague of Athens,... First Describ'd in Greek by Thucydides; Then in Latin by Lucretius; Now attempted in English...* (1659), bears, in fact, only a tenuous relation to Book 6 of *De Rerum Natura*, being effectively a free-standing meditation, more imitative of Abraham Cowley than of Lucretius, on the precariousness and uncertainty of human existence.[25] The rendering of a large section of *De Rerum Natura* 1 by Sir

[21] Olinthus Gregory, *Memoirs of the Life, Writings, and Character, Literary, Professional and Religious, of the Late John Mason Good, M. D.* (London, 1828), p. 85.

[22] John Mason Good, *The Nature of Things: A Didactic Poem. Translated from the Latin of Titus Lucretius Carus*, 2 vols (London, 1805), 1. ciii. Quotations from Good's translation below are taken from this edition.

[23] Good, *The Nature of Things*, 1. lxxxii–lxxxiii.

[24] Good, *The Nature of Things*, 1. lxix.

[25] See Raymond A. Anselment, 'Thomas Sprat's *The Plague of Athens*: Thucydides, Lucretius, and the "Pindaric Way"', *Bulletin of the John Rylands University Library of Manchester*, 78 (1996), 3–20 (13).

Edward Sherburne (1616–1702),[26] in contrast, follows Lucretius' Latin closely. Omitting the opening sections of the *De Rerum Natura*, Sherburne concentrates on Lucretius' exposition (1. 162–710) of Epicurean cosmology and mechanistic philosophy. Such an emphasis accords with Sherburne's strong mathematical, scientific, and philosophical concerns, and with his interest in Gassendi, a philosopher on whom his own notes survive. Another of the separate versions, 'Of Nature's Changes' by Dryden's brother-in-law, Sir Robert Howard (1626–98),[27] renders Lucretius description (5. 235–415) of the processes of cyclical regeneration in the world, and its final destruction by the strife of elements. Howard seems to have been fired by Lucretius' grand vision of natural dissolution and rebirth, but, just as Sherburne had been careful to omit the overtly anti-religious sentiments near the beginning of Book 1 of *De Rerum Natura*, Howard subtly Christianizes Lucretius' account of the warring elements, asserting that water's defeat was brought about by the actions of a 'greater Being', rather than merely 'aliqua ratione' ('by some means or other': *De Rerum Natura*, 5. 409).

The two fragments of Lucretius rendered by the celebrated courtier and rake, John Wilmot, Earl of Rochester, display, as one might expect, a less inhibited response to Lucretian heterodoxy, one being a sensuously expansive translation of the opening of Lucretius' invocation to Venus (1. 1–4), and the other a close rendering of the Roman poet's evocation (2. 646–51; 1. 44–9) of the perfect peace enjoyed by the gods:

> The *Gods*, by right of Nature, must possess
> An Everlasting Age, of perfect Peace:
> Far off remov'd from us, and our Affairs:
> Neither approach'd by *Dangers*, or by *Cares*:
> Rich in themselves, to whom we cannot add:
> Not pleas'd by *Good* Deeds; nor provok'd by *Bad*.[28]

[26] Sherburne's translation remained in manuscript until it was published in *The Poems and Translations of Sir Edward Sherburne (1616–1702), Excluding Seneca and Manilius*, ed. F. J. Van Beeck, S.J. (Assen, 1961).

[27] First published anonymously, as 'By a Person of Quality' in *Sylvae: or the Second Part of Poetical Miscellanies* (London, 1685), pp. 406–17.

[28] John Wilmot, Earl of Rochester, *Works*, ed. Harold Love (Oxford, 1999), p. 108.

Among other poets of the period, Thomas Flatman, for whom Lucretius is said to have been 'a favourite',[29] rendered a short fragment from *De Rerum Natura* 3 on the loss of one's loved ones in death,[30] John Glanvill translated the opening of *De Rerum Natura* 2,[31] previously rendered by Dryden, and James Beattie made a version of the opening of Book 1 of *De Rerum Natura*, 'written at the particular desire of a Friend, whose commands the Translator hath reason to honour',[32] and apparently designed to temper the surging vigour of Dryden's version with a more measured, Popeian elegance and balance.

It is in the versions of John Dryden that we encounter by far the fullest translatorly engagement with Lucretius, short of a complete rendering.[33] These translations, published in 1685, mark the poet's coming-of-age in verse translation. Though Dryden had a longstanding interest in Epicurean atomic theory, the intensification of his engagement with Lucretius in the 1680s was part of a larger body of religio-philosophical stocktaking in which 'Christian' and 'pagan' elements came into various kinds of complex and paradoxical interaction.[34] From the 1670s, Dryden seems to have been associating his own growing reservations about Restoration courtly and theatrical culture with the critique of worldly ambition and libertine morality to be found in the writings of Epicurus and Lucretius, as newly expounded by Gassendi and his English epigones. In the Dedication to *Aureng-Zebe* (1676) he had invoked Lucretius in support of his declaration that 'True greatness, if it be any where on Earth, is in a private Virtue; remov'd from the notion of Pomp and Vanity, confin'd to a contemplation of it self, and centring on it self' (*Works*, 4. 153). But Dryden's interest in Lucretius seems simultaneously to have been motivated by an attraction of opposites: a desire

[29] George Saintsbury, ed., *Minor Poets of the Caroline Period*, 3 vols. (Oxford, 1905), 3. 280.

[30] Thomas Flatman, *Poems and Songs* (3rd edition, London, 1682), pp. 139–40.

[31] John Glanvill, *Poems* (London, 1725), pp. 188–92. In his Preface (sig. b$^{v}$) Glanvill declares that he has borrowed nothing from Dryden's version.

[32] James Beattie, *Poems* (London, 1760), p. x; the translation is printed on pp. 77–81.

[33] Dryden renders *De Rerum Natura*, 1. 1–40, 2. 1–61, 3. 830–1094, 4. 1052–1287, and 5. 222–34.

[34] See David Hopkins, *John Dryden* (Cambridge, 1986), pp. 90–133.

to comprehend and inhabit a poetic mind and temperament which he felt to be, in important respects, very different from his own. The 'distinguishing Character' of Lucretius' 'Soul and Genius', Dryden wrote in the preface to the collection containing the translations,

> is a certain kind of noble pride, and positive assertion of his Opinions. He is every where confident of his own reason, and assuming an absolute command not only over the vulgar Reader, but even his patron *Memmius*. For he is always bidding him attend, as if he had the Rod over him; and using a Magisterial authority, while he instructs him.
>
> (Preface to *Sylvae*; *Works*, 3. 10)

Lucretius' insistent pursuit of his mission, Dryden declares, sometimes constrained 'the quickness of his Fancy': on occasions, he was 'so much an Atheist, that he forgot to be a Poet'. But in the 'Descriptions, and... Moral part of his Philosophy' Lucretius' 'sublime and daring Genius', 'fiery temper', and 'Masculine' 'thoughts' find apt expression in a 'loftiness of... Expressions' and in a 'perpetual torrent' of verse. In order to convey such qualities in his own translations, Dryden says, he has 'lay'd by [his own] natural Diffidence and Scepticism for a while, to take up that Dogmatical way of his'. Lucretius' 'Opinions concerning the mortality of the Soul', Dryden insists, are morally undesirable and psychologically unsustainable, but there are, he says, other arguments in Book 3 of *De Rerum Natura* 'which are strong enough to a reasonable Man, to make him less in love with Life, and consequently in less apprehensions of Death'. These arguments are 'pathetically urg'd', 'beautifully express'd', 'adorn'd with examples', and 'admirably rais'd by the *Prosopopeia* of Nature, who is brought in speaking to her Children, with so much authority and vigour'. Lucretius' treatment of love in Book 4 of *De Rerum Natura*, moreover, offers 'the truest and most Philosophical account both of the Disease and Remedy which [he] ever found in any Author'. Dryden was confident of the success of his versions: 'I must take the liberty to own, that I was pleas'd with my endeavours, which but rarely happens to me, and that I am not dissatisfied upon the review, of any thing I have done in this Author' (*Works*, 3. 10–12).

How successful are the various seventeenth- and eighteenth-century translations of Lucretius in discovering or creating a convincing

English poetic voice for the Roman poet? When discussing Lucretius' style, E. J. Kenney observed a striking 'discrepancy in tone and emotional impact' between the grander and more emotionally charged sections of the *De Rerum Natura* and the 'scientific, or expository' passages which lay out, in systematic detail and with painstaking clarity, the physical basis of Lucretius' larger cosmological, moral, and social vision.[35] Lucretius' style in the expository passages, Kenney argues, is carefully calculated for its task. The poet eschews elegant balance and complex periodic structuring in favour of a cogently-unfolding verse-argument, in which there is a high degree of coincidence between metrical and syntactical structures, and in which thesis-statement, supportive illustration, and summative recapitulation follow one another in a clearly-differentiated sequence. As a sustained illustration of this expository manner, Kenney offers some lines (323–49) from Book 3 of *De Rerum Natura.* Body and soul, Lucretius argues in this passage, are integrally related and cannot be separated without the destruction of both. Mind and body can no more be divided, or experience feeling separately from one another, than the scent can be separated from a lump of frankincense while still leaving that lump intact. The body is neither born in separation from the soul, nor can the two live separately after death. While water can be heated and then lose that heat without changing its essential nature, human life, from its inception in the womb, involves a mutual, and inseparable, connection of body and soul.

How is this passage rendered by the English translators? Lucy Hutchinson's translation of Lucretius has recently been praised in general terms for the way in which its long compound sentences, heavy enjambment, frequent elisions, and comparative lack of parallelism, alliteration, and assonance – features which differentiate it strongly from the more polished couplet verse of the eighteenth century – create a forward-surging movement which is particularly suitable for rendering the most urgent and impetuous of Roman poets.[36] But though such qualities may be appropriate for the more

[35] *Lucretius: De Rerum Natura, Book III*, ed. E. J. Kenney (Cambridge, 1971), pp. 14–29.

[36] See Hugh de Quehen, 'Ease and Flow in Lucy Hutchinson's Lucretius', *Studies in Philology*, 93 (1996), 288–303.

impassioned parts of the *De Rerum Natura*, they seem less apt for the more discursive passages, where clarity of exposition is all important. In the present instance, the continuously-flowing forward movement of Hutchinson's verse, and the looseness of her sentence structure tend to obscure the clearly-articulated contours of Lucretius' argument:

> They in their first beginning are combind
> Nor in lifes tedious voyage ere disjoynd
> Nor can they singly suffer violence
> What either feeles afflicts the others sence
> In all commotions beare an equal share,
> Whatever tumults in the entrailes are.
> The bodie is not borne, nor grows alone,
> Nor after death subsists, the soule being gone.
> Though water heated, when that heate doth goe
> Reteins its being still, yet tis not soe
> With bodies quitted by the vitall heate,
> Corruption there dissolves the empty seate.
>
> (339–50)

But Hutchinson's rendering is a model of elegant lucidity when compared with Evelyn's, in which a regular disjunction of metre and syntax, serving no obvious conceptual or expressive function, makes Lucretius' argument seem clotted and contorted:

> So from th' whole
> Body, to separate the Mind & Soule
> Is difficult; but that together all
> Dissolve: since from their first original
> The Principles so implicated be
> And in a life conforme knit mutually.
> So that the Mind acts not by't Selfe, nor one
> Body, without anothers helpes alone.
>
> (327–34)

Creech's version adds details that have no direct source in the Latin. In his rendering, it is 'with provident care' that the soul protects the 'life and health' of the body; the smell of frankincense is 'ravishing'; embryos spend time in the womb 'Before they pass the confines of the Night'. But Creech is so scrupulously attentive to Lucretius' rhetorical shaping that the reader's mind is led elegantly and effortlessly to a conclusion that seems to emerge convincingly from the examples presented – a characteristic that is in evidence throughout his translation, and which makes it the most continuously readable of the complete versions:

> Besides, the *Body*, is not born alone,
> Nor grows, nor lives, when *Mind* and *Soul* are gone;
> For tho the water heated o'er the fire
> May lose some *Vapours*, yet remain entire;
> The *Limbs*, when *Mind* and *Soul* are fled, submit
> To the same fate, and die, and rot with it:
> Nay more, before the Infants see the light,
> Before they pass the confines of the Night,
> Whilst yet within their Mothers Womb they lie,
> If these *two* separate, they fail and die:
> Whence learn, that since the *cause of Life*'s combin'd
> And lies in both, their *natures* too are joyn'd.
>
> (p. 78)

Good's version of the passage resembles Creech's both in its embroidery of the original and in its attentiveness to Lucretius' rhetorical shaping. But Good's Miltonic inversions – a regular occupational hazard of eighteenth-century blank verse – sometimes create a stilted effect –

> So live they mutual, so, from earliest birth,
> In intertwin'd existence, that apart,
> Nor this nor that perception can possess, . . .

– as does his infelicitous choice of diction ('the tepid lymph', 'Fly off profuse'):

> This frame, moreo'er, alone can never spring,
> Can never thrive, the dread attack of death
> Can never conquer. For, with aim sublime,
> Though the light vapour from the tepid lymph
> Fly off profuse, while yet the lymph itself
> Exists uninjur'd – the deserted limbs
> Nor harmless, thus, can bear the soul's escape,
> Doom'd to one ruin, and one common grave.
>
> (341–3, 346–53)

When one turns from the expository sections of the *De Rerum Natura* to those passages in which Lucretius presents the larger moral, emotional, and philosophical upshot of his physical and cosmological convictions, all four full-length versions are clearly outclassed by Dryden.[37] Dryden's ability to offer a more convincing English Lucretius than any other translator seems due, at least in part, to the overlap which, as we have seen, he believed to exist between some of the Roman poet's most passionately held beliefs and his own. Dryden's own disillusionment with the 'wits' of the Restoration court, for example, seems to have fuelled his rendering of Lucretius' scornful denunciation of false hedonists at *De Rerum Natura* 3. 912–15:

> Yet thus the fools, that would be thought the Wits,
> Disturb their mirth with melancholy fits,
> When healths go round, and kindly brimmers[38] flow,
> Till the fresh Garlands on their foreheads glow,
> They whine, and cry, let us make haste to live,
> Short are the joys that humane Life can give.
> ('Lucretius . . . Against the Fear of Death', 97–102; *Works*, 3. 50)

And Dryden's rendering of Lucretius' portrayal of Sisyphus – a figure, Lucretius insists, to be found not in a mythological Hades but this side of the grave – is clearly informed by his observation of the destructive ambition of seventeenth-century politicians:

> The *Sisyphus* is he, whom noise and strife
> Seduce from all the soft retreats of life,
> To vex the Government, disturb the Laws;
> Drunk with the Fumes of popular applause,
> He courts the giddy Crowd to make him great,
> And sweats & toils in vain, to mount the sovereign Seat.
> For still to aim at pow'r, and still to fail,
> Ever to strive and never to prevail,
> What is it, but in reasons true account
> To heave the Stone against the rising Mount;
> Which urg'd, and labour'd, and forc'd up with pain,
> Recoils & rowls impetuous down, and smoaks along the plain?
> ('Lucretius . . . Against the Fear of Death', 200–11; *Works*, 3. 53)

[37] Dryden does not translate *De Rerum Natura*, 3. 323–49.
[38] A vogue word for 'brimming cups'.

Dryden's awareness of Lucretius' contemporary resonance is fully matched by his responsiveness to the Roman poet's verbal artistry, here particularly notable in his direct imitation (in its final fourteener) of Lucretius' rhythmic mimicry of the ascent and descent of the stone (*De Rerum Natura*, 3. 1002).

But Dryden was also able to identify himself in the act of poetic composition with Lucretian sentiments and beliefs to which, in ordinary life, he would have denied all commitment. Consider, for example, the uninhibited relish with which he renders Lucretius' vehement declaration that individual existence ceases at the point of death (3. 830–41):

> What has this Bugbear Death to frighten Man,
> If Souls can die, as well as Bodies can?
> For, as before our Birth we felt no pain
> When Punique arms infested Land and Mayn,
> When Heav'n and Earth were in confusion hurl'd
> For the debated Empire of the World,
> Which aw'd with dreadful expectation lay,
> Sure to be Slaves, uncertain who shou'd sway:
> So, when our mortal frame shall be disjoin'd,
> The lifeless Lump, uncoupled from the mind,
> From sense of grief and pain we shall be free;
> We shall not feel, because we shall not *Be*.
> ('Lucretius ... Against the Fear of Death', 1–12; *Works*, 3. 48)

Here Dryden combines argumentative cogency with dramatic urgency: the passage culminates in a powerful concluding couplet in which the strong antithesis on the two simple monosyllabic words 'feel' and '*Be*' acquires greater weight from the cumulative tension built up over the previous eight lines by a continuous flow of sense across line endings. In contrast, the enjambments in Lucy Hutchinson's equivalent passage create a shapeless, rambling effect, which lacks the point and urgency of Dryden's version or Lucretius' original:

> As of past ages we no sence reteine
> When the worlds terror the fierce African
> Now on his march, the whole earth shooke with feare,
> And tumults in th affrighted nations were,
> When mankind looking for one suddaine fall,

Doubted which empire should entomb them all.
Whither in Sea-fights or land battailes slaine
The earth or sea should their dead trunkes reteine.
Soe when death shall dissolve that union
By which our soules and bodies now are one,
When we shall cease to be, noe accidents
Shall waken our dead sence, no sad events
Shall moove us then, . . .

(903–15)

The dramatic vividness of Dryden's version is even more strikingly apparent in the diatribe in which Nature rebukes man for squandering her precious gifts:

What does thou mean, ungrateful wretch, thou vain,
Thou mortal thing, thus idly to complain,
And sigh and sob, that thou shalt be no more?
For if thy life were pleasant heretofore,
If all the bounteous blessings I could give
Thou hast enjoy'd, if thou hast known to live,
And pleasure not leak'd thro' thee like a Seive,
Why doest thou not give thanks as at a plenteous feast
Cram'd to the throat with life, and rise and take thy rest?
('Lucretius . . . Against the Fear of Death', 123–31; *Works*, 3. 51)

Once again, Dryden's masterful control of the interplay between tight metrical form and larger argumentative trajectory throws the emphasis unerringly on the key words, as in the fervently emotional, yet artfully controlled, rhetoric of what Kenney calls Lucretius' 'pathetic' style. 'If thou hast known to live' (128) has no direct equivalent in Lucretius' Latin, but perfectly captures the Lucretian Nature's distinction between mere existence and a life lived in full and conscious relish of its goods, leading directly into the triumphant swagger of the final Alexandrine. Evelyn's Nature, by contrast, sounds like a splenetic pedant:[39]

Why Mortal, dos't indulge to sadnesse so?
Why so at death repine, and weeping goe?
If thy past life so pleasant were to thee
And that so many ungratefull troubles be

[39] Dryden, however, incorporated some details from Evelyn in his own renderings: see my review of Repetzki's edition of Evelyn's Lucretius, *Translation and Literature*, 11 (2002), 114–18.

(As from a Vessell craz'd which doth conteyne
Them) run out, why sated, dost not refraine
Retiring from thy life as from a feast?
And (foole) contentedly take thy safe rest?

(976–83)

Considerations of space preclude further discussion of Dryden's versions.[40] Suffice it to say that poetic excellence of his version of the closing passage of Book 3 of *De Rerum Natura* is also evident in his rendering of the opening of Book 1, which combines a hymn-like elegance with a delighted appreciation of the fecundity of the natural processes presided over by Venus, and of the passage on love in Book 4, where Dryden's only rival is the stiff-jointed Good, and where a satirical detachment is miraculously combined with a tumultuous depiction of the power of sexual passion which W. B. Yeats described as 'the finest description of sexual intercourse ever written'.[41]

Direct translation, however, only represents part of Lucretius' presence in seventeenth- and eighteenth-century English poetry, since Lucretian form, rhetoric, and imagery were deployed by English poets of the period in more partial and oblique ways. The piecemeal use of Lucretius by English poets was in part encouraged by the long-standing tradition of *florilegia*: thematically-organized collections of poetic 'beauties', offered both for intrinsic pleasure and as models for poetic composition. In the eighteenth century, collections such as Henry Baker's *Medulla Poetarum Latinorum* (1737), Charles Gildon's *Complete Art of Poetry* (1718), and Edward Bysshe's *Art of English Poetry* (1702; final version, 1718) and *British Parnassus* (1714),

[40] For further discussions, see Paul Hammond, 'The Integrity of Dryden's Lucretius', *Modern Language Review*, 78 (1983), 1–23; 'John Dryden: The Classicist as Sceptic', *The Seventeenth Century*, 4 (1989), 165–87; 'Dryden, Milton, and Lucretius'. *The Seventeenth Century* 16 (2001), 158–76; Emrys Jones, 'A "Perpetual Torrent": Dryden's Lucretian Style', in *Augustan Studies: Essays in Honor of Irvin Ehrenpreis*, ed. Douglas Lane Patey and Timothy Keegan (Newark DE, 1985), pp. 47–63; Tom Mason, 'Is There a Classical Tradition in English Poetry?', *Translation and Literature*, 5 (1996), 203–19, and ' "Et Versos Digitos Habet": Dryden, Montaigne, Lucretius, Virgil and Boccaccio in Praise of Venus', *Translation and Literature*, 10 (2001), 89–109.

[41] Interview with John Sparrow (May 1931), transcribed in A. Norman Jeffares, *W. B. Yeats: Man and Poet* (2nd edition, London, 1962), p. 267.

presented copious selections from Lucretius (usually in the versions of Creech and Dryden), which present the great 'visionary' passages from the *De Rerum Natura*, complemented by Lucretian descriptions of the physical, natural, and human world under such diverse headings as 'Ambition', 'Bird', 'Cloud', 'Disease', 'Dreams', 'Lightning', 'Metals', 'Passions', 'River', and 'Wind'. The miscellaneous influence of such Lucretian 'beauties' is visible in many poems of the period. In some famous lines in his 'Elegy written in a Country Churchyard', for example, –

> For them no more the blazing hearth shall burn,
> Or busy housewife ply her evening care:
> No children run to lisp their sire's return,
> Or climb his knees the envied kiss to share.
>
> (21–4)

– Thomas Gray drew on a celebrated passage in Lucretius (*De Rerum Natura*, 3. 894–6) which had previously been translated by Flatman and Dryden, anthologized by Bysshe and Baker, and incorporated by James Thomson in *The Seasons*:

> In vain for him th' officious Wife prepares
> The Fire fair-blazing, and the Vestment warm;
> In vain his little Children, peeping out
> Into the mingling Storm, demand their Sire,
> With Tears of artless Innocence. Alas!
> Nor Wife, nor Children, more shall he behold,
> Nor Friends, nor sacred Home.
>
> ('Winter', 311–17)

Similarly, Matthew Prior drew on Lucretius' much anthologized opening invocation to Venus for his own 'Hymn to Venus, upon a Marriage', and Mark Akenside incorporated Lucretius' description of seashells (*De Rerum Natura*, 2. 374–6) in *The Pleasures of the Imagination* (1772):

> thus the pearl
> Shines in the concave of its purple bed,
> And painted shells along some winding shore
> Catch with indented folds the glancing sun.
>
> (1. 526–9)

But in addition to such piecemeal Lucretian borrowings, English poets sometimes displayed a more extensive engagement with the tone and substance of *De Rerum Natura*. Lucretius was, for example, frequently invoked in the debates about Newtonian physics found in the scientific poetry of the period, in both English and Latin.[42] James Sambrook has described the 'shadowy' presence of Lucretius behind the design of Thomson's *Seasons*, a poem in which Sir Isaac Newton replaces Epicurus as the leading source of poetic inspiration, and in which 'a Lucretian grandeur and passion' are reoriented to serve very different theological ends.[43] Other poems of the period were more forthrightly – even crudely – explicit in their exploitation of Lucretian form and rhetoric for decidedly un-Lucretian purposes. The most explicit of all is *Anti-Lucretius* (1766), George Canning's translation of Books 1–5 of the celebrated neo-Latin poem by Cardinal Melchior de Polignac (1661–1741).[44] Just as Polignac had closely imitated Lucretius' Latin style in a point-by-point refutation of the Latin poet's arguments on the gods and the mortality of the soul, so Canning launches, in English Lucretian style, a lucidly systematic attack on Epicurean teachings about pleasure (Book 1), the void (Book 2), atoms (Book 3), motion (Book 4) and the mind (Book 5). If *Anti-Lucretius* conducts a systematic imitative refutation of the more technical aspects of Lucretius' poetic teaching, Sir Richard Blackmore's *Creation: A Philosophical Poem, In Seven Books* (1712) harnesses Lucretius' tone of lofty and passionate contempt to more emotional, though no less anti-Lucretian, ends, imitating the Roman poet's insistent questions, and passionately enjambed versification, to pour scorn on every aspect of his theological and scientific teaching. John Dennis may – like Samuel Johnson, who endorsed his judgement – have been to some extent betraying his own religious bias when he wrote that *Creation* had 'equalled' the *De Rerum Natura* 'in the Beauty of its Versification, and infinitely surpass'd it, in the Solidity and Strength of its Reasoning'.[45] But modern readers hitherto only

[42] See Patricia Fara and David Money, 'Issac Newton and Augustan Anglo-Latin Poetry', *Studies in the History and Philosophy of Science*, 34 (2004), 549–71; T. J. B. Spencer, 'Lucretius and the Scientific Poem in English', in D. R. Dudley, ed., *Lucretius* (London, 1975), pp. 131–64.

[43] James Thomson, *The Seasons*, ed. James Sambrook (Oxford, 1981), p. xxiv.

[44] De Polignac's poem, first published in 1745, runs to nine books *in toto*.

[45] John Dennis, *Critical Works*, ed. Edward Niles Hooker, 2 vols. (Baltimore, 1939–43), 2. 120; Samuel Johnson, *The Lives of the Most Eminent English Poets*, ed. Roger Lonsdale, 4 vols. (Oxford, 2006), 2. 78.

acquainted with Blackmore's dismal Arthurian epics might be surprised to encounter the tonal assurance and rhythmic energy of his vehement denunciation of Lucretian teaching about 'the Self-existent, Independent and Eternal Being of Atomes': up to here

> Tell us, fam'd *Roman*, was it e'er deny'd,
> That Seeds for such Productions are supply'd?
> That Nature always must Materials find
> For Beasts and Trees, to propagate their Kind?
> All Generation the rude Peasant knows
> A pre-existent Matter must suppose.
> But what to Nature first her Being gave?
> Tell whence your Atomes their Existence have?
> We ask you whence the Seeds Constituent spring
> Of ev'ry Plant, and ev'ry Living Thing,
> Whence ev'ry Creature should produce its Kind,
> And to its proper Species be confin'd?
> To answer this, *Lucretius*, will require
> More than sweet Numbers and Poetic Fire.
>
> (*Creation* (1712), pp. 116–17)

The most impressive indirect responses to the *De Rerum Natura* in the period, however, are to be found, not surprisingly, in the work of two of the period's greatest poets. John Milton's knowledge of Lucretius is evident from the outset of his career in 'Naturam non pati senium' (That Nature does not suffer from old age), a Latin poem supporting the Baconian claim that the world is not in a state of terminal decay.[46] Milton's response to Lucretius in *Paradise Lost* (1667; revised 1674)[47] forms part of his larger endeavour to forge a new style of epic poetry in which the wisdom and imaginings of the classical pagan world are both assimilated and transcended, and in which elements of long-established poetic genres are fused in new combinations and to new ends. At the heart of *Paradise Lost* (5. 469–533), the archangel Raphael discourses to Adam on the nature of God's universe. His 'miniature *De Rerum*

[46] For the Lucretian echoes in this poem, see John K. Hale, *Milton's Languages: The Impact of Multilingualism on Style* (Cambridge, 1997), p. 40.

[47] Quotations below are from the 1674 edition.

*Natura*'[48] offers, like Lucretius (*De Rerum Natura*, 1. 351–7), an analogy from the world of plants to characterize the nature of the material universe, but asserts, in a way markedly different from Lucretian atomism, the divine origins and telos of the primal 'first matter' which constitutes all things and 'which is capable of various degrees of refinement as it nourishes progressively higher forms of life.'[49] Later in his poem, Milton remembers Lucretius' account of creation, elaborating the Roman poet's account of the birth of flora from the earth (*De Rerum Natura*, 5. 781–91) with even greater sensuousness, as we are told (*Paradise Lost* 7. 313–24) how 'Herbs of every leaf' 'sudden flowr'd / Op'ning thir various colours, and made gay / Her bosom smelling sweet' and how 'the clust'ring Vine' 'forth flourish'd thick'. Later still (7. 453–70) Milton similarly embellishes Lucretius' account of the earth generating creatures from several wombs (*De Rerum Natura*, 5. 795–924) in his own depiction of the earth 'Op'ning her fertile womb' and pouring forth 'Innumerous living Creatures, perfet forms' – such as the lion, who, 'pawing to get free / His hinder parts... springs as broke from Bonds, / And Rampant shakes his Brinded mane'. Such animal vigour is for Milton, however, not the product of random atomic collision but of 'the prodigious vitality of a divine Father, who makes his creature vigorous, active, and potent, and sustains them in continuous processes of growth and generation'.[50] In a similar vein, Milton gives his own, distinctively Christian, colouring to the Lucretian claim to be leading readers from darkness into light.[51] He offers his inspiring deity Urania (*Paradise Lost*, 7. 1) as a heavenly alternative to Lucretius' *alma Venus* (*De Rerum Natura*, 1. 2).[52] And, drawing on the traditional association of Pan with the music of the spheres,[53] he reverses

[48] Barbara Kiefer Lewalski, Paradise Lost *and the Rhetoric of Literary Forms* (Princeton NJ, 1985), p. 40.

[49] Ibid., p. 41.

[50] Ibid. p. 135.

[51] *De Rerum Natura*, 1. 921–7; 1. 146–8 = 2. 59–61; 3. 91–3; 6. 39–41; cf. *Paradise Lost*, 3. 1–26). See Philip Hardie, 'The Presence of Lucretius in *Paradise Lost*', *Milton Quarterly*, 29 (1995), 13–24 (13–15).

[52] See William B. Hunter, 'Lucretius', in William B. Hunter, ed., *A Milton Encyclopedia*, 5 vols. (Lewisburg PA, 1978–83), 5. 39.

[53] See John Milton, *Paradise Lost*, ed. Alastair Fowler (2nd edition, London, 1998), p. 260 (on *Paradise Lost* 4. 681–4); Hardie, 'The Presence of Lucretius', 15.

Lucretius' scornful dismissal (*De Rerum Natura* 4. 580–92) of countrymen's superstitious attribution of hillside echoes to the revelling of woodland deities, in his own rapt evocation of the 'Celestial voices' of the 'Millions of spiritual creatures' who, in *Paradise Lost,* 'walk the earth / Unseen, both when we wake, and when we sleep' (4. 677–8, 682). And in his depictions of Satan's Icarus-like fall into Chaos (2. 927–38) and Phaethon-like assault on heaven (Book 6), Milton offers an implicit critique of Lucretius' vision of a godless, material universe that is ever falling and decaying, affirming in the process God's role as the preserver and sustainer of cosmic order.[54] Milton's 'imitation' of Lucretius 'through opposition'[55] is strikingly combined in *Paradise Lost* with a unique ability to convey in English some of the most notable features of Lucretius' poetic style. 'Even at its most prosaic and ratiocinative,' Charles Martindale has observed, '[Lucretius'] is a sublime voice, weighty, craggy, ponderous, at times even galumphing.'[56] Milton's responsiveness to such a voice is nowhere more evident than in his evocation of Chaos, where specific Lucretian echoes ('a dark / Illimitable Ocean without bound', 'embryon Atoms') are combined with the weighty, heavily enjambed verse-music, markedly reminiscent of Lucretius' sublime manner, in which Milton evokes a landscape

> where eldest Night
> And *Chaos,* Ancestors of Nature, hold
> Eternal *Anarchie,* amidst the noise
> Of endless Warrs, and by confusion stand.
>
> (*Paradise Lost,* 2. 891–2, 900, 894–7)[57]

Another notable 'redirection' of Lucretius' poetic voice in our period occurs in a poem that some might be surprised to find discussed in such a context at all: Alexander Pope's *Essay on Man* (1733–4). Lucretius' presence in the poem is, in fact, well

[54] See David Quint, 'Fear of Falling: Icarus, Phaethon, and Lucretius in *Paradise Lost*', *Renaissance Quarterly,* 57 (2004), 847–81.

[55] Hardie, 'The Presence of Lucretius', 15.

[56] Charles Martindale, *Latin Poetry and the Judgement of Taste: An Essay in Aesthetics* (Oxford, 2005), p. 197.

[57] For further discussion of Lucretius' and Milton's Chaos, see J. Leonard, 'Milton, Lucretius, and "the void profound of unessential light"', in *Living Texts: Interpreting Milton,* ed. K. A. Pruitt and C. W. Durham (Selinsgrove PA, 2000), pp. 198–207.

documented.[58] Pope himself referred to his emulation of the Roman poet's 'grave march' in the first two parts of the poem, and the presence has been discerned throughout much of the *Essay* of 'the hortatory, "magisterial" mode generally associated with Lucretius'.[59] The 'grave' Lucretian 'march' has been heard, for example, in such lines as the following:[60]

> Oh blindness to the future! kindly giv'n,
> That each may fill the circle mark'd by Heav'n;
> Who sees with equal eye, as God of all,
> A hero perish, or a sparrow fall,
> Atoms or systems into ruin hurl'd,
> And now a bubble burst, and now a world.
>
> (*An Essay on Man*, 1. 85–90; *TE*, 3i. 24–5)

Pope told Joseph Spence that he had originally intended to include in the *Essay* 'an address to our Saviour, imitated from Lucretius' compliment to Epicurus',[61] and in one of the manuscripts of the poem its addressee, Lord Bolingbroke, is twice referred to as 'Memmius'.[62] The opening of 'Epistle 1' contains prominent echoes of Dryden's version of the opening of *De Rerum Natura* 2.[63] And commentators have also demonstrated the conspicuous presence in Pope's poem of Lucretian satire, and of structural patternings derived from the *De Rerum Natura*.[64]

But it is equally apparent that, despite some contemporaries' suspicions that *An Essay on Man* was a heterodox, even crypto-pagan, work displaying 'strong traces of Infidelity',[65] Pope's poem is

[58] See Bernard Fabian, 'Pope and Lucretius: Observations on *An Essay on Man*', *Modern Language Review*, 74 (1979), 524–37; Miriam Leranbaum, *Alexander Pope's 'Opus Magnum', 1729–1744* (Oxford, 1977).

[59] *The Correspondence of Alexander Pope*, ed. George Sherburn, 5 vols. (Oxford, 1956), 3. 433; Leranbaum, *Alexander Pope's 'Opus Magnum'*, p. 42.

[60] Spencer, 'Lucretius and the Scientific Poem in English', pp. 140–1.

[61] Joseph Spence, *Anecdotes of Books and Men*, ed. James M. Osborn, 2 vols. (Oxford, 1966), 1. 135.

[62] Maynard Mack, ed., *The Last and Greatest Art: Some Unpublished Poetic Manuscripts of Alexander Pope* (Newark DE, 1984), pp. 207, 283.

[63] See Fabian, 'Pope and Lucretius', 530–1.

[64] See Fabian, 'Pope and Lucretius', 531–3, Leranbaum, *Alexander Pope's 'Opus Magnum'*, pp. 43, 45–6, 55–62.

[65] *TE*, 3.i, xvii.

no straightforward imitation of Lucretius. Beside his draft of the couplet –

> The blest today is as completely so,
> As who began a thousand years ago.
> (*Essay on Man*, 1. 75–6; *TE*, 3i. 23)

– which clearly echoes Dryden's translation of Book 3 of *De Rerum Natura*:

> The Man as much to all intents is dead,
> Who dyes to day, and will as long be so,
> As he who dy'd a thousand years ago.
> ('Lucretius ... Against the Fear of Death', 319–21; *Works*, 3. 56)

– Pope wrote, 'Lucretius of death reverst',[66] a phrase which has been described as 'an appropriate motto not just for this echo but for the entire *Essay*'.[67] And Pope's opening proclamation that the only man capable of plumbing the mysteries of God is

> He, who thro' vast immensity can pierce,
> See worlds on worlds compose one universe,
> (1. 23–4; *TE*, 3i. 15–16)

has been seen as 'implicitly a reply to Lucretius's celebration of Epicurus',[68] an observation supported by the fact that the lines appear in the manuscript as

> He who can all the flaming limits pierce
> Of Worlds on worlds, that form one Universe,

– lines which directly echo the *flammantia moenia mundi* of *De Rerum Natura* 1. 73.[69] It has, moreover, been argued that Pope's optimistic assertion of the interdependent order of 'Nature's Chain' (*Essay*, 1. 245–58) is offered as a deliberate *riposte* to Lucretius' depiction of the ultimate dissolution of things.[70]

[66] Mack, *The Last and Greatest Art*, p. 210.
[67] Leranbaum, *Alexander Pope's 'Opus Magnum'*, p. 50.
[68] *TE*, 3.i, 15.
[69] Mack, *The Last and Greatest Art*, p. 209.
[70] At *De Rerum Natura*, 5. 104–9.

Should we, then, see Pope's *Essay* as a simple 'inversion' of Lucretius, more sophisticated in method but fundamentally similar in intent to Blackmore's *Creation* and the Polignac/Canning *Anti-Lucretius*? The *Essay* has often been regarded, by both admirers and detractors, as a systematizing piece of versified philosophy: an attempt to situate the emotional, moral, and social nature of man definitively within the larger scheme of things. But an important recent study has drawn attention to the ways in which the poem's local movements complicate its apparently totalizing design, subtly counterpointing, without simply contradicting, its tendency to philosophical system-building, with a sceptical resistance that resists exclusive commitment to any fixed philosophy, and finds ultimate satisfaction in a Montaignian surrender to life's flux and inconstancy. According to such an interpretation, Pope's celebrated pronouncement that 'Whatever is, is RIGHT' (*Essay*, 1. 294) should be seen not so much as an abstract and complacent affirmation of philosophical optimism but as 'the report of an experience . . . in which rational inquiry, through the very process by which it establishes its own inadequacy, finds itself yielding to the current of nature, and finds in that yielding a paradoxical sense of rightness'.[71] Might one see, in Pope's deployment of Lucretius in the *Essay*, an ambivalence or fluidity similar to that which is evident in his attitudes to 'philosophy' in the poem as a whole? On such a reading, Pope is both attracted by Lucretius' dogmatically assertive tone, and, in a complex dialectic of engagement and disengagement, unwilling to align himself with its insistence and evangelical commitment – not merely because it did not accord with his own Christianity but because he would not align himself wholeheartedly with *any* totalizing philosophical certainty. Lucretius is thus appropriated in a way that hovers ambivalently between sympathetic alignment and sceptical distance, affirmative solidarity and self-conscious self-differentiation. Whereas Dryden had revealed his simultaneous attraction to and distance from Lucretius by assuming a Lucretian voice that would later be complemented by equally empathetic assumptions of other, very different, poetic voices (principally those of Homer, Juvenal, Ovid,

[71] Fred Parker, *Scepticism and Literature: An Essay on Pope, Hume, Sterne, and Johnson* (Oxford, 2003), p. 31.

and Virgil),[72] Pope's *Essay*, like *Paradise Lost* before it, signals its distance from Lucretius *at the same time* as imitating and rendering Lucretius' 'grave march'. Samuel Johnson suggested that Dryden was the first English poet who effectively 'joined argument with poetry'.[73] The evidence presented in this chapter suggests, I believe, that some of the greatest English poets' capacity to 'join argument with poetry' was crucially enhanced by their attempts to assume an English 'Lucretian voice' – even when those attempts sometimes served interests distinctly different from, even directly opposed to, Lucretius' own.

[72] For this view of Dryden, see Hammond, 'John Dryden: The Classicist as Sceptic'; David Hopkins, *Writers and their Work: John Dryden* (Tavistock, 2004), pp. 57–62.

[73] Johnson, *Lives of the Most Eminent English Poets*, 2. 155.

# 4

# 'If He Were Living, and an *Englishman*': Translation Theory in the Age of Dryden

The writings of John Dryden constitute the most substantial and influential body of thinking about translation in the late seventeenth and early eighteenth centuries, and soon established a framework of principles and assumptions which would be constantly invoked in discussions of the subject. Dryden's first essay on translation, the Preface to *Ovid's Epistles* (1680), was immediately cited by other practitioners,[1] and quotations from Dryden dominate the section 'Concerning Translations' in Sir Thomas Pope Blount's collection of commonplaces about poetry.[2] But to describe Dryden's writings on the subject as 'translation theory' might suggest an original, comprehensive, static, and consistent body of doctrine, rather than – as is the case – a constantly-evolving set of programmatic statements and reflections, often developing from the work of predecessors, composed over the course of two decades as a working translator, and deriving their authority as much from the poet's practice as from their cogency in the abstract. Dryden's major statements on translation all occur in prefaces or dedications attached to particular works or collections: *Ovid's Epistles* (1680), *Sylvae* (1685), *The Satires of Juvenal and Persius* (1692, dated 1693), *Examen Poeticum* (1693), *Virgil's* Aeneis (1697), and *Fables Ancient and Modern* (1700). Like the rest of Dryden's literary criticism, his discussions of translation

[1] See [Thomas Hoy], *Two Essays. The Former Ovid De Arte Amandi... the First Book. The Later Hero and Leander of Musaeus* (London, 1682), sig. A1$^{r}$; *Ovid's Elegies, or a Translation of his Choicest Epistles* (London, 1683), sig. a3$^{v}$.

[2] Sir Thomas Pope Blount, *De Re Poetica: Or, Remarks upon Poetry* (London, 1694), pp. 106–12.

bear the distinct marks of their 'occasional' provenance. To be sure, Dryden remained broadly true throughout his translating career to many of the principles set out in introducing his first work as a translator in 1680. But those principles were continually, and sometimes radically, modified in response to the challenge of specific tasks, and in the light of the poet's larger thoughts about the nature of literature, of literary tradition, and of life itself.

Dryden's writings on translation offer relatively little detailed insight into his own translating practice at the line-by-line level – into the way, for example, in which (like his contemporaries and successors) he regularly incorporated not only the thoughts and words of numerous scholarly commentators and translator-predecessors but those of other poets ancient and modern, sometimes even abandoning his original altogether for a quite different source.[3] But his prefaces return regularly to a number of large questions about translation. What kinds of knowledge and experience – scholarly, artistic, human – need a translator possess? What degree and kind of fidelity to his original should he seek? How should he best preserve that original's distinctive 'character' and 'spirit'? Should he reproduce his author's vices as well as his virtues? Should he 'update' the manners, customs, and beliefs of his source-text to make them more accessible to a modern audience? What kinds of pleasure should a translator seek to give his readers? What part might the activity of translation play in the larger linguistic and literary culture of the nation?

Some of these issues had been on the critical agenda from antiquity. Many of them had received extensive recent consideration in France, most notably in the work of Nicolas Perrot D'Ablancourt (1606–64),[4] and this body of French thought had been a formative influence on a

[3] On this topic, see J. M. Bottkol, 'Dryden's Latin Scholarship', *Modern Philology*, 40 (1943), 241–54; Helene M. Hooker, 'Dryden's *Georgics* and English Predecessors.' *Huntington Library Quarterly*, 9 (1946), 273–310; Arvid Løsnes, 'Dryden's *Aeneis* and the Delphin *Virgil*', in Maren-Sophie Røstvig et al., *The Hidden Sense and Other Essays* (Oslo, 1963), pp. 113–57; Arthur Sherbo, 'Dryden's Translation of Virgil's *Eclogues* and the Tradition', *Studies in Bibliography*, 39 (1985), 262–76, and 'Dryden and the Fourth Earl of Lauderdale', *Studies in Bibliography*, 39 (1986), 199–210.

[4] See T. R. Steiner, 'Precursors to Dryden: English and French Theories of Translation in the Seventeenth Century', *Comparative Literature Studies*, 7 (1970), 50–81; *English Translation Theory, 1650–1800* (Assen, 1975), pp. 13–18.

group of writers – particularly Sir John Denham and Abraham Cowley – who had sojourned on the continent during the Interregnum, and whom Dryden and his contemporaries regarded as the founding fathers of English 'translation theory'.

Writing from the vantage point of 1779, Samuel Johnson judged Denham to have been 'one of the first that understood the necessity of emancipating translation from the drudgery of counting lines and interpreting single words',[5] and quoted with approval Denham's praise of Sir Richard Fanshawe's translation of Guarini's *Il Pastor Fido* (1648):

> That servile path thou nobly dost decline
> Of tracing word by word, and line by line.
> Those are the labour'd births of slavish brains,
> Not the effects of Poetry, but pains;
> Cheap vulgar arts, whose narrowness affords
> No flights for thoughts, but poorly sticks at words.
> A new and nobler way thou dost pursue
> To make Translations and Translators too.
> They but preserve the Ashes, thou the Flame,
> True to his sense, but truer to his fame.[6]

Denham's lines had been cited by Dryden in his Preface to *Ovid's Epistles*, in the course of his tripartite division of translation into 'metaphrase', 'or turning an Authour word by word and Line by Line, from one Language into another'; 'paraphrase', 'or Translation with Latitude, where the Authour is kept in view by the Translator, so as never to be lost, but his words are not so strictly follow'd as his sense, and that too is admitted to be amplyfied, but not alter'd'; and 'imitation', 'where the Translator (if he has not lost that Name) assumes the liberty not only to vary from the words and sence, but to forsake them both as he sees occasion: and taking only some general hints from the Original, to run division on the ground-work, as he pleases' (*Works*, 1. 114–15). Dryden conscripts Denham in support of his own conviction that the kind of 'metaphrase' adopted by Ben Jonson in his translation of Horace's *Ars Poetica* is an unsatisfactory

[5] See Samuel Johnson, *The Lives of the Most Eminent English Poets*, ed. Roger Lonsdale, 4 vols. (Oxford, 2006), 1. 239.

[6] Sir John Denham, *Poems*, ed. Theodore Howard Banks (2nd edition, Hamden CT, 1969), pp. 143–4.

method of translation, since ''tis almost impossible to Translate verbally, and well, at the same time'. The 'Verbal Copyer', Dryden argues,

> is to consider at the same time the thought of his Authour, and his words, and to find out the Counterpart to each in another Language: and besides this he is to confine himself to the compass of Numbers, and the Slavery of Rhime. 'Tis much like dancing on Ropes with fetter'd Leggs: A man may shun a fall by using Caution, but the gracefulness of Motion is not to be expected.
>
> (*Works*, 1. 115–16)

Dryden's argument here closely resembles that of another work by Denham, the Preface to *The Destruction of Troy* (1656):

> whosoever offers at Verbal Translation, shall have the misfortune of that young Traveller, who lost his own language abroad, and brought home no other instead of it: for the grace of the Latine will be lost by being turned into English words; and the grace of the English will be lost by being turned into the Latine Phrase.[7]

Denham's emphasis on 'gracefulness' in translation, and his stated intention to make Virgil 'speak not only as a man of this Nation, but as a man of this age', have been interpreted in narrowly political terms, as an attempt to assimilate his originals to the 'noble' values of the English aristocracy, rather than employ the 'vulgar', 'servile', and 'slavish' methods of pedagogues and grammarians.[8] But Denham's remarks are firmly grounded in the irreducible fact that the 'Graces and Happinesses peculiar to every Language' which give 'life and energy to the words'[9] cannot be transposed into another tongue without seeming bizarrely unidiomatic. In this respect, Denham's thought is close to that of the emphatically non-aristocratic Aphra Behn, who, in the 'Essay on Translated Prose' prefixed to her translation of Fontenelle's *Entretiens sur la pluralité des deux mondes* (1688), stressed the impossibility of reproducing the 'apostrophes'

[7] Denham, *Poems*, pp. 159–60.

[8] Lawrence Venuti, 'The Destruction of Troy: Translation and Royalist Cultural Politics in the Interregnum,' *Journal of Medieval and Renaissance Studies*, 23 (1993), 197–219; *The Translator's Invisibility: A History of Translation* (London, 1995), pp. 44–65.

[9] Denham, *Poems*, p. 159.

and the 'flourishes and embroideries' of French prose in English without the result being 'worse than French tinsel' and 'no translation' at all.[10] As well as stressing the need for idiomatic translation, Denham had argued for a principle of compensation according to which 'a new spirit' must be added in the 'transfusion' of literature from one language to another, to remedy the inevitable losses involved in the process. Without such remedial action, Denham suggested, nothing would remain of the original 'but a *Caput mortuum*' – a worthless residue.[11]

In his own arguments against 'imitation', Dryden is at pains to distance himself from Denham, who had, he says, encouraged an unacceptably free mode of translation according to which a 'later Poet' might feel entitled to abandon both 'words' and 'Sense' of his original, merely setting his author 'as a Pattern' and writing 'as he supposes, that Authour would have done, had he liv'd in our Age, and our Country' (*Works*, 1. 116). Denham's theory of compensation will, Dryden argues, license a kind of rendering so free as to be 'almost the creation of another hand'. Dryden is equally sceptical about the freedoms advocated by Cowley in the Preface to his *Pindarique Odes* (1656):

> If a man should undertake to translate *Pindar* word for word, it would be thought that one *Mad man* had translated *another*; as may appear, when he that understands not the *Original*, reads the verbal Traduction of him into *Latin Prose*, than which nothing seems more *Raving*.[12]

Like Denham, Cowley had written (in the same preface) of the need for translators 'to supply the lost Excellencies of another *Language* with new ones in their own'.[13] In his 'Account of the Life and Writings of Mr. Abraham Cowley' (1668) Cowley's friend and executor Thomas Sprat had distinguished carefully between the extreme freedom of the *Pindarique Odes*, 'which may perhaps be thought rather a new sort of Writing than a restoring of an Ancient', and the method deployed in Cowley's other translations, in which the poet had achieved 'wonderfully happy' results by virtue of his possession of

[10] Aphra Behn, *Works*, ed. Janet Todd, 7 vols. (London, 1992–6), 4. 75–6.
[11] Denham, *Poems*, p. 159.
[12] Abraham Cowley, *Poems*, ed. A. R. Waller (Cambridge, 1905), p. 155.
[13] Ibid. p. 156.

'not only the Elegance of both the Languages, but the true spirit of both the Poetries'.[14]

In the Preface to *Ovid's Epistles*, Dryden offered a less sanguine view. Though, he concedes, Denham 'advis'd more Liberty than he took himself', and though Cowley's more extreme pronouncements had, he acknowledges, been made with specific reference to a 'wild and ungovernable Poet' who had to be translated freely if he were to be intelligible at all, both poets' programmatic statements had encouraged a 'liberty' which 'is the most advantagious way for a Translator to shew himself, but the greatest wrong which can be done to the Memory and Reputation of the dead' (*Works*, 1. 117). Dryden's misgivings had been anticipated in the early 1660s by Katherine Philips, who took exception to the 'great liberty' which had been taken by 'the wits' (Edmund Waller and others) in their translation of Corneille's *Pompée* 'in adding, omitting and altering the original as they please themselves'. 'This way of garbling authors', she declared, 'is fitter for a paraphrase than a translation' and is 'a liberty not pardonable in translators'.[15]

Though Cowley and Denham had advocated freedom in translation ('imitation' in Dryden's sense), they had seldom in practice interpreted this as a licence to 'update' their originals by interpolating references to modern persons and *mores* ('imitation' in the sense that became familiar during the eighteenth century). Cowley's sole attempts at modernizing (his versions of Horace, *Odes* 1. 5 and 'The Country Mouse' – discussed in Chapter 2 above) became influential in the 1670s when their influence blended with that of the French poet Boileau to encourage English poems which either, in Cowley's manner, followed the specific contours of one Latin original, substituting English characters and situations for Roman, or, in the manner of Boileau's *Satires*, drew more generally on ancient sources for novel effects. John Wilmot, Earl of Rochester, composed poems of both types. 'An Allusion to Horace' follows its source (Horace, *Satires*, 1. 10) consecutively, in the manner of Cowley's moderniza-

[14] J. E. Spingarn, ed., *Critical Essays of the Seventeenth Century*, 3 vols. (Oxford, 1908), 2. 132.

[15] Katherine Philips, *The Collected Works*, ed. Patrick Thomas, G. Greer, and R. Little, 3 vols. (Stump Cross, 1990–93), 2. 103.

tions. 'Timon' and 'A Satyre against Reason and Mankind' imitate Boileau with a freedom reminiscent of Boileau's imitations of the Latin satirists. Rochester's admirer John Oldham was initially drawn to Drydenian 'paraphrase',[16] but soon resolved to attempt a modernizing version of Horace's *Ars Poetica*. His comments on this version, however, reveal his respect for Dryden's strictures on excessive freedom. Oldham declares his decision to follow Cowley and Rochester's precedents by shifting Horace's 'scene' from Rome to London, and making 'use of *English* names of Men, Places, and Customs' so that his version will be 'more agreeable to the relish of the present Age'. But, in deference to Dryden's fears that 'imitation' was merely a licence for egotistical display, Oldham declares himself to have been 'religiously strict' to the 'sence' of Horace's poem, departing from it only when it was absolutely 'necessary for carrying on [his] propos'd design'.[17]

Dryden's advocacy of 'paraphrase' in the Preface to *Ovid's Epistles* is accompanied by a number of other important affirmations. A translator of poetry, he argues, must himself have a 'Genius to' (temperamental inclination towards) that art himself. He must be 'a Master both of his Authours Language, and of his own', and render those qualities in his author that 'distinguish, and as it were individuate him from all other writers'. In so doing, he must 'conform' his 'genius' to that of his original, following the 'Sacred and inviolable' sense of his author even to a fault, and resisting any temptation to 'improve' his source: 'If the Fancy of *Ovid* be luxuriant, 'tis his Character to be so, and if I retrench it, he is no longer *Ovid*' (*Works*, 1. 118).

The later perception of Denham's centrality in the reorientation of English translation theory in the mid-seventeenth century was closely connected with a larger reorientation of English poetic taste and practice which was thought to have occurred around the same date, in which regard Denham's name was regularly linked with that of his contemporary, Edmund Waller. In his Preface to *The Second*

[16] See his *The Passion of Byblis* (London, 1681).

[17] John Oldham, *Poems*, ed. Harold F. Brooks, with Raman Selden (Oxford, 1987), pp. 87–8; for discussion, see Harold F. Brooks, 'The "Imitation" in English Poetry, Especially in Formal Verse Satire, before the Age of Pope,' *Review of English Studies*, 25 (1949), 124–40.

*Part of Mr. Waller's* Poems (1690) Francis Atterbury described Waller as 'the parent of English verse, and the first that showed us our tongue had beauty and numbers in it'. 'Before his time,' Atterbury continued,

> men rhymed indeed, and that was all: as for the harmony of measure, and that dance of words which good ears are so much pleased with, they knew nothing of it. Their poetry then was made up almost entirely of monosyllables; which, when they come together in any cluster, are certainly the most harsh, untuneable things in the world. If any man doubts of this, let him read ten lines in Donne, and he will be quickly convinced. Besides, their verses ran all into one another, and hung together, throughout a whole copy, like the hooked atoms that compose a body in Des Cartes. There was no distinction of parts, no regular stops, nothing for the ear to rest upon; but as soon as the copy began, down it went like a larum, incessantly; and the reader was sure to be out of breath before he got to the end of it: so that verse, in those days, was but downright prose tagged with rhymes. Mr. Waller removed all these faults, brought in more polysyllables, and smoother measures, bound up his thoughts better, and in a cadence more agreeable to the nature of the verse he wrote in; so that wherever the natural stops of that were, he contrived the little breakings of his sense so as to fall in with them; and, for that reason, since the stress of our verse lies commonly upon the last syllable, you will hardly ever find him using a word of no force there. I would say, if I were not afraid the reader would think me too nice, that he commonly closes with verbs, in which we know the life of language consists.[18]

In Sir William Soame's translation of Boileau's *L'art poétique* (revised by John Dryden, and published in 1683), in which Boileau's French examples are replaced by English equivalents, a similar account is offered of the development of English verse. As in Atterbury's Preface, the state of the poetic language in former times is seen as crude and barbarous:

> Our ancient Verse, (as homely as the Times,)
> Was rude, unmeasur'd, only Tagg'd with Rhimes:
> Number and Cadence, that have Since been Shown,
> To those unpolish'd Writers were unknown.

[18] *The Second Part of Mr. Waller's Poems* (London, 1690), sigs. A5$^{v}$–A7$^{r}$.

Then, after some pioneering developments in the direction of greater elegance from Fairfax, Spenser, and Davenant, came the significant breakthrough:

> *Waller* came last, but was the first whose Art
> Just Weight and Measure did to Verse impart;
> That of a well-plac'd Word could teach the force,
> And shew'd for Poetry a nobler Course:
> His happy Genius did our Tongue Refine,
> And easie Words with pleasing Numbers joyn:
> His Verses to good method did apply,
> And chang'd harsh Discord to Soft Harmony.
> All own'd his Laws; which, long approv'd and try'd,
> To present Authors now may be a *Guide.*
>
> (*The Art of Poetry*, 111–14; 131–40; Dryden, *Works*, 2. 127–8)

Finally, looking back on the developments described by Soame from the vantage point of the early eighteenth century, Alexander Pope exhorted his readers to 'praise the *Easie Vigor* of a Line, / Where *Denham's* Strength, and *Waller's* Sweetness join'[19] (*An Essay on Criticism*, 360–1). The stylistic innovations so fruitfully pioneered by Denham and Waller, Pope thought, were partly connected with a salutary transfusion of French refinement into English culture, and had been brought to their full perfection by Dryden:

> We conquer'd France, but felt our captive's charms;
> Her Arts victorious triumph'd o'er our Arms:
> Britain to soft refinements less a foe,
> Wit grew polite, and Numbers learn'd to flow.
> Waller was smooth; but Dryden taught to join
> The varying verse, the full resounding line,
> The long majestic march, and energy divine. [20]
> ('The First Epistle of the Second Book of *Horace*', 263–9; *TE*, 4. 217)

The eighteenth-century belief that English verse had been invested with potential for new harmony, eloquence, and expressive vigour by the 'reform of our numbers' associated with Denham and Waller has often been regarded with scepticism, or even derision. It prompted Robert Southey, for example, to dismiss the whole period from the

[19] *An Essay on Criticism*, 360–1; *TE*, 1. 280.

[20] *The First Epistle of the Second Book of Horace*, 263–9; *TE*, 4. 217.

Restoration to the death of Pope as a 'dark age' of English poetry, inhabited by superficial 'versifiers', 'wits', and 'reasoners' who were unhealthily besotted with the rule-mongering aesthetics of contemporary France.[21] But a more considered scrutiny of the taste and ideals that motivated the 'reform' helps us realize that the 'harmony' and 'easy vigour' sought by poets and critics of the period was more than a merely superficial fluency and elegance, and can suggest why, to later seventeenth-century ears, many of the translations of classical and modern European poems produced in the Elizabethan, Jacobean, and Caroline periods – such as Arthur Golding's Ovid, Chapman's Homer, and Barten Holyday's Juvenal – now seemed ripe for replacement by more metrically adroit, lucidly expressive, and rhetorically coherent versions.[22] The appetite for new translations was thus simultaneously an appetite for a greater fidelity to the 'spirit' (as opposed to the mere 'letter') of the original, and an appetite for versions which would manifest the new harmony and eloquence which, it was felt, English verse had recently achieved, and could thus stand on an equal footing with the best modern verse.

John Oldham's and the Earl of Rochester's attempts in the 1670s to explore new possibilities for translation were not an isolated venture. A group of scholars active in Oxford in the early 1680s sought similarly to follow the French lead in making the classics available to the general reader, leading to such projects as Thomas Creech's translation of Lucretius (1682) and Theocritus (1684), White Kennett's version of Erasmus' *Praise of Folly* (1683), and composite versions of Anacreon (1683) and the Roman historian Cornelius Nepos (1684). One of the prefatory poems to Creech's Lucretius is by Dryden's publisher, Jacob Tonson,[23] who laments the unwillingness of English writers to emulate the skill of the French in translation with the eagerness that they had adopted French sartorial fashions. But the following year, Matthew Morgan, in his prefatory poem to Kennett's *Praise of Folly*, confidently claimed that the English

[21] See Upali Amarasinghe, *Dryden and Pope in the Early Nineteenth Century* (Cambridge, 1962), p. 154.

[22] A discerning and sympathetic account of the issue is offered by Robin Sowerby, *The Augustan Art of Poetry: Augustan Translation of the Classics* (Oxford, 2006).

[23] On Tonson's (surreptitious) authorship of this poem, see Sarah Lewis Carol Clapp, ed., *Jacob Tonson in Ten Letters by and about him* (Austin TX, 1948), p. 11.

had now surpassed the French in translation. The French – particularly Boileau – were pioneers in the field, but their accomplishment has now degenerated into vulgar popularization, whereas recent English achievements like Creech's Lucretius are likely to prove more enduring. A year later, in 1684, Gilbert Burnet looked forward, more cautiously but nevertheless with a degree of quiet confidence, to a renewal in English translation activity. 'The French,' Burnet writes, 'took no ill Method, when they intended to reform and beautify their Language, in setting their Best Writers on Work to translate the Greek and Latin Authors into it'. Certain recent linguistic developments in England, he believes, have made it likely that translation, engagement in which is sometimes thought of as 'a sign of a slow Mind', will, in the hands of some writers that 'have appeared of late . . . bring that way of writing in credit':

> The English language has wrought it self out, both of the fulsome Pedantry under which it laboured long ago, and the trifling way of dark and unintelligible Wit that came after that, and out of the course extravagance of Canting that succeeded this . . . We are now so much refined, that how defective soever our Imaginations or Reasonings may be, yet our Language has fewer Faults, and is more natural and proper, than it was ever at any time before.[24]

Dryden's Preface to *Ovid's Epistles* established a number of principles to which the poet remained broadly faithful for the rest of his life. But his proposal of 'paraphrase' as a classical *via media* between two undesirable extremes, though rhetorically neat, was to prove simplistic in the light of his developing experience.[25] His revision of Sir William Soame's translation of Boileau's *Art poétique*, quoted above, shows his interest in Oldham's style of modernized translation. And his work would soon embrace some of the other freedoms which he had earlier deplored.

An important stimulus to Dryden's developing thought about translation in the early 1680s was provided by Wentworth Dillon, Fourth Earl of Roscommon (1637–85), whose *Essay on Translated Verse* (1684) was the by-product or manifesto of an Academy which

[24] [Gilbert Burnet], *Utopia: Written in Latin by Sir Thomas More, Chancellor of England: Translated into English* (London, 1684), sigs. A3$^{r}$–A4$^{v}$.

[25] See Maurice O'Sullivan Jr, 'Running Division on the Groundwork: Dryden's Theory of Translation,' *Neophilologus*, 64 (1980), 144–59.

he had recently established, to encourage the 'refining our Language, without abating the force of it' by enriching the native literary tradition through translation.[26] The details of Roscommon's venture remain obscure, and its dating controversial, but covert allusions in the *Essay* seem to indicate that he saw Dryden as the natural leader of the new generation of translator-poets which his Academy had sought to encourage.[27] Dryden, for his part, hailed Roscommon's *Essay* enthusiastically in a verse epistle of 1684 (*Works*, 2. 172–4) and declared in his Preface to *Sylvae* (1685) that Roscommon's poem had 'made him uneasie till [he] try'd whether or no [he] was capable of following his Rules, and of reducing the speculation into practice' (*Works*, 3. 3).

Roscommon's *Essay on Translated Verse* contains a number of memorable formulations which anticipate later developments in Dryden's translating career. Roscommon, for example, places particular emphasis on the translator's need to combine the scrupulousness of a scholar with the intuitive responsiveness of a poet in determining the sense of his original:

> Take pains the *genuine* Meaning to explore,
> There *Sweat*, there *Strain*, tug the laborious *Oar*:
> Search *ev'ry Comment*, that your Care can find,
> Some here, some there, may hit the Poets *Mind*.

And elsewhere Roscommon stresses the bond of sympathy, even identification, that must exist between a successful translator and his original:

> Then, seek a *Poet* who *your* way do's bend,
> And chuse an *Author* as you chuse a *Friend*.
> United by this *Sympathetick Bond*,
> You grow *Familiar*, *Intimate* and *Fond*;
> Your *thoughts*, your *Words*, your *Stiles*, your *Souls* agree,
> No Longer his *Interpreter*, but *He*.

[26] Knightly Chetwood, 'A Short Account of Some Passages of the Life & Death of Wentworth late Earle of Roscommon', ed. Greg Clingham, *Restoration*, 25 (2001), 117–38; Greg Clingham, 'Roscommon's "Academy", Chetwood's "Life of Roscommon", and Dryden's Translation Project,' *Restoration*, 26 (2002), 15–26; Andrew Barclay, 'Dating Roscommon's Academy,' *Restoration*, 26 (2002), 119–26.

[27] See Clingham, 'Roscommon's "Academy"'; H. A. Mason, 'Clique Puffery in Roscommon's *Essay on Translated Verse*', *Notes and Queries*, 235 (1990), 296.

Roscommon also celebrates the great benefits which translation can bring to modern civilization, as evidenced by the recent achievements of the French:

> There (cultivated by a Royal Hand)
> Learning grew fast, and spread, and blest the Land;
> The choicest Books, that *Rome*, or *Greece* have known,
> Her excellent *Translators* made her own:
> And *Europe* still considerably gains,
> Both by their good *Example* and their *Pains*.[28]

Empathetic engagement of the kind desiderated by Roscommon is clearly evident in Dryden's next major statement on translation. The commercial success of *Ovid's Epistles* had paved the way for the series of miscellanies and volumes of translated verse, single-author and collaborative, which Dryden's publisher Jacob Tonson was to issue during the 1680s and 1690s, and in which Dryden was to feature prominently as author, editor, recruiter of contributors, and general source of leadership and inspiration.[29] It was in the second Tonson miscellany, *Sylvae* (1685), that Dryden published his first unqualifiedly masterly translations: of four poems by Horace and the five passages from Lucretius' *De Rerum Natura* discussed in Chapter 3 above. Dryden's exuberant Preface to the volume is a breathlessly excited dispatch from the field. The poet speaks of the 'hot fit' of creativity which has resulted in poems in which he has, to his delight and surprise, found 'something that was more pleasing' than in his 'ordinary productions' (*Works*, 3. 3). Dryden's main critical focus is on the translator's paramount need to maintain 'the Character of an Author, which distinguishes him from all others', and to convey 'the Spirit which animates the whole' of each of his originals, just as a good portrait painter captures the inner life, rather than merely the appearance, of his sitters. 'A good Poet', Dryden maintains, 'is no more like himself, in a dull Translation, than his Carcass would be to his living Body.' The translator must modify his own style and

[28] Wentworth Dillon, fourth Earl of Roscommon, *An Essay on Translated Verse* (2nd edition, London, 1685), pp. 12, 7, 3.

[29] See Stuart Gillespie and David Hopkins, eds., *The Dryden–Tonson Miscellanies, 1684–1709*, Cultural Transformations: The Eighteenth Century, 6 vols. (London and Toyko, 2008).

temperament to accommodate it whole-heartedly to that of his original. Consequently, when translating Lucretius, Dryden has 'lay'd by' his 'natural Diffidence and Scepticism for a while, to take up that Dogmatical way of his, which ... is so much his Character, as to make him that individual Poet' (*Works*, 3. 11).

But if Dryden is aware of the distinctiveness of his originals, he is simultaneously conscious of the mysterious sympathy or affinity which drew him to each of them in the first place. His versions are of those passages which have 'most affected' him 'in the reading' (*Works*, 3. 3). Buoyed up with his own confidence at having conveyed the 'noble pride, and positive assertion of his Opinions' which characterize Lucretius, and the 'Briskness', 'Jollity', and 'good Humour' which is 'the most distinguishing part' of Horace, Dryden is now prepared to allow the translator a far greater freedom than previously. In these versions, he declares, echoing the very sentiments in Denham which he had earlier dismissed,

> I have both added and omitted, and even sometimes very boldly made such expositions of my Authors, as no *Dutch* Commentator will forgive me. Perhaps, in such particular passages, I have thought that I discover'd some beauty yet undiscover'd by those Pedants, which none but a Poet cou'd have found. Where I have taken away some of their Expressions, and cut them shorter, it may possibly be on this consideration, that what was beautiful in the *Greek* or *Latin*, wou'd not appear so shining in the *English*: And where I have enlarg'd them, I desire the false Criticks wou'd not always think that these thoughts are wholly mine, but that either they are secretly in the Poet, or may be fairly deduc'd from him: or at least, if both those considerations should fail, that my own is of a piece with his, and that if he were living, and an *Englishman*, they are such, as he wou'd probably have written.
>
> (*Works*, 3. 3–4)

The translator's right to take such freedoms derives, Dryden believes, from the breadth of experience which he brings to his task, experience which involves a far wider range of human qualities and aptitudes than the merely scholastic or linguistic:

> There are many who understand *Greek* and *Latin*, and yet are ignorant of their Mother Tongue. The proprieties and delicacies of the *English* are known to few; 'tis impossible even for a good Wit, to understand and practice them without the help of a liberal Education, long Reading, and

digesting of those few good Authors we have amongst us, the knowledge of Men and Manners, the freedom of habitudes and conversation with the best company of both Sexes; and in short, without wearing off the rust which he contracted, while he was laying in a stock of Learning.

(*Works*, 3. 4–5)

Dryden was to repeat his conviction that the insights of poet-translators were potentially superior to those of scholarly commentators, when, in the Dedication to *Examen Poeticum* (1693) he wrote, apropos of his recent translations from Ovid:

If I Flatter not my self, or if my Friends have not Flatter'd me, I have given my Author's Sense, for the most past truly: for to mistake sometimes, is incident to all Men: And not to follow the *Dutch* Commentatours alwaies, may be forgiven to a Man, who thinks them, in the general, heavy gross-witted Fellows; fit only to gloss on their own dull Poets.

(*Works*, 4. 370–1)

Dryden's experience eight years after *Sylvae*, when preparing the translations included in *The Satires of Juvenal and Persius* (1692, dated 1693), convinced him that even further freedoms were legitimate, or at least unavoidable, when rendering poetry of such dense topical reference, circumstantial detail, and textual obscurity as that of the Roman satirists. The method employed by Dryden and his collaborators in this volume has been, he says, 'a kind of Paraphrase; or somewhat which is yet more loose, betwixt a Paraphrase and Imitation', in which he and his associates have sometimes caused Juvenal to 'express the Customs and Manners of our Native Country, rather than *Rome*', 'either when there was some kind of Analogy, betwixt their Customes and ours; or when, to make him more easy to Vulgar Understandings, we gave him those Manners which are familiar to us' (*Works*, 4. 89). Without such freedoms, a translator of Juvenal will inevitably miss the poet's 'Soul' and 'Poetry', thereby failing, like the crabbed and unidiomatic 'metaphrastic' versions by Barten Holyday (1673) and Sir Robert Stapylton (1647, revised 1660), to offer the reader that 'Pleasure' without which any satirical 'Instruction' 'is but a bare and dry Philosophy' (*Works*, 4. 88–9).

Dryden's old enemy Thomas Shadwell disagreed. In the Epistle Dedicatory to this version of *The Tenth Satyr of Juvenal* (1687) he had affirmed his loyalty to the older style of translation, explicitly eschewing the 'arrogant' freedoms advocated by Dryden's Preface to *Sylvae*, and declaring:

I have endeavour'd in this Translation to come as near the words and thoughts of my Author, as my skill in bothe Languages could enable me. I have omitted no part of his Sence, nor have I varied from it, nor added to it, but in some few places where it was necessary to a meer English Reader, for explanation.[30]

Dryden was undeterred. His conviction that his freedoms were justified rested, indeed, on an increasing awareness of the needs of the 'meer English Reader', and particularly of the important female element in his audience. His predecessor, the learned Barten Holyday, he says, 'wrote for Fame, and wrote to Scholars'. But Dryden and his associates

write only for the Pleasure and Entertainment of those Gentlemen and Ladies, who tho they are not Scholars are not Ignorant: Persons of Understanding and good Sense; who not having been conversant in the Original, or at least not having made *Latine* Verse so much their business, as to be Critiques in it, wou'd be glad to find, if the Wit of our Two great Authors, be answerable to their Fame, and Reputation in the World.

('Discourse Concerning . . . Satire'; *Works*, 4. 87)

The success in the market place of Dryden and Tonson's translating ventures over these years indicates a productive coincidence between Dryden's theoretical preferences and the tastes of an expanding English audience for such work.[31]

The Dedication and Postcript to Dryden's translation of Virgil's *Aeneid* (1697) are the only essays in which Dryden's main emphasis falls on the difficulties – even the impossibility – of translation, rather than on its discoveries and delights. Dryden now describes his activity as that of a 'Slave' forced to 'labour on another Man's Plantation'. He has, he says, omitted and expanded details in Virgil's text, but hopes that his omissions are 'but of Circumstances, and such as wou'd have no grace in *English*', and that his additions 'will seem . . .

[30] Thomas Shadwell, *The Tenth Satyr of Juvenal, English and Latin* (London, 1687), sig. A3$^{v}$.

[31] See Gillespie and Hopkins, eds., *The Dryden–Tonson Miscellanies*, 1. xv–lxix, *passim.*

not stuck into him, but growing out of him'. But the task of making one's original speak 'as... if he had been born in *England*, and in this present Age' is, he acknowledges, supremely difficult in the case of a poet peculiarly renowned for the euphonious elegance, sweetness, and conciseness of his style in Latin – a language Dryden believes to be inherently superior to English in its economy, harmoniousness, and variety. He has, he claims, perhaps been 'the first *Englishman*... who made it his design to copy [Virgil] in his Numbers, his choice of Words, and his placing them for the sweetness of the sound'. In this regard, he has taken the trouble to avoid excessive elision of vowels so that his verse does not display an un-Virgilian 'roughness', and has drawn on Spenser as well as Virgil for stylistic inspiration. Nevertheless, he is conscious of the burden – unprecedented in his translating career – of having 'the weight of a whole Author on [his] shoulders'. He is, nevertheless, unapologetic about one feature of his version: its Latinizing. His numerous borrowings from Latin will, he claims, valuably extend the resources of his own tongue: 'I Trade both with the Living and the Dead, for the enrichment of our Native Language' (*Works*, 5. 319–36).

But if the Dedication and Postcript to the *Aeneis* are at times disconsolate, even despairing in tone, the Preface to Dryden's last volume, *Fables Ancient and Modern* (1700), returns to the buoyant delight of the Preface to *Sylvae*. In this essay, and one of the poems in the collection with which it is closely connected, Dryden moves onto a different plane of 'translation theory', subsuming considerations of literary style and technique within a lofty conception of translation as the local expression and embodiment of the larger processes of flux, transformation, and renewal which pervade the human and natural world at every level. Since, in the *Fables*, Dryden's translation theory becomes even more inextricably and intimately intertwined with his translatorly practice, and since, here, even more surely than before, he 'proves his right of judgement by his power of performance',[32] discussion of this final phase of Dryden's reflection on the translator's art will be postponed till Chapter 9, by which time we will have considered some of the poems that lie at the heart of his achievement in the field in the last decade of his life.

[32] Johnson, *Lives of the Most Eminent English Poets*, 2. 120.

# 5

# Dryden and the Tenth Satire of Juvenal

Recent commentary on Dryden's translations of Juvenal can be broadly divided into four main categories. One group of scholars has devoted itself to assembling the range of materials which the poet had before him while composing his versions. As is now well established, Dryden did not simply work from plain texts of his originals, but drew on a remarkably wide variety of commentaries and earlier translations, continually incorporating, adapting, and combining interpretative glosses, phrasing, diction, rhymes, and end-words from these sources in his own rendering. Scholarship over the last fifty years has gone a long way towards establishing the particular editions and translations of Juvenal with which Dryden worked, and on whose phrasing and insights he drew when composing his own versions.[1]

A second body of commentators has discussed Dryden's Juvenal in the light of seventeenth-century debates about the nature of satire and about the theory and practice of translation. Such critics have frequently followed an agenda set by Dryden's own prose prefaces – most notably the Preface to *Ovid's Epistles* (1680), with its famous tripartite division of translation into metaphrase, paraphrase, and imitation, discussed in Chapter 4 above.[2]

[1] See particularly the commentaries in *Works*, 4 and *Poems*, 4. The pioneer studies of Dryden's translation methods were J. McG. Bottkol, 'Dryden's Latin Scholarship', *Modern Philology*, 40 (1943), 241–54, and H. M. Hooker, 'Dryden's *Georgics* and English Predecessors', *Huntington Library Quarterly*, 9 (1946), 273–310.

[2] For this group of critics, see particularly G. L. Broderson, 'Seventeenth-Century Translations of Juvenal', *Phoenix*, 7 (1953), 57–76; William Frost, *John Dryden: Dramatist, Satirist, Translator* (New York, 1988), pp. 41–70; William Kupersmith, *Roman Satirists in Seventeenth-Century England* (Lincoln NB, 1985); Raman Selden,

The third category of commentary on Dryden's Juvenal comprises a single, extended item: H. A. Mason's celebrated article, 'Is Juvenal a Classic?'.[3] Mason's essay stands apart from other studies of Dryden's Juvenal in the prominent use it makes of Dryden's translation as part of an attempt to define the distinctive poetic qualities of Juvenal himself. Mason argues against the influential conception of Juvenal as high-minded moralist and scourge of the vice and corruption of imperial Rome – a wounded soul whose caustic vehemence and hysterical bitterness were the direct result of frustrations and disappointments in his own career and private life. Instead, Mason maintains, Juvenal's art is that of an opportunistic entertainer with a penchant for hyperbole and indiscriminate derision, whose moral stance is deliberately inconsistent, and whose private opinions and motives can never simply be identified with any expressed in his work. In all these respects, Mason argues, Dryden's version is far closer in tone and spirit to Juvenal than Samuel Johnson's celebrated imitations of Juvenal's Third and Tenth Satires, which substitute for Juvenal's 'witty' opportunism (where even the sublime epic register is deployed to remorselessly belittling effect) a moral weight and earnestness which is quite alien to the original.

The final (and perhaps currently dominant) group of commentators has stressed the political dimension of Dryden's Juvenal, seeing this as part of a larger pattern of covert topical comment running throughout Dryden's later work.[4] Such critics sometimes take their

'Juvenal and Restoration Modes of Translation', *Modern Language Review*, 68 (1973), 481–93, and *English Verse Satire, 1590–1795* (London, 1978); Michael Wilding, 'Dryden and Satire: "Mac Flecknoe, Absalom and Achitophel, The Medall", and Juvenal', in *Writers and their Background: John Dryden*, ed. Earl Miner (London, 1972), pp. 191–233.

[3] Mason's article was first published in *Arion*, 1 (1962), 8–44 and 2 (1962), 5–77. It was reprinted in *Critical Essays on Roman Literature: Satire*, ed. J. P. Sullivan (London, 1963), pp. 91–176 (from which quotations in the present chapter are taken). The essay has been much debated by classicists: see, for example, W. S. Anderson, *Essays on Roman Satire* (Princeton NJ, 1982), pp. 370–93; John Bramble, 'Martial and Juvenal', in *The Cambridge History of Classical Literature, Vol. II: Latin Literature*, eds. E. J. Kenney and W. V. Clausen (Cambridge, 1982), pp. 606–9; Niall Rudd, *Themes in Roman Satire* (London, 1986), pp. 33–4. For a later account of Juvenal which substantially endorses Mason's findings, see G. O. Hutchinson, *Latin Literature from Seneca to Juvenal: A Critical Study* (Oxford, 1983), pp. 32–3, 100–1, 136–8.

[4] For this approach, see James Anderson Winn, *John Dryden and his World* (New Haven CT and London, 1987), pp. 457–8, and '"Complying with the Times":

cue from Dryden's application of Juvenal's Sixteenth Satire to the 'standing armies' debate of the 1690s, and from the clear element of self-identification between Dryden and Juvenal's Umbricius in 'The Third Satyr'. In Dryden's translation, the poem's main speaker (called 'Umbritius' in the English version) is leaving Rome in disgust for a life of retirement at Cumae on the Bay of Naples, and voices his discontents in the following terms:

> Since Noble Arts in *Rome* have no support,
> And ragged Virtue not a Friend at Court,
> No Profit rises from th' ungrateful Stage,
> My Poverty encreasing with my Age,
> 'Tis time to give my just Disdain a vent,
> And, Cursing, leave so base a Government.
>
> (39–44)

A few lines later Umbritius declares:

> For want of these Town Virtues, thus, alone,
> I go conducted on my way by none:
> Like a dead Member from the Body rent;
> Maim'd and unuseful to the Government.
>
> (85–8)

A cursory comparison with Juvenal's Latin reveals that it contains no direct equivalent for Dryden's references to the 'Court', 'th' ungrateful Stage', or the 'base' 'Government'. All these allusions, however, fit Dryden's own situation and sentiments in the early 1690s very precisely. After the Revolution of 1688–9, he had lost his former position as quasi-official spokesman for the Court, had seen his Poet Laureateship conferred on his old enemy Thomas Shadwell, and had been forced, for financial reasons, to resume the career as a playwright

Dryden's Satires of Juvenal and Persius (1693)', *Eighteenth-Century Life*, 12 (1988), 76–87; Kirk Combe, 'Clandestine Protest against William III in Dryden's Translations of Juvenal and Persius', *Modern Philology*, 87 (1989), 36–50; Rachel Miller, '"Physic for the Great": Dryden's Satiric Translations of Juvenal, Persius and Boccaccio', *Philological Quarterly*, 68 (1989), 53–75; William Myers, *Dryden* (London, 1973), pp. 152–8. For the stress on politics as the central preoccupation of Dryden's work in general, see David Bywaters, *Dryden in Revolutionary England* (Berkeley and Los Angeles CA, 1991), and Stephen N. Zwicker, *Politics and Language in Dryden's Poetry: The Arts of Disguise* (Princeton NJ, 1974).

which he had often found uncongenial, and which had never brought him adequate monetary reward. Juvenal's Umbricius describes himself simply as 'mancus et extinctae corpus non utile dextrae' (48; maimed, and a useless body with the right hand lost). The implication in the English version, that it is Umbritius himself who is 'Like a dead Member', since he is now excluded from the activities of the body politic and 'unuseful to the Government', is Dryden's personal adaptation of a gloss in Ludovicus Prateus' 'Delphin' edition of 1684: 'Quasi membrum inutile civitati discedo' (I leave like a member unuseful to the state).[5]

On the strength of such examples, several recent commentators have concluded that Dryden was merely using the opportunity of translating Juvenal as a 'cover' for the articulation of his own sentiments – those of a court satirist and political writer no longer able to practise his art in the mainstream public forum, and now forced to voice his Jacobite resentment by covert innuendo and indirect rhetorical stratagem.

All four categories of scholarship described above have generated information and insights for which any student of Dryden's Juvenal will be grateful. But all four also have certain limitations for a reader seeking enlightenment about the distinctive poetic significance and pleasures which Dryden's renderings of Juvenal contain and convey. Readers, for example, who attempt to work their way through the commentary on the poems in the California edition of Dryden's *Works* might well come away baffled and overwhelmed by the sheer quantity and diversity of source material quoted, and uncertain about the precise bearing of each element of this copious workshop activity on their understanding of Dryden's finished text. Without specific guidance it is difficult to distinguish those key borrowings, interpolations, or tonal colourings which might take one to the heart of Dryden's sense of the larger import and meaning of Juvenal's poems from the numerous borrowings from commentators and earlier translations which contributed continuously, but in a less immediately significant way, to the verbal texture of his version.

Slightly different problems occur when one turns to the criticism focused on questions of satiric genre and translation theory. For while it is clear that no reader of Dryden's Juvenal can afford to

[5] See *Works*, 4. 608.

ignore seventeenth-century critical opinion on both subjects, it would be misleading to assume that such material constitutes the exclusive framework within which the qualities and characteristics of the translations themselves can or should be understood and assessed. For all the quasi-theoretical claims scattered throughout his critical prose, Dryden was in many respects an intuitive and inspirational artist, whose poetic practice did not always simply square with his stated principles, and who was not always able or willing to expound fully in discursive prose the discoveries which he had made in the act of composition. As we saw in Chapter 4, Dryden described his Juvenal translations (alluding to his own earlier tripartite classification) as 'a kind of Paraphrase; or somewhat which is yet more loose, betwixt a Paraphrase and Imitation' ('Discourse Concerning . . . Satire'; *Works*, 4. 87). But when examined at the line-by-line level, they can be seen to cross the boundaries of all three categories in an almost infinitely variable and flexible way. Dryden sometimes supplies a literal, word-for-word, rendering of a particular phrase or line in the original, sometimes expands on Juvenal's text without apparently departing far from its main drift, and sometimes interpolates words and phrases which have no obvious basis in the original at all. Dryden's theoretical categories, that is, give only the very broadest sense of the complexity and fluidity of his local engagement with his original. And something analogous might be said about his prose comments on satire and on the individual Roman satirists. While these sometimes provide suggestive hints about the deeper imaginative reaches of his engagement with Juvenal, the qualities which Dryden discovered in the Roman poet are only fully revealed in the translations themselves.

H. A. Mason's 'Is Juvenal a Classic?' is in many ways the most stimulating of all the modern engagements with Dryden's Juvenal, and performed an invaluable service in reminding readers of the crucial 'witty' dimension of Juvenal's work, at a time when many were still disposed to treat him as an earnest and simple-minded moralist. Yet, for all its learning and critical suggestiveness, the essay seems, in retrospect, somewhat disappointing (at least as far as Dryden is concerned) in the light of its own stated intentions. At first sight, Mason seems to be offering to investigate and describe the distinctive poetic characteristics of Juvenal, differentiating them from those of satirists with whom his readers will be more familiar, with the aim of recapturing a rare and neglected mode of literary pleasure. Near the beginning of his essay, he states his intention 'to communicate delight, or to make comprehensible what Dryden may have meant when he said of Juvenal, "he gives me as much pleasure as I can bear"' (p. 94). Later he notes that, despite its contemptuous and belittling tendencies, 'Juvenal's best wit seems to elevate rather than depress the mind' (p. 122). The conclusions of the essay, however, seem rather more negative than such remarks might lead one to expect. On his last page, Mason appears to concede the objections of an imagined reader that he has made 'the prospect of pleasure seem... very much less than Dryden's remark promised' and that Juvenal's brand of wit, in his (Mason's) description, is 'something if not inferior yet very much more specialized' than that of T. S. Eliot and Ezra Pound. Earlier in the piece, Mason had described Juvenal as being notably deficient in 'the most precious form of intelligence', the 'incomparably finer moral interest, which reveals itself... locally as a much greater intellectual grasp' to be found in Johnson's *The Vanity of Human Wishes* (p. 108). Juvenal is thus, it seems, ultimately being condemned in the name of the very kind of moral satire from which Mason had initially set out – without censorious intent – to differentiate him. And Dryden's version, by virtue of its very overall faithfulness (in Mason's view) to Juvenal's tone, is implicitly associated with Juvenal's own deficiencies. Mason, moreover, insinuates further doubts about Dryden's version when he identifies in it a 'playful flippancy' (p. 113) and 'affable irreverence' (p. 115) which go beyond anything in Juvenal, and which are 'very much of the Restoration' (p. 113).

The tendency of the fourth and final group of commentators to see covert political commentary not merely as one important strand in Dryden's later work but as its prime *raison d'être* is perhaps ultimately attributable to current assumptions about the relations between literature and politics which go far beyond the bounds of Dryden scholarship. Suffice it to say in the present context that those recent studies which have placed an exclusive stress on the political dimension of the Juvenal translations have rested on a somewhat selective consideration of the text. When one looks closely at the personal and political allusions in the Juvenal, one begins to see that they are, in fact, even more numerous than the critics have suggested, but also (paradoxically) often larger in resonance, less narrowly Jacobite in implication, and more complicatedly intertwined with other strands in the poems' textures and meanings than has been acknowledged.

To illustrate this point, let us consider some of the 'topical' allusions in Dryden's rendering of what has often been considered Juvenal's masterpiece: the poem which Dryden called the 'Divine' Tenth Satire. Such an investigation should serve, simultaneously, as a useful *entrée* to a number of the key critical questions which are raised in Mason's essay: what distinctive kinds of pleasure did Dryden take in Juvenal's poem? How did these pleasures relate to Dryden's other interests as a man and poet? And, in the light of Dryden's belief that, in satire, 'there can be no pleasantry where there is no Wit: No Impression can be made, where there is no Truth for the Foundation' (*Works*, 4. 60), what connections can we see between Dryden's rendering of Juvenal's characteristic 'wit' in the Tenth Satire, and any 'Truth' which he might have considered to be both its basis and end product?

Let us first remind ourselves of the general design of the Tenth Satire. The poet's professed aim is to reveal the folly of the various longings of mankind, by listing, and providing telling *exempla* of, those human prayers which have resulted in ruin. Juvenal disposes, in turn, of the desires for political power (Sejanus), eloquence (Cicero and Demosthenes), military glory (Hannibal, Alexander, Xerxes), long life (Nestor, Priam, Marius, Pompey), and good looks (Hippolytus, Bellerophon, Silius). The poem concludes with an affirmation that, despite the vanity of the human wishes depicted in the main body of the poem, there are still a few things for which it might, nevertheless, be possible for men to pray.

The first of Dryden's personal and contemporary interpolations occurs shortly after the opening of his version. Surveying the topics which will be the subject of the main body of the satire, Dryden refers to the 'Laurels' with which some eloquent men 'have fatally been Crown'd' (11).[6] The hint is taken up later, when, in his rendering of Juvenal's description of Demosthenes (198–205), he deploys

[6] For the application to Dryden's own Laureateship, see Winn, '"Complying with the Times"', p. 78.

vocabulary which is as applicable to his own career in the theatre as to an orator addressing the Assembly at Athens. Where Juvenal simply speaks (129) of Demosthenes' having been born 'dis . . . adversis . . . fatoque sinistro' (with the gods and an unpropitious fate against him), Dryden refers to his having been born 'beneath a boding Horoscope' (202). The poet, we may remember, was a keen amateur astrologer, whose 'nativity', preserved in the Bodleian Library, shows him to have been born under the adverse sign of Saturn.[7] Moreover, Dryden's contemptuous description of Demosthenes' rhetoric as 'th' unlucky Art of wheedling Fools' (205) has no direct equivalent in the Latin, but is close in tone and sentiment to the many passages in which Dryden had referred, sardonically, to the thankless task of trying to please the theatre audiences of Restoration London.[8]

Two paragraphs later, when reflecting on the fate of the famous, and noting that even the lapidary inscriptions which celebrate great men's achievements are destroyed by the effects of time (here in the shape of a fig tree, whose roots crack a great man's tomb from below), Dryden's reference to the 'lying verse' on the crumbling tomb (231) seems to glance at his own lengthy career as a writer of panegyrics.[9] And, two paragraphs later still, when preparing for his portrayal of the exile and suicide of Hannibal, Dryden's Juvenal asks sardonically:

> Now what's his End, O Charming Glory, say
> What rare fifth Act, to Crown this huffing Play?
>
> (256–7)

The absence of any reference to 'plays' in the Latin, together with the adjective 'huffing', suggests strongly that Dryden is here thinking, at least in part, of the notorious extravagance of his own heroic dramas.[10]

[7] See Simon Bentley and Paul Hammond, 'The Nativities of John and Charles Dryden', *Restoration*, 9 (1985), 56–60.

[8] See my *John Dryden* (Cambridge, 1986), pp. 91–4.

[9] See Alexander Lindsay, 'Dryden and Juvenal' (Unpublished PhD thesis, Trinity College, Dublin, 1982), p. 242.

[10] In *The Rehearsal* (4. 1. 214–5), the swaggering hero 'Drawcansir', a figure who partly parodies Almanzor in Dryden's *The Conquest of Granada*, declares: 'I drink, I huff, I strut, look big and stare; / And all this I can do, because I dare'. See *Plays,*

Earlier in the poem, when Juvenal was speaking of the dangers of Nero's Rome, Dryden had inserted two small but significant allusions to civic disturbances of his own days. In Nero's 'Arbitrary time' (itself, one notes, a phrase with obvious resonance in seventeenth-century political debate), Dryden had written,

> A Troop of Cut-Throat Guards were sent, to seize
> The Rich Mens Goods, and gut their Palaces:
>
> (25–6)

whereas

> The Mob, Commission'd by the Government,
> Are seldom to an Empty Garret, sent.
>
> (27–8)

Here, the word 'Guards' and the reference to government-commissioned mob violence would seem to suggest the celebrated 'Guards' of contemporary London (the élite troops of the later Stuart monarchy, prominent on state occasions, and in their suppression of public insurrections), and the accusations of government-orchestrated violence levelled during the Exclusion Crisis of 1681–3.[11] A few lines later, Dryden imagines the terrors of a 'Fearful Passenger'

> who Travels late,
> Charg'd with the Carriage of a Paltry Plate,
> Shakes at the Moonshine shadow of a Rush;
> And sees a Red-Coat rise from every Bush.
>
> (29–32)

*Poems, and Miscellaneous Writings Associated with George Villiers, Duke of Buckingham*, ed. Robert D. Hume and Harold Love, 2 vols. (Oxford, 2007), 1. 437. It might be noted that Henry Higden (see below) refers to Hannibal as 'this grum bulk of Huff and Storm' and to the 'Catastrophe of Fate' which destroyed him. See *A Modern Essay on the Tenth Satyr of Juvenal* (London, 1687), p. 27. For the possible theatrical overtones of 'catastrophe', see *OED*, *s.v.* 'Catastrophe', *sb.* 1.

[11] On the Guards, see David Ogg, *England in the Reign of Charles II* (2nd edition, Oxford, 1956), pp. 253–4; *The Diary of Samuel Pepys*, ed. Robert Latham and William Matthews, 11 vols. (London, 1970–83), 3. 267–8, 7. 415, 8. 28, 9. 129, 130, 132; Tim Harris, *London Crowds in the Reign of Charles II* (Cambridge, 1987), p. 82. On government-orchestrated riots, see Harris, p. 171.

Juvenal has no equivalent for Dryden's last line. But, as the *OED* reminds us, 'Red-Coat' was commonly used for the troopers of the Cromwellian army. Later (70–2), when depicting the absurd pomposity of a Roman *praetor* in procession, Dryden inserts obvious jibes at the flattery and corruption of courtiers (one of his own recurrent themes) and at the notorious place-selling of William III's régime.[12]

When describing Democritus, the 'laughing philosopher' (with whose scoffing view of human folly he identifies his own), Juvenal had observed the improbability of such a great thinker having been born in Abdera in Thrace, where (in the words of the early seventeenth-century translator, Sir Robert Stapylton) 'the inhabitants are barbarous and gross-witted Clowns, their brains being like their country, ever in a fog'.[13] At the equivalent point in his version, Dryden unmistakably glances at William III and Holland, the country of the King's birth:

> a Land of Bogs
> With Ditches fenc'd, a Heaven Fat with Fogs,
> May form a Spirit fit to sway the State;
> And make the Neighb'ring Monarchs fear their Fate.
>
> (75–8)

And in the depiction of Sejanus' fall, William seems again to have been on Dryden's mind, when Tiberius is referred to as 'The Saviour of the Nation and the Prince' (107). Gilbert Burnet reports William's own claim that he 'came to save [England's] religion and liberties',[14] and the King was regularly referred to in loyalist sermons and

[12] The 'Quirites' (Roman citizens) of Juvenal's l. 45 are promoted up the social scale and become 'Nobles' (Dryden, 70). A whole section (pp. 100–12) is devoted to place-selling under William III in *Poems on Affairs of State: Augustan Satirical Verse, 1660–1714, Vol. V: 1688–1697*, ed. William J. Cameron (New Haven CT and London, 1971). For Dryden on the corruption of courtiers, see my *John Dryden*, pp. 92–3.

[13] Sir Robert Stapylton, *Juvenal's Sixteen Satyrs, or A Survey of the Manners and Actions of Mankind* (London, 1647), p. 195.

[14] Gilbert Burnet, *History of his own Time, with Notes by the Earls of Dartmouth and Hardwicke, Speaker Onslow, and Dean Swift*, 6 vols. (2nd edition, London, 1833), 4. 77; see also 4. 394. Dryden's allusion is made even more probable by the identification of William with Tiberius in Jacobite satire of the period. See *Poems on Affairs of State: V*, p. 121. Paul Hammond notes that 'saviour of the nation' had also been applied to Titus Oates by his supporters during the Exclusion Crisis: see *Dryden and the Traces of Classical Rome* (Oxford, 1999), p. 189.

panegyrics of the late 1680s and early 1690s as the 'deliverer', 'redeemer', and 'restorer' of the English nation from Popish tyranny.[15] A few lines later, the fickleness of the Roman mob (as fervent now in their condemnation of Sejanus as they would have been in their enthusiasm, had his plans succeeded) is explicitly transformed into the behaviour of the mob in Dryden's own day:

> How goes the Mob, (for that's a Mighty thing?)
> When the King's Trump, the Mob are for the King:
> They follow Fortune, and the Common Cry
> Is still against the Rogue Condemn'd to Dye.
>
> (112–15)

Under the Republic, declares Juvenal (79), it was the Roman people itself which bestowed 'imperium, fasces, legiones, omnia' (empire, the trappings of magisterial power, legions, all things), but now 'duas tantum res anxius optat / panem et circenses' (180–1; it anxiously desires two things only, bread and the public games). Dryden reshapes Juvenal's passage thus:

> Our Wise Fore-Fathers, Great by Sea and Land,
> Had once the Pow'r, and absolute Command;
> All Offices of Trust, themselves dispos'd;
> Rais'd whom they pleas'd, and whom they pleas'd, Depos'd.
> But we who give our Native Rights away,
> And our Inslav'd Posterity betray,
> Are now reduc'd to beg an Alms, and go
> On Holidays to see a Puppet show.
>
> (124–31)

Here the additions seem not only to refer to the open-air puppet shows of seventeenth-century London[16] but to allude to the belief of some seventeenth-century political writers that, in the words of J. P. Kenyon, 'as far back into the misty Saxon past as men could delve, the

[15] See Matthew Prior, *Literary Works*, ed. H. Bunker Wright and Monroe K. Spears, 2 vols. (2nd edition, Oxford, 1971), 1. 96, 125; Thomas Shadwell, *Complete Works*, ed. Montague Summers, 5 vols. (London, 1927), 5. 340; *Poems on the Reign of William III*, ed. Earl Miner (Los Angeles CA, 1974), pp. iii–iv.

[16] See Pepys's *Diary*, entries for 30 August 1667, 4 September 1667, 20 August 1668, 31 August 1668, 21 September 1668.

rights of the English people had been known, ascertained and respected, kings had been elected... and the people's will had been expressed in popular assemblies'.[17] They also appear to allude to the Jacobite conviction that, in accepting William, the English people had violated constitutional legality and willingly subjected themselves to a foreign tyranny.[18]

A few lines later, Juvenal rounds, characteristically, on the reader who might by this stage have been entertaining a complacent superiority towards Sejanus:

> Visne salutari sicut Seianus, habere
> tantumdem atque illi summas[19] donare curules?
> illum exercitibus praeponere?
>
> (90–2)

(Do you wish to be hailed as Sejanus was? To have as much wealth, and to bestow on one person the seats of highest office, and on another the command of armies?)

Again, the phrasing of Dryden's rendering involves clear applications of Juvenal's insistent questions to contemporary politics and Court life:

> Now tell me truly, would'st thou change thy Fate
> To be, like him, first Minister of State?
> To have thy Levees Crowded with resort,
> Of a depending, gaping, servile Court:
> Dispose all Honours, of the Sword and Gown,
> Grace with a Nod, and Ruin with a Frown.
>
> (144–9)

Various commentators have argued that Dryden is suggesting specific parallels between the flight and exile of James II and Juvenal's descriptions of Hannibal's ignominious banishment (259–63) and of the death of Priam (402–17).[20] Dryden's pointed references to

[17] J. P. Kenyon, *Stuart England* (Harmondsworth, 1978), p. 30.

[18] See Tim Harris, *Politics under the Later Stuarts: Party Conflict in a Divided Society, 1660–1715* (London, 1993), p. 213.

[19] Seventeenth-century texts read 'sellas... curules' (ceremonial chairs).

[20] See Miller, "Physic for the Great", p. 61; Myers, *Dryden*, pp. 157–8.

Priam's sons as '*Hector* with the Race / Of Royal Bastards' and to Priam's 'Loyal Daughters' would certainly both seem to glance at the monarchs of Dryden's day: Charles II's begetting of illegitimate progeny was a standing joke, and in the anti-Williamite polemic of the late 1680s and early 1690s much was made of the conspicuous *dis*loyalty of Queen Mary in acquiescing in her husband's deposition of her father.[21] Earlier in the poem, Dryden had strengthened his rendering of Juvenal's discussion of Pompey and Julius Caesar by observing that 'few Usurpers to the Shades descend / By a dry Death, or with a quiet End' (178–9). There is, one notes, no direct equivalent in Juvenal's Latin for Dryden's 'Usurpers'.

The quantity of personal and contemporary reference in 'The Tenth Satyr', however, should not lead us to assume that the poem has merely been transformed by Dryden into an anti-Williamite tract or personal *cri de coeur*. Many of the examples noted above are not specifically or exclusively Tory or Jacobite in their resonance. The reference to 'Red Coats' in the passage on the 'Fearful Passenger', for example, alludes, as we have seen, to the Cromwellian period of Dryden's youth rather than to the early 1690s, and in any case, the allusion, in context, seems less to focus on a narrowly political point than to convey (in a tone which is neither merely horrifying nor horrified) the sheer fertility of a nocturnal traveller's imagination when fuelled by fear. Dryden's allusions to the 'Guards', to the fickle allegiances of the mob, to the 'first Minister of State', 'servile Courts', 'Royal Bastards', and government-commissioned mobs, seem to be applicable as much, or more, to the Stuarts and their supporters as to the new, Williamite, regime. Puppet shows were not peculiar to post-Restoration London.[22] Furthermore, Dryden's glances at his own career as dramatist and writer of panegyrics seem, in context, wryly rueful rather than bitterly self-defensive. The reference to the dark fate awaiting 'usurpers' might apply to William III, but the word 'usurpe' occurs at the equivalent point (p. 182) in Stapylton's translation, first published in 1647. Moreover, enthusiasm for the popular election of monarchs, of the kind invoked in Dryden's recreation of Juvenal's

[21] See *Poems on Affairs of State: V*, pp. 52, 60, 156–7, 236, 298–302.

[22] The references cited in n. 16 above all relate to the 1660s. For puppet shows in the Commonwealth period, see Pepys, *Diary*, 3. 80.

depiction of the golden age of Roman republicanism, was the hallmark of those at the furthest possible remove in the political spectrum from Dryden himself: the radical 'True Whigs' and 'Commonwealthmen'. In 1689 the Tory Lords had specifically objected that any attempt on Parliament's part to determine the succession would imply 'that the crown was thereby become elective'. And in 1692 the 'Whiggish Jacobite' Sir James Montgomery deplored the fact (as he saw it) that the Revolution had 'turned our hereditary monarchy into an elective'.[23]

Furthermore, a number of the parallels between Juvenalian and seventeenth-century situations which are glanced at by Dryden *en passant* are too inextricably blended with insistent reminders of the poem's original Roman settings to suggest an exclusively modern resonance. Often they are pursued in a conspicuously loose and unsystematic way. The loss of Dryden's Laureateship, though a bitter blow, had not, of course, like the eloquence of Cicero and Demosthenes, proved 'fatal'. And Dryden's renderings of Juvenal's portrayals of the exiled Hannibal and the dying Priam are not sufficiently reshaped to insist on the parallel between the fate of these men and that of James II. Perhaps most surprising of all, Dryden's clearest interpolated reference to William III (the reference to Holland, the 'Land of Bogs'), seems, in context, more of a *compliment* to William than an attack on him. The King is, after all, being likened at this point in the poem to Democritus, 'the laughing philosopher', whose stance towards human folly, in Dryden as much as in Juvenal, is closely identified with the poet's own. The parallel seems not to suggest 'what evil people come from awful places like Holland', but rather, 'even such an unpropitious place as Holland can produce a

[23] See *Journals of the House of Lords, XIV*, p. 117; Paul Kléber Monod, *Jacobitism and the English People: 1688–1788* (Cambridge, 1989), p. 26. On the 'True Whigs' and their relation to the more conservative parliamentary Whigs, see Mark Goldie, 'The Roots of True Whiggism: 1688–94', *History of Political Thought*, 1 (1980), 195–236, and J. G. A. Pocock, 'The Varieties of Whiggism from Exclusion to Reform: A History of Ideology and Discourse', in *Virtue, Commerce and History: Essays on Political Thought and History, Chiefly in the Eighteenth Century* (Cambridge, 1985), pp. 215–310 (esp. pp. 224–9). For Dryden and the tradition of reading Juvenal as a 'zealous vindicator of Roman liberty' and an opponent of arbitrary tyranny, see Howard D. Weinbrot, *Augustus Caesar in 'Augustan' England: The Decline of a Classical Norm* (Princeton NJ, 1978), pp. 161–3.

great man, just as Abdera produced Democritus'. The allusion, that is, seems to emanate from amused wonder rather than simple contempt or hatred.[24]

Dryden's rendering of Juvenal's portrait of Democritus is a passage in which one can locate clearly the three inseparable elements which hold the clue to the nature of his interest in the Roman satirist: the distinctive kinds of pleasure which Juvenal's work gave him, the tone and style which were the indispensable vehicles for the communication of that pleasure (and for which he knew he must find a viable English equivalent), and the body of philosophico-poetic reflection linking him with Juvenal in a bond of congeniality which ensured that, in rendering the Latin poet, Dryden was (in the words of T. S. Eliot quoted in Chapter 2 above) both 'giving the original through himself, and finding himself through the original'.[25]

> When faced by the infinite follies of mankind, we are told,
> *Democritus*, cou'd feed his Spleen, and shake
> His sides and shoulders till he felt 'em ake;
>
> (47–8)

Democritus' laughter, however, is no mere cynicism or *Schadenfreude* but constitutes a kind of philosophical wisdom which is proof against the vicissitudes of existence, and which, it is suggested, is a general model for humanity:

> He laughs at all the Vulgar Cares and Fears;
> At their vain Triumphs, and their vainer Tears:
> An equal Temper in his Mind he found,
> When Fortune flatter'd him, and when she frown'd.
> 'Tis plain from hence that what our Vows request,
> Are hurtful things, or Useless at the best.
>
> (79–84)

[24] It may be relevant that Ludovicus Prateus' note on the line in the 'Delphin' edition of Juvenal (1684) cross-refers the reader to Horace's suggestion (*Epistles*, 2. 1. 231–44) that Alexander the Great's poor taste in literature might have led one to believe that he was nurtured in the dull climate of Boeotia. William III was frequently likened to Alexander in contemporary panegyric.

[25] T. S. Eliot, 'Introduction: 1928' in *The Selected Poems of Ezra Pound* (London, 1948), p. 13.

There are clear connections in thought and phrasing between these descriptions of Democritus and Dryden's account of the pleasures given him by the poetry of Juvenal himself. In a key passage from the 'Discourse Concerning... Satire', Dryden describes his response to Juvenal as follows:

> *Juvenal*... gives me as much Pleasure as I can bear: He fully satisfies my Expectation, he Treats his Subject home: His Spleen is rais'd, and he raises mine: I have the Pleasure of Concernment in all he says; He drives his Reader along with him; and when he is at the end of his way, I willingly stop with him: If he went another Stage, it wou'd be too far, it wou'd make a Journey of a Progress, and turn Delight into Fatigue. When he gives over, 'tis a sign the Subject is exhausted; and the Wit of Man can carry it no farther.
>
> (*Works*, 4. 63)

For Dryden, as for Juvenal's Democritus, the purpose of 'raising the spleen' is not merely to agitate and disturb the reader but a means to the essential 'End or Scope of Satire' which is 'to purge the Passions' (*Works*, 4. 77). The passions are engaged and inflamed in a way that mounts exhilaratingly to a climax and finally leaves the mind in a state of satisfied calm. Such a process of 'purgation', Dryden thinks, can only be achieved via poetic pleasure, without which the satirist's 'Instruction is but a bare and dry Philosophy' (*Works*, 4. 88). Juvenal's principal previous English translators, Barten Holyday and Stapylton, Dryden argues, were unable to suggest anything of the specifically 'Poetical part of [Juvenal] his Diction and Elocution' (*Works*, 4. 88), both because of their intrinsic lack of poetic gifts and because of the antiquated, literal method of translation to which they had tied themselves. Little sense of Juvenal's 'sounding' and 'eloquent' verse can consequently be gained from their versions, and thus little sense of the larger aesthetic and emotional effect of his work.

As the *OED* records, the word 'spleen' encompassed in the seventeenth century a range of meanings which carried connotations both (on the one hand) of merriment, delight, and content, and (on the other) of melancholy, ill-temper, peevishness, indignation, and depression.[26] That Dryden saw an intimate connection between these two emotional spheres, both in Juvenal's art itself and in its

[26] See also Dustin Griffin, 'Venting Spleen', *Essays in Criticism*, 40 (1990), 124–35.

effect on the reader, is confirmed by a dedicatory poem which he had written in 1687 for *A Modern Essay on the Tenth Satyr of Juvenal*, an experimental translation by the lawyer and wit Henry Higden. In this poem, Dryden had reflected on the potentially beneficial aspects of the Tenth Satire (in Higden's version), and had partially attributed to them certain positive emotional and philosophical reorientations which he had recently effected in himself. Higden's poem, he suggests, has raised his 'Spleen' in order to 'laugh it away':

> Oh! were your Author's Principle receiv'd,
> Half of the lab'ring World wou'd be reliev'd;
> For not to Wish, is not to be Deceiv'd!
> *Revenge* wou'd into *Charity* be chang'd,
> Because it costs too Dear to be *Reveng'd*:
> It costs our *Quiet* and *Content of Mind*;
> And when 'tis compass'd, leaves a Sting behind.
> Suppose I had the better End o'th' Staff,
> Why should I help th' ill-natur'd World to laugh?
> 'Tis all alike to them, who gets the Day;
> They Love the Spight and Mischief of the *Fray*.
> No; I have Cur'd my Self of that *Disease*;
> Nor will I be provok'd, but when I please;
> But let me half that *Cure* to You restore;
> You gave the *Salve*, I laid it to the *Sore*.
> Our kind Relief against a Rainy Day,
> Beyond a Tavern, or a tedious Play;
> We take your Book, and laugh our Spleen away.
>
> ('To My Ingenious Friend, Mr. Henry Higden', 22–39;
> *Works*, 3. 116–17)

There are good reasons for believing that during the 1680s Dryden had gone through a complex period of what might be called spiritual reorientation, one result of which was his conversion to Catholicism, another his delighted rediscovery, as a translator, of a number of episodes and poems by Lucretius and Horace. Dryden's renderings of these two Roman poets dramatize, in various ways, the means by which an individual might achieve an active, defiant, personal triumph over Fortune, the capricious power which enslaves Man and destroys his quiet of mind by inspiring him with vain desires –

political ambition, the quest for fame, sexual love – and the fear of an arbitrary and inscrutable universe.[27] In his translation of Horace *Odes*, 1. 9, in the miscellany *Sylvae* (1685) Dryden had written of the need to 'Lay hold upon the present hour, / And snatch the pleasures passing by, / To put them out, of Fortune's pow'r' (20–2). In his version of Horace *Odes*, 3. 29 in the same volume, he had similarly exhorted his reader to 'Enjoy the present smiling hour; / And put it out of Fortune's pow'r' (50–1).

That he continued to see a personal significance in these Horatian sentiments can be seen in the Epistle Dedicatory to *Don Sebastian* (1690), where, having reflected on the 'ambitious meteors' of the Court, who 'will not permit their own hearts to be at quiet' and who thus 'disturb the repose of all beside them', he offers his own ideal of political conduct:

> How much happier is he . . . who centring on himself, remains immovable, and smiles at the madness of the dance about him. He possesses the midst, which is the portion of safety and content: He will not be higher, because he needs it not; but by the prudence of that choice, he puts it out of Fortunes power to throw him down.
>
> (*Works*, 15. 60)

In the Dedication to his next play, *Amphitryon* (also 1690), Dryden explicitly linked this image of contented Horatian quietism in the midst of a world of turbulent passion with his own state of equanimity after the 1688 Revolution, and identified himself, most significantly in the present context, with Democritus:

> I suffer no more than I can easily undergo; and so long as I enjoy my Liberty, which is the Birth-right of an *English* Man, the rest shall never go near my Heart. The Merry Philosopher, is more to my Humour than the Melancholick; and I find no disposition in my self to Cry, while the mad World is daily supplying me with such Occasions of Laughter.
>
> (*Works*, 15. 224)

[27] For discussion of this phase in Dryden's career see Hopkins, *John Dryden*, pp. 90–133; Stuart Gillespie, 'Dryden's *Sylvae*' (Unpublished PhD thesis, University of Cambridge, 1987), pp. 84–118; Paul Hammond, 'Dryden's Philosophy of Fortune', *Modern Language Review*, 80 (1985), 769–85.

Dryden says he has refrained in the 'Discourse... Concerning Satire' from responding to the many libels which have been levelled against him. He has 'suffer'd in silence; and possess'd [his] Soul in quiet' (*Works*, 4. 60).

There is ample evidence in the translation of Juvenal's Tenth Satire that Dryden was fully conscious of the similarity between the vain wishes depicted in the poem and the 'madness' – the restless, anxious energies and passions, destructive of all contented self-possession – which he saw in the world around him, and which he had so tellingly evoked in his earlier renderings of Lucretius and Horace. The Democritus of Dryden's 'Tenth Satyr' laughs, as we have seen, not only at the 'Cares' of the multitude (as in the Latin) but also at the 'Fears' which, as in Lucretius' Third Book, make their life an anxious hell-on-earth. Juvenal's 'praetor' (in the passage mentioned above) is described, in Dryden's version, as a 'mighty madman' (66). The trappings of military ambition are characterized as 'Toys' (218) representing a resignation of 'solid Quiet, to obtain / The windy satisfaction of the Brain' (218–19). Hannibal is seen as having, like the political and religious subversives of the 1680s, an 'untam'd' and 'turbulent' mind (266),[28] and is, like the desperately 'driven' human beings in Dryden's translation from Lucretius' Book 3, 'uneasie' (249) until he has sealed his former triumphs by entering Rome itself.[29] Alexander the Great is 'restless' (275) – again like Lucretius' fearful mortals. Parents of beautiful children, like the men and women in Lucretius who live in daily fear of death, suffer 'Anxious Nights' (457). Silius, the young Roman noble pursued by the lustful Empress Messalina, even if he submits to her wishes can only look forward to 'A day or two of Anxious Life' (526). (In all these cases the key word has no direct equivalent in Juvenal's text.) Dryden adapts Juvenal's image (105–7) of Sejanus erecting a mighty tower from the top of which he fell to his ruin, to have the ambitious man crushed by his edifice, when he

[28] Cf. 'Lucretius: The Beginning of the Second Book', 44–5; *Absalom and Achitophel*, 153; *The Hind and the Panther*, 3. 20 (*Works*, 3. 47; 2. 10; 3. 161).

[29] Cf. 'Translation of the Latter Part of the Third Book of Lucretius: Against the Fear of Death', 227, 279, 281, 267 (*Works*, 3. 55).

> Rais'd a Top-heavy Tow'r, of monst'rous height,
> Which Mould'ring, crush'd him underneath the Weight.
>
> (170–1)

Sejanus' fate is thus approximated to the perpetual fears of Lucretius' Tantalus, who 'dreads th' impending Rock to crush him from on high'.[30] And Dryden introduces a subtle but significant change at the end of the poem, when Juvenal's celebrated exhortation (356) to pray for 'mens sana in corpore sano' (a sound mind in a sound body) is transformed into a prayer for 'Health of Body, and *Content* of Mind' (549; my emphasis) – the very state which Dryden had said in the poem to Higden is destroyed by vengeful passions, and which he has attempted to preserve by refusing to respond to the numerous attacks upon him.

But Dryden's association of Juvenal's Tenth Satire with the Lucretian/Horatian diagnosis of the 'anxious cares' which destroy 'Sweet peace of Mind'[31] should not lead us to assume that he has simply assimilated the one body of verse to the other, effectively transforming Juvenal's poem, in his rendering, into a replay of the Lucretian and Horatian material which he had translated in *Sylvae*. As we have already seen, Dryden was acutely aware that the unique potency of Juvenalian satire was bound up with the distinctive 'impetuosity' of Juvenal's rhetoric and the exhilarating momentum of his 'wit', whereby he produces 'the Pleasure of Concernment in all he says', moves our 'Indignation', and 'drives his Reader along with him' (*Works*, 4. 63, 72). Juvenalian 'wit', for Dryden, is clearly something quite distinct from the 'noble pride and positive assertion of his opinions', the 'Magisterial authority' and 'Dogmatical way' which, for him (as we saw in Chapter 4), characterize Lucretius (*Works*, 3. 10), or the 'Briskness', 'Jollity', and 'good Humour' which he associated with Horace, and said he had 'chiefly endeavour'd to Coppy' in his own versions of that poet (*Works*, 3. 16).

In attempting to discover a fitting English equivalent for Juvenal's characteristic 'wit', Dryden drew on a large number of predecessors,

[30] 'Against the Fear of Death', 186 (*Works*, 3. 53).

[31] Charles Dryden's phrase, in his important but little-known poem 'On the Happyness of a Retir'd Life... Sent to his Father from Italy', first published in *The Annual Miscellany: for the Year 1694* (London, 1694), pp. 195–201 (p. 198).

but seems to have received particularly significant assistance from the very version which he had so warmly commended five years previously – that of Henry Higden. Higden's version of Satire 10, like his earlier rendering of Satire 13, is a free rendering in octosyllabic couplets, in which Higden for the most part preserves Juvenal's Roman settings, but also incorporates extensive passages of 'imitation', in which the Roman poet's scenes and characters are temporarily transposed to seventeenth-century London. In the prefaces to his two versions, Higden asserts that he has aimed 'to abate something of [Juvenal's] serious Rigour', to express the Roman poet's sense 'in a sort of Verse apt for Raillery, without debasing the dignity of the Author', and to give 'Life and Spirit to his Author, by making him English, in a Modish and Familiar way'.[32] Higden's touch, to be sure, is sometimes uncertain, and his octosyllabics often produce precisely the kind of merely trivializing effect, the 'Boyish kind of Pleasure' so aptly characterized by Dryden in his remarks on Hudibras in the 'Discourse... Concerning Satire' (*Works*, 4. 81). Higden's rendering of Juvenal's account of the death of Priam, for example, brings the original close to pure burlesque:

> E're Fair *Cassandra* Fate fore-knowing
> Bewayl'd sack'd *Troy*, with eyes o're-flowing;
> Had he been dead as any Herring,
> E're *Paris* went a privateering;
> For Whores and Plunder play'd leud Tricks,
> Which to the Gutts provok'd the Greeks.
>
> (pp. 43–4)

Elsewhere, however, Higden can manage a plain sententiousness, which, while a long way from Juvenal's epic stateliness, attains its own kind of lapidary dignity:[33]

> 'Tis the immoderate thirst of Fame
> Much more than Vertue does inflame:
> Which none for worse or better take
> But for her dower and trappings sake.

[32] *A Modern Essay on the Thirteenth Satyr of Juvenal* (London, 1686), sig. b2; *A Modern Essay on the Tenth Satyr*, sig. (a)4.

[33] See Selden, 'Juvenal and Restoration Modes of Translation', 492.

The fond Ambition of a few
Many vast Empires overthrew;
While their Atchievements with their dust
They vainly to their Tombstones trust.
For sepulchres like bodyes ly
Swallow'd in Deaths obscurity.

(p. 24)

Higden cannot, however, always satisfactorily integrate the lighter and more dignified elements in his version, and the translation consequently fails to achieve overall tonal coherence. But the 'witty' elements in Higden's poem – and it should be remembered that Higden's is the only English rendering of the Tenth Satire before Dryden's that can be described as 'witty' in any sense of the term – provided Dryden with some crucial clues as to how Juvenalian 'wit' and moral sententiousness might be viably combined in a more consistently coherent and purposeful manner than Higden had himself achieved.

The closeness with which Dryden had attended to Higden's version can be seen not only in the sheer quantity of his borrowings, but from the fact that he transposes distinctive colourings from one place in Higden's version to quite different passages in his own. Dryden seems to have been particularly drawn to visual or circumstantial details in Higden's translation which help to bring each scene vividly alive in the reader's imagination. In the lines on the fearful traveller, for example, Dryden took from Higden the notions that the traveller is a servant who has been commissioned to carry the plate for his master (in Juvenal, the traveller's social status and the purpose of his journey are unspecified), and that the wayfarer's imagination actually causes him to mistake the moonlit bushes for robbers (in Juvenal, the traveller simply trembles at the shadow of a reed shaken in the moonlight). Later, Dryden asks the reader contemptuously whether he would not, instead of seeking political greatness, prefer to

choose a small Renown,
To be the May'r of some poor Paltry Town,
Bigly to Look, and Barb'rously to speak;

(163–4)

– remembering Higden's mayor, who at an earlier point in the poem 'Looks big, as if install'd o'th' Garter' (p. 11). And in his description of the destruction of Sejanus' statue Dryden has drawn on a touch in Higden which powerfully reinforces the indignity of Sejanus' fall:

> That Head lately ador'd, and reckond
> In all the Universe the Second,
> Melted new forms and shapes assumes,
> Of Pispots, Frying-pans, and Spoons.
>
> (Higden, p. 13)

> *Sejanus* almost first of *Roman* Names,
> The great *Sejanus* crackles in the Flames:
> Form'd in the Forge, the Pliant Brass is laid
> On Anvils; and of Head and Limbs are made,
> Pans, Cans, and Pispots, a whole Kitchin Trade.
>
> (Dryden, 93–7)

The editions of Juvenal by Henricus Christianus Henninius (1685), Ludovicus Prateus (1684), and Cornelius Schrevelius (1648),[34] all used by Dryden when composing his translation, give the final set of utensils into which Sejanus' statue is transformed as 'patellae' (small pans), and the same reading is included in the text printed at the foot of the page in Higden's translation. Higden's rendering, however, follows, or guesses at, the reading 'matellae' (chamber pots) contained in the Codex Pithoeanus, and now generally accepted by editors of Juvenal – and Dryden follows suit.

Later, Higden treats Juvenal's depiction of the ambition of Alexander the Great thus:

> One World's too mean a trifling thing
> For the Young *Macedonian* King,
> He raves like one in Banishment
> In a narrow craggy *Island* pent:
> In one poor Globe does sweat and squeeze,
> Wedg'd in and crampt in *Little-Ease.*
>
> (p. 29)

[34] Dryden used material not incorporated before the 1684 edition of Schrevelius.

Dryden develops Higden's suggestions of the sheer physical frustration of the penned-up Alexander:

> One World suffis'd not *Alexander*'s Mind;
> Coop't up, he seem'd in Earth and Seas confin'd:
> And, strugling, stretch'd his restless Limbs about
> The narrow Globe, to find a passage out.
>
> (273–6)

And, in the description of the miseries of old age, Dryden follows Higden in his fanciful likening of an old man's sexual incapacities to a defeat in battle (Higden is quoted first):

> Nor beauty moves, nor Cupids dart:
> Forgetfulness has seiz'd that part.
> Long since he there has been bewitcht,
> 'Tis a long Age since last he itcht.
> Obsequious hand cannot excite
> The bafled Craven to the fight;
> From hoary loynes, and sapless trunk,
> In vain strives the industrious punk
> To raise the nerve quite num'd and shrunk.
>
> (p. 35)

> His taste, not only pall'd to Wine and Meat,
> But to the Relish of a Nobler Treat.
> The limber Nerve, in vain provok'd to rise,
> Inglorious from the Field of Battel flies:
> Poor Feeble Dotard, how cou'd he advance
> With his blew Head-piece, and his broken Lance?
>
> (326–31)

In each of these examples Dryden is indebted to Higden for observations and imaginings which, however fanciful they may seem at first sight, are nevertheless grounded in shrewdly observed particulars. But in each case Dryden has developed Hidgen's hints and combined them with other notes, so that the overall effect of each passage is both complex in itself and more satisfactorily related to its surrounding context than its equivalent in the earlier version.

Dryden, for example, renders with far greater plausibility than Higden Juvenal's daring transition from the ignominious fall of Sejanus to the moment where the poet rounds on his readers to include them in the scope of his scornful tirade. In Higden's version, this stretch of Juvenal's text is rendered in a uniformly jaunty manner:

> Would you on these Conditions, Sir,
> Be Favourite and Prime-Minister,
> As was *Sejanus*? Stand possest
> Of Honours, Power and Interest;
> Dispose supream Commands at will,
> Promote, disgrace, preserve, or kill:
> Be guardian to a careless King
> Who in all pleasures takes his swing:
> Cloyst'red in Bawdy Grots and Cellers,
> With Pimps, Buffoones, and Fortune-Tellers.
> Have Foot and Horse-Guards, the Command
> Of Armys both by Sea and Land.
> Why not? Though Good-men would not kill,
> Yet in their pow'r they'd have it still.
>
> (pp. 18–19)

In his equivalent passage, Dryden clearly benefited from the way in which Juvenal's satirical strokes had been applied by Higden with equal accuracy to Tiberius' 'Favourite and Prime-Minister' and those nearer home. And he perhaps particularly relished the way in which the power of Higden's Sejanus to 'Promote, disgrace, preserve, or kill' had been made to sound remarkably similar to that of the malicious goddess Fortune, who, in his own version of Horace *Odes*, 3. 29, 'Promotes, degrades, delights in strife, /And makes a Lottery of life' (79–80; *Works*, 3. 84). But Dryden's rendering of Juvenal's passage achieves a far greater expressive range than its predecessor. Dryden's Juvenal first insidiously invites our complicity with the scorn he is venting against Sejanus, and then, by a surprising tonal transition and change of rhetorical tack, springs his satirical trap on us, with a final couplet which, though indebted to Higden, has a far more disturbing power:

> Now Tell me truly, wou'dst thou change thy Fate
> To be, like him, first Minister of State?
> To have thy Levees Crowded with resort,
> Of a depending, gaping, servile Court:
> Dispose all Honours, of the Sword and Gown,

Grace with a Nod, and Ruin with a Frown;
To hold thy Prince in Pupill-Age and sway,
That Monarch, whom the Master'd World obey?
While he, intent on secret Lusts alone,
Lives to himself, abandoning the Throne;
Coopt in a narrow Isle, observing Dreams
With flatt'ring Wisards, and erecting Schemes!
I well believe, thou wou'd'st be Great as he;
For every Man's a Fool to that Degree:
All wish the dire Prerogative to kill;
Ev'n they wou'd have the Pow'r, who want the Will.

(144–59)

Dryden's rendering of the final couplet in this passage – one of the 'sentences' for which the Roman poet was famous – takes on an extra sharpness from 'Prerogative', the term used in seventeenth-century political writing to denote specifically royal power.

Dryden's description of Alexander draws on, but moves beyond, the merely physical fancy of Higden's imagining of the monarch 'sweating' and 'squeezing' 'in one poor Globe'. Dryden's emphasis on Alexander's great 'mind', and his avoidance of Higden's 'low terms', allow him to transcend the mere deflation of Higden's lines, where Alexander 'for all his huffing / Finds ample room in narrow Coffin', proving that 'Man swells with bombast of inventions: / When strip'd Death shews his true dimensions' (p. 30). Dryden hints at the pathos as well as the absurdity of the minute, fragile, physical body in which the greatest human aspirations were conceived. As a result, his rendering of the inscription on Alexander's tomb – '"Death only this Mysterious Truth unfolds, / The mighty Soul, how small a Body holds"' (279–80) – has a powerful generalizing weight which transcends mere irony or contempt. And in his description of the old man's sexual defeat, Dryden sharpens, by the physical specificity of his additions, our sense of the grotesque fatuity of the old man's actions, while simultaneously conveying, by a skilful deployment of a heroic diction which is not exclusively belittling in effect, a sense of the agony of the old man's plight. As a result, the phrase 'Poor Feeble Dotard' in line 330, while certainly not denoting straightforward pity, nevertheless seems, in context, more than merely a sneer.

Elsewhere Dryden has, quite independently of Higden, responded with relish to the numerous touches of observed detail which Juvenal had incorporated in his *exempla* of the vanity of human wishes, and has added further details of his own which it is tempting to think he would have claimed (as he did of the interpolations in his Virgil) were 'not stuck into' but 'growing out of' his original (*Works*, 5. 329). There is, for example, the fanciful description of the 'Unwieldy Sums of Wealth, which higher mount / Than Files of Marshall'd Figures can account' (18–19), beside which the wealthy stores of Croesus 'Wou'd look like little Dolphins, when they sail / In the vast Shadow of the *British* Whale' (21–2);[35] of the 'praetor' in procession 'with dumb Pride, and a set formal Face' (56); of the smith carefully preparing his hammer for the stroke which will destroy Sejanus' statue (91); of the exiled Hannibal being 'Repuls'd by surly Grooms' who wait on the king of Bithynia (262); of the grotesque resemblance between behaviour of old people and 'an old Grandam Ape, when, with a Grace, / She sits at squat, and scrubs her Leathern Face' (311–12); of the similarity between an old person needing to be fed, and 'a young Swallow, when with weary Wings, / Expected Food, her fasting Mother brings' (367–8); of the moment when, having seen his son on a funeral pyre, Nestor 'turn'd and Weeping, ask'd his Friends, what Crime / Had Curs'd his Age to this unhappy Time?' (398–9). All these examples, though they go beyond anything warranted by the literal meaning of the original, contain qualities – whether of pathos, surreal fancy, studied observation, or delicately imagined beauty – which have been identified as characteristic features of Juvenal's writing in general.[36]

Are we now in a position to draw some general conclusions about the qualities in Juvenal's Tenth Satire which Dryden found so profoundly pleasurable, and which he attempted to recreate in his version? Can we now determine the kind of relationship which Dryden thought existed between Juvenal's 'wit' and the truth-telling,

[35] Here Dryden was perhaps prompted by Higden's reference (pp. 4–5) to 'Upstarts' 'Whose Estate's audit so immense / Exceeds all Prodigal Expence'.

[36] See particularly Richard Jenkyns's excellent chapter on 'Juvenal the Poet' in his *Three Classical Poets: Sappho, Catullus and Juvenal* (London, 1982), pp. 151–221.

'purgative' properties of his satire? Is it possible to divine the principles according to which Dryden felt free to incorporate allusions to his own life and times into the rendering of a Roman poet, while still being able to claim that his version was a genuine translation, rather than merely an updating or 'imitation' of his original?

On the strength of the examples already considered, we might offer some suggestions along the following lines. Judging from his translation, Dryden seems to have believed that Juvenal's celebrated satire on the vanity of human wishes had been written not in a state of bitterness, nihilism, cynicism, or single-minded moral righteousness but from a position of heady confidence, in which the full appallingness of human life could be boldly and frankly faced and evoked, without the evasiveness which is the mark of both the cynic and the sentimentalist; in which the poet's exuberant scurrilousness and gift for daring hyperbole and caricature simultaneously sharpened the accuracy and bite of his onslaught, and metamorphosed what might otherwise have been an intolerably depressing catalogue of misery, despair, and fatuity into something absorbingly and exhilaratingly pleasurable. Such a stance allowed the poet the freedom to evoke the beauty and pathos of life in the very midst of revealing its hellishness and absurdity. On a stylistic level, Juvenal was able to create vertiginously risky, but ultimately plausible and satisfying transitions between extreme, exaggerated, or fanciful *exempla*, and general statements of ungainsayable acuteness and power. The Juvenalian tone, in Dryden's reading, both emanated from, and culminated in the statement of, a confident attitude from which the most painful events of individual human lives and of the larger sweep of history could be contemplated with a vigorous contempt. To recreate such a stance in the act of translation was, for Dryden, simultaneously to attain a point of view from which the painful events of his *own* life and his *own* century could be similarly faced, known, and contemplated. To incorporate references to one's own times into a rendering of Juvenal would thus not be a matter of smuggling personal apologia or party-political points into a classical translation but rather of discovering, in the act of translation, a set of circumstances whereby one's own political convictions and artistic aspirations, and the events of one's own times, could be seen from a distinctive and delightful new perspective.

Such an account might explain Dryden's capacity to achieve, in the first paragraph of his version of 'The Tenth Satyr', a tone which, while far removed from the grand epic register of Juvenal's opening, nevertheless attains a note of masterful, comprehensive survey. In Dryden's passage this sense of a grand sweep is combined with a tone of effortless conversational intimacy, in which the poet's words seem, playfully, to glance at the 'conduct' and 'design' of his own writing as well as at the larger pattern of human hopes and aspirations, and in which, thus, even the poet's own professional activities are included in the scope of his generalization. In these lines we are, surely, a long way from the 'playful flippancy' and 'affable irreverence' which H. A. Mason saw as the chief characteristics of Dryden's Juvenal:

> Look round the Habitable World, how few
> Know their own Good; or knowing it, pursue.
> How void of Reason are our Hopes and Fears!
> What in the Conduct of our Life appears
> So well design'd, so luckily begun,
> But, when we have our wish, we wish undone?
>
> (1–6)[37]

The subversive wit, tonal flexibility, and philosophical assurance of Dryden's Juvenalian imaginings are simultaneously evidenced and justified in the closing paragraphs of the poem, to which we should now turn. Before this close, we recall, Dryden's Juvenal has been surveying the disastrous consequences of praying for physical beauty. After two examples of the predatory lusts of beautiful woman taken from the remote world of Greek myth – those of Hippolytus and Bellerophon – Juvenal turns to his culminating instance, which, though more extreme and bizarre than the others, is taken not from legend but from fairly recent Roman history, and which he knows his readers will recognize not as mere fantasy but as a 'true story'. In AD 48, the consul-designate, Gaius Silius, described by

[37] In his *John Dryden* (Cambridge, 1950), David Nichol Smith speculates (p. 69) that this passage may have been one of those which Samuel Johnson excepted from his general opinion that the Dryden *Juvenal* fails to convey the 'grandeur' of the original.

Tacitus (*Annals*, 11. 12) as 'iuventutis Romanae pulcherrimus' (the most beautiful flower of Roman youth), had attracted the illicit passion of Messalina, wife of the Emperor Claudius. The Empress had insisted that they celebrated a public marriage ceremony while Claudius was absent from Rome. Dryden's Juvenal begins his narration of the story with an insistent rhetorical command, involving the reader directly in the drama of Silius' predicament:

> Now *Silius* wants thy Counsel, give Advice;
> Wed *Caesar*'s Wife, or Dye; the Choice is nice.
> Her Comet-Eyes she darts on ev'ry Grace;
> And takes a fatal liking to his Face.
> Adorn'd with Bridal Pomp she sits in State;
> The Publick Notaries and *Auspex* wait:
> The Genial Bed is in the Garden drest;
> The Portion paid, and ev'ry Rite express'd,
> Which in a *Roman* Marriage is profest.
> 'Tis no stol'n Wedding, this; rejecting awe,
> She scorns to Marry, but in Form of Law:
> In this moot case, your Judgment: To refuse
> Is present Death, besides the Night you lose.
> If you consent, 'tis hardly worth your pain;
> A Day or two of Anxious Life you gain:
> Till lowd Reports through all the Town have past,
> And reach the Prince: For Cuckolds hear the last.
> Indulge thy Pleasure, Youth, and take thy swing:
> For not to take, is but the self same thing:
> Inevitable Death before thee lies;
> But looks more kindly through a Ladies Eyes.
>
> (512–32)

The hopelessness of Silius' plight is stressed by Juvenal and heightened still further in Dryden's rendering by his emphasis on the 'fatal' inauspiciousness of the 'Comet-Eyes' with which Messalina weighs up the young man's charms, and by Dryden's salacious suggestion (for which Juvenal provides no direct precedent) that, besides being killed by Messalina if he refuses, Silius will miss out on the opportunity of a night in her bed. Dryden's Juvenal, borrowing a throwaway colloquialism from Higden, scornfully exhorts Silius to 'have his swing' – that is, both to 'enjoy himself', 'have his fling', and simultaneously (by a grisly pun) to 'hang himself'.[38] The paragraph culminates in a 'sentence', which gathers up the previous suggestions of Messalina's murderous beauty and glances at a larger truth: 'Inevitable Death' lies before *all* of us, the readers who have been attending to this story as much as Silius. Dryden's Juvenal then moves to his consolatory conclusion: –

> What then remains? Are we depriv'd of Will?
> Must we not Wish, for fear of wishing ill?
> Receive my Counsel, and securely move;
> Intrust thy Fortune to the Pow'rs above,
> Leave them to manage for thee, and to grant
> What their unerring Wisdom sees thee want:
> In Goodness as in Greatness they excel;
> Ah that we lov'd our selves but half so well!
> We, blindly by our headstrong Passions led,
> Are hot for Action, and desire to Wed;
> Then wish for Heirs: But to the Gods alone
> Our future Offspring, and our Wives are known;
> Th' audacious Strumpet, and ungracious Son.
> Yet, not to rob the Priests of pious Gain,
> That Altars be not wholly built in vain;
> Forgive the Gods the rest, and stand confin'd
> To Health of Body, and Content of Mind:
> A Soul, that can securely Death defie,
> And count it Nature's Priviledge, to Dye;
> Serene and Manly, harden'd to sustain
> The load of Life, and Exercis'd in Pain;
> Guiltless of Hate, and Proof against Desire;
> That all things weighs, and nothing can admire:
> That dares prefer the Toils of *Hercules*
> To Dalliance, Banquets, and Ignoble ease.
> The Path to Peace is Virtue: What I show,
> Thy Self may freely, on Thy Self bestow:
> Fortune was never Worshipp'd by the Wise;
> But, set aloft by Fools, Usurps the Skies.
>
> (533–61)

[38] See the quotations dated 1587 and 1698 under *OED* 'swing', *sb.*[1], 5, and 1589 under 'swing', *sb.*[1], 8a. Higden had used the phrase on p. 18.

The only behaviour, Dryden's Juvenal suggests, that would be fully adequate to the absurd and intractable dilemmas of the human condition would be to exercise no longings or desires whatever. The very passions from which we cannot escape, and indeed which ensure the survival of the human species, are those which destroy us all. But such behaviour, the poet realizes, is itself beyond human capacities. Therefore, since it is impossible for us to renounce all prayers and wishes, we should confine ourselves to praying for the physical health and mental tranquillity which will enable us to look steadily at the world, including our own inevitable dissolution, and to reconciling ourselves, proudly, boldly, and without self-pity, to the world's vicissitudes in a 'serene and manly' spirit.

To some readers of Juvenal, Dryden's conclusion might seem a shade more self-consciously 'noble' than that of his original. His rendering certainly has something of the triumphantly self-possessed tone of his earlier translations of Horace – particularly in his bold claim that when the time comes he will treat death as 'Nature's Priviledge' – a great *benefit* bestowed by a benign power.[39] Also Horatian is Dryden's interpolated suggestion that the wise man is neither mesmerized by life's vanities nor upset by its disappointments (a clear allusion to the 'nil admirari' of Horace's *Epistles*, 1. 6). However, the gods envisaged in 'The Tenth Satyr' are beneficent deities, altogether unlike the remote, uncaring divinities of Horatian or Lucretian Epicureanism. And though the position of resolute clear-sightedness advocated in the passage has clear affinities with Stoicism, it is far removed from the variety of that philosophy anathematized by Dryden in the Dedication to *Don Sebastian*, in which the folly of the Stoic is seen to lie in his affectation of 'saying he suffers not what he knows he feels' and of straining 'himself beyond the nature of his Being; either to become a Deity, by being above suffering, or to debase himself into a Stock or Stone, by pretending

[39] Here Dryden is indebted to *The Tenth Satyr of Juvenal Done into English Verse. By J[ohn] H[arvey] Esq.* (London, [1693]), p. 18: 'Let's pray for Health and Wisdom, pray to have / A Mind so great, Death's Terrors can't enslave, / As knowing he that quits this Life, but pays / A due and priviledge which Nature has'. On Dryden's (pre-publication) use of this translation, see, further, my 'Dryden, John Harvey and the Tenth Satire of Juvenal', *Notes and Queries*, 240 (1995), 54–6, and *Poems*, 4. 96.

not to feel it' (*Works*, 15. 62). In sharp contrast, the wise man is, in the Drydenian Juvenal's sense of things, '*Exercis'd* in Pain'.

In translating Juvenal, Dryden was able to adopt or discover a stance towards the world which could be summed up in a grand, defiant shrug of the shoulders, a note of triumph derived not from any reassuring moral code or set of theological beliefs but conjured up by some mysterious, unpredictable power from the depths of his own soul. According to the Juvenalian Dryden, it is futile to attempt to resolve, elude, or explain away the delusions and disasters of life: one must simply look them squarely and derisively in the face, acknowledge them for what they are in a spirit of scornful delight, and carry on.

It would clearly be a gross oversimplification to identify this stance in any straightforward way with the attitudes of Dryden the man in the early 1690s. Dryden's sympathies and convictions, both as a man and a poet, were always too *ondoyant et divers* to be reduced to any single principle or formula. On the strength of the evidence already presented, however, it is tempting to speculate that Dryden's discovery of (to adapt a phrase of C. S. Lewis)[40] 'the possible Juvenal in himself' was not unconnected with his ability to rise, with remarkable rapidity and ease, above the disappointments and difficulties which followed the collapse of his official career in 1689, and to go on, throughout the last decade of his life, to write thousands of lines of the most sprightly, vivid, exuberant, varied, and musical verse in the English language.

[40] See C. S. Lewis, *A Preface to 'Paradise Lost'* (Oxford, 1942), p. 63: 'The possible Lucretius in myself interests me more than the possible C. S. Lewis in Lucretius.'

# 6

## Dryden's 'Baucis and Philemon'

In a letter to William Wycherley of 26 December 1704, Alexander Pope wrote of Dryden that 'those Scribblers who attack'd him in his latter times, were only like Gnats in a Summer's evening, which are never very troublesome but in the finest and most glorious Season; (for his fire, like the Sun's, shin'd clearest towards its setting).'[1] Pope's remark may seem strange to the modern reader accustomed to regard Dryden as primarily a political poet, and the satires and religious poems of the 1680s as the summit and core of his achievement. However, Pope's would have been the more familiar view to readers in the century after Dryden's death. The poet's friend Sir Samuel Garth wrote in 1717 that 'as his earlier Works wanted no Maturity, so his latter wanted no Force, or Spirit.'[2] Similarly, and in the same year, William Congreve, another friend, and Dryden's chosen literary heir, wrote that Dryden's 'Parts did not decline with his Years: But . . . he was an improving Writer to his last, even to near seventy Years of Age; improving in Fire and Imagination, as well as in Judgement: Witness his Ode on St. *Cecilia's* Day, and his Fables, his latest Performances'.[3] Later in the eighteenth century, in the second volume of his *Essay on the Genius and Writings of Pope* (1782), Joseph Warton wrote that 'It is to his fables, though wrote in his old age, that Dryden will owe his immortality . . . The warmth and melody of these pieces, has never

[1] Alexander Pope, *Correspondence*, ed. G. Sherburn, 5 vols. (Oxford, 1956), 1. 2.

[2] *Ovid's Metamorphoses, in Fifteen Books. Translated by the Most Eminent Hands* [ed. Sir Samuel Garth] (London, 1717), p. xx.

[3] William Congreve, *The Mourning Bride, etc.*, ed. B. Dobrée (Oxford, 1928), pp. 482–3.

been excelled in our language'.[4] Even as late as 1845 we find 'Christopher North' (John Wilson) writing in similar terms in the pages of *Blackwood's Edinburgh Magazine*:

> [The *Fables*], as they are the works of Dryden's which the most fasten themselves with interest upon a mind open to poetry and free from preconceived literary opinion, so do they seem to us to be . . . those which a versed critic must distinguish as stamped, beyond the others, with the skilled ease, the flow as of original composition, the sustained spirit, and force, and fervour – in short, by the mastery, and by the keen zest of writing . . . no detriment of time is here perceptible; youthful fire and accomplished skill have the air of being met in these remarkable pieces.[5]

Indeed, I think it would be true to say that, with the possible exception of Samuel Johnson, most readers in the century or so after his death, and many for much longer, would have agreed with Dryden's own suggestions, in the Preface to the *Fables* and the letters of the late 1690s, that the poet, now in his late 60s, was working with an unsurpassed vigour and youthful enthusiasm:

> What Judgement I had, increases rather than diminishes; and Thoughts, such as they are, come crowding in so fast upon me, that my only Difficulty is to chuse or to reject; to run them into Verse, or to give them the other Harmony of Prose.
>
> (Preface to *Fables*; *Works*, 7. 26–7)

*Fables Ancient and Modern* was published in March 1700, two months before the poet's death. It contains seventeen translations – five from Chaucer (one – 'The Flower and the Leaf' – of a poem no longer believed to be genuinely Chaucerian), eight from Ovid, three from Boccaccio, and one from Homer, together with four non-translated poems, and the originals of the Chaucerian translations, printed – for the first time ever – in Roman typeface. Various attempts have been made to suggest an overarching architectonic or thematic design to the volume as a whole. Earl Miner, for example,

[4] Joseph Warton, *An Essay on the Genius and Writings of Pope*, 2 vols. (4th edition, Oxford, 1782), 2. 12.

[5] [John Wilson], *Specimens of the British Critics, by Christopher North*, introd. David Hopkins (Delmar NY, 1979), p. 206 [first published in *Blackwood's Edinburgh Magazine*, 57 (1845)].

has suggested that *Fables* was loosely organized round a number of recurrent preoccupations – love, the good life, war, fate, and determinism – with Christian consolations against life's vicissitudes being set against pagan doctrines of materialism and metempsychosis.[6] Judith Sloman has interpreted the volume as a systematic attempt to demonstrate the superiority of Christian virtue and humility over the martial heroism and amoral passions of the ancient world.[7] James D. Garrison has judged that Dryden was offering in *Fables* a balanced view of human nature that does justice both to its violently passionate and morally pious impulses, avoiding both despair and naive idealism.[8] And, in the most important – and only book-length – study of the volume to date, Cedric D. Reverand II has argued that *Fables* is organized on a sceptical, exploratory, and dialectical pattern, in which the affirmations of one poem are constantly undermined by others, so that the reader is not allowed to rest secure in the consolation provided by any single system of assumptions, values or beliefs. Such a structure, Reverand suggests, reflects Dryden's own sense of uncertainty at the collapse of ideals and institutions to which he had devoted himself earlier in his career.[9]

These accounts – particularly Reverand's – offer valuable suggestions about the larger considerations informing *Fables* – considerations that make the volume so much more than a mere miscellany. *Fables* is certainly concerned to explore, from a variety of viewpoints, and in a variety of modes and tones, a number of topics with which Dryden had been recurrently preoccupied throughout his work: the possibility of human happiness and the conditions under which it might be achieved; the nature of personal and civic virtue; the deceitfulness and violence of political debate; the glory, brutality, and absurdity of martial heroism; the nature of true nobility; the affective power of music and poetry; the grandeur, folly, and destructiveness of love; the competing claims of 'human' and 'natural' law;

[6] Earl Miner, *Dryden's Poetry* (Bloomington IN, 1967), pp. 287–323.

[7] Judith Sloman, 'An Interpretation of Dryden's *Fables*', *Eighteenth-Century Studies*, 4 (1970–1), 199–211, later incorporated in the same author's *Dryden: The Poetics of Translation* (Toronto, 1985).

[8] James D. Garrison, 'The Universe of Dryden's *Fables*', *Studies in English Literature*, 21 (1981), 409–23.

[9] Cedric D. Reverand II, *Dryden's Final Poetic Mode: The* Fables (Philadelphia PA, 1988).

the destructive and creative effects of time and change. But the circumstances of the poems' composition and publication suggest that one should exercise caution in assuming too elaborate a degree of architectonic organization or organic interrelatedness in the volume's structure. We do not know for certain whether Dryden or Tonson was ultimately responsible for the ordering of its items. The Ovid translations which it contains may represent, at least in part, unfinished business from an earlier plan of Dryden's for a complete English version of the *Metamorphoses.*[10] The translation of 'The First Book of Homer's *Ilias*' seems to have been conceived as a pilot experiment for a complete version of the Greek epic.[11] And two of the 'original' poems in *Fables* had already entered the public domain in very different contexts.[12] Moreover, an excessive preoccupation with the volume's larger themes and structuring might cause one to overlook some of its local quiddities and nuances, and particularly the details of Dryden's engagement with the classical and medieval poems which he was translating. My approach, therefore, in this and the next three chapters will be to look closely at three of the versions from Ovid in *Fables* in and for themselves, paying close attention to Dryden's dialogic engagement with a poet whose work he had (albeit with important reservations) long admired.[13]

'Baucis and Philemon', perhaps one of the most immediately attractive of the *Fables*, offers a good example of Dryden's drawing out in his version various possibilities latent in the Latin, and refashioning and reliving the episode as a modern English poem. Dryden's own description of the poem as a 'good natur'd story' (*Works*, 6. 24) should not lead us into regarding it as a charming but essentially lightweight product of his dotage. Its power lies in its refusal to press or

[10] See my 'Dryden and the Garth-Tonson *Metamorphoses*', *Review of English Studies*, 39 (1988), 64–74, and 'Charles Montague, George Stepney, and Dryden's *Metamorphoses*,' *Review of English Studies*, 51 (2000), 83–9.

[11] See the letter of ?October 1699, in *The Letters of John Dryden*, ed. Charles E. Ward (Durham NC, 1942), pp. 120–1, quoted on p. 18 above.

[12] *Alexander's Feast* had been printed as a separate folio pamphlet in connection celebrations on St Cecilia's Day (22 November) in 1697. 'The Monument of a Fair Maiden Lady, Who dy'd at *Bath*' had been inscribed on the tomb of Mary Frampton in Bath Abbey in 1698.

[13] On Dryden's lifelong interest in, and criticisms of, Ovid, see Dryden, *Poems*, 4. 229.

argue its point in any obviously didactic way, allowing the reader to view the events of the story from a series of what might initially seem mutually contradictory perspectives but which, in Dryden's treatment, blend to create a subtle and distinctive re-presentation of Ovid's episode. The lightness of Dryden's touch in achieving his effects might easily lead us to overlook the artistry with which he has fused a number of disparate elements from his reading in the composition of the poem. For he has drawn significant details, not only from the Latin commentaries on Ovid available to him[14] but also from previous translators who had relished this passage in the *Metamorphoses*, and from the greatest poem of his greatest English poetic contemporary.

When we compare Dryden's poem with Ovid's text we immediately find several interests not obvious from a casual perusal of the Latin. Dryden has put more emphasis than Ovid, for example, on the deep affection which Baucis and Philemon feel for each other, and on the almost sacred regard with which they view their marriage. In his initial description, he characterizes them (in phrases which have no direct equivalent in the Latin) as 'a happy Pair' who have grown 'old in Love' (33–4), perhaps remembering the stress on their abiding passion to be found in Jean de La Fontaine's French rendering of the story:

> Ni le temps ni l'hymen n'éteignirent leur flame; . . .
> L'amitié modéra leurs feux sans les détruire.[15]

There is also no direct equivalent in the Latin for some of Philemon's words to Jupiter, after the god has asked the couple what they desire most:

> et quoniam concordes egimus annos,
> auferat hora duos eadem, nec coniugis unquam
> busta meae videam, neu sim tumulandus ab illa.
> (708–10)

[14] The study which first demonstrated and documented Dryden's use of contemporary editions of Ovid was J. McG. Bottkol, 'Dryden's Latin Scholarship', *Modern Philology*, 40 (1943), 241–54.

[15] Jean de La Fontaine, 'Philémon et Baucis', in *Fables, Contes et Nouvelles*, eds. René Groos and Jacques Schiffrin (Paris, 1954), p. 323. The poem was first printed in *Ouvrages de prose et de poésie des sieurs de Maucrois et de La Fontaine* (Paris, 1685), 1. 78–98.

(and since we have spent our lives in constant company, we pray that the same hour may bring death to both of us – that I may never see my wife's tomb, nor be buried by her.)

> And since not any Action of our Life
> Has been polluted with Domestick Strife,
> We beg one Hour of Death; that neither she
> With Widows Tears may live to bury me,
> Nor weeping I, with wither'd Arms may bear
> My breathless Baucis to the Sepulcher.
>
> (171–6)

Dryden's telling phrase 'polluted with Domestick Strife' (which he used as a contrast to the blissful married state of Palamon and Emily at the end of his version of Chaucer's Knight's Tale[16]) adds more pathos to the carefully chosen 'wither'd Arms' and 'breathless Baucis': we momentarily catch a glimpse of the old man imagining the scene for himself, and we feel all the more for him.

Besides encouraging us to view the old couple with the seriousness and inward sympathy which this passage forces on us, Dryden can also, with no sense of strain or contradiction, reinforce and extend the comic wit which caused George Sandys to comment that Baucis' and Philemon's 'homely and hearty entertainment is most conceitedly expressed by our wittiest of authors',[17] and allows us to view the old couple, at times, with a charitable detachment. Baucis, for example, merely an 'anus' (old woman) in Ovid (661), becomes, in Dryden a 'good old Huswife' (82), a domesticating touch which enhances our sympathetic amusement at her gusto and enthusiasm as she scuttles around the cottage, eager to please her guests. Such a touch typifies the skill at which Dryden excels throughout the poem, to hit on telling details in his treatment both of the human and divine protagonists and of the setting. It is these details which perhaps first interested him in Ovid's fable and prompted the remark in the Preface: 'I see Baucis and Philemon as perfectly before me, as if some ancient Painter had

[16] 3. 1149; *Works*, 7. 195.

[17] George Sandys, *Ovids Metamorphosis Englished, Mythologiz'd, and Represented in Figures* (Oxford, 1632), p. 296 (italics reversed).

drawn them' (*Works*, 6. 31).[18] Some sense of the kind of significance Dryden may have seen in the details of Ovid's portrayal, and amplified in his own version, is provided by a celebrated passage in Pope's notes to his translation of Homer's *Iliad*, which takes up the same topic (Pope is discussing Homer's use of telling detail in his depiction of the last parting of Hector and Andromache in Book 6):

> All these are but small Circumstances, but so artfully chosen, that every Reader immediately feels the force of them, and represents the whole in the utmost Liveliness to his Imagination. This alone might be a Confutation of that false Criticism some have fallen into, who affirm that a Poet ought only to collect the great and noble Particulars in his Paintings. But it is in the Images of Things as in the Characters of Persons; where a small Action, lets us more into the Knowledge and Comprehension of them, than the material and principle Parts themselves. As we find this in a History, so we do in a Picture, where sometimes a small Motion or Turn of a Finger will express the Character and Action of a Figure more than all the other Parts of the Design . . . There is a vast difference betwixt a small Circumstance and a trivial one, and the smallest become important if they are well chosen, and not confused.
>
> (*TE*, 7. 355–6)

It is in his choice of 'small Circumstances' that we can see to best advantage Dryden's mind working over his predecessors, and using them creatively for his own purposes.

Dryden has taken particular care to depict the precise details of the meal which the old couple set before their divine visitors. To increase the rusticity of his terminology Dryden went back beyond George Sandys's *Metamorphoses*, his quarry for many verbal details throughout his translations from Ovid, to Arthur Golding's version of 1567.[19] Though Sandys had also used Golding – so that it is often difficult to determine precisely when Dryden had consulted Golding directly – we can see Dryden taking over words like 'coleworts' (58), 'sallow' (78), and 'sherd' (86), as well as several details of phrasing, from the earlier version, and from Sandys and Golding combined he introduced for the first time into his poetry the words 'bacon' (62),

[18] Dryden here paraphrases a note in Crispinus' edition: see *Poems*, 5. 63.

[19] Dryden used both the main editions of Sandys's translation (1626, 1632). See my 'Dryden and the Two Editions of Sandys's Ovid', *Notes and Queries*, 221 (1976), 552–4, and the notes on Dryden's Ovid translations in Dryden, *Poems*, *passim*.

'brushwood' (54), 'chips' (54), 'cushions,' 'kettle' (54), 'pickled' (93), and 'settle' (44). He also expanded Ovid's already full and specific portrayal of the rustic banquet to make more vivid the effect of the scene on our senses. For his description of the mint with which Baucis scrubs the table, as: 'A wholesome Herb, that breath'd a grateful Scent' (89) Dryden went to the 'Delphin' edition of Ovid (Lyon, 1689) by the Swiss scholar Daniel Crispinus, whose note on the word 'mentae' read: 'Quae attritu gratum odorem emitterent' (which give off a pleasant smell when rubbed).[20] And in his description of 'The party-colour'd Olive, Black and Green' (91) Dryden combined a line from Sandys ('Whereon they party-colour'd oliues set') with the gloss on Ovid's word 'bicolor' in Borchard Cnipping's Variorum Ovid of 1670: 'Olivae virides & nigrae' (olives, green and black). The Delphin edition is the source for the 'smoking Lard' (107) which, in Dryden, the boiling kettle sends to the table: Crispinus had glossed Ovid's 'epulas . . . calentes' (671; warm feast) as 'lardum'. Dryden also added details of his own. The dates, described by Ovid as 'rugosi' (which Sandys translated as 'rugged') are made, more specifically, 'wrinkled' in Dryden's version (114), and Dryden combines English custom with Ovid's Italian scene, when he portrays Philemon boiling the bacon, 'To tame the Flesh, and drain the Salt away' (69).

But Dryden's 'rustic' details do not suggest that he is merely imitating the recording eye of an observer in the countryside. Dryden sometimes also enhances the fanciful and magical elements in Ovid's tale. Towards the end of the banquet, the 'Beechen Bowls' reveal their divine origin more delightfully in Dryden's version by being endowed in the verse with a life of their own. We are told that they: 'Ran without Feet, and danc'd about the Board' (125), a touch similar to that moment in his version of 'The First Book of Homer's *Ilias*' (785), where Dryden draws on various seventeenth-century predecessors to evoke the spontaneous mirth of the divine banquet where 'The laughing Nectar overlook'd the Lid' (785).[21] Moreover, in

[20] In his edition of Ovid (1662), Cornelius Schrevelius had noted that 'mentha suavissimi odoris est herba' (mint is a herb of the most pleasant smell).

[21] For analogues and possible sources, see Dryden, *Poems*, 5. 331. Robert Cummings (*Seventeenth-Century Poetry: An Annotated Anthology* (Oxford, 2000), p. 513) notes that the line in 'Baucis and Philemon' may also recall the moving tripods made by Homer's Hephaestus (*Iliad*, 18. 372–8).

rendering Ovid's rural feast, Dryden has enriched his translation with subtle but unmistakable echoes of another celebrated feast in which a human couple entertain a divine guest: that provided by Adam and Eve for the archangel Raphael in Milton's *Paradise Lost*.[22] After a series of rural *hors d'oeuvres*, Ovid's old couple produce bacon and wine for their guests:

> parva mora est, epulasque foci misere calentes,
> nec longae rursus referuntur vina senectae
> dantque locum mensis paulum seducta secundis:
>
> (671–3)

(A moment and the hearth sent forth its steaming banquet, and wine of no great age was brought out, which was then pushed aside to give a small space for the second course.)

Dryden rendered the passage thus:

> By this the boiling Kettle had prepar'd.
> And to the Table sent the smoaking Lard;
> On which with eager Appetite they dine,
> A sav'ry Bit, that serv'd to rellish Wine:
> The Wine itself was suiting to the rest,
> Still working in the Must, and lately pressd.
>
> (106–11)

There is no mention in the Latin (or in Golding or Sandys) of the diners' 'eager Appetite' or of the 'sav'ry' taste of the bacon. But the words 'savoury' and 'appetite' occur twice in close conjunction in Milton's descriptions of Adam and Eve's divinely-favoured meals (*Paradise Lost*, 4. 327–31, 335; 5. 303–5). It is, moreover, we remember, the 'savourie' smell of the fruit which increases Eve's desire, in her dream, to eat from the forbidden tree (5. 84–6). And a similar 'savorie

[22] For a persuasive suggestion that Milton was himself thinking of Ovid's Baucis and Philemon episode when composing the *theoxenia* which occupies the central books of *Paradise Lost*, see Charles Martindale, *John Milton and the Transformation of Ancient Epic* (London, 1986), pp. 184–7. Dryden seems here (as so often) to have been reading a classical text through an intermediary which had itself been influenced by his original.

odour' arouses her 'eager appetite' during her temptation (9. 740–10). Furthermore, Dryden's description of Baucis and Philemon's wine (for which, again, there is no direct source either in Ovid's Latin or in Dryden's English predecessors) seems to recall the moment in *Paradise Lost* where Eve prepares a drink for their angelic guest:

> for drink the Grape
> She crushes, inoffensive moust, and meathes
> From many a berrie, and from sweet kernels prest
> She tempers dulcet creams.
>
> (5. 344–7)

That Dryden's Miltonic borrowings are not merely gratuitous but contribute significantly to his overall artistic purpose can be seen when they are viewed in connection with another aspect of the poem, one prominent in a passage discussed earlier: Philemon's words to the gods about the old couple's marriage.

Our ability to take Philemon's words so seriously at that point in the narrative seems attributable in no small part to Dryden's portrayal of Ovid's gods. Here he has taken several oblique glances at an influential interpretation of Ovid's episode which he would have found in many of his predecessors, not least in the allegorical commentaries printed in the 1632 and 1640 editions of Sandys's Ovid, and the footnotes of the pious Jesuit, Crispinus. Practically all commentators on Ovid, and many pictorial representations of the episode, had been anxious to point out the obvious parallels between the story of the visit of Jupiter and Mercury to the old couple and the story of the angels visiting Lot in Sodom, told in the Book of Genesis.[23] That Dryden was well aware of this tradition, and used it for his own purposes, can be seen particularly in three passages.

When the gods arrived at the cottage, the old couple, in Dryden's version 'bath'd their Feet, / And after with clean Towels dry'd their Sweat' (75–6). In Ovid's original, it is merely their 'artus' (limbs) that are dried. Even more significant are Jupiter's words (not in Ovid's Latin) to the couple when he has exempted them from the dreadful

[23] See Wolfgang Stechow, 'The Myth of Philemon and Baucis in Art', *Journal of the Warburg and Courtauld Institutes*, 4 (1941), 103–13; M. Beller, *Philemon und Baucis in der europäischen Literatur* (Heidelberg, 1967).

calamity that will overcome their neighbours: 'Leave these accurs'd; and to the Mountains Height / Ascend; nor once look backward in your Flight' (145–6). Here we are surely to recall the angels' words to Lot: 'Escape for thy life; look not behind thee, neither stay thou in all the plain; escape to the mountain, lest thou be consumed' (Genesis 19). And for Ovid's 'flexere oculos' (they turned their eyes) (696), Dryden, again glancing at the story of Lot, substitutes: 'They turn their now no more forbidden Eyes' (151).

It is inconceivable, I think, that Dryden included these touches, or his Miltonic colourings of Baucis and Philemon's hospitality, merely to scoff at those who had seen religious significances in the pagan tale. For, though we smile when they arrive sweating and not looking to their dignity, and though we remember that, as an admirer of Lucian and adapter of Molière's *Amphitryon,* Dryden was by no means averse to portrayals of the classical gods in ridiculous and humiliating circumstances, the gods in this poem are figures of real power, and the destruction they mete out is genuinely terrible. Like the gods in Dryden's translation of the first Book of the *Iliad*, they are simultaneously amusing and formidably potent – very different from the buffoons and charlatans who form the gods in the two burlesque versions of the Baucis and Philemon story composed in the early eighteenth century by Matthew Prior and Jonathan Swift. Prior's Jupiter, for example, reveals himself to the old couple thus:

> You have to Night beneath your Roof
> A Pair of Gods: (nay never wonder)
> This Youth can Fly, and I can Thunder.
> I'm JUPITER, and he MERCURIUS,
> My Page, my Son indeed, but spurious.
>
> ('The Ladle', 124–8)[24]

But neither has Dryden promoted any simple allegorical identification of the pagan gods with Lot's angels, or any straightforward identification of Baucis and Philemon with Milton's Adam and Eve. By aligning his classical deities momentarily with divine powers close to those worshipped by his own audience, Dryden has preserved the

[24] Matthew Prior, *Literary Works*, ed. H. B. Wright and M. K. Spears, 2 vols. (2nd edition, Oxford, 1971), 1. 206.

awe and respect with which his readers could regard them (incidentally enabling them to take the old couple's piety more seriously), while at the same time doing nothing to obscure the aspects of the story that are incompatible with Christian notions of divinity. Avoiding any hint of the blasphemous, he subtly blends Judaeo-Christian depictions of God and his angels visiting human beings on earth with a fantastical pagan story that culminates in a grotesque metamorphosis of an elderly married couple into a pair of trees. Elements from his own culture combine with elements of his classical original to create a common middle ground, neither purely Christian nor purely pagan, but fully deserving of the epithet 'religious' by virtue of its moving, albeit unsentimental, celebration of long-standing love, devotion, and piety, and its awesome, albeit not merely solemn, demonstration of godly power. Dryden's balancing of the religious and secular, and comic and serious, elements in his portrayal is so sure-footedly adroit that the parodies of Prior and Swift, witty though they are in many respects, leave Dryden's poem, at which they seem specifically directed, substantially unharmed.[25]

The interests of the poem all come together in the episode of the goose:

> One Goose they had, ('twas all they cou'd allow)
> A wakeful Cent'ry, and on Duty now,
> Whom to the Gods for Sacrifice they vow:
> Her, with malicious Zeal, the Couple view'd;
> She ran for Life, and limping they pursu'd:
> Full well the Fowl perceiv'd their bad intent,
> And wou'd not make her Masters Compliment;
> But persecuted, to the Pow'rs she flies,
> And close between the Legs of Jove she lies:
> He with a gracious Ear the Suppliant heard,
> And sav'd her Life; then what he was declar'd,
> And own'd the God.
>
> (130–41)

[25] For Swift's poem as a parody of Dryden's, see E. Rothstein, 'Jonathan Swift as Jupiter: "Baucis and Philemon"', in *The Augustan Milieu: Essays Presented to Louis A. Landa*, ed. H. K. Miller, E. Rothstein, and G. S. Rousseau (Oxford, 1970), pp. 205–24.

In the first two lines of this passage, Dryden has blended English rural custom (geese were regularly kept as 'watchdogs') with a hint from Crispinus' note, reminding us that it was the geese on the Capitol that saved Rome from the Gauls. But though this goose too is 'A wakeful Cent'ry, and on Duty now,' his owners determine in their 'malicious Zeal' to sacrifice her on the spot. Here is one of the moments where Dryden has distanced us ironically from the old couple, partly by letting us see the action momentarily, in the phrase 'malicious Zeal' and in the lines: 'Full well the Fowl perceiv'd their bad intent, / And wou'd not make her Masters Compliment' from the goose's point of view. Besides being a goose, independent-minded and unencumbered by any human notions of reverence, she performs the most intimately human of all gestures, that of submissive suppliance to the god. Dryden has shown her at one and the same moment as a farmyard animal and an emblem of pious and vulnerable humanity prostrate before the deity. In this passage occurs perhaps the most inspired of all Dryden's borrowings from his predecessors. For whereas Ovid's goose had merely fled 'ad ipsos deos' (to the gods themselves), Dryden's 'lies' 'close between the Legs of Jove' (138), a detail borrowed from the same moment in La Fontaine's version:

> La volatille échappe à sa tremblante main;
> Entre les pieds des dieux elle cherche un asile.[26]

Dryden now effects the extraordinary change to Jupiter's sentence of death on the neighbourhood, by making his Jupiter sound like a god whom we should take seriously:[27]

> Speak thy Desire, thou only Just of Men;
> And thou, O Woman, only worthy found
> To be with such a Man in Marriage bound.
>
> (164–6)

The sonority of these lines carries our minds back to Lelex's equally sonorous statement, at the beginning of the poem, of the truth that we are now being shown in action:

[26] *Contes et Nouvelles*, p. 324.

[27] Schrevelius notes that Jupiter's words are 'sententia gravi viro maxime conveniens' (a pronouncement fully befitting a serious man).

Heav'ns Pow'r is Infinite: Earth, Air, and Sea,
The Manufacture Mass, the making Pow'r obey.

(13–14)

The goose passage exemplifies most clearly my earlier suggestion that Dryden's interest in visual detail is creative and not merely documentary. The details of the goose's behaviour exist both in their own right and also as a vehicle for the main concerns of the poem.

In his adroit manipulation of transitions, most notably from the comedy of the goose to the destruction of the valley, Dryden can be seen to have exemplified the qualities idealized by Boileau in lines which, many years earlier, he (or Sir William Soame) had rendered thus:[28]

Happy, who in his Verse can gently steer,
From Grave, to Light; from Pleasant, to Severe.

(*The Art of Poetry*, 1. 75–6; *Works*, 2. 126)

And his discerning depiction of the 'Passions' and 'Habits' of Baucis and Philemon via a telling choice of detail would also, perhaps, have earned the admiration of the same critic, who, later in the same work, had written:

Nature in various Figures does abound;
And in each mind are diff'rent Humors found:
A glance, a touch, discovers to the wise;
But every man has not discerning eyes.

(*The Art of Poetry*, 3. 798–801; *Works*, 2. 148)

[28] The Soame/Dryden translation of Boileau's *L'Art poétique* (for which, see further Chapter 4) was published anonymously in 1683. In *The Fourth Part of Miscellany Poems* (1708), an 'Advertisement' by the publisher Jacob Tonson stated that Dryden had made 'very considerable Alterations' to Soame's manuscript 'particularly, the beginning of the 4th Canto', but it is not otherwise known precisely which parts of the translation should be attributed to which writer.

# 7

## Nature's Laws and Man's: Dryden's 'Cinyras and Myrrha'

In turning from the 'good natur'd Story' of Baucis and Philemon from Book 8 of Ovid's *Metamorphoses* to the more disturbing tale of Cinyras and Myrrha from Book 10, Dryden was engaging with an episode which he had long admired for its presentation of its heroine 'in the violence of her passions'.[1] The story is one of a sequence of tales narrated by Orpheus after the loss of his wife, Eurydice. Myrrha, daughter of Cinyras, King of Cyprus, is consumed with an incestuous passion for her father. So disturbed is she by her feelings that she resolves to commit suicide by hanging herself. She is discovered in the act by her nurse, who worms her secret out of her and then, after an initial expression of horror, offers to help Myrrha to consummate her desires. While Cinyras' wife is away, officiating at the feast of Ceres, the nurse approaches him and offers him a mistress 'of about the same age as his daughter'. Myrrha is brought to the royal bed-chamber under cover of darkness, and the incestuous act is committed on this occasion and several times subsequently. Eventually, desiring to see his young mistress's face, Cinyras brings a lighted torch which reveals that she is his own daughter. He is outraged and tries to kill her, but she flees, eventually arriving in Arabia where she prays to be relieved of life but not to be sent into the underworld. Her prayer is answered and she is transformed into a myrrh tree, in the shape of which she preserves both the beauty and the agony of her life. Her tears are changed into a fragrant perfume, and the child

[1] See 'An Account of the Ensuing Poem', prefixed to *Annus Mirabilis* (1667); *Works*, 1. 54.

born of the union with her father turns out to be Adonis, the future beloved of Venus herself.

Several features of Ovid's handling of the story are immediately striking. The subject matter shows the clear influence of Greek tragedy, and the prominence of the heroine's lengthy soliloquy, together with the obviously stylized nature of Ovid's telling, might seem to reinforce the connexion. Yet throughout the episode the narrator's manner of proceeding signals to readers that they are listening to a tale which is being related to them in a mood of relative calm: no profound emotional demands are therefore going to be made of the kind which we associate with the dramatic presentations of similar material by Euripides and Racine. Furthermore, while, as everyone agrees, Ovid is deeply interested in the thoughts of his heroine, his interest is clearly of a very different kind from that of a realistic novelist.

Modern commentators have been widely divided on the question of where Ovid stands in relation to the events in his tale and how he expects his readers to react to it, and have consequently valued the episode very differently. Some, for example, have seen it as a frigid, melodramatic, and even repulsive piece which allows no sympathy for the heroine and finally sees her callously degraded to the level of the subhuman. Such commentators sometimes stress what they take to be the gratuitous presence in the episode of the Latin poet's stylistic mannerisms: the rhetorical patternings, antitheses, and wordplay which had often been said by critics from Roman times onwards (including Dryden himself in some of his prose prefaces) to have marred Ovid's presentation of serious and harrowing situations.[2] Other commentators, however, have found Myrrha being afforded an impressive dignity by Ovid's handling, a dignity somehow enhanced rather than diminished by the witty verse and the final fanciful transformation.[3]

[2] See, for example, M. M. Crump, *The Epyllion from Theocritus to Ovid* (London, 1931), pp. 230–2; W. W. Sellar, *Roman Poets of the Augustan Age: Horace and the Elegiac Poets* (Oxford, 1892), p. 7; G. Lafaye, *Les Métamorphoses d'Ovide et leurs modèles grecs* (Paris, 1904), p. 171; Brooks Otis, *Ovid as an Epic Poet* (2nd edition, Cambridge, 1970), p. 229. Dryden's own critical prose sometimes echoed the stock disapproval of Ovid's 'boyisms' and 'wit out of season': see Chapter 7 below.

[3] See H. Fränkel, *Ovid: A Poet Between Two Worlds* (Berkeley and Los Angeles CA, 1956), p. 100; J.-M. Frécaut, *L'Esprit et l'humour chez Ovide* (Grenoble, 1972), p. 254; G. K. Galinsky, *Ovid's Metamorphoses: An Introduction to the Basic Aspects* (Oxford,

The problem of determining Ovid's precise stance and tone faces us at the outset with the narrator's warning to the reader:

> dira canam; procul hinc natae, procul este parentes,
> aut, mea si vestras mulcebunt carmina mentes,
> desit in hac mihi parte fides, nec credite factum,
> vel, si credetis, facti quoque credite poenam.
>
> (300–3)

(A horrible tale I have to tell. Far hence be daughters, far hence, fathers; or, if your minds find pleasure in my songs, do not give credence to this story, and believe that it never happened; or, if you do believe it, believe also in the punishment of the deed.)

On the face of it, Ovid (in using the formula employed by the Romans to warn off the irreligious who might profane the purity of a rite) is telling the reader that here is a story of sacrilegious horror, rendered tolerable only by the sternly moral nature of its conclusion and the strictness of the retribution meted out to the sinner. It was certainly as a grim cautionary tale that the episode was interpreted in the two principal English translations of Ovid before Dryden, those of Arthur Golding (1567) and George Sandys (1626, 1632). In the 'Epistle' included with his translation Arthur Golding had written:

> The tenth booke cheefly dooth containe one kynd of argument
> Reproving most prodigious lusts of such as have bene bent
> Too incest most unnaturall.[4]

Sandys, in his commentary on Book 10 in the revised edition of his translation (1632), described Myrrha as an 'impious soule' with 'hellish affections', and a later seventeenth-century translator, P. Du-Ryer, in his Brussels Ovid of 1677, judged that the point of the story was to encourage the reader to avoid such vice as Myrrha's, and attributed her transformation into a precious, rather than an

1975), p. 10; *Ovid: Metamorphoses: Books VI–X*, ed. W. S. Anderson (Norman OK, 1971), p. 504.

[4] *Shakespeare's Ovid: Being Arthur Golding's Translation of the Metamorphoses*, ed. W. H. D. Rouse (London, 1904), p. 5.

odious, tree to the fact that, like Mary Magdalene, she repented of her sin.[5]

Yet there are elements present in Ovid's telling which might cause us to be dissatisfied with such readings. Why, for example, does he immediately raise the suggestion that the reader might get pleasure from the tale? And why, if the tale is to be one of just retribution for a moral outrage, is the poet so equivocal about both the source of Myrrha's passion and the nature of the power which finally brings about her transformation? For it is only at the end of the episode (and then only obliquely) that Ovid seems to follow the tradition, preserved in the handbook versions of the story by Apollodorus (*Library*, 3. 14. 4) and Hyginus (*Fabulae*, 38) that Myrrha's passion was a punishment inflicted on her by Venus because of her mother's impiety to the goddess. At the beginning of the story he rather peremptorily attributes her passion to one of the Furies. In Dryden's rendering:

> *Cupid* denies to have inflam'd thy Heart,
> Disowns thy Love, and vindicates his Dart:
> Some Fury gave thee those infernal Pains,
> And shot her venom'd Vipers in thy Veins.
>
> (22–5)

In the light of Ovid's handling of the end of the poem one must see Myrrha's final transformation as a *relief*, the blessed and mysterious answer to her prayers, rather than as a just and degrading punishment. The transformation is, after all, exactly what she had asked for. In Dryden's rendering again:

> Ye Pow'rs, if any so propitious are
> T' accept my Penitence, and hear my Pray'r;
> Your Judgments, I confess, are justly sent;
> Great Sins deserve as great a Punishment:
> Yet since my Life the Living will profane,
> And since my Death the happy Dead will stain,
> A middle State your Mercy may bestow,

[5] George Sandys, *Ovid's Metamorphosis, English'd, Mythologiz'd and Represented in Figures* (Oxford, 1632), p. 362; P. Du-Ryer, *Les Metamorphoses d'Ovide . . . , avec des nouvelles explications historiques, morales et politiques, sur toutes les fables* (Brussels, 1677), p. 333.

Betwixt the Realms above, and those below;
Some other Form to wretched *Myrrha* give,
Nor let her wholly die, nor wholly live.

(326–35)

It is significant that the child of her incestuous union, though 'male conceptus' (badly conceived; 503), turns out on birth to be 'formosissimus' (most beautiful; 522), and that although the myrrh tree into which Myrrha is transformed is twisted and weeping it is also beautiful and fragrantly-perfumed, part of the fabled sumptuous opulence of Arabia.

The tone of the opening caution, then, should perhaps be seen as finely poised: the narrator registering that he is about to tell of events which might ordinarily be thought of as loathsomely sinful, and simultaneously alerting his reader to the possibility that this is not the only legitimate way in which they might be envisaged. Such a double-edged note is certainly present in Dryden's subtly-modulated rendering:

I sing of Horrour; and could I prevail,
You shou'd not hear, or not believe my Tale.
Yet if the Pleasure of my Song be such,
That you will hear, and credit me too much,
Attentive listen to the last Event,
And with the Sin believe the Punishment.

(5–10)

A sharp contrast is provided by the exclamatory horror of Sandys's opening (on which Dryden nevertheless drew):

I sing of Horror! Daughters, farre ô farre
From hence remove! and You, who fathers are!
Or if my winning verse your minds allure:
Let them no credit in this part procure.
Or if you will beleeve the same for true:
Beleeve with all the judgments that insue.

(1632 edition, p. 344)

A similar poise to that of the opening can, I think, be observed in Ovid's treatment of his heroine.

While the Romans seem to have thought of many moral issues on a purely secular level, incest, we are told by historians of Roman religion, was generally regarded as one of the few offences to fall under divine rather than merely human jurisdiction, the punishment of incestuous crimes being considered to be the preserve of the Penates.[6] In keeping with the formalistic and legalistic nature of Roman religion, and its emphasis on the supreme importance of forms of words in religious ceremonies, the iniquity of incest was felt to reside not least in the confusion of relationships and the consequent destruction of the bonds of 'pietas' which result from an incestuous act. A passage in Cicero's speech *Pro Cluentio* makes the point neatly, and in terms which have a close bearing on Myrrha's reflections on her predicament. Giving full vent to his horror at the marriage of his client's mother to her son-in-law, Cicero calls it a 'scelus incredibile et praeter hanc unam in omni vita inauditum' (an unbelievable crime, and scarcely heard of in the whole of life except for the case of this woman), wonders why she did not fear the gods' revenge, and concludes:

Atque etiam nomina necessitudinum, non solum naturae nomen et iura mutavit; uxor generi, noverca filii, filiae pellex: eo enim denique adducta est, uti sibi praeter formam nihil ad similitudinem hominis reservavit.[7]

(Nay more; as the wife of her son-in-law, the step-mother of her son, the rival of her daughter, she has changed not merely the names and ordinances which nature gives, but even the name we give to relationships; and she is come at last to such a pass that she has lost all semblance of humanity save only her outward form.)[8]

By changing the names which symbolize human relationships, Cicero quite clearly assumes, this woman has forfeited her right to be considered human in any meaningful sense of the term. It is the fact that she will be confounding the form of words in which family

[6] See J. H. W. G. Liebeschuetz, *Continuity and Change in Roman Religion* (Oxford, 1979), pp. 41–3, 45.

[7] *Pro Cluentio*, 199. It was a passage which Cicero himself particularly admired. See *De Oratore*, 107.

[8] 'Rival' is an inadequate translation of 'pellex' (or 'paelex'), 'a mistress installed as a rival or in addition to a wife' (*Oxford Latin Dictionary*). English has no word for the phenomenon.

relationships are properly expressed that is one of the principal causes of Myrrha's feelings of revulsion against her passion:

> et quot confundas et iura et nomina, sentis?
> tune eris et matris paelex et adultera patris?
> tune soror nati genetrixque vocabere fratris?
>
> (346–8)

(Think how many ties, how many names you are confusing! Will you be the rival of your mother, the mistress of your father? Will you be called the sister of your son, the mother of your brother?)

But if incest was thought of by one powerful body of Roman opinion as going against 'naturae nomen et iura' (the name and laws of nature), there was another sense in which it could be thought of, paradoxically, as profoundly in accord with Natural Law.

The writings of Cicero can be seen as standing in what one might call the mainstream of ancient thinking about Natural Law, the tradition leading from Aristotle through the Stoics to the later Roman jurists and thence to Christendom.[9] In a famous passage in the *Rhetoric* (1373b), Aristotle had distinguished between two kinds of law: particular (*idios*) and general (*koinos*). General laws, he argued, were based on Nature (*phusis*). All men have a 'general idea of just and unjust in accordance with nature' and that idea is common to peoples between whom there has been no direct communication. For the Stoics, Natural Law was nothing less than the recognition, by the Reason of the individual, of the larger Reason which is the moving principle of that single unified organism that constitutes the world. Thus the principle of 'living according to Nature' (however difficult it might be in practice to determine precisely what it entailed) was central to Stoic doctrine. Cicero had been profoundly influenced in his own philosophical writing by Stoic teaching, but, in accordance with the instincts of his temperament towards the law, rather than towards moral philosophy *per se*, he had developed the Stoic notion of Natural Law in the direction of seeking

[9] See Gerard Watson, 'The Natural Law and Stoicism', in *Problems in Stoicism*, ed. A. A. Long (London, 1971), pp. 216–38. For later developments, see Richard McCabe, *Incest, Drama, and Nature's Law* (Cambridge, 1993) and R. S. White, *Natural Law in English Renaissance Literature* (Cambridge, 1996).

'natural' support for those bonds and duties which are most conducive to public order and a stable community.

But coexisting with what I have called this 'philosophical mainstream' was an alternative tradition, first prominent in the teachings of the Sophists and continuing after them in the work of the Cynics, which appealed to the precedent of animal behaviour for the 'natural laws' which should govern human conduct.[10] Though derided by, among others, Aristophanes,[11] this tradition nevertheless survived (the Cynics, for example, arguing that the animals had preserved in their behaviour a 'natural' state which human civilization had obscured or abandoned) and served as a constant reminder of the problems and ambiguities latent in the whole idea of Natural Law, problems which persist in the statements of some of the later Roman jurists.[12]

This second tradition of thought about Natural Law has also left its mark on Myrrha's soliloquy. Having rebuked herself for her 'scelus' (crime), she then reflects:

> si tamen hoc scelus est. sed enim damnare negatur
> hanc Venerem pietas: coeunt animalia nullo
> cetera dilectu, nec habetur turpe iuvencae
> ferre patrem tergo, fit equo sua filia coniunx,
> quasque creavit init pecudes caper, ipsaque, cuius
> semine concepta est, ex illo concipit ales.
> felices, quibus ista licent! humana malignas
> cura dedit leges, et quod natura remittit,
> invida iura negant. gentes tamen esse feruntur,
> in quibus et nato genetrix, et nata parenti
> iungitur, ut pietas geminato crescat amore.
>
> (323–33)

(if indeed it is a crime. But I am not sure, for piety refuses to condemn such love as this. Other animals mate as they will, nor is it thought base for a heifer to be mounted by her father, nor for his own daughter to be a horse's wife; the goat goes in among the flocks which he has fathered, and the very

[10] See W. K. C. Guthrie, *The Sophists* (Cambridge, 1971), p. 104.

[11] *Clouds*, 1427–31; *Birds*, 753–68.

[12] See Barry Nicholas, *An Introduction to Roman Law* (1962; reprinted Oxford, 1975), pp. 54–6.

birds conceive from those by whose seed they were conceived. Happy they who have such privilege! Human civilization has made spiteful laws, and what nature allows, the jealous laws forbid. And yet they say that there are tribes among whom mother with son, daughter with father mates, so that natural love is increased by the double bond.)

Ovid creates sympathy for Myrrha's predicament, I would suggest, by revealing in her the workings of the conflicting claims of Natural Law. Unlike Cicero he is not content to relegate someone with feelings like hers to the category of subhuman. But neither is he blind to the power of the traditional claims of 'pietas' and the traditional Roman loathing of incest as 'nefas' and 'scelus'. The witty poise of his treatment, with (in the example just quoted) its deft and surprising juxtaposition of human and animal terms, is his means of alerting us to the reality of the problem encapsulated in Myrrha's predicament, while at the same time keeping us at a sufficient distance, and allowing our minds a freedom, so that we maintain a complex attitude to the girl, never lapsing into a position of simple approval or disapproval. All the time we are conscious of the poet's mind playing around and beyond his character's. Yet the precision and acuteness of the details reassure us that Ovid is not merely being irrelevantly witty at Myrrha's expense, or merely using the scene as an opportunity to indulge a prurient interest in the subject. Commentators on the passage just quoted have sometimes written off Myrrha's arguments as mere sophistry. 'Gentes tam efferatas et immanes umquam fuisse credibile non est' (It is not credible that there were ever peoples so bestial and savage), remarks the editor of the 1825 Oxford Variorum Ovid, and then offers fables of the gods and rumours about the Troglodytes, Ethiopians, and Attila the Hun as possible 'evidence'. But Ovid would certainly have known about the reality of the incestuous unions of Persia and Egypt, and he could have read about animal incest (if he had not observed it at first hand) in Aristotle.[13]

Ovid's fascination with the paradoxical workings of Natural Law in the mind of his heroine lies at the centre of Dryden's interest in the Myrrha episode. In his rendering of Myrrha's complaint, he has given her words an extra note of earthy vigour to increase our

[13] *Historia Animalium*, 6. 22.

consciousness of the pervasiveness and power of animal sexuality. In this he was assisted in particular by two of the previous renderings. One is James Gresham's little-known *The Picture of Incest. Lively Portraicted in the Historie of Cinyras and Myrrha* (London, 1626):

> The little Heifar scarce yet ag'd a yeare
> Her own begetter on her backe may beare
> Yet not be turpious, And the lustie steed
> Cover the Mare which sprung from his own seed
> The leacherous Goat too, leapes the female she
> From whom himselfe was gendred: and that hee
> Proceeding from them both by carnall use
> Oft tups the Dam that did himselfe produce.
> Birds with each other too do mate and by
> The so up hatch'd doe like fructifie.
>
> (p. 3)

The other is by Golding:

> The Hecfer thinkes no shame
> Too beare her father on her backe: The Horse beestrydes the same
> Of whom he is the syre: The Gote dooth bucke the Kid that hee
> Himself begate: and birdes doo tread the self same birdes wee see
> Of whom they hatched were before.
>
> (*Shakespeare's Ovid*, p. 208)

Dryden has also emphasized Myrrha's insistence that the laws and prohibitions imposed upon mankind, far from being principles derived by inexorable logic from the indisputable order of things, are in fact sometimes little more than arbitrary and intolerable burdens imposed upon Man by officious, even malevolent, lawgivers. Here he drew for assistance on the version of the episode, 'The Story of Cinyras and Myrrha' in *Epistolary Poems: On Several Occasions* (1694), by his younger contemporary, Charles Hopkins:

> But, foolish Man, against himself conspires,
> Inventing Laws, to curb his free desires.
> Industrious, to destroy his own content,
> He makes those bars, which Nature never meant.
>
> (p. 34)

The laws which Man has devised, Myrrha suggests in Dryden's version, go against the very grain of humanity itself:[14]

> Ah *Myrrha!* whither wou'd thy Wishes tend?
> Ye Gods, ye sacred Laws, my Soul defend
> From such a Crime, as all Mankind detest,
> And never lodg'd before in Humane Breast!
> But is it Sin? Or makes my Mind alone
> Th' imagin'd Sin? For Nature makes it none.
> What Tyrant then these envious Laws began,
> Made not for any other Beast, but Man?
> The Father-Bull his Daughter may bestride,
> The Horse may make his Mother-Mare a Bride;
> What Piety forbids the lusty Ram
> Or more salacious Goat, to rut their Dam?
> The Hen is free to wed the Chick she bore,
> And make a Husband, whom she hatch'd before.
> All Creatures else are of a happier Kind,
> Whom nor ill-natur'd Laws from Pleasure bind,
> Nor Thoughts of Sin disturb their Peace of mind.
> But Man, a Slave of his own making lives;
> The Fool denies himself what Nature gives:
> Too busie Senates, with an over-care
> To make us better than our Kind can bear;
> Have dash'd a Spice of Envy in the Laws,
> And straining up too high, have spoil'd the Cause.
> Yet some wise Nations break their cruel Chains,
> And own no Laws, but those which Love ordains:
> Where happy Daughters with their Sires are join'd,
> And Piety is doubly paid in Kind.
> O that I had been born in such a Clime,
> Not here, where 'tis the Country makes the Crime!
>
> (35–63)

Dryden has strengthened those elements in Ovid's episode which seem to support Myrrha's vision of a world seething beneath its 'respectable' surface with unbridled sexuality. In the English translation Cinyras is made a drunken lecher, not simply 'gravem vino'

[14] For an excellent analysis of this speech, see Cedric Reverand II, *Dryden's Final Poetic Mode: The* Fables (Philadelphia PA, 1988), pp. 153–4.

(heavy with wine) as in the Latin (438), but also (his wife is away at a religious festival) 'Easie with Wine, and deep in Pleasures drown'd, / Prepar'd for Love' (249). He takes particular pleasure in being told by the nurse that the mistress she has procured for him is the same age as his daughter. Again the tiniest hint in the Latin is expanded and made more explicit. Ovid has 'quaesitis virginis annis, / "par" ait "est Myrrhae." quam postquam adducere iussa est . . .' (440–1): (When he asked the maiden's age, she said: 'The same as Myrrha's.' Bidden to fetch her, . . . ). Dryden has

> the Monarch ask'd her Years,
> And she reply'd, The same thy *Myrrha* bears.
> Wine and commended Beauty fir'd his Thought;
> Impatient, he commands her to be brought.
>
> (252–5)

The behaviour of the nurse, too, contributes to the general impression. Earlier, after having discovered Myrrha about to attempt suicide and having concluded that love was the cause, she had been very ready to procure Myrrha a secret lover to satisfy her desires. Even when she discovers the real focus of those desires and reacts to the discovery with horror, it is not long before we see 'The crafty crone, officious in her Crime' (247) bustling off to the king, expertly fanning his desires, and then assisting Myrrha to overcome her inhibitions and accomplish the deed: Dryden got the hint for the adjective 'officious' from the Latin *interpretatio* (running Latin prose paraphrase) printed in Daniel Crispinus's 'Delphin' Ovid (Lyon, 1689), where the nurse is called 'perversè officiosa nutrix' (the wrongheadedly industrious nurse).

But most significant of all is the depiction of the incestuous act itself. Ovid's description alerts us, delicately but definitely, to the fact that 'ordinary' lovers' behaviour often has implications and dimensions which come uncomfortably close to incest, and that this closeness is reflected in the very texture of love language itself:

> virgineosque metus levat hortaturque timentem.
> forsitan aetatis quoque nomine 'filia' dixit,
> dixit et illa 'pater,' sceleri ne nomina desint.
>
> (466–8)

(It chanced, by a name appropriate to her age, he called her 'daughter', and she called him 'father', that names might not be lacking to their guilt.)

It is useful to be reminded by a modern scholar that the festival of Ceres, at which Cinyras' wife is officiating while the act is taking place, was one dedicated to the celebration of the intimacy of the bond between mother and daughter. On this occasion it was specifically forbidden for fathers to be mentioned: the very words 'pater' and 'filia', we are told in Servius' commentary on the *Aeneid* (4. 58), were under interdict.[15] It is therefore doubly significant that it is these very words which are being used at this moment in the royal bedchamber. Dryden's rendering causes us to remember Cinyras' alacrity in pursuing the affair when the nurse told him that his mistress was to be Myrrha's age:

> He found she trembl'd, but believ'd she strove
> With Maiden-Modesty, against her Love,
> And sought with flatt'ring Words vain Fancies to remove.
> Perhaps he said, My Daughter, cease thy Fears,
> (Because the Title suited with her Years;)
> And Father, she might whisper him agen,
> That Names might not be wanting to the Sin.
>
> (297–302)

The parenthesis in Dryden's rendering, '(Because the Title suited with her Years;)', gives, in its very (apparent) disingenuousness, the hint that the explanation being offered is not the full one. There was, we reflect, perhaps an ironic point when Myrrha remarked earlier, apropos of Cinyras, 'No thoughts like me his Sinless soul profane' (99). Many aspects of the sexual world created in the episode, therefore, make it less easy to shrug off Myrrha's animal parallels or to see the heroine herself merely as a monster or a freak.

In what I have said so far I may seem to have implied that Dryden saw in Ovid's episode and developed in his own version interests similar to those expressed by Freud in the *Introductory Lectures on Psychoanalysis*: that disgust at what we call 'sexual perversions', and

15 See Marcel Detienne, *The Gardens of Adonis: Spices in Greek Mythology* (1972), trans. Janet Lloyd (Hassocks, 1977), pp. 79–82.

incest in particular, is the product of nurture not nature; that the barriers against the temptations to incest are created, not inherent.[16] Dryden would certainly have remembered the essay, *Apologie de Raymond Sebond*, in which one of his favourite prose writers, Montaigne, had drawn specifically on this episode of Ovid's to support one of his own favourite (and very un-Ciceronian) arguments: that what we call Natural Law is merely the improper imputation of universal validity to the system of practices to which we are most accustomed.

In his treatise *De la sagesse* Montaigne's friend and disciple the philosopher Pierre Charron had also discussed the relationship of Natural Law to incest. Nature's laws, Charron argued (building on Stoic doctrine) are synonymous with those of God:

> The Model and Pattern, the Spring and Source of... Integrity, is the Law of Nature; by which I mean Universal Equity and Reason, that Candle of our Maker lighted up in every Breast, to guide, and shine in us perpetually. For This is the Dictate and Direction of God himself; He is the King, and this the Fundamental Law of the Universe, a Ray and Beam of the Divine Nature, that flows from, and hath a necessary Connexion and Dependance upon that Eternal and Immutable Law, which the Almighty prescribes to his own Actions.[17]

Man might, Charron suggests, recapture his sense of what observing Nature's laws might entail by observing the animals, as long as he avoids those animals whose behaviour has been corrupted by living in close proximity to Man. Man's avoidance of incest, Charron argues in a later chapter, is the product not of any prohibition by Nature but of the operations of specifically human laws and customs:

> Whence I pray, comes it to pass that Fathers never fall in Love with their own Daughters, though never so charming and desirable Creatures? Or why are Sisters seldom or never smitten with their own Brothers, though infinitely handsomer, better accomplish'd, and more engaging than Strangers? This Reservation and Coldness does not properly proceed from Nature; She makes no such Distinctions; These are the Effects of general Customs and

[16] See pp. 245–7 and 378 in the Pelican edition (Harmondsworth, 1973). Freud is here treating matters which are dealt with at greater length in other works, notably *The Interpretation of Dreams* (1900) and *Totem and Taboo* (1912–13).

[17] *Of Wisdom*, trans. George Stanhope, 3 vols. (2nd edition, London, 1707), 2. 54 (Book 2, Chapter 3).

Positive Laws, who forbid such Mixtures, pronounce them Scandalous, and Horrid, Incestuous and Wicked; but again, I say, these Characters are fix'd by Divine or Human Institutions; for Nature knows no such thing as Incest, nor condemns any Alliances, let the Line or Relation be what it will.[18]

Man should avoid incestuous unions, Charron goes on to suggest, not because they violate Natural Law but because he must, for the sake of social order, respect those customs and laws which obtain in the community in which he lives.

Charron's treatment of the subject, however, contains at one point an ambivalence which bears interestingly on Dryden's poem. Human customs and laws, Charron argues (Book 2, Chapter 8), generally forbid incestuous unions. Mosaic law, however, sometimes relaxed its own vetoes, allowing marriages, for example, between a man and his brother's wife, and even between a man and his father's wife. But, Charron goes on, liaisons between persons in 'a Right Line in Blood' do seem to be not merely a violation of custom or law but 'a Crime against Nature' ('du tout contre Nature'). But even *here*, the argument continues, there are sometimes exceptions: the liaison of Lot's daughters with him seems to have been brought about by Nature herself, who feared that the end of the human race might occur if Lot's daughters were forbidden to have sexual relations with their father. At any rate, it is on such grounds as these, Charron argues, that the conduct of Lot's daughters has been defended by 'some great Men'.[19]

A more straightforwardly iconoclastic handling of the subject is to be found in the writings of the later French sceptical philosopher, François La Mothe Le Vayer. In 'Le Banquet sceptique', the second of his *Quatre dialogues faits à l'imitation des anciens*, Le Vayer reviews the evidence relating to the incest prohibition. Having first entertained the view that 'les premiers degrez de paranté semblent devoir ester raisonnablement respectés' (it seems that the first degrees of kinship ought in reason to be respected), Le Vayer then proceeds to suggest that the 'standard' modern view of the subject is merely one among many:

[18] Chapter 8; *Of Wisdom*, 2. 174.

[19] Stanhope's translation of this passage misrepresents Charron's original by making it seem as if Charron is dismissing the 'great men's' interpretation of the story, rather than conceding truth to their views.

Si est-ce que beaucoup ont estimé legitime de joindre et unir les liens d'amour, et de parenté, puis que *duo vincula uno fortiora*; et comme dit Ovide,

> *gentes tamen esse feruntur*
> *In quibus et nato genitrix, et nata parenti*
> *Iungitur, et pietas geminato crescit amore.*

Ainsi ces vieux Chaldéens disoient *iustum esse matri ac filiae misceri*, au rapport de Sotion,... Ainsi Chrysippus aux livres de sa police, estimoit indifferent d'avoir affaire avec sa mere, sa soeur, ou sa fille... Sur ce fondement Periander, l'un des sept sages de la Grece, ne fit point de scrupule de connoistre sa mere Cratea. Les Anglois, au rapport de Cesar, en usoient de mesme à l'esgard de leurs soeurs et filles. *Hiberni palam cum matribus et sororibus concumbebant*, dit Strabon, asseurant le mesme des Mages de Perse avec leurs meres, et des Egyptiens avec leurs soeurs, dont le Mausolée et les Obelisques rendent assez de tesmoignage; et en un autre endroit il adjouste le mesme des Arabes. Les Romains, qui ont fait plus de conscience de ces incestes, leur donnerent neantmoins un nom si leger, qu'ils montrerent assez qu'ils n'en faisoient pas grand cas;... Aussi voyons-nous que l'Empereur Caligula se vantoit publiquement que sa mere estoit venuë de l'inceste commis par Auguste avec sa fille Livia; et quant à luy, *cum omnibus sororibus suis stupri consuetudinem fecit.* L'Empereur Claudius ayant espousé sa niepce Agrippine, les incestes furent permis par authorité du Senat. Et nous sommes contraints d'advoüer que ce qui est inceste aujourd'hy, estoit innocence à la naissance du monde. Les voyages d'Americ Vespuce nous ont appris, qu'en toutes les Indes Occidentales il n'y avoit aucune acception de parenté pour cela. Marc Polo soustient le mesme des Indes d'Orient. Et les Druses du Liban vivent encores aujourd'huy de la sorte. Pour ce qui est de ce pretendu respect des animaux, les chiens, les chats, et autres semblables nous montrent journellement le contraire. Aussi Aristote s'est contredit luy-mesme, advoüant que, *equi vel suas matres et filias superveniunt.* D'ailleurs, quelqu'un à qui on faisoit cette objection, *non sic amant bestiae*, se contenta de respondre, *neque enim Philosophantur.* Ce sont des revers de la medaille.[20]

[20] 'Orasius Tubero', *Quatre dialogues faits à l'imitation des anciens* (Frankfurt, 1506), pp. 121–4 (with marginal references omitted). As well as appearing pseudonymously, Le Vayer's dialogues were originally published with false dates. The probable date of the edition cited (in which '1506' seems, in any case, a misprint for '1606') is 1632 or 1633. See René Pintard, *La Mothe Le Vayer – Gassendi – Guy Patin: Études de bibliographie et de critique suivies de textes inédits de Guy Patin*, Publications de l'Université de Poitiers, Série des sciences de l'homme, 5 (Paris, 1943), p. 13. On Charron, Le Vayer, and the post-Montaignian sceptical tradition in France, see Alan M. Boase, *The Fortunes of Montaigne: A History of the Essays in France, 1580–1669* (London, 1935).

(And yet, many people have considered it acceptable to combine the chains of love and kinship, since 'two bonds are better than one', and as Ovid says, 'they say there are peoples among whom mother mates with son, and daughter with father, and piety increases by the double tie of love'. Thus the Ancient Chaldeans allowed men to marry their mothers and daughters, as Sotion of Alexandria reports . . . Thus Chrysippus in his *Politics* was unperturbed by relations with a mother, a sister or a daughter . . . On that basis, Periander, one of the seven sages of Greece, had no scruples about having intercourse with his mother Cratea. The Angles, according to Caesar, had the same attitude regarding their sisters and daughters. 'The Hiberni lay openly with their mothers and sisters,' says Strabo, insisting that the same applies to the Persian Magi with their mothers, and the Egyptians with their sisters, as is amply attested by the evidence of the Mausoleum and Obelisks, and in another place he adds the same point with regard to the Arabs. The Romans were more perturbed by this sort of incest, yet even they gave it a relatively mild name, indicating that they did not take it very seriously: . . . Thus we see that the Emperor Caligula boasted in public that his mother was the result of incest committed by Augustus with his daughter Livia, and he himself 'lived in habitual incest with all his sisters'. When the Emperor Claudius married his niece Agrippina, their incest was authorised by the Senate. We are thus constrained to admit that what is incest today was considered innocent at the dawn of the world. The voyages of Amerigo Vespucci have taught us that the West Indies had no sense of kinship in this respect, Marco Polo makes the same claim for the East Indies, and the Druses of Lebanon live in the same manner to this day. Concerning the alleged respect demonstrated by animals, we are daily shown the opposite by dogs, cats and other species. Thus Aristotle, contradicting his own statement, admitted that 'horses mount their own mothers and sisters'. Moreover, someone to whom the objection was made that 'beasts don't love in this way' made no more reply than that 'they do not philosophize either'. These are two sides of the same coin.)[21]

Dryden, as we have seen, took such arguments very seriously, and gave them much imaginative extension in his version. In this respect, by the side of translator-predecessors for whom scriptural indictments of incest weighed more heavily than they seem to have done for professing Christians like Montaigne, Charron, and Le Vayer, and who were thus rendered incapable of portraying Myrrha's plight with any real sympathy, Dryden can be seen to have been strikingly uninhibited by his Christianity. But he did bring to the poem an

[21] Translation by Edward Forman.

interest which can be thought of as deriving, however subtly and indirectly, from his own faith. Ovid, despite his feeling for Myrrha, was never merely dismissive of the older Roman notions of 'pietas' and the Ciceronian idea of the 'naturae nomen et iura' (name and laws of nature). Dryden introduces a thought into his version which goes subtly beyond anything to be found in Ovid's text in giving to his Myrrha, when expressing her revulsion at the feelings she recognizes within her, terms which inevitably have a charge that derives from the Christian tradition.

Dryden seems, on the evidence of this translation, to have seen the human mind as operating, as it were, on three levels. Beneath the habitual surface layer, he suggests (the codes and conventions which we sometimes, improperly, think of as embodiments of Natural Law), lie powerful desires which are quite at odds with that 'Law', yet still perfectly deserving of the name 'human':

> Too busie Senates, with an over-care
> To make us better than our Kind can bear,
> Have dash'd a Spice of Envy in the Laws,
> And straining up too high, have spoil'd the Cause.
>
> (54–7)

This is the area so boldly and acutely exposed in the writings of Freud and of Montaigne and the French sceptics. But beneath that layer is a deeper one still, a tendency of the human mind (or, as Dryden significantly puts it, 'soul'), its mysterious and – one cannot avoid the word – 'natural' compulsion to recognize certain sanctions, distinctions, and categories, and to recoil in revulsion when those sanctions are threatened or abandoned.

Earlier, when quoting his version of Myrrha's complaint against the restricting laws which are laid on mankind, I commented on the vigorous manner in which Dryden had rendered Myrrha's lament that it was merely because of arbitrary prescriptions that Man is barred from the earthy promiscuous sexuality in which the animals can freely indulge. But as well as alerting us there to the similarity between human and animal sexuality, Dryden is able, like Ovid, to bring home simultaneously – in a way that Myrrha herself does not seem to realize – what an entirely different sexual world mankind and the animals inhabit:

> The Hen is free to wed the Chick she bore,
> And make a Husband, whom she hatch'd before.
> (47–8)

Despite his harsh words in the Preface to *Fables* about Ovid's inappropriate use of wit 'in strong Passions',[22] Dryden has, in fact, heightened the rhetorical patterning of Myrrha's speech, adding witty 'turns' of his own to complement those already existing in Ovid's Latin.[23] In the lines just quoted, the alliteration on 'Husband/hatch'd' produces something of the effect of an Ovidian 'turn on the words'. A more direct imitation of Ovid's distinctive stylistic trait occurs when Dryden's Myrrha remarks that 'the Perverseness' of her 'Fate' 'is such'

> That he's not mine, because he's mine too much:
> (71)

A few lines later, she longs to 'travel to some Foreign Shore':

> So might I to my self my self restore;
> (78)

In so doing, she thinks, her mind might remove her 'impious Thoughts',

> And ceasing to behold, might cease to love.
> (80)

The accumulation of antitheses, heightened by Dryden's additions, can be seen to serve a positive function in holding us at some distance from Myrrha's passion, while simultaneously focusing us on the paradoxical aspects of her plight.

It is only because the reader's mind is kept so subtly poised, in a way that would be impossible in a more realistic treatment, that Dryden is able without any sense of strain or contradiction – despite

[22] See *Works*, 7. 32–3, and, for further discussion, Chapter 7 below.

[23] Dryden discusses the 'Elegant turns, either on the words or thought' that characterize Ovid's style in the 'Discourse Concerning... Satire' prefixed to his translation of Juvenal and Persius (1692, dated 1693). See *Works*, 4. 84–6, and, for discussion of Dryden's examples, *Poems*, 3. 441–5. For the play of wit in Ovid's original, see Garth Tissol, *The Face of Nature: Wit, Narrative, and Cosmic Origin in Ovid's* Metamorphoses (Princeton NJ, 1997), pp. 36–42. For Dryden's expansions of Ovidian wit in general, see Garth Tissol, 'Dryden's Additions and the Interpretive Reception of Ovid', *Translation and Literature*, 13 (2004), 181–93.

the daring transitions in thought – to allow Myrrha to use vocabulary with a serious charge from his own religion when she is voicing her doubts about the feelings which possess her. The train of thought is subtly prepared throughout her soliloquy. Near the beginning she implores the 'sacred Laws' to 'defend' her 'Soul' (36). The animals, she realizes, have no 'Thoughts of Sin' to 'disturb their Peace of mind' (51). If she achieves her wishes she recognizes that she will be breaking 'all Statutes Humane and Divine' (85). But the full expression of the thought is retained for the end of the speech:

> But thou in time th' increasing Ill controul,
> Nor first debauch the Body by the Soul;
> Secure the sacred Quiet of thy Mind,
> And keep the Sanctions Nature has design'd.
>
> (94–7)

The reader steeped in Dryden's other works will be aware that the notion of the 'quiet mind' had often been invested by the poet elsewhere with a special depth and weight.[24] But such knowledge is not necessary to appreciate the charge of significance generated by Dryden's using the epithet 'sacred' to characterize what Myrrha feels she will be losing and violating in succumbing to her passion.

Related thoughts are touched upon at the important moment when the nurse returns from her mission to Cinyras:

> Pleas'd with her Charge perform'd, she hies her home,
> And gratulates the Nymph, the Task was overcome.
> *Myrrha* was joy'd the welcome News to hear;
> But clogg'd with Guilt, the joy was unsincere:
> So various, so discordant is the Mind,
> That in our Will, a diff'rent Will we find.
>
> (256–61)

The last two lines of that quotation (one of those 'penetrating remarks on human nature' for which Samuel Johnson thought Dryden 'seems to have been peculiarly formed')[25] have no direct equivalent in the Latin, and provide strong confirmation that Dryden

[24] See the note on l. 51 of 'Cinyras and Myrrha' in Dryden, *Poems*, 5. 270.

[25] See Samuel Johnson, *The Lives of the Most Eminent English Poets*, ed. Roger Lonsdale, 4 vols. (Oxford, 2006), 2. 130.

thought that he had found in Ovid's Myrrha story a profound exploration of the contradictions and cross-currents working away in the obscurer regions of the human mind.

One's sense of the depth and mastery of Dryden's handling of the relationship between incest and Natural Law in the Myrrha translation is confirmed by a glance at his presentation of similar subjects in earlier works. He had touched on the subject of incestuous passion on five previous occasions, all but one of them in his writings for the stage. In the heroic play *Aureng-Zebe* the wicked Empress Nourmahal had made a direct declaration of her passion for her son, the noble Aureng-Zebe. In *Oedipus* (1679; written in collaboration with Lee) the hero had lamented the confusion of relationships brought about by his acts. In the letter of Canace to Macareus, included in the composite translation of *Ovid's Epistles* (1680), Canace had confessed her incestuous love for her brother. The subject of incest is also treated by Dryden in two of his later plays. In *Don Sebastian* (1690) the hero discovers that he has unwittingly married his half-sister, Almeyda. Consumed with remorse, Sebastian becomes an anchorite and Almeyda takes the veil. In *Love Triumphant* (1694) Alphonso, consumed with passion for Victoria whom he believes (falsely, as it turns out) to be his sister, finds a parallel for his own predicament in the situation of Canace and Macareus and quotes from Dryden's 1680 translation to console himself.

In two of these works the treatment of the incest theme is so different from that of the Myrrha translation that they need not occupy us long. In both *Don Sebastian* and *Oedipus* the central incestuous act is committed unwittingly. To be sure, Sebastian and Oedipus both lament, in a way broadly similar to Myrrha, the fact that incest confuses the very names by which human relationships are expressed. Sebastian also makes a passing reference (5. 1. 629) to the fact that incest is a violation of 'Laws Divine, and Humane' which do not apply in the animal world, and expresses a desire to hide from the rest of mankind in the deserts of Africa, which are 'wide enough to hold / Millions of Monsters' (5. 1. 550–1; perhaps a momentary reminiscence of the Myrrha story).[26] But in neither play is Dryden much concerned with the larger exploration of the problems inherent in incestuous love which is so central to the translation.

[26] The specific mention of 'deserts' perhaps suggests that Dryden's mind is on the Myrrha story as much as on the contemporary and proverbial treatments of African monsters cited in *Works*, 15. 428.

In *Love Triumphant* the feelings of Alphonso and Victoria turn out in the end not to be incestuous at all. But even when they think that they are in the grip of an 'unnatural' passion, Dryden makes the lovers express their predicament not in a manner which impresses upon us the acuteness of their dilemma but by a series of stagey antitheses, where neither element is invested with any of the power of the contradictions which fight in Myrrha's mind:

> *Victo.* Incendiary Book, polluted Flame,
> Dare not to tempt the Chaste *Victoria*'s Fame.
> I love, perhaps, more than a Sister shou'd:
> And Nature prompts; but Heav'n restrains my Blood.
> Heav'n was unkind, to set so strict a Bound:
> And Love wou'd struggle to forbidden Ground.
> Oh let us gain a *Parthian* Victory;
> Our only way to conquer, is to fly.
>
> (2. 1. 68–75; *Works*, 16. 196)

In this speech, and in the whole scene from which it comes, Dryden is merely toying with the issues which are fully focused in the translation, in order to create for his audience a vague aura of languishing and illicit (or pseudo-illicit) passion without investing any real imaginative capital in his presentation of either the characters or their situation. The slackness of his hold on his material comes out most clearly in the string of clichés and posturings which make up Alphonso's final speech:

> *Alph.* Oh Raging, Impious, and yet hopeless Fire;
> Not daring to possess what I desire:
> Condemn'd to suffer what I cannot bear;
> Tortur'd with Love, and Furious with Despair.
> Of all the Pains which wretched Mortals prove,
> The fewest Remedies belong to Love:
> But ours has none: for if we should enjoy,
> Our fatal Cure must both of us destroy.
> Oh Dear *Victoria*, cause of all my Pain!
> Oh dear *Victoria*, whom I would not gain!
> *Victoria*, for whose sake I would survive:
> *Victoria*, for whose sake I dare not live.
>
> (2. 1. 102–13; *Works*, 16. 197)

'Languishing and illicit passion' also gives a fair indication of Dryden's interest in the incest theme in his epistle of Canace. By concentrating in that poem so exclusively on Canace's feelings, rather than exploring those larger Laws of Nature which prompted the feelings in the first place, Dryden has paradoxically prevented the reader from having any appreciation of Canace's emotional state beyond the level of prurient male fantasy. This comes out most clearly in a passage which is substantially Dryden's addition to Ovid's original. Canace is recalling the moment when she declared her incestuous passion for her brother. The revealing note is the uneasy blend of sighing regret and gloating gush with which Dryden has invested Canace's words:

> Forc'd at the last, my shameful pain I tell:
> And, oh, what follow'd we both know too well!
> 'When half denying, more than half content,
> 'Embraces warm'd me to a full consent:
> 'Then with Tumultuous Joyes my Heart did beat,
> 'And guilt that made them anxious, made them great.
>
> (37–42; *Works*, 1. 121)

It is significant that this is the very passage quoted by Alphonso and Victoria in *Love Triumphant.*

Of all the treatments of incest before 'Cinyras and Myrrha', it is only in *Aureng-Zebe* that Dryden makes more than momentary attempts to open out the larger speculative questions which the subject provokes and which are so searchingly explored in the translation. In the scene where Nourmahal declares her passion for Aureng-Zebe to her favourite slave Zayda, Zayda protests to her mistress in terms which in some respects anticipate Myrrha's revulsion at her feelings:

> *Zay.* Though all th'Idea's you can form be true,
> He must not, cannot be possess'd by you.
> If contradicting int'rests could be mixt,
> Nature her self has cast a bar betwixt.
> And, ere you reach to this incestuous Love,
> You must Divine and Humane Rights remove.
>
> (3. 1. 348–53; *Works*, 12. 202–3)

Nourmahal's reply similarly anticipates some of Myrrha's sense of the inexorable power of passion and of the difference which names make in matters of love:

> Why was that fatal knot of Marriage ti'd,
> Which did, by making us too near, divide?
> Divides me from my Sex! for Heav'n, I find
> Excludes but me alone of Woman-kind.
> I stand with guilt confounded, lost with shame,
> And yet made wretched onely by a name.
> If names have such command on humane Life,
> Love sure's a name that's more Divine than Wife.
> That Sovereign power all guilt from action takes,
> At least the stains are beautiful it makes.
>
> (3. 1. 360–9; *Works*, 12. 203)

Later, in her scene with Aureng-Zebe, Nourmahal defends her passion by a direct appeal to Natural Law:

> *Nour.* Custom our Native Royalty does awe;
> Promiscuous Love is Nature's general Law:
> For whosoever the first Lovers were,
> Brother and Sister made the second Pair,
> And doubled, by their love, their piety.
>
> (4.1. 131–5; *Works*, 12. 213)

In writing *Aureng-Zebe*, Dryden was clearly turning over in his mind some of the issues and problems which were to fascinate him over twenty years later when making the Myrrha translation. But in the play his treatment of these matters remains partial and embryonic, and lacks the depth and artistic cogency which is so evident in the translation. The verse of *Aureng-Zebe*, though far superior to that of *Love Triumphant*, has (as my quotations will confirm) little of that sustained rhythmical assurance, wit, and range of implication which are to be found almost everywhere in 'Cinyras and Myrrha'. Nourmahal, moreover, is a grotesquely unsympathetic figure, and partly because of that, and partly because they occur in a play where far-fetched reversals of fortune and tedious plot-manoeuvrings take up so much attention, her general reflections tend to sound in context more like sonorous platitudes, unconvinced and unconvincing, than propositions with a real power to impress or disturb.

Dryden seems to have found in the format of the Ovidian narrative fable the opportunity both to focus the reader's mind more concentratedly on the essential issues and their implications and to allow a more subtle and diverse play of mind over the complexities of the subject than he had ever found possible in his dramatic handlings of similar material or in the epistolary form of the *Heroides*. The challenge of rendering the Myrrha episode, it appears, forced Dryden to probe more deeply into matters which had interested him for a long time but which he had hitherto been able to treat with only limited artistic success. In searching out what he took to be the essential meaning of Ovid's tale, Dryden was simultaneously perfecting his own art and handling the subject of incestuous passion with a wit, range, economy, depth, and unsalacious sympathy which went far beyond anything he had achieved in this area hitherto.

In his Preface to *Fables*, Dryden wrote that Ovid (like Chaucer) 'understood the Manners; under which Name I comprehend the Passions'.[27] In a famous passage, René Rapin, one of Dryden's favourite contemporary literary critics, had described 'the Manners' thus:

> The *Manners* are, as it were, the first *springs* of all humane *actions*... the Poet represents the *minds* of Men by their *Manners*:... The sovereign Rule for treating of *Manners*, is to copy them after *Nature*, and above all to study well the *heart* of Man, to know how to distinguish all its motions. 'Tis this which none are acquainted with: the heart of man is an *abyss*, where none can sound the bottom: it is a *mystery*, which the most quick sighted cannot pierce into, and in which the most cunning are mistaken.[28]

In his Myrrha episode, Dryden seems to have thought, Ovid had shown himself to be one of those rare spirits gifted with insight into these mysterious regions. In his own rendering of that episode Dryden was inspired to produce an English poem which not only far surpasses his earlier handlings of similar themes but also rivals, and perhaps in some respects even transcends, its Latin original.

[27] *Works*, 7. 31.

[28] René Rapin, *Reflections on Aristotle's Treatise of Poesie*, trans. Thomas Rymer (London, 1674), pp. 36–8.

# 8

# Dryden and Ovid's 'Wit out of Season': 'The Twelfth Book of Ovid his *Metamorphoses*' and 'Ceyx and Alcyone'

One of the oldest and most persistent of the charges which have been levelled against the Ovid of the *Metamorphoses* is that the poet trivializes his depictions of pain, anxiety, and suffering by prolixity, by a callous impassivity, and by displays of tastelessly inappropriate wit. Again and again in the poem acts of violence and destruction are treated by Ovid with fanciful playfulness, and characters in the extremity of distress are made to burst into puns, epigrams, or strings of obtrusive rhetorical figures. This habit, it is alleged, reveals Ovid's essential frigidity and frivolousness, his lack of sensitivity to human suffering, and his 'Alexandrian' weakness for the display of his own verbal brilliance, whatever the demands of his subject.

The first recorded instances of such criticisms occur in the work of a commentator who had known Ovid personally. In his *Controversiae* the elder Seneca (who had been an eye-witness of the poet's declamations in Arellius Fuscus' rhetorical school) commented on Ovid's propensity to proliferate to a fault the brilliant verbal formulations of which he was so fond.[1] The example which Seneca cites is taken from an incident which Ovid narrates in Book 13 of the *Metamorphoses*, and which had been one of the subjects of Euripidean tragedy. Troy has fallen, and the Trojan women are now prisoners of the Greeks. The ghost of Achilles has appeared and demanded the sacrifice of

[1] See *Controversiae*, 2. 2. 8–12, in Seneca the Elder, *Declamations*, ed. M. Winterbottom, 2 vols. (Cambridge MA and London, 1974), 1. 259–65.

Polyxena, Hecuba's daughter. The ritual slaughter has been performed and Hecuba is lamenting her lot. Achilles when alive, she says, had killed her sons and laid her city waste. Now, when she had finally thought herself safe from his malign power, the Greek hero has spoken from the grave to wreak yet more havoc on her family:

> cinis ipse sepulti
> in genus hoc pugnat.
>
> (Even the ashes of the buried man fight our family.)

This comment, says Seneca, would have sufficed to convey Hecuba's sentiments eloquently and pointedly, but Ovid has the Queen go on: 'tumulo quoque sensimus hostem' (We have felt our enemy, even in his grave)... and on – this time with a grisly fancy and a display of obtrusive alliteration: 'Aeacidae fecunda fui' (I was fertile – for Achilles). Seneca comments:

> Aiebat autem Scaurus rem veram: non minus magnam virtutem esse scire dicere quam scire desinere.
>
> ([The orator] Scaurus was quite right in saying that to know how to stop is as important a quality as to know how to speak.)[2]

Quintilian, too, criticized Ovid for being 'lascivus' (extravagant, frivolous) in the higher genres of poetry, where more seriousness was required, and for being 'nimium amator ingenii sui' (unduly enamoured of his own gifts).[3] And the younger Seneca, in his *Naturales Quaestiones*, commented, in the course of some speculations of his own about the destruction of the world by flood, that Ovid had, characteristically, ruined his own portrayal of the flood, undercutting those parts of his description in which he had effectively conveyed the grandeur and momentousness of the scene by descending 'ad pueriles ineptias' (to childish sillinesses). In depicting the wolf swimming among the sheep and the lions carried along by the waves, Seneca remarks, Ovid had exercised his imagination in ways which were irrelevant and distracting, rather than restricting his tone and treatment to an appropriately grave solemnity.[4] He had thus made the

[2] *Declamations*, 2. 324–5.
[3] Quintilian, *Institutio Oratoria*, ed. Donald A. Russell, 5 vols. (Cambridge MA and London, 2001), 4. 298.
[4] Ovid is here making deliberate play with Horace, *Ars Poetica*, 29–30.

flood seem paltry and absurd: 'Non est res satis sobria lascivire devorato orbe terrarum' (To make the annihilation of the world a subject for frivolity shows insufficient seriousness).[5]

The criticisms of Ovid voiced by Quintilian and the two Senecas were re-echoed, with minor additions and shifts of emphasis, down the centuries, so that, for example, Adrien Baillet's compilation of Renaissance and seventeenth-century testimonia on Ovid in his *Jugemens des Savans* (1685–6) consists, for the most part, of Roman sentiments re-expressed in modern terms. Ovid's works, say the critics cited by Baillet, for all their 'esprit' and 'facilité', lack 'règle' and 'mesure', and abound in 'des jeunesses', 'le mauvais goût', 'les faux brillans', and 'les superfluités'. The Roman and Renaissance criticisms of Ovid were reinforced by Romantic demands for 'seriousness', 'pathos', and 'sincerity' (in all of which Ovid was found conspicuously wanting)[6] and have thus survived to our own century.

The strength and persistence of the Roman objections to Ovid, together with the widespread familiarity with and affection for Ovid's works among educated readers, made it inevitable that Ovid should feature prominently in the critical debates of the seventeenth century about the role which verbal and imaginative exuberance and playfulness might properly play in dramatic, heroic, and lyric poetry.[7] These were debates in which John Dryden took a special interest, and to which he made frequent contributions in his critical prose.

In one of his earliest essays, the 'Account of the Ensuing Poem' prefixed to to *Annus Mirabilis* (1667), Dryden praised Ovid's depictions of his passionate heroines for precisely those qualities which had been denied by many critics, arguing that Ovid is so anxious to produce 'concernment' in the reader for his distressed ladies that

> his words . . . are the least part of his care, for he pictures Nature in disorder, with which the study and choice of words is inconsistent. This is the proper wit of Dialogue or Discourse, and, consequently, of the *Drama*, where all

[5] Seneca the Younger, *Naturales Quaestiones*, ed. T. H. Corcoran, 2 vols. (Cambridge MA and London, 1971–2), 1. 278–81.

[6] See Adrien Baillet, *Jugemens des savans sur les principaux ouvrages des auteurs*, 4 vols. (Paris, 1685–86), and the remarks of Johann Christian Jahn quoted and translated by W. S. Anderson in 'Playfulness and Seriousness in Ovid's *Metamorphoses*', *Mosaic*, 12. 1–2 (1981), 192–210.

[7] See G. Williamson, *The Proper Wit of Poetry* (London, 1951).

that is said is to be suppos'd the effect of sudden thought; which, though it excludes not the quickness of wit in repartees, yet admits not a too curious election of words, too frequent allusions, or use of Tropes, or, in fine, any thing that showes remoteness of thought, or labour in the Writer.

(*Works*, 1. 53–4)

But by the time he came to write the Preface to Tonson's composite version of *Ovid's Epistles* (1680), Dryden, while still maintaining much of his earlier admiration for Ovid's portrayal of women in love, had moved significantly closer to the 'Roman' view:

the copiousness of his Wit was such, that he often writ too pointedly for his Subject, and made his persons speak more Eloquently than the Violence of their Passion would admit: so that he is frequently witty out of season: leaving the Imitation of Nature, and the cooler dictates of his Judgment, for the false applause of Fancy.

(*Works*, 1. 112)

Dryden went on to reiterate the Roman criticisms of Ovid at various points in his later prose, and nowhere more memorably than in the Preface to his last volume, *Fables Ancient and Modern* (1700). There, having expressed a general preference for the poetry of Chaucer over that of Ovid, he remarked:

The Vulgar Judges, which are Nine Parts in Ten of all Nations, who call Conceits and Jingles Wit, who see *Ovid* full of them, and *Chaucer* altogether without them, will think me little less than mad, for preferring the *English-man* to the *Roman*: Yet, with their leave, I must presume to say, that the Things they admire are only glittering Trifles, and so far from being Witty, that in a serious Poem they are nauseous, because they are unnatural. Wou'd any Man who is ready to die for Love, describe his Passion like *Narcissus*? Wou'd he think of *inopem me copia fecit*, and a Dozen more of such Expressions, pour'd on the Neck of one another, and signifying all the same Thing? If this were Wit, was this a Time to be witty, when the poor Wretch was in the Agony of Death? This is just *John Littlewit* in *Bartholomew Fair*, who had a Conceit (as he tells you) left him in his Misery; a miserable Conceit. On these Occasions the Poet shou'd endeavour to raise Pity: but instead of this, *Ovid* is tickling you to laugh.

If Ovid had been called upon to write Arcite's dying speech in Chaucer's *Knight's Tale*, Dryden speculates,

He would certainly have made *Arcite* witty on his Death-bed. He had complain'd he was farther off from Possession, by being so near, and a thousand such Boyisms, which *Chaucer* rejected as below the Dignity of the Subject.

(*Works*, 7. 32–3)[8]

Dryden here alludes silently to a specific example of Ovid's wit-in-a-serious-circumstance which he had himself recently translated,[9] and endorses the Roman verdict on Ovid to the letter. The 'Boyisms' of the Preface to *Fables* are the direct descendants of the younger Seneca's 'pueriles ineptiae'.

It is, however, a striking fact that, in the very translations from the Preface to which these remarks are quoted, Dryden, far from attempting to play down or expunge Ovid's 'Boyisms', renders them with verve, skill, and uninhibited relish. As so often, Dryden's stated critical position stands in a complex relation to his poetic practice. In the last chapter, some suggestions were made about the function which Dryden seems to have thought Ovid's distinctive wit played in the soliloquy of the tormented Myrrha. This chapter will explore further the qualities in Ovid's witty, playful, or aloof handlings of 'serious' situations which undermined Dryden's conscious defences and caused him, when exercising his art, to delight in aspects of the Roman poet's work which, as a critic, he felt obliged to deplore.

Two of the translations in *Fables* offer themselves as appropriate test cases for such a further investigation. Modern commentators have been almost universal in their condemnation of the long passage in Book 12 of the *Metamorphoses* which depicts the battle between the Lapiths and the Centaurs, and the terms of the critics' disapproval show them as true heirs of the Roman tradition. The episode has been called 'tedious and otiose', and even 'repulsive'. Critics have seen in it an 'ingenious gruesomeness' and have condemned it for its

[8] Joseph Addison closely echoed Dryden's remarks about Ovid's treatment of Narcissus in the notes to his translation of Book 3 of the *Metamorphoses* in *Poetical Miscellanies: the Fifth Part* (London, 1704), 591. For the possibility that Addison's notes may pre-date Dryden's remarks, see *Poems*, 5. 65.

[9] See 'Cinyras and Myrrha', 72–3: 'Our Kindred-Blood debars a better Tie; / He might be nearer, were he not so nigh.' For discussion, see Chapter 6.

'succession of *outré* killings' and its 'lurid and suggestive detail which today is the hallmark of reporting on capital crime in the tabloid press'. Ovid has been thought to have been 'revelling' in this episode 'in ever new ways of imagining how bodies can be mangled, maimed and disintegrated'.[10] Dryden, however, praises the passage strongly, remarking in the headnote to his complete translation of Book 12 that '*The Fight of* Achilles *and* Cygnus, *and the Fray betwixt the* Lapythae *and* Centaurs, *yield to no other part of this Poet*' (*Works*, 7. 406).

The story of Ceyx and Alcyone from Book 11, unlike the episode of the Lapiths and Centaurs, has been warmly praised by several modern scholars and has been, down the ages, one of the most frequently excerpted and imitated of all the tales in the *Metamorphoses*.[11] But even here the critical verdict has been mixed. Georges Lafaye, the translator of the *Metamorphoses* for the Budé series, charged Ovid with displaying 'mauvais goût' (bad taste) in his description of Ceyx's drowning and in Alcyone's lament for her dead husband, and a recent English commentator on Book 11 has accused the poet of having undercut 'the pathos of his own narrative by pursuing fancy to the brink of the preposterous', of having allowed his interest in 'the setting' to 'distract from the tragedy itself', and of having depicted the last moments of Ceyx 'mercilessly', allowing his 'visual realism'... 'to puncture a general effect of dignified pathos'.[12] Yet Dryden's version of the episode shows him to have lavished all his poetic skill on emulating precisely those qualities in his original which are singled out for particular censure by the modern critics.

[10] See Brooks Otis, *Ovid as an Epic Poet* (2nd edition, Cambridge, 1970), p. 281; H. Fränkel, *Ovid: A Poet Between Two Worlds* (Berkeley and Los Angeles CA, 1956), p. 232; L. P. Wilkinson, *Ovid Recalled* (Cambridge, 1955), p. 168; Otis, *Ovid as an Epic Poet*, p. 39; G. K. Galinsky, *Ovid's 'Metamorphoses': An Introduction to the Basic Aspects* (Oxford, 1975), p. 137.

[11] See particularly Otis, *Ovid as an Epic Poet*, pp. 331–61, 421–3. Galinsky, *Ovid's 'Metamorphoses'* (pp. 146–6) sees the main pleasure to be had from the piece as that of a connoisseur for a bravura display of literary parody, though he also comments very appreciatively (p. 146) on Ovid's distinctive blend of lightness and seriousness in his handling of Ceyx and Alcyone's love, calling it (p. 159) 'a humor which does not mean to wound or hurt but keeps just the right equilibrium between detached amusement and sympathy'.

[12] See G. Lafaye, ed., *Ovide: les Métamorphoses*, 3 vols. (Paris, 1928–30), 3. 21, 25; G. M. Murphy, ed., *Ovid: Metamorphoses, Book XI* (Oxford, 1972), pp. 71–2.

An examination of Dryden's renderings of these two episodes would thus seem to provide a particularly useful basis for a further attempt to comprehend, and thus perhaps to share, some of the English poet's pleasure in the distinctively Ovidian handling of violence and pain.

Modern scholars have offered various explanations of Ovid's poetic intent in the episode of the Lapiths and Centaurs. Some have seen the passage as having been written out of, and designed to appeal to, the 'lurid curiosity for novel kinds of agony' characteristic of a society whose favourite entertainment was gladiatorial combat.[13] Others have attempted to explain the episode's appeal to the Roman intelligentsia by drawing analogies with the penchant displayed by some twentieth-century sophisticates for 'the spattering of blood and brains and furniture' in the 'Spaghetti Western'.[14] Others, again, have seen the whole of the later books of the *Metamorphoses* as an attempt on Ovid's part to bring his longest poem to an 'Augustan' culmination by concentrating on deeds of arms (an attempt for which, they say, he was temperamentally unsuited, and which therefore failed),[15] or conversely have seen the 'lurid' and 'grotesque' elements in the later books as a deliberate attempt at '*anti*-Augustanism': a parody or *reductio ad absurdum* of epic combat which wickedly subverts the heroic ideals embraced by Augustus and Maecenas.[16] This last group of critics has stressed the obtrusively 'literary' quality of the final section of the *Metamorphoses* – Ovid's deployment for his own very different purposes of subject matter and language which his audience would immediately recognize from other (chiefly Homeric and Virgilian) contexts. A further group of commentators, while similarly stressing the allusiveness of the later books, has held that this practice constituted, itself, the *raison d'être* of these sections of the poem: Ovid, they say, was parodying, inverting, and varying the epic material with which his sophisticated

[13] Fränkel, *Ovid*, p. 102; see also Galinsky, *Ovid's 'Metamorphoses'*, pp. 126–8 and G. Lafaye, *Les Métamorphoses d'Ovide et leurs modèles grecs* (Paris, 1904), p. 117.

[14] O. S. Due, *Changing Forms: Studies in the Metamorphoses of Ovid*, Classica et Mediaevalia: Dissertations x (Copenhagen, 1974), p. 148.

[15] See, for example, the first edition of Otis (Cambridge, 1966).

[16] See, for example, the second edition of Otis, and R. Coleman, 'Structure and Intention in the *Metamorphoses*', *Classical Quarterly*, 21 (1971), 461–77.

readers were already familiar, his primary intention being to produce a 'purely literary' pleasure and to turn attention onto the virtuosity of the narrator himself, rather than to reorientate his audience's perceptions of the human situations and problems with which epic literature deals.[17]

But none of these responses seems to account for the particular kinds of interest and pleasure which Dryden's translation shows him to have taken in the episode. The version clearly demonstrates Dryden's sense of the sophistication and control exercised by Ovid throughout Book 12, a control quite incompatible with neurotic or depraved blood-lust. Dryden does not seem to have detected any ideological purpose in the episode, nor did he make any consistent attempt to apply the passage to the politics of his own day.[18] He would have been little interested in poetry which was designed to display a 'purely literary' virtuosity. And he was not influenced by the allegorical interpretations which had seen the battle of the Lapiths and Centaurs as a solemn warning against the dire effects of wine and lust.[19]

Dryden's version of Book 12 of the *Metamorphoses* has, in fact, received little critical attention. Most accounts of the poet's work pass over the translation cursorily with, at most, a few (usually unenthusiastic) general remarks.[20] So it would seem necessary at this point to examine a number of short crucial passages, with a view to establishing some sense of the nature of Dryden's engagement with his

[17] See Galinsky, *Ovid's Metamorphoses*, and D. L. Arnaud, 'Aspects of Wit and Humor in Ovid's *Metamorphoses*' (Unpublished PhD dissertation, Stanford 1968).

[18] Despite an occasional local inclusion of a modern colouring in the rendering – for example, allusions to the violence of the Civil War and to Roman Catholic religious practices in 344–5.

[19] See, for example, Alexander Ross, *Mystagogus Poeticus* (2nd edition, London, 1648), pp. 55–7; P. Du-Ryer, *Les Métamorphoses d'Ovide... avec de nouvelles explications historiques, morales et politiques sur toutes les fables* (Brussels, 1677), p. 395; N. Renouard, *Les Métamorphoses d'Ovide... avec quinze discours contenant l'explication morale des fables* (Paris, 1640), p. 229; Natalis Comes, *Mythologiae* (Venice, 1567), p. 255; George Sandys, *Ovid's Metamorphosis, English'd, Mythologiz'd and Represented in Figures* (Oxford, 1632), pp. 418–19; *Shakespeare's Ovid: Being Arthur Golding's Translation of the Metamorphoses*, ed. W. H. D. Rouse (London 1904), p. 6.

[20] See, for example, Mark Van Doren, *John Dryden: A Study of his Poetry* (revised edition, Bloomington IN, 1963), p. 219; William Myers, *Dryden* (London, 1973), p. 185.

original at the detailed, local, level. It may then be possible to move to some more general suggestions about his interest in the imaginative potential of Ovid's battle.

The central section of Ovid's Twelfth Book (210–535 in the Latin, 292–705 in Dryden's version) depicts the carnage and destruction which ensues when one of the Centaurs, who have been invited as guests to the Thessalian wedding of Perithous and Hippodamia, attempts to rape the bride. Most of the lengthy passage is taken up with detailed descriptions of the maimings and deaths of various of the Centaurs and their opponents the Lapiths, culminating in the burial under an immense pile of logs of the invulnerable Caeneus, whose metamorphosis into a golden-feathered bird brings the episode to its close. One of the first to be maimed in the conflict is Grineus, a Centaur who has just hurled a huge altar stone into the midst of the Lapiths, instantly killing several of their number. The Lapith Exadius vows vengeance, and immediately seeks a means of putting his vow into effect:

> He look'd about, where on a Pine were spred
> The votive Horns of a Stags branching Head:
> At *Grineus* these he throws; so just they fly,
> That the sharp Antlers stuck in either Eye:
> Breathless and Blind he fell; with Blood besmear'd;
> His Eye-balls beaten out, hung dangling on his Beard.
>
> (374–9)

Dryden has been especially struck by the ordered precision with which the incident is narrated. The teller in the translation (as in the original) gives the impression of being entirely untroubled as he narrates Grineus' gruesome fate. There is mordant punning in Dryden's characterization of the antlers' flight as 'just': they effect the desired revenge for Grineus' initial crime and also strike so 'justly' (exactly) that both eyeballs are extruded by the single blow. The effect of clinical, impassive, observation is reinforced by the brisk, businesslike, step of line 377 ('That the sharp Antlers stuck in either Eye'). But the manner of narration is also flexible and leisurely enough to include a beautiful Miltonism ('a Stags branching Head'[21]) to

[21] Cf. *Paradise Lost*, 7. 471.

describe the majestic votive offering which has effected the atrocity, and the last two lines of the passage quoted are notable for their obtrusive alliterative patterning which, as well as adding force to the description, simultaneously reminds readers that they are being given not raw uncensored violence but material which has been carefully processed and fashioned by an artist's hand. Here Dryden offers an English analogue of the effect created in the Latin by the patterned deliberateness of Ovid's 'pars . . . pars' construction:

> eruiturque oculos. quorum pars cornibus haeret,
> pars fluit in barbam concretaque sanguine pendet.
>
> (269–70)

(And his eyeballs were gouged out. One of these stuck to the horn and the other rolled down upon his beard and hung there in a mass of clotted blood.)[22]

A little after the maiming of Grineus, Aphidas meets his fate:

> Amid the Noise and Tumult of the Fray,
> Snoring and drunk with Wine, *Aphidas* lay.
> Ev'n then the Bowl within his Hand he kept:
> And on a Bear's rough Hide securely slept.
> Him *Phorbas* with his flying Dart, transfix'd;
> Take thy next Draught, with *Stygian* Waters mix'd,
> And sleep thy fill, th'insulting Victor cry'd;
> Surpris'd with Death unfelt, the Centaur dy'd;
> The ruddy Vomit, as he breath'd his Soul,
> Repass'd his Throat; and fill'd his empty Bowl.
>
> (435–44)[23]

Here, if anywhere, we might have expected Dryden's translation to show the influence of moralistic readings of the episode as an indictment of drunken abandon. Yet he has followed Ovid in deliberately avoiding any censorious emphasis, and in stressing, rather, the peaceful oblivion of Aphidas' slumber and the consequent painlessness of

[22] In his commentary on Book 2 of the *Aeneid* (Oxford 1964), R. G. Austin comments that Ovid 'hideously develops' the idea in Virgil's l. 277.

[23] In ll. 435–6, Dryden reworks and develops Sandys: 'Vnwakened with the tumult of this fray / Dissolu'd in death-like sleep, *Aphidus* lay'.

his death. Though Dryden can incorporate an irony in the adverb 'securely' used to characterize Aphidas' sleeping (and in Phorbas' exhortation to him to 'sleep' – we might have expected 'drink' – his fill), the central detail around which he clearly thought Ovid had shaped his little scene was the way in which the bowl held in the sleeping Centaur's hand was conveniently at the ready to receive the blood which flowed from his throat at the point of death. Dryden has been struck by the way in which the Centaur's idle and accidental retention of the bowl has now provided a neat and apt receptacle for the 'ruddy Vomit'. The balanced antithesis of his last line mirrors Ovid's precise specification of the 'Vomit's' destination in the Latin ('inque . . . inque'):

> plenoque e gutture fluxit
> inque toros inque ipsa niger carchesia sanguis.
>
> (325–6)

(and from his full throat out upon the couch and into the very wine-cup the dark blood flowed.)

Ovid's treatment had stressed the bizarre incongruity of the event. But he had also observed a number of telling miscellaneous details in the imagined scene. He had noted, for example, the precise materials from which the death-dealing spear had been made. He had reminded readers of the potential pathos of the scene: the Centaur is a 'iuvenis' (323). A beautiful Greek-derived poetic plural ('carchesia') had been used to describe the drinking vessel into which Aphidas' blood was disgorged. Even the fabulous origin (Mount Ossa) of the bearskin on which Aphidas lay had been noted. And the whole was shaped into a poetic entity by Ovid (in a way carefully imitated by Dryden) with subtle patterns of assonance and alliteration.

Towards the end of the battle, Ovid interjected a digression depicting 'the Loves and Death of *Cyllarus* and *Hylonome*, the Male and Female Centaur', which Dryden singled out as 'wonderfully moving' (*Works*, 7. 406). Cyllarus, a particularly handsome Centaur, is loved by Hylonome, a beautiful Centaur 'Maiden'. Both have come to the wedding feast and both now fight side by side. Cyllarus is pierced by a stray spear and dies in the arms of his beloved, who then takes the weapon from her lover's heart and uses it to kill herself.

Commentators have often seen the description of Cyllarus' and Hylonome's love as providing attractive and welcome relief from the lengthy catalogue of slaughters which have preceded it.[24] Dryden responded to this change of mood and pace in Ovid's text, and also discovered in the passage an opportunity to explore one of his favourite poetic subjects – the similarities and differences between sexual love in the human and animal worlds. His initial description of Hylonome (like that in his original) contains lines which, if excerpted, could be taken for an evocation of a beautiful human maiden or a wood-nymph:

> ut sit coma pectine levis,
> ut modo rore maris, modo se violave rosave
> inplicet, interdum candentia lilia gestet,
> bisque die lapsis Pagasaeae vertice silvae
> fontibus ora lavet, bis flumine corpora tinguat.
>
> (409–13)

(so that her long locks are smoothed with a comb; now she twined rosemary, now violets or roses in her hair; and sometimes she wore white lilies. Twice each day she bathed her face in the brook that fell down from a wooded height by Pagasa, and twice dipped her body in the stream.)

> For him she dress'd: For him with Female Care
> She comb'd, and set in Curls, her auborn Hair.
> Of Roses, Violets, and Lillies mix'd
> And Sprigs of flowing Rosemary betwixt
> She form'd the Chaplet, that adorn'd her Front:
> In Waters of the *Pagasaean* Fount,
> And in the Streams that from the Fountain play,
> She wash'd her Face; and bath'd her twice a Day.
>
> (542–53)

And the couple's life together is even momentarily assimilated, in the English version, to the paradisal bliss of Milton's Adam and Eve:

[24] R. S. Lang, ed., *P. Ovidii Nasonis Metamorphoseon Liber XII* (Oxford, 1927), p. 65; *P. Ovidii Nasonis Opera, e textu Burmanni*, 5 vols. (Oxford 1826), 4. 286.

With equal Flame
They lov'd: Their *Sylvan* Pleasures were the same:
All day they hunted: And when Day expir'd,
Together to some shady Cave retir'd.

(554–7)[25]

Yet in both the original and the English version we are also never allowed to forget that the couple are half-horses. The description of Hylonome quoted above is prefixed in Ovid's text by the proviso:

haec et blanditiis et amando et amare fatendo
Cyllaron una tenet, cultu quoque, *quantus in illis*
esse potest membris.

(407–9, my italics)

(She, by her coaxing ways, by loving and confessing love, alone possessed Cyllarus; and by her toilet, too, *so far as such a thing was possible in such a form.*)

Dryden's version, though much gentler, offers essentially the same reminder:

*Hylonome*, for Features, and for Face
Excelling all the Nymphs of double Race:
Nor less her Blandishments, than Beauty move;
At once both loving and confessing Love.

(540–3)

Here Dryden has been careful to imitate Ovid's *polyptoton* ('et amando et amare fatendo') in his own version ('At once both loving and confessing Love'). The effect works both to reinforce the reader's sense of the intensity and frankness of Hylonome's affections, and simultaneously draws attention to the very incongruity involved in such feelings being displayed by a creature 'of double Race'. The poet makes no attempt to conceal his part in controlling the reader's response.

The constant reminders of the couple's (partial) horsiness allow both Ovid and Dryden to bring an unexpected blend of emotions

[25] Cf. *Paradise Lost*, 4. 720; 5. 137, 377.

into play in the reader's mind when the two Centaurs die. We remember, with equal force, the couple's devotion and beauty and the fact that this beauty is one in which 'the Beast was equal to the Man' (531). The vocabulary of Dryden's version exploits the age-old English reverence for equine splendour: Cyllarus has a 'Back proportion'd for the Seat', a brawny 'Chest' and a 'Coal-black' coat which 'shone' 'like Jet' (534–6). At the moment of the couple's death, the English version incorporates two strokes of wit, both of them characteristically 'Ovidian' but neither of them directly prompted by the Latin. When Cyllarus falls, mortally wounded, Hylonome rushes to him,

> And while her Hand the streaming Blood oppos'd,
> Join'd Face to Face, his Lips with hers she clos'd.
> Stiffled with Kisses, a sweet Death he dies.
>
> (566–8)

It is possible to detect a slight raise of the eyebrows in the very deliberateness with which the joining of faces and lips is described. Ovid, at the equivalent place in the original (425) seems, in saying that 'animae fugienti obsistere tentat' ([Hylonome] strove to hold from its passing the dying breath), to be alluding to the belief that one should catch the departing breath of a loved one with a kiss, and perhaps thus prevent death occurring, since a dying man's expiring breath carried his soul from his body.[26] Dryden redirects the fancy, suggesting that, in her anxiety to smother her lover with kisses, Hylonome was part cause of his death, which, nevertheless, was found sweet by Cyllarus because it was accompanied by her embraces.

The death of Hylonome herself is described thus by Ovid:

> telo, quod inhaeserat illi,
> incubuit moriensque suum conplexa maritum est.
>
> (427–8)

(She threw herself upon the spear which had pierced Cyllarus and fell in a dying embrace upon her lover.)

Dryden expands the moment considerably:

[26] *Opera, e textu Burmanni*, 4. 288; Lang, p. 67.

In madness of her Grief, she seiz'd the Dart
New-drawn, and reeking from her Lover's Heart;
To her bare Bosom the sharp Point apply'd;
And wounding fell; and falling by his Side,
Embrac'd him in her Arms; and thus embracing, dy'd.

(572–6)

The double *polyptoton* of the last two lines, plus the conclusion of the paragraph with a triplet plus an Alexandrine, gives Hylonome's end a conspicuously stylized cast. The effect is to concentrate and epitomize the ambivalent impressions which the Centaur-lovers have made from the start. Hylonome dies to a poetical flourish which simultaneously aggrandizes and, in its neatly patterned antitheses, distances us from her, allowing the reader to perceive the moment as both an impassioned *Liebestod* and a slightly melodramatic, almost 'hammy', gesture from a creature who is, after all, only half human.

A few lines after the suicide of Hylonome, the Centaur Phaeocomes kills the Lapith Tectaphos, son of Olenus:[27]

codice qui misso, quem vix iuga bina moverent,
Tectaphon Oneleniden a summo vertice fregit;
fracta volubilitas capitis latissima, perque os
perque cavas nares oculosque auresque cerebrum
molle fluit, veluti concretum vimine querno
lac solet utve liquor rari sub pondere cribri
manat et exprimitur per densa foramina spissus.

(432–8)

(Hurling a log which the combined force of two yokes of cattle could scarce move, he struck Tectaphos, the son of Olenus, a crushing blow upon the head. The broad dome of his head was shattered, and through his mouth, through the hollow nostrils, eyes, and ears oozed the soft brains, as when curdled milk drips through the oaken withes, or a thick liquid mass trickles through a coarse sieve weighted down, and is squeezed our through the crowded apertures.)

[27] The Lapith is called 'Phonolenides' ('the son of Phonolenus') in the seventeenth-century editions of Ovid used by Dryden, and in Sandys's translation. In modern texts, he is called 'Tectaphos Olenides' ('Tectaphos, son of Olenus'). Borchard Cnipping's edition gives 'Phololenides' ('the son of Phololenus') as a possible variant.

Dryden translates:

> He threw at *Pholon*; the descending Blow
> Divides the Skull, and cleaves his Head in two.
> The Brains, from Nose and Mouth, and either Ear
> Come issuing out, as through a Colendar
> The curdled Milk or from the Press the Whey
> Driv'n down by Weights above, is drain'd away.
>
> (585–90)

Ovid's lines have been much criticized. 'Res foeda', commented the editor of the Oxford Variorum Ovid of 1826 dryly, 'poterat sine similitudine transmitti' (The foul event could have been conveyed without a simile)[28] and the passage has been rejected from some editions of the *Metamorphoses*, one editor finding it 'totally unworthy of Ovid'.[29]

Though one of Dryden's editions informed him that the slaying of Tectaphus/Phonolenides did not appear in some manuscripts of the *Metamorphoses*, the poet may have recollected a passage in the *Fasti* where Ovid had used a similar image of whey being squeezed through a wickerwork sieve in the cheese-making process.[30] At any rate, he evidently regarded the simile (suitably tidied up and purged of the slight obscurities which have puzzled scholars) as very much in accord with the general spirit of the Lapiths and Centaurs episode. For there were other moments in Book 12 where Ovid had drawn the reader's attention to the precise physical laws which the processes of destroying living limbs, tissue, features, and bones in battle manifest in common with other, apparently totally dissimilar, activities and occurrences in the peacetime world.

Just as, earlier, Ovid (in Dryden's rendering) had likened the 'shriveling' 'crackle' of burning hair to 'dry Stubble fir'd' (386) and to the hissing of 'red hot Iron, within the Smithy drown'd' (390), and

[28] *Opera, e textu Burmanni*, 4. 289.

[29] Lang, p. 68; Franz Bömer, in his edition of Books 12–13 of the *Metamorphoses* (Heidelberg, 1982) questions (pp. 145–7) the lines' authenticity on the grounds that they do not appear in the best MSS, and that 438 contains a metrical irregularity. On the obscurities of the passage (which Bömer considers to have been overstressed), see Lang, p. 68.

[30] See Borchard Cnipping's note on l. 433; the 'parallel' passage is in *Fasti*, 4. 769–70.

had likened the firebrand with which Rhoetus had beaten Comoetes to a 'Lever' which 'drives the batter'd Skull, within the Brains' (401), so, here, the poet's attention is on the precise similarity of pressure and texture between crushed brains passing through the apertures of an impacted skull and the manner in which whey is extracted in cheese-making. No attempt whatever is made to encourage sympathy or fellow feeling with the Lapith on whom the action is being performed.

The point has now been reached where it may be possible to make some larger suggestions about the nature of Dryden's interest in the episode of the Lapiths and Centaurs as a whole. It might first be noted that Ovid took much care to establish a particular context for his battle, a context which Dryden, by rendering the whole of Book 12, was able to preserve intact. The story of the Lapiths and Centaurs is told, in a period of respite from the fighting round Troy, by the traditionally garrulous and aged Nestor, for the benefit of Achilles. Achilles in Ovid's narrative is not totally divested of his aura of Homeric heroism, but Ovid's treatment also allows the reader a certain amused delight in Achilles' boyish naiveté, and at the undignified situations in which he finds himself, particularly his exasperated attempts to defeat the invulnerable Cygnus. Nestor's tale, itself told in a legendary past, refers his audience to a yet more distant past (when he was in the second of the three centuries which, according to Ovid, he had lived so far) and deals with semi-mythical creatures in a semi-mythical and remote region of northern Greece. Before the narration of the battle even begins, therefore, the reader has been positioned at several stages removed from the conflict. And the narrative itself is constantly punctuated by reminders that the deaths and dismemberments which we are witnessing are of 'Brutes', 'Monsters', and 'Beasts', not of beings which too closely resemble any which we might expect to encounter in life. As we have seen, moreover, Ovid's style constantly serves to remind us, obtrusively, that we are experiencing a highly fashioned work of art, not attending to anything which could for a moment be confused with the world of day-to-day reality.

An advantage of this elaborate process of verbal and narrative distancing is that, once established, it allows the poet various kinds of freedom and flexibility in his depictions of violent fighting which might not have been possible if his readers' sympathies had been more straightforwardly and wholeheartedly engaged with the emotions and fortunes of the characters in the drama. Ovid's narrative allows readers to entertain thoughts about and attitudes towards human conflict which might not have been possible if human conflict had been his overt subject. We can, for example, focus, in this battle, on the sheer arbitrariness and inconsequentiality of much of what happens once any hand-to-hand fighting has commenced. Freed by his fantastic setting from any pressing obligation to pass moral judgement or to take sides, the poet can concentrate with scrupulous exactness and fascinated attention (but without gloating or attempting to produce vicarious thrills) on the precise physical processes involved in the disintegration of flesh and bone. He can register the curious resemblances between actions on the battlefield and other actions which the reader has seen or experienced in quite different regions of life. He can see symmetry and shape in actions which, looked at in almost any other conceivable frame of mind, would seem merely chaotic and confused. He can register the potential for beauty and humour and horror at one and the same moment in one and the same action, and his verbal wit and rhetorical patterning can be his means of containing and focusing these paradoxical responses.

The poetic stance adopted by Ovid in Book 12 might thus seem less simple-mindedly callous and less gratuitously tasteless than it appears at first sight. And the positive appeal of such a stance for a poet of Dryden's temperament is not difficult to appreciate. It has always been recognized that Dryden particularly relished poetic situations which enabled him to adopt an oblique, distanced, or analytical relation to his subject. And the sceptical attitude towards martial heroism which is such a prominent feature of his later writing[31] may have made him particularly well disposed towards an episode which, though many of its individual acts of violence have their parallels in the *Iliad* or *Aeneid*,[32] tends to concentrate on the

[31] See Michael West, 'Dryden's Ambivalence as a Translator of Heroic Themes', *Huntington Library Quarterly*, 36 (1972–73), 17–38; Cedric D. Reverand II, *Dryden's Final Poetic Mode: The* Fables (Philadelphia PA, 1988), pp. 24–35.

[32] With Ovid, 245–53 (Celadon's eyeballs extruded), cf. *Iliad*, 13. 616–17, 16. 740–2; with Ovid, 254–7 (Amycus spitting out blood and teeth), cf. *Aeneid*, 5. 470; with Ovid, 270–9 (Charaxus' hair set alight), cf. Aeneid, 12. 300–1; with Ovid, 293–5 (Evagrus speared through the mouth), cf. *Iliad*, 16. 346–50; with Ovid, 335–6 (Helops speared through both ears), cf. *Iliad*, 20. 472–4; with Ovid, 380–92 (Dorylas disembowelled), cf. *Iliad*, 21. 180–2.

ultimate weakness and insignificance of fighting men rather than, like Homer, viewing heroic combat as the moment which simultaneously asserts life's frightening vulnerability and its supreme preciousness and grandeur, or, like Virgil, seeing it as a painful but perhaps necessary means to the establishing of a great civilization.

Yet both Ovid's battle and Dryden's version are still open to serious objections, of a kind similar to those which Samuel Johnson levelled against the 'metaphysical' poets:

> they... wrote rather as beholders than partakers of human nature; as Beings looking upon good and evil, impassive and at leisure; as Epicurean deities making remarks on the actions of men, and the vicissitudes of life, without interest and without emotion.[33]

Ovid and Dryden, it can be objected, are using their mythological narrative to affect a godlike superiority to the painful dimensions of earthly life, a more-than-human view of humanity which ignores the poets' own participation and implication in the human condition, and which consequently strikes the reader as sub- rather than suprahuman.

Another of Johnson's criticisms of the metaphysical poets might also be pressed against Ovid's episode:

> Their attempts were always analytick: they broke every image into fragments: and could no more represent, by their slender conceits and laboured particularities the prospects of nature, or the scenes of life, than he, who dissects a sunbeam with a prism can exhibit the wide effulgence of a summer noon.[34]

In the battle of the Lapiths and Centaurs, Ovid and his English translator display an acute eye for the incongruous detail, the strange resemblances 'in things apparently unlike', the bizarre arbitrariness of the situation depicted, but these might seem to remain opportunist and isolated strokes, never connecting in the reader's mind so that they all appear to emanate from an imaginatively coherent general conception of life. They might seem, that is, never to attain what

[33] Samuel Johnson, *The Lives of the Most Eminent English Poets*, ed. Roger Lonsdale, 4 vols. (Oxford, 2006), 1. 201.

[34] *Lives*, 1. 201.

Johnson thought to be the characteristic quality of the best witty imaginings of poets: they never seem 'at once natural and new'.[35]

However, the impulse to write about human life from a standpoint in some ways resembling that of a god, looking down on humanity with a broader, more comprehensive, view than human beings can ordinarily attain, is not necessarily coldly sub-human or vainly and self-deludedly presumptuous. On two occasions Dryden published memorable renderings of famous moments in Latin poetry where the poet, or his persona, had imagined the pleasure of rising above the human condition to see it from a larger, and therefore more complete and truthful, vantage point. Dryden had begun his rendering of the opening of Lucretius' Second Book thus:

> 'Tis pleasant, safely to behold from shore
> The rowling Ship; and hear the Tempest roar:
> Not that anothers pain is our delight;
> But pains unfelt produce the pleasing sight.
> 'Tis pleasant also to behold from far
> The moving Legions mingled in the War:
> But much more sweet thy lab'ring steps to guide,
> To Vertues heights, with wisdom well supply'd,
> And all the Magazins of Learning fortifi'd:
> From thence to look below on humane kind,
> Bewilder'd in the Maze of Life, and blind.
>
> (1–11; *Works*, 3. 46)

And in his version of Pythagoras' discourse from Book 15 of the *Metamorphoses*, Dryden warmed to the Greek philosopher's desire

> To leave the heavy Earth, and scale the height,
> Of *Atlas*, who supports the heav'nly weight;
> To look from upper Light, and thence survey
> Mistaken Mortals wandring from the way
> And wanting Wisdom, fearful for the state
> Of future Things, and trembling at their Fate!
>
> ('Of the Pythagorean Philosophy', 215–30; *Works*, 7. 490)

The details of the speakers' positions in Dryden's two originals differ considerably. But his versions show that he saw affinities between the

[35] *Lives*, 1. 200.

Lucretian and Pythagorean desires to look down on mankind not 'without interest and without emotion' but, rather, having attained a comprehensive view of life, encompassing both sympathetic involvement and objectifying distance, in which the pains and glories, follies and pleasures, pathos and comedy, of the human condition could all be given no more and no less than their due, and could thus be contemplated and enjoyed in untroubled calm.

In the fable of Ceyx and Alcyone from Book 11 of the *Metamorphoses* Dryden seems to have found an episode in which Ovid had attained such a stance. For this episode, in Dryden's rendering, achieves a perspective on human life which, though freer and larger than many to be found in fiction, is not (like the battle of the Lapiths and Centaurs) vulnerable to the charge that the poet has forsaken his own humanity in the pursuit of an 'analytick' impassivity.

But if the narrator's stance in 'Ceyx and Alcyone' can be described as (in some ways) 'godlike', it is not that of any of the gods who appear in the episode itself. In his reworking of his sources, Ovid seems to have transformed the tale from one of divine vengeance for impiety into a story in which the gods' part in the affair is altogether more mysterious.[36] Ceyx and Alcyone, in Ovid's version, have committed no crime, and the malignity of the storm which destroys Ceyx seems as strangely arbitrary as the reaction of Juno to Alcyone's prayers of distress, or Somnus' to Iris' request that a dream be sent to inform Alcyone of her husband's fate. Both deities act not out of any sense of duty, justice, or compassion but to rid themselves of their petitioners' tiresome pestering.[37]

Yet the narrator-poet sees beyond the arbitrariness which constitutes one aspect of the gods' activity, to include the beneficence which is also part of their character. For the tale ends not on a note of frustration, dejection, or bafflement, but with Ceyx's and Alcyone's beautiful metamorphosis and consequent release from their grief and separation, a metamorphosis which is itself the work

[36] Otis, *Ovid as an Epic Poet*, p. 232; E. Fantham, 'Ovid's Ceyx and Alcyone', *Phoenix*, 33 (1979), 330–45.

[37] Niall Rudd, however, suggests (privately) that Ovid's 'non ... sustinet' (584–5) could imply that Juno gives way not out of impatience but because she can no longer bear to do nothing.

of gods, now for a moment as mysteriously merciful as they had previously been indifferent, impotent, or heartless.

If the poet can acknowledge both the arbitrariness and the beneficence of the gods, so can he see his human characters' behaviour in a greater variety of lights than is usual in narrative fictions. This largeness of vision is strikingly noticeable in his treatment of his heroine. Begging her husband not to go on his intended sea voyage, Alcyone reminds Ceyx of the closeness of their relationship: 'iam potes Halcyone securus abesse relicta?' (423; Can you now abandon your Alcyone with no thought of her?). Dryden heightens the pathos and seriousness of her request by having his heroine evoke her marriage in a phrase which had been used by Milton's Adam to characterize his relationship with Eve, the crown of his happiness in Eden:

> Can *Ceyx* then sustain to leave his Wife,
> And unconcern'd forsake the Sweets of Life?
>
> (19–20)[38]

And when Alcyone begs to be allowed to travel with Ceyx, she is given, in the English version, a tone of ardently romantic insistence:

> Go not without thy Wife! but let me bear
> My part of Danger with an equal share,
> And present, what I suffer only fear:
> Then o'er the bounding Billows shall we fly,
> Secure to live together, or to die.
>
> (49–53)

Dryden has given a heady flourish to the close, but in a way that also, with unobtrusive irony, anticipates future events. In his fidelity to the precise tenor of Alcyone's request in Ovid, Dryden conveys more of her discreetly intelligent realism, as well as her passion, than is apparent in the more straightforwardly confident (and therefore more than a little self-deluding) romanticism of Charles Hopkins's Alcyone:

[38] Cf. *Paradise Lost*, 8. 182–4; Raphael has taught Adam 'to live, / The easiest way, nor with perplexing thoughts / To interrupt the sweet of Life, . . .'; Dryden puts the phrase 'the sweets of life' into the mouth of Diomedes in his *Aeneis*, 11. 417, when the hero is describing all that the cruelty of the gods has denied him.

> Take me along, let me your Fortunes share,
> There's nought too hard for Love like mine to bear.
> In Storms, and Calms, together let us keep,
> Together brave the dangers of the Deep,
> The grant of this, my flattering Love assures,
> Which knows no Joys, and feels no Griefs but yours.[39]

The sentiments of Dryden's Alcyone are also sometimes voiced with a super-scrupulous exactness which reveals an acute psychological understanding on the poet's part, but which simultaneously allows the reader something approaching a smile at her precision and earnestness. A good example occurs at the moment when she is warning Ceyx about the difficulty which her father Aeolus has in controlling the turbulence of the sea winds. At this point Ovid's Alcyone remarks:

> quo magis hos novi (nam novi et saepe paterna
> parva domo vidi), magis hos reor esse timendos.
>
> (437–8)

(The more I know (for I do know them, and have often seen them when a child in my father's home) the more I think them to be feared.)

Dryden here remembered George Sandys's version:

> These knew I, and oft saw their rude comport;
> While yet a Girle, within my fathers Court.
>
> (p. 378)

In his own rendering, he took his cue from Ovid's repetition of 'novi' and from the emphatic parenthesis in the Latin, and made the smallest changes in Sandys's wording to turn Alcyone's remark into an insistent reminder of what, as a child, she had noted down for future reference:

> I know them well, and mark'd their rude Comport,
> While yet a Child, within my Father's Court.
>
> (41–2)

[39] Charles Hopkins, *Epistolary Poems; on Several Occasions* (London, 1694), p. 58. On Dryden's use of this volume, see my 'Two Hitherto Unrecorded Sources for Dryden's Ovid Translations', *Notes and Queries*, 21 (1974), 419–20.

Dryden then extended the thought by taking up the hint from Sandys's 'Court' and, in an addition of his own, likening Aeolus' fear of his subjects to that which had been recently experienced by more than one English monarch:

> In times of Tempest they command alone,
> And he but sits precarious on the Throne.
>
> (43–4)

But Dryden's momentary likening of the winds to the (in his view) subversive and anarchic forces which had twice shaken the English throne in his own lifetime was not undertaken in any spirit of fear or disgust. Aeolus' impotence is imagined with a relish, and the winds' wayward gusto and malice with a vigour which gives the reader an access to the imagined spectacle which is pleasantly independent of any authorial censoriousness. And we are allowed something approaching a smile at the solemn insistence with which Alcyone makes her point, while simultaneously registering the seriousness of what might be at stake. The poet's sympathies are everywhere at once – with the helpless king, with the headstrong winds, with the desperate wife telling all this in a passionate attempt to prevent her husband's departure:

> Nor let false Hopes to trust betray thy Mind,
> Because my Sire in Caves constrains the Wind,
> Can with a Breath their clam'rous Rage appease,
> They fear his Whistle, and forsake the Seas;
> Not so, for once indulg'd, they sweep the Main;
> Deaf to the Call, or hearing hear in vain;
> But bent on Mischief bear the Waves before,
> And not content with Seas insult the shoar,
> When Ocean, Air, and Earth, at once ingage
> And rooted Forrests fly before their Rage:
> At once the clashing Clouds to Battle move,
> And Lightnings run across the Fields above.
>
> (29–40)[40]

[40] Dryden took the hint for l. 33 from Hopkins: 'They sweep ore all the earth, swell all the Main'.

Ovid's combination of sympathy and distance can be seen, too, in his treatment of Ceyx. One characteristic touch occurs when, having tried many arguments in vain to persuade Alcyone of the necessity of his voyage, Ceyx eventually prevails by telling her that his journey will only be of two months' duration. Ceyx's breakthrough is likened to a lucky strategy devised by a lawyer to win his case. Hitherto all his arguments have failed:

> non tamen idcirco causam probat; addidit illis
> hoc quoque lenimen, quo solo flexit amantem:
>
> (449–50)

(For all that he did not prove his case. He added this comforting condition, also, by which alone he convinced his loving wife.)

Dryden preserved the legal metaphor, thus allowing the reader to stand back a little from Ceyx's predicament. While never doubting the genuineness of his affection, we observe him fixed (as human beings so often are) in his own resolve, searching for an unanswerable argument, rather than making any real attempt to face or answer his wife's objections:

> Nor these avail'd; at length he lights on one,
> With which, so difficult a Cause he won.
>
> (60–1)

As the couple part, Dryden follows Ovid in allowing us to view the scene both from the vantage point of the departing ship (it is the land which recedes) and of Alcyone (we also see the boat going down, in carefully defined stages, over the horizon). He imitates and heightens the orderly cause-and-effect explicitness and balance with which Ovid had described the successive stages of Alcyone's reaction. We are thus able to observe the whole situation, and particularly the Queen's behaviour, with a cool attentiveness:

> The Queen recover'd rears her humid Eyes,
> And first her Husband on the Poop espies
> Shaking his Hand at distance on the Main;
> She took the Sign; and shook her Hand again.
> Still as the Ground recedes, contracts her View
> With sharpen'd Sight, till she no longer knew

The much-lov'd Face; that Comfort lost supplies
With less, and with the Galley feeds her Eyes;
The Galley born from view by rising Gales
She follow'd with her Sight the flying Sails:
When ev'n the flying Sails were seen no more
Forsaken of all Sight, she left the Shoar.

(75–86)

Dryden has delicately pointed up the momentary similarity of Alcyone's plight to that of Virgil's Dido, by rendering Ovid's

vacuum petit anxia lectum
seque toro point: renovat lectusque locusque
Alcyonae lacrymas et quae pars admonet absit

(471–3)

(Heavy-hearted she sought her lonely couch and threw herself upon it. The couch and the place renewed Alcyone's tears, for they reminded her of the part that was gone from her.)

thus:

Then on her Bridal-Bed her Body throws,
And sought in sleep her weary'd Eyes to close:
Her Husband's Pillow, and the Widow'd part
Which once he press'd, renew'd the former Smart,

(87–90)[41]

recalling the moment in Book 4 of the *Aeneid* which he had rendered:

She last remains, when ev'ry Guest is gone,
Sits on the Bed he press'd, and sighs alone;
Absent, her absent Heroe sees and hears.

(117–19)[42]

[41] Dryden remembered Golding, 547–8: 'The chamber did renew a fresh her smart, / And of her bed did bring to mynd the deere departed part'.

[42] Dryden may have been prompted to make the connection by his feeling that Virgil, too, had viewed his heroine in a way that included both sympathy and objective distancing. The obtrusive rhetorical figure (polyptoton) in the last line of the quotation – a characteristically 'Ovidian' device – is in direct imitation of the equivalent moment in Virgil's Latin: 'illum absens absentem auditque videtque' (*Aeneid*, 4. 83).

Ovid's evocation of the storm which destroys Ceyx, and his depiction of the shipwreck and drowning itself are, it might be remembered, the sections of the episode which have prompted the most serious objections from modern critics. Here Ovid's wit and fancy, and his adapting to his own purposes of previous literary storm scenes,[43] are exercised to their full extent. As in the earlier descriptions of Aeolus, Dryden aligns Ovid's storm with tempestuous events of a kind experienced in his own century:

> In this Confusion while their Work they ply,
> The Winds augment the Winter of the Sky,
> And wage intestine Wars; the suff'ring Seas
> Are toss'd, and mingled as their Tyrants please.
>
> (111–14)

But, as before, the thought of civil strife is entertained in a way that seems closer to appreciative delight than appalled horror. Dryden has extended the hint contained in Ovid's animistic characterization of the waves as 'indignantia' (aggrieved, complaining) to give an exhilarated sense of the way the winds seem to delight in the extent of their tyrannical power over the seas, a power which reduces the vast bulk of the oceans to something which can be 'toss'd' and 'mingled'.

Even more surprising is the poet's attitude when contemplating the storm's effects on its human victims:

> ipse pavet nec se, quid sit status, ipse fatetur
> scire ratis rector, nec quid iubeatve vetetve:
> tanta mali moles tantoque potentior arte est.
>
> (492–4)

(The captain himself is in terror and admits that he does not know how the vessel stands, nor what either to order or forbid; so great is the impending weight of destruction, more mighty than all his skill.)

> The Master wou'd command, but in despair
> Of Safety, stands amaz'd with stupid Care,
> Nor what to bid, or what forbid he knows,

[43] For a full discussion of this aspect of the episode, see Arnaud, 'Aspects of Wit', pp. 104–36.

Th'ungovern'd Tempest to such Fury grows:
Vain is his Force, and vainer is his Skill.

(115–19)

Here the antitheses, marked alliteration and *paranomasia* on 'bid'/ 'forbid' (all directly imitative of stylistic features in Ovid's Latin), together with the deliberate exploitation of the two meanings of 'stupid' (stunned with surprise/obtuse) seem, cumulatively, both to evoke the nonplussed exasperation which the captain is feeling and, by their very obtrusiveness, to embody and provoke an attitude towards that exasperation which keeps us at a quizzical distance from the captain's plight.

Dryden's imitation and extension of Ovid's fanciful animism reaches its height at the moment when the waves mount their final assault on the vessel:

Now all the Waves, their scatter'd Force unite,
And as a Soldier, foremost in the Fight
Makes way for others: And an Host alone
Still presses on, and urging gains the Town;
So while th'invading Billows come a-brest,
The Hero tenth advanc'd before the rest,
Sweeps all before him with impetuous Sway,
And from the Walls descends upon the Prey;
Part following enter, part remain without,
With Envy hear their Fellows conqu'ring Shout:
And mount on others Backs, in hope to share
The City, thus become the Seat of War.

(161–72)[44]

The simile likening the decisive 'tenth wave' to a soldier leading an assault on a city is redeemed from seeming childishly extravagant by the precision and aptness of its fanciful logic. Ovid had attributed to his waves not merely a human will but also competitiveness, envy, vainglory, muscle-power, and tactical skill. Dryden extends the fancy, making the waves, explicitly, 'invaders', evoking their *élan* in the vivid onrush of his verse (167), and imagining the waves overcresting each

[44] Dryden took a hint for his depiction of the tenth wave (165–6) from Hopkins: 'With more than common ardour in his breast, / And higher hopes, spurr'd further than the rest'.

other as climbing on one another's backs in envious eagerness to enter the city and share the spoils of war.

The inexorable force of a stormy sea (which to a human observer can seem almost wilful in its destructiveness) and the murderousness of looting insurgents could not possibly be enjoyed by anyone whose life was in direct danger from either. But such personal involvement in any hazardous action necessarily produces a certain myopia, a refusal to register aspects of the situation which might be apparent to a more distanced, and therefore in some senses more clear-sighted, observer. Ovid's witty analogy, we might say, allows the reader to entertain the senses in which a turbulent sea and an invading army might be thought of as impelled by a single grand spirit or power, whose anarchic and exuberant vigour can be legitimately conceived in a spirit of appreciative delight rather than merely being deplored or feared.

If Ovid can encourage us to relish a destructive storm, can he also allow us to view the predicament of a drowning man quizzically, without reproaching ourselves after the event for unpardonable callousness? Here are three excerpts from Dryden's rendering of the death of Ceyx:

> All *Ceyx* his *Alcyone* employs,
> For her he grieves, yet in her absence joys;
> His Wife he wishes, and wou'd still be near,
> Not her with him, but wishes him with her:
>
> (188–91)

> But yet his Consort is his greatest Care;
> *Alcyone* he names amidst his Pray'r,
> Names as a Charm against the Waves, and Wind;
> Most in his Mouth, and ever in his Mind:
>
> (214–17)[45]

> As oft as he can catch a gulp of Air,
> And peep above the Seas, he names the Fair,
> And ev'n when plung'd beneath, on her he raves,
> Murm'ring *Alcyone* below the Waves:

[45] Dryden was here perhaps recollecting a couplet in Cowley's poem, *On the Queens repairing Somerset-House*: 'For the distrest and the afflicted lye, / Most in their Care, and always in their Eye'. The couplet is (mis)quoted in the Epistle Dedicatory to *Don Sebastian* (*Works*, 15. 62).

At last a falling Billow stops his Breath,
Breaks o'er his Head, and whelms him underneath.

(222–5)

Here the diction ('peep', 'gulp'), the pat antitheses which (among other things) seem almost to mimic the bobbing motion of a body in water, and the near-comic potential (combined with great precision) of lines 217 and 190–1 (the latter substantially Dryden's invention) ensure that the reader's reaction to the events is far removed from that of Shakespeare's Miranda in similar circumstances:

O! I have suffered
With those that I saw suffer. A brave vessel
(Who had, no doubt, some noble Creature in her)
Dash'd all to pieces! O, the cry did knock
Against my very heart. Poor souls, they perish'd.

(*The Tempest*, 1. 2. 5–9)

Yet we perhaps too often underestimate the ease with which what we call 'sympathy', in life and literature, can slide into a self-cherishing sentimentality, and a consequent failure of real imaginative engagement with and attentiveness to the situation we are purportedly contemplating. In any case, the Ovid/Dryden handling of Ceyx's drowning is not one which automatically and consistently excludes feelings at the more tender and pathetic end of the spectrum. These lines follow immediately after the first of the extracts quoted above:

Now with last looks he seeks his Native Shoar,
Which Fate has destin'd him to see no more;
He sought, but in the dark tempestuous Night
He knew not whether to direct his Sight.
So whirl the Seas, such Darkness blinds the Sky,
That the black Night receives a deeper Dye.

(191–7)

The treatment of Ceyx's drowning allows the reader to register many different reactions to the king's death: the ignominy of such a man being tossed like driftwood on the ocean, his part-devoted, part-superstitious, part-selfless, part-desperate obsession with his wife as he goes down, his precarious and pathetic vulnerability to the destructive forces about him.

One commentator on Book 11 spoke for many readers of the *Metamorphoses*, past and present, when he praised the episode depicting the Cave of Sleep for its 'hushed and trance-like' quality, drew attention to the way in which the very sound patterns of Ovid's verse contribute to that effect, and remarked that 'Somnus . . . incorporates the very essence of sleepiness in live detail'.[46] Somnus is indeed an embodiment of the repose and release from worldly care which sleep provides. The surroundings of his cave are evoked in Dryden's version with a soothing melodiousness analogous to that which the commentators find in Ovid's original. And when, in Dryden's version, Iris addresses Somnus:

> O sacred Rest,
> Sweet pleasing Sleep, of all the Pow'rs the best!
> O Peace of Mind, repairer of Decay,
> Whose Balm renews the Limbs to Labours of the Day,
> Care shuns thy soft approach, and sullen flies away!
> (308–12)

the poet seems to be recalling the desperate yearnings of Shakespeare's Macbeth for the sacred restorative powers of sleep:

> innocent sleep,
> Sleep that knits up the ravell'd sleave of care,
> The death of each day's life, sore labor's bath,
> Balm of hurt minds, . . .
>
> (*Macbeth*, 2. 2. 33–6)

But Ovid's godlike inclusiveness of view extends to the gods themselves, and in this poem Somnus is a figure who also embodies the comic dimensions of sleep. The very poppies round his cave are 'nodding', both in reverence to the god and because they themselves can hardly keep awake. And as he hears Iris' address, Somnus' chin knocks his bosom in weariness, and his utterances are punctuated by yawns. As he wakes he (Sleep-as-god) has to 'shake off' himself

[46] *Ovid: Metamorphoses, Book XI*, ed. Murphy, pp. 73–4.

(Sleep-as-process). He only accedes to Iris' request to send a dream to warn Alcyone of Ceyx's death because to do so will allow him to go back to sleep all the sooner.[47]

It is just after hearing the news of her husband's death that Alcyone is given what is perhaps the most striking piece of Ovidian word-play in the whole episode:

> nunc absens pereo, iactor quoque[48] fluctibus absens,
> et sine me me pontus habet.
>
> (700–1)

(But now far from myself I have perished; far from myself also I am tossed about upon the waves, and without me the sea holds me.)

Dryden finds his own equivalents for Ovid's *ploche* ('Nunc . . . nunc'; 'absens . . . absens') and *anadiplosis* (' . . . me me . . . '):

> Now I die absent, in the vast profound;
> And Me without my Self the Seas have drown'd.
>
> (423–4)

This would seem to be the moment in the poem where one might be most inclined to pose Dryden's question: 'Were this a Time to be witty?' Indeed, one commentator has described the lines as 'an Ovidian paradox pursued to verbal breaking point' and 'the most extreme example of a type of word-play to which Ovid was addicted'.[49] Yet, in the light of the arguments already advanced, it is possible to see the lines as something more than a mere exercise in wanton and unfeeling ingenuity. Ovid uses his rhetorical figures to reassert the intimate *rapport* between the couple while simultaneously distancing the reader from Alcyone's grief, allowing us to appreciate at the very same moment the element of self-absorption and self-regard which is perhaps an inevitable part of all human expressions of both grief and love. The effect is confirmed a little

[47] It is no accident that, in composing his version of the scene, Dryden both drew on and contributed to the tradition of mock-heroic poetry. See my 'Dryden's Cave of Sleep and Garth's *Dispensary*', *Notes and Queries*, 23 (1976), 243–5.

[48] Seventeenth-century texts read 'nunc'.

[49] *Ovid: Metamorphoses, Book XI*, ed. Murphy, p. 77.

later, at the moment when Alcyone first begins to recognize the corpse floating towards her as that of Ceyx:

> quod quo magis illa tuetur,
> hoc minus et minus est mentis vae![50] iamque propinquae
> admotum terrae, iam quod cognoscere posset,
> cernit.
>
> (722–5)

(The more she regarded it, the less and less the woman was in possession of her mind. And now it had come close to land, now that it was something she could recognize, she perceived it fully.)

> The more she looks, the more her Fears increase,
> At nearer Sight; and she's her self the less:
> Now driv'n ashore, and at her Feet it lies,
> She knows too much, in knowing whom she sees.
>
> (460–3)

Dryden has strengthened Ovid's emphasis on Alcyone's greed for knowledge which she already half knows she does not want to possess, a greed which makes her almost forsake her normal personality (she becomes 'amens' (out of her mind) in the seventeenth-century texts) only to come to an all too sharp realization of the position she is now in. The irony is all the more piquant in the light of her determination, only a few lines earlier, to treat the (as yet unidentified) corpse floating towards her *as if* it were Ceyx's, and her exclamation that the unknown wretch is unhappy, 'but *more* [his] widdow'd Wife' (Dryden 457; my italics).

Yet Ovid's distance from Alcyone's grief in no way detracts from the sense of release and joy which is felt when the final metamorphosis occurs. Since at this culminating moment Dryden has responded with remarkable fullness to the challenge of his original, the passage must be given entire:

> to the neighb'ring Mole she strode,
> (Rais'd there to break th'Incursions of the Flood;)
> Headlong from hence to plunge her self she springs,
> But shoots along supported on her Wings,

[50] Seventeenth-century texts read 'amens sua'.

A Bird new-made about the Banks she plies
Not far from Shore; and short Excursions tries;
Nor seeks in Air her humble Flight to raise,
Content to skim the Surface of the Seas:
Her Bill, tho' slender, sends a creaking Noise,
And imitates a lamentable Voice:
Now lighting where the bloodless Body lies,
She with a Funeral Note renews her Cries.
At all her stretch her little Wings she spread,
And with her feather'd Arms embrac'd the Dead:
Then flick'ring to his palid Lips, she strove,
To print a Kiss, the last essay of Love:
Whether the vital Touch reviv'd the Dead,
Or that the moving Waters rais'd his Head
To meet the Kiss, the Vulgar doubt alone;
For sure a present Miracle was shown.
The Gods their Shapes to Winter-Birds translate,
But both obnoxious to their former Fate.
Their conjugal Affection still is ty'd,
And still the mournful Race is multiply'd:
They bill, they tread; *Alcyone* compress'd
Sev'n Days sits brooding on her floating Nest:
A wintry Queen: Her Sire at length is kind,
Calms ev'ry Storm, and hushes ev'ry Wind;
Prepares his Empire for his Daughter's Ease,
And for his hatching Nephews smooths the Seas.

(470–99)

This passage seems to epitomize the distinctive blend of involvement and distance, pathos and near-humour, psychological precision and extravagant fancy, discretion and daring, which are so characteristic of Ovid's episode. Dryden has responded to those touches in the Latin which evoke the miniature delicacy of the newly metamorphosed Alcyone. Where Ovid had, for Alcyone's leap from the breakwater, used the verb 'insiluit', a word which 'suggests a birdlike movement and so contains a hint of what is to come',[51] Dryden adopted the word 'springs' from his predecessors Sandys and Hopkins, but his combination of this with the phrase 'shoots along' to

[51] *Ovid: Metamorphoses, Book XI*, ed. Murphy, p. 78.

describe her new-found motion gives a far more vivid impression of her sudden sensation of the lightness of her own body than had been apparent in either of their versions.[52] The touching tentativeness of her flight is equally aptly captured in the 'short Excursions'[53] which she 'tries' (both nervousness and modesty prevent her attempting more ambitious flight), and we are reminded of the agile gracefulness of her movement in the way she 'skims' the seas and hovers 'flick'r-ing' in her vain attempts to kiss her husband's corpse with her 'slender Bill' and to embrace the body with arms which are now 'tiny' and 'feather'd'. These last touches remind us of both the delicate beauty and the disconcerting awkwardness of her transformation. She can now only emit eerie 'creaking' sounds which are a weird miniaturization of her former groans of human misery. When Ceyx, too, is transformed, the couple are perceived to preserve in their changed state both the devotion and the sadness they had known in human life. Dryden daringly draws attention to the changed nature of their sexuality in his boldly witty and technically precise 'bill', 'tread',[54] 'compress'd', 'brooding', 'Nest',[55] and 'hatching', but these touches seem to fuse with, rather than merely undercut, the beauty and dignity of the new-formed union. Alcyone is felt genuinely to be a 'wintry Queen',[56] the mother of a 'Race'. In the most daringly witty stroke of all, Dryden makes play with his own Catholicism, in asserting that their transformation, the work of gods far removed from the God of Christianity (Aeolus now seems able to exercise without difficulty the power over his subjects which had formerly eluded him), is 'a present Miracle',[57] a demonstration that, by mysterious means to

[52] Cf. Sandys: 'Thither forth-with (ô wonderfull!) she springs; / Beating the passive ayre with new-growne wings'; Hopkins: 'Thither (almost beyond belief) she springs, / Born thro' the yielding air, on new-grown wings'.

[53] On the afterlife of the phrase, see Philip Smallwood, 'Pope's "Short Excursions" and Dryden: An Unrecorded Borrowing', *Notes and Queries*, 26 (1979), 243–5.

[54] Borrowed from Golding, 857: 'They treade, and lay, and bring foorth yoong'.

[55] Cf. Sandys: 'Alcyon sits upon her floating nest'; Hopkins: 'Seven days she sits upon her floating Nest'.

[56] Dryden's contemporaries would perhaps have recalled Elizabeth (1569–1662), the eldest daughter of James 1 and sister of Charles 1, whose brief stay in Prague as Queen of Bohemia (October 1619–November 1620) caused her to be known as 'the Winter Queen'.

[57] Dryden possibly alludes to the proverbial belief that 'miracles are ceased' (for which, see Shakespeare, *Henry V*, 1. 1. 67; *All's Well that Ends Well*, 2. 3. 1).

which only the gods are privy, human grief *can* be transcended and overcome, just as the storms of Winter are transformed into the calm of the 'halcyon days'.

Ovid's refusal to align himself, or the reader, in a position of straightforward empathy with the characters in the drama allows him and us a distance which enables us to see their conduct and thoughts in many different lights – appreciative, critical, quizzical, sympathetic, indulgent, clinical – without any of these predominating. Ovid puts into practice the principle enunciated in a couplet which Dryden inserted into his translation of the story of Cinyras and Myrrha:

> Eyes and their Objects never must unite,
> Some Distance is requir'd to help the Sight.
>
> (74–5)

To be allowed to share the poet's large vision has a consolatory, calming effect on the reader. For the mind, as Johnson knew, can only repose on the stability of truth. The Ovidian vision allows readers to face, comprehend, and thus enjoy, in a state of untroubled equanimity and delight, a view of human life as simultaneously glorious and futile, dignified and absurd, precious and dispensable, ordered and arbitrary, the care of the gods and of no concern to them at all, at one in its transience with the rest of Nature, with which it is involved in a continuous process of transformation, metamorphosis, and flux. Such a vision is perhaps a more adequate attempt to see life steadily and whole, for *all* that it contains, than many apparently more 'serious' literary endeavours. This may go some way towards explaining the endless fascination which, despite a hostile critical press, the best parts of the *Metamorphoses* have continued to provoke down the centuries, to the creation of which Ovid's notorious 'wit out of season' has made such an indispensable contribution.

# 9

# Translation, Metempsychosis, and the Flux of Nature: Dryden's 'Of the Pythagorean Philosophy'

To turn from Dryden's earliest discussions of translation to his last is to experience a shift from criticism focused primarily on questions of genre, method, and technique to writing which contemplates, in language of extraordinary metaphorical resonance and suggestiveness, the most fundamental processes of inheritance, influence, transmission, and transformation – in nature and history as well as in art. In his earliest and most famous essay on translation, the Preface to *Ovid's Epistles* (1680), Dryden, as we saw in Chapter 4, had proposed his celebrated tripartite division of translation into 'Metaphase', 'Paraphrase', and 'Imitation', in which 'Paraphrase' ('or translation with Latitude, where the Author is kept in view by the Translator, so as never to be lost, but his words are not so strictly follow'd as his sense, and that too is admitted to be amplyfied but not alter'd') had been offered as a *via media* between the crabbed obscurity of 'Metaphrase' and the unacceptable licence of 'Imitation'. But by the late 1690s Dryden was less concerned to discriminate between the proprieties of different modes or styles of translation, than to defend his own practice with reference to the fundamental ties of lineage, consanguinity, and congeniality of soul by which he felt bound to each of his originals, and to the larger processes of nature and fate which had led him to translate them in the first place. In the Dedication to *Examen Poeticum* (1693) Dryden described Ovid as 'more according to [his] Genius' than some of the other poets whom he had been translating recently (*Works*, 4. 369). He was to repeat the formula, this time with reference to Homer, in a letter of 1699 and in the Preface to his *Fables Ancient and Modern* (1700), the volume which saw the first appearance of his translation of Book 1 of the *Iliad*.[1] His use of the word 'Genius' seems primarily designed to suggest that the poetic temperaments of Ovid and Homer were particularly in accord with his own 'characteristic disposition, inclination, bent, turn or temper of mind' (*OED*, '*genius*' 3a). But his use of the term perhaps also carries some of its original classical associations, as the word for 'the tutelary god or attendant spirit allotted to every person at his birth, to govern his fortunes and determine his character, and finally to conduct him out of the world' (*OED*, '*genius*', 1). Such a notion of supernatural guidance is certainly present in his description of his relationship with another of the poets whose work he translated for *Fables*: Geoffrey Chaucer. Dryden had, he declares, been 'embolden'd' to prune redundancies and to supplement deficiencies in Chaucer's original texts by a realization that he had a 'Soul congenial' to that of the medieval poet, and 'had been conversant in the same Studies' (*Works*, 7. 40). A few lines later (*Works*, 7. 41), Dryden uses the word 'Transfusion' to describe his translating activity. He had employed this term earlier in the same Preface to characterize the process whereby influence and inspiration is transmitted within the 'Lineal Descents and Clans' of the poets. '*Spencer*', he had observed, 'more than once insinuates, that the Soul of *Chaucer* was transfus'd into his Body; and that he was begotten by him Two hundred years after his Decease' (*Works*, 7. 25). Dryden's own 'Veneration' for Chaucer has, he says, been enhanced by his discovery that, at the very same time as he has been preparing his own renderings, a new version of Chaucer was being prepared in France.[2] This fact, he suggests, has caused him to think 'that there is something in it like Fatality; that after certain Periods of Time, the Fame and Memory of Great Wits should be renew'd'. 'If this be wholly Chance', he continues, ''tis extraordinary; and I dare not call it more, for fear of being tax'd with Superstition' (*Works*, 7. 42). Dryden's sense of having almost been fated to translate his originals by the benign influence of some

[1] *The Letters of John Dryden*, ed. C. E. Ward (Durham NC, 1942), p. 121; *Works*, 7. 28.

[2] The rumoured contemporary French translation of Chaucer by Mademoiselle de Scudéry seems never to have appeared.

higher process or power is confirmed by the epigraph which he appended to *Fables*, taken from the speech in Book 5 of Virgil's *Aeneid* in which Aeneas tells his comrades that they have been brought to (in Dryden's translation) the 'blest Remains' of his father Anchises, 'Not, as I deem, without the Will of Heav'n' (*Works*, 5. 489).

The metaphors of spiritual congeniality, consanguinity, transfusion, and reincarnation with which the Dryden of 1699 describes the processes of literary influence and translation had, to be sure, been used by a number of earlier writers on the subject. John Florio, George Chapman, Nicolas Perrot d'Ablancourt, and Sir John Denham had all used the trope of metempsychosis to describe the way in which writers are given new life in later reworkings.[3] Dryden, as we have seen, noted Spenser's use of the same figure to describe his relation to Chaucer, and had himself previously used metaphors of 'traduction' and 'transfusion' to speculate on the poet Anne Killigrew's possible indebtedness to her dramatist-father.[4] William Congreve had hinted that the success of Dryden's translation of Persius was perhaps attributable to Dryden's having been 'the recipient of Persius' transmigratory soul'.[5] There is an analogous precedent in Denham's Preface to *The Destruction of Troy* (1656) for Dryden's use of 'transfusion' as a synonym for translation.[6] And Dryden's expressions of his felt congeniality of soul with his originals were partly anticipated by the Earl of Roscommon's celebrated exhortation in his *Essay on Translated Verse* to 'seek a *Poet* who *your* way do's bend, / And chuse an *Author* as you chuse a *Friend*', so that 'Your *thoughts*, your *Words*, your *Stiles*, your *Souls* agree, / No Longer his *Interpreter*, but *He*.'[7] They might also be thought of as a putting-into-effect of

[3] See *Western Translation Theory, from Herodotus to Nietzsche*, ed. Douglas Robinson (Manchester, 1997), pp. 134, 160; T. R. Steiner, *English Translation Theory, 1650–1800* (Assen, 1975), pp. 10–12; *The Poems of Sir John Denham*, ed. Theodore Howard Banks (2nd edition, Hamden CT, 1969), pp. 149–52.

[4] 'To the Pious Memory of... Mrs Anne Killigrew' (1685, dated 1686), 23–6 (*Works*, 3. 110).

[5] See Richard Terry, *Poetry and the Making of the English Literary Past, 1660–1781* (Oxford, 2001), pp. 156–68, citing Congreve's 'To Mr Dryden, on his Translation of Persius', first printed in *The Satires of Juvenal and Persius* (London, 1692, dated 1693), sigs. A2$^{r-v}$ (second pagination).

[6] *The Poems of Sir John Denham*, p. 159. See further Chapter 4 above.

[7] Wentworth Dillon, fourth Earl of Roscommon, *An Essay on Translated Verse* (2nd edition, London, 1685), p. 7. See further Chapter 4 above.

Dryden's own earlier aspiration (discussed in Chapter 4 above) to render the sentiments of each of his originals in such a way that 'if he were living, and an *Englishman*, they are such, as he wou'd probably have written' (Preface to *Sylvae*; *Works*, 3. 4).

But the presentation in the Preface to *Fables* of translation as a kind of spiritual self-identification or reincarnation is given a distinctively new edge and depth by virtue of the powerful support and endorsement which it receives from one of the poems in the volume itself. Close similarities in vocabulary and phrasing reveal unmistakable connections between the Preface to *Fables* and the translation 'Of the Pythagorean Philosophy', Dryden's rendering of the extended passage from Book 15 of Ovid's *Metamorphoses*, in which the Greek philosopher Pythagoras expounds, to an audience which includes Numa, the future King of Rome, his belief in vegetarianism, the transmigration of souls, and the continuous processes of change to which the whole of human, animal, and inanimate nature is subject. The overlaps between Preface and poem provide a telling confirmation of Dryden's own sense of the inextricability of his poetic and critical activity in the composition of *Fables*: 'Thoughts . . . come crowding in so fast upon me, that my only Difficulty is to chuse or to reject; to run them into Verse, or to give them the other Harmony of Prose' (Preface to *Fables*; *Works*, 7. 26–7).

The cosmological aspects of the philosophy of Pythagoras had exercised a powerful influence on the thought and poetry of the Renaissance,[8] but the Greek philosopher's commitment to metempsychosis had proved more controversial, being sometimes treated as the butt of jokes, and sometimes as a more serious threat to Christian belief.[9] Pythagorean metempsychosis was, indeed, a focus for heated debate during the 1690s. In 1692 the moralist and Anglican apologist Whitelocke Bulstrode (1650–1724) had published *An Essay of Transmigration, in Defence of Pythagoras: Or, A Discourse of Natural Philosophy*, a work explicitly designed 'to vindicate the Honour of Pythagoras' and to 'defend him from the Calumny of the World so unjustly cast upon him, as the Author of an erroneous Doctrine'.[10]

[8] See S. K. Heninger, Jr., *Touches of Sweet Harmony: Pythagorean Cosmology and Renaissance Poetics* (San Marino CA, 1974), *passim*.

[9] Heninger, *Touches of Sweet Harmony*, pp. 267–8.

[10] Whitelocke Bulstrode, *An Essay of Transmigration* (2nd edition, London, 1693), sigs. a5$^{v}$–a6$^{r}$ (italics romanized).

The transmigration of souls envisaged by Pythagoras, Bulstrode argues, is not of the 'Rational Soul' which is unique to Man but of the 'Sensitive and Vegetative Spirit' which man shares with other animals and vegetables. There is, therefore, no incompatibility between his teachings and the Christian doctrine of the Resurrection.[11] But Bishop William Lloyd, in a pamphlet published in 1699, was in diametrical disagreement. 'There is,' he wrote,

more than idle Fancy in [the teachings of Pythagoras]. They shew plainly a pernicious Devilish design, to confound those two Doctrines that have so great an influence into Men's minds, to make them do good, and eschew evil: the Doctrines of the Immortality of the Soul, and of the Resurrection of the Body. For if those Fictions were true, there would be no difference between the Soul of a Man, and the Soul of a Brute, or a Plant; and there would be many more Bodies than there would be Souls to animate them at the Resurrection. What would not the Devil give to have these things believ'd by all Mankind?[12]

Ovid had placed Pythagoras' speech on the transmigration of souls in a position of great prominence at the beginning of the final book of his greatest poem. Modern scholars are generally unwilling to accept the passage as any kind of adequate summary or distillation of the essential vision of the *Metamorphoses*, some even seeing it as a burlesque of Pythagorean teaching.[13] But Dryden's translator-predecessor Arthur Golding had seen the episode as a 'sum of all the former woorke'.[14] And Golding's Caroline successor George Sandys had noted the 'more lofty pitch, both in matter and expression' to which Ovid had risen in Pythagoras'

[11] Bulstrode, *An Essay of Transmigration*, pp. 5, 82 and *passim*.

[12] William Lloyd, *A Chronological Account of the Life of Pythagoras* (London, 1699), p. ix (italics romanized).

[13] See Joseph Solodow, *The World of Ovid's 'Metamorphoses'* (Chapel Hill NC, 1988), pp. 162–8; for the suggestion of burlesque, see G. K. Galinsky, *Ovid's Metamorphoses: An Introduction to the Basic Aspects* (Oxford, 1975); C. P. Segal, 'Myth and Philosophy in the *Metamorphoses*: Ovid's Augustanism and the Augustan Conclusion of Book XV', *American Journal of Philology*, 90 (1969), 257–90.

[14] *Shakespeare's Ovid, Being Arthur Golding's Translation of the Metamorphoses*, ed. W. H. D. Rouse (London, 1904), p. 6; Golding (p. 1) refines Pythagoras' teaching to distinguish the 'soule or lyfe' which human beings share with 'brute beasts' from the 'soule whereby / We are endewd with reason and discretion from on hie'.

discourse.[15] In the Preface to *Fables* and the headnote to his translation, Dryden singles out Ovid's story of Numa's studies with Pythagoras and his presentation of 'the Moral and Natural Philosophy of *Pythagoras*' as 'the Master-piece of the whole *Metamorphoses*' and 'the most learned and beautiful Parts' of Ovid's poem (*Works*, 7. 24, 484). This indicates that he, too, saw the episode as possessing a unique *gravitas* and significance.

Various touches in 'Of the Pythagorean Philosophy', as Cedric D. Reverand II has shown, reveal the deposed Laureate subtly aligning some of the sentiments of Ovid's Pythagoras with his own situation and concerns.[16] The Greek philosopher is depicted (in a series of subtle expansions of the Latin) as an independent-minded and eloquent hater of tyrants who could not 'bear / The Chains which none but servile Souls will wear' (77–9). He has the 'Strength of Mind' to 'tread th'Abyss above; / And penetrate with his interiour Light / Those upper Depths, which Nature hid from Sight' (82–4), and offers advice of the broadest philosophical import to a chaste, saintly, and peace-loving king (the antithesis of William III) who has himself, at the beginning of the episode, retired 'to cultivate his Mind' (213), and who is later received in Rome, 'by Gift his own:/ A willing People, and an offer'd Throne' (714).

A number of features of Dryden's version further extend our sense of Dryden's personal involvement in Pythagoras' discourse, in terms both of his life experience and of his artistic beliefs and practices. As he rises to the height of his theme, the Ovidian Pythagoras (in Dryden's rendering) begins to discourse on the fundamental processes of time and change which operate throughout nature:

Nature knows
No stedfast Station, but, or Ebbs, or Flows:
Ever in motion; she destroys her old,

[15] George Sandys, *Ovid's Metamorphosis Englished, Mythologiz'd, and Represented in Figures* (Oxford, 1632), p. 511. There seems to have been no separate English translation of the passage before Dryden. There is a version of part of the episode by John Glanvill (?1664–1735), published in his *Poems* (1725), pp. 280–2, which shares some phrasing with Dryden's translation. But in his Preface (sig. b1$^{v}$), Glanvill explicitly claims that he is not indebted to Dryden's version.

[16] Cedric D. Reverand II, *Dryden's Final Poetic Mode: The* Fables (Philadelphia PA, 1988), pp. 164–84. Reverand offers some suggestive comparisons between Pythagoras' speech and that of Theseus in 'Palamon and Arcite'.

And casts new Figures in another Mold.
Ev'n Times are in perpetual Flux; and run
Like Rivers from their Fountain rowling on;
For Time no more than Streams, is at a stay:
The flying Hour is ever on her way;
And as the Fountain still supplies her store,
The Wave behind impels the Wave before;
Thus in successive Course the Minutes run,
And urge their Predecessor Minutes on,
Still moving, ever new: For former Things
Are set aside, like abdicated Kings:
And every moment alters what is done,
And innovates some Act till then unknown.

(262–77)

The sense conveyed in this passage (powerfully reinforced by Dryden's insistent patterns of alliteration and repeated rhyme) is of ceaselessly and inexorably innovative motion which encompasses the whole of human endeavour and natural activity. Dryden has here combined echoes of Francis Bacon, who in his essay 'Of Vicissitudes of Things' had written of the way in which 'matter is in a perpetual flux, and never at a stay', of his former colleague, Andrew Marvell, who in 'An Horatian Ode on Cromwell's Return from Ireland' had described Cromwell's endeavour 'To ruine the great Work of Time, / And cast the Kingdome old / Into another Mold', of the Book of Revelation's proclamation that 'the former things are passed away', and of the Earl of Rochester's lament for the passing of 'Love and Life' ('All my past life is mine no more, / The flying hours are gone').[17] Dryden's use (for the first time in his non-dramatic verse) of the key Miltonic adjective 'successive',[18] simultaneously, and significantly, incorporates a punning allusion to William III's 'succession' to the English throne after his 'predecessor' James II – for Dryden the most momentous recent instance of political 'innovation'. The allusion is reinforced by the mention of 'abdicated Kings', a phrase with no precedent in Ovid's Latin, but with obvious

[17] See Tom Mason, 'Dryden's Chaucer' (Unpublished PhD thesis, University of Cambridge, 1977), pp. 117–19, in which these sources are noted. The echo of Bacon is also noted by Reverand, p. 175.

[18] *Paradise Lost*, 4. 612–16, also noted in Mason, 'Dryden's Chaucer'.

application to English events. As is well known, one of the key issues in recent political debate had been whether James II's flight to France in December 1688 had constituted an 'abdication' of the English throne. Dryden's phrasing teasingly preserves the linguistic ambiguity, by which 'abdicated' could mean (in the active sense) 'having abdicated' or (in the passive) ('having *been* abdicated', i.e. 'deposed').[19] Dryden had used the verb transitively in his Dedication to *Examen Poeticum* (1693; *Works*, 4. 365), and was perhaps also remembering some lines from the anonymous Prologue to *The Late Revolution; or The Happy Change* (1690), where the author, noting the political implications of Dryden's play, *Don Sebastian*, had linked James's loss of his throne with Dryden's loss of the Laureateship:

> *Sebastian* better does the trick,
> With Bobs and Innuendo's thick,
> Which Abdicated Laureat brings
> In praise of Abdicated Kings.[20]

The final line of Dryden's passage ('And innovates some Act till then unknown') – translating Ovid's 'fitque quod haut fuerat' (that which was not has come to be) – incorporates a further punning allusion to the Acts of Parliament[21] which had consolidated the new régime after James's departure. A related colouring had been in evidence earlier in the poem, when Pythagoras was speaking of the changing impressions left in softened wax:

> And, as the soften'd Wax new Seals receives,
> This Face assumes, and that Impression leaves;
> Now call'd by one, now by another Name;
> The Form is only chang'd, the Wax is still the same:
> (247–51)

[19] On the controversy surrounding James II's 'abdication', see J. P. Kenyon, *Revolution Principles: The Politics of Party, 1689–1720* (2nd edition, Cambridge, 1990), especially pp. x–xv, 5–13; Thomas P. Slaughter, '"Abdicate" and "Contract" in the Glorious Revolution', *Historical Journal*, 24 (1981), 323–37; John Miller, 'The Glorious Revolution: "Contract" and "Abdication" Reconsidered', *Historical Journal*, 25 (1982), 541–55.

[20] *The Prologues and Epilogues of the Restoration*, ed. Pierre Danchin, 6 vols. (Nancy, 1981–88), 4. 783–4.

[21] Likely candidates are 1 Gul. & Mar. sess 1, cap. 1 and 8.

Ovid's Latin contains no mention of 'seals' or 'faces'. But an attentive contemporary reader of Dryden's poem would have recalled the central symbolic role which James II's casting of the Great Seal into the river Thames on his departure had played in the constitutional crisis of 1688–9, and particularly in the debates about James's supposed 'abdication'. In the words of the Whig Gilbert Burnet, 'the Great Seal's being cast into the *Thames*... seems to imply this at least, That either he did not think of returning again, or that if he should return, that he would no more Govern by the shew of Law, of which the Great Seal seems always to carry some prints'.[22]

As well as pointing up the relevance of Pythagoras' discourse to recent events, Dryden appears to have discovered a more intimately personal significance in some of the Greek philosopher's words. In the passage in which Pythagoras likens the progress of the seasons to the ages of man, Dryden amplifies Ovid's text to incorporate glances at the philosophical equipoise which he had claimed for himself in several of his later Prefaces ('Not froze with Fear, nor boiling into Rage' (313)), and at his own physical appearance. His references to an old man's 'brown Locks' which 'repine to mix with odious Grey' (315) and to his 'ragged Fleece' which 'is thin, and thin is worse than bare' (319), recall the image so memorably captured in Sir Godfrey Kneller's great portrait of the previous year (now in Trinity College, Cambridge), depicting a wigless Dryden in informal mode, and might also remind us of the image affectionately invoked in the later tribute to Dryden by his friend, Sir Samuel Garth: 'The falling off of his Hair, had no other Consequence, than to make his Lawrels be seen the more'.[23]

Even more remarkable than these political and personal allusions, however, are the ways in which Dryden sees implications in Pythagoras'

[22] *A Pastoral Letter* (1689), quoted in J. A. Downie, *To Settle the Succession of the State: Literature and Politics, 1678–1750* (London, 1994), p. 37. Illustrations of the Great Seals of James II, of William III and Mary, and of William III alone are provided in C. H. Firth's edition of Macaulay's *History of England*, 6 vols. (London, 1914), 3. 1172–3, 1294–5; 5. 2478).

[23] *Ovid's Metamorphoses, in Fifteen Books. Translated by the most Eminent Hands* [ed. Sir Samuel Garth] (London, 1717), p. xx.

discourse for his specifically poetic activity. A number of striking elaborations of Ovid's Latin make plain the connections which he saw between Pythagoras' discourse and the reflections on poetic mortality, immortality and rebirth with which, as we have seen, he was so preoccupied in the Preface to *Fables*. Ovid's Pythagoras follows his description of the seasons and the ages of man with a general celebration of nature's ceaseless change. Dryden has here expanded his original (Ovid's 252–8) considerably:

> Thus are their Figures never at a stand,
> But chang'd by Nature's innovating Hand;
> All Things are alter'd, nothing is destroy'd,
> The shifted Scene, for some new Show employ'd.
> Then to be born, is to begin to be
> Some other Thing we were not formerly:
> And what we call to Die, is not t' appear,
> Or be the Thing that formerly we were.
> Those very Elements which we partake,
> Alive, when Dead some other Body make:
> Translated grow, have Sense, or can Discourse,
> But Death on deathless Substance has no force.
>
> (386–97)

An obvious affiliation can be discerned between the Drydenian Pythagoras' assertion that 'All Things are alter'd, nothing is destroy'd' and Dryden's remark in the Preface (apropos of Chaucer's Canterbury pilgrims) that 'Mankind is ever the same, and nothing lost out of Nature, though every thing is alter'd' (*Works*, 7. 37–8). And Dryden's punning interlingual use of the word 'Translated' both renders the primary meaning of Ovid's 'translata' (shifted, moved; 258), and implicitly applies Pythagoras' words to the very literary process by which they are being communicated to English readers: translation. The self-referential colouring accords with Dryden's earlier sly incorporation of the title of his own volume when rendering Pythagoras' dismissal of the horrors of death as 'Vain Themes of Wit, which but in Poems pass, / And *Fables* of a World, that never was' (225–6; my italics). It also mirrors the reflexive and self-referential tendencies which are such recurrent features of Ovid's language throughout the *Metamorphoses*.[24]

The vocabulary in which Dryden renders Pythagoras' reflections on the 'translation' of matter suggests that he was also possibly connecting the passage with another of his profoundly personal concerns. Attention has been drawn to resemblances between Dryden's conception of translation and the Catholic stress on the physical re-embodiment of Christ in the Eucharist.[25] In his use of the words 'elements' and 'substance' when conveying Pythagoras' vision of permanence-in-change (neither term has any direct source in Ovid's Latin), Dryden possibly incorporates passing allusions to contemporary scientific discourse (Robert Boyle had recently argued for the replacement of the traditional belief in four basic 'elements' with a corpuscular or mechanical theory of matter, and the word 'elements' had been regularly used for the atoms of the Democritean/Lucretian system[26]), and to Catholic theology, according to which the '*real Presence* of Christ's body' and its 'very *substance*' were believed to be present in the 'elements' of Eucharistic bread and wine.[27]

My suggestion, however, is not that Dryden has merely used the occasion of his rendering from Book 15 of Ovid's *Metamorphoses* as an opportunity to smuggle in opportunistic allusions to contemporary politics and science, or to his own life, art, and religious beliefs. It seems, rather, that, in translating the speech of the Ovidian Pythagoras, Dryden entered an imaginative realm in which historical events, individual lives, the mysteries of religion (both classical and

[24] This topic features prominently in recent Ovidian scholarship. See, for example, *Ovidian Transformations: Essays on Ovid's 'Metamorphoses' and its Reception*, ed. Philip Hardie, Alessandro Barchiesi, and Stephen Hinds, Proceedings of the Cambridge Philological Society, Supplementary Volume No. 23 (Cambridge, 1999).

[25] See Greg Clingham, 'Another and the Same: Johnson's Dryden', in *Literary Transmission and Authority: Dryden and Other Writers*, ed. Earl Miner and Jennifer Brady (Cambridge, 1993), pp. 149–50.

[26] See *English Science: Bacon to Newton*, ed. Brian Vickers (Cambridge, 1987), p. 67; John Arthos, *The Language of Natural Description in Eighteenth-Century Poetry* (Ann Arbor MI, 1949), pp. 142–3.

[27] See Abraham Woodhead's [as R. H.'s] *A Compendious Discourse on the Eucharist* (Oxford, 1688), cited in Dryden, *Poems*, 3. 56. For the connection of 'translate' with 'transubstantiation', compare Laurence Ramsey, *The Practise of the Diuell* (London, ?1577), p. [4]: 'Of Bread into Flesh, I think it conuenient, / And Wine into Blood, quicke for to translate: / I might be more finer, with transubstantiate'.

Christian), the processes of literary creation and re-creation, and the poet's own imminent dissolution in death and achievement of immortality through his work, could be encompassed in a single, all-inclusive vision, in which it is difficult to separate the political, autobiographical, religious, and literary elements, or to differentiate the 'beliefs' expressed in the poetry from the deepest convictions of their author – however oddly they might seem to square with his officially-professed faith. For Dryden, the processes whereby a modern poet can discover a congeniality or identity of soul with several illustrious predecessors from the distant past, in acts of simultaneous self-surrender and self-discovery which seem almost the work of some larger power or Fate, are analogous with, or illustrative of, mysterious processes of nature, in which, in a perpetual cycle of annihilation and renewal, destruction, despair, and decay are constantly counterpointed by rebirth and hope. Dryden's very capacity to render the vision of the Ovidian Pythagoras seems to constitute, for him, proof of that vision's essential validity. The flux of nature which is the poem's subject matter, and the processes whereby it was conceived and composed, are, in the poet's conception, inexorably connected one to another.

# 10

## Some Varieties of Pope's Classicism

Educated eighteenth-century English culture was permeated at every level by the art, history, mythology, philosophy, and literature of ancient Greece and Rome.[1] School and university curricula were dominated by the study of classical (and particularly Latin) texts, in ways that had changed little since the Renaissance. Schoolboys and undergraduates were drilled not only in classical poetry, philosophy, and oratory but also in the historical, geographical, medical, mathematical, and legal lore of the ancient world. Figures from republican Rome attained the status of cult heroes among the English ruling classes. Eminent politicians and land-owning grandees had themselves sculpted in the manner and garb of virtuous Romans.[2] Young aristocrats and gentlemen on the Grand Tour visited the monuments of Rome, and later Herculaneum and Pompeii, and brought back with them physical relics of the classical past.[3] (Travel to Greece became more common as the century progressed.[4]) Parliamentary speakers modelled their orations on those of Cicero and Demosthenes. Classical

[1] For an overview, see the sections on 'Roman' and 'Grecian' in Chapter 7 of James Sambrook, *The Eighteenth Century: The Intellectual and Cultural Context of English Literature, 1700–1789* (2nd edition, London, 1993), pp. 195–209.

[2] See Philip Ayres, *Classical Culture and the Idea of Rome in Eighteenth-Century England* (Cambridge, 1997).

[3] See G. S. Bowersock, 'The Rediscovery of Herculaneum and Pompeii', *The American Scholar*, 47 (1978), 461–70; Francis Haskell and Nicholas Penny, *Taste and the Antique: The Lure of Classical Sculpture, 1500–1900* (New Haven CT, 1981); Jonathan Scott, *The Pleasures of Antiquity: British Collectors of Greece and Rome* (New Haven CT, 2003).

[4] See T. J. B. Spencer, *Fair Greece, Sad Relic: Literary Philhellenism from Shakespeare to Byron* (London, 1954); Timothy Webb, ed., *English Romantic Hellenism, 1700–1824* (Manchester, 1982).

heroism served as a model for those forging an expanding British empire.[5] The country's great landscape gardens were adorned, sometimes according to complex iconographic schemes, with Graeco-Roman temples, their grottoes sporting statues of classical river- and sea-deities.[6] Portrait painters depicted their female subjects in the guise of classical goddesses and the Muses. The architecture of country houses imitated Graeco-Roman practice and design.[7] Operatic plots regularly drew on ancient myth. Periodical essays were prefaced by quotations from the Roman poets.[8] A burgeoning print culture was making available the majority of ancient writing of all kinds in translation, for the benefit those whose Latin and Greek was rusty, or who had been denied by social status or gender the classical education enjoyed by the largely moneyed, largely male élite.

Eighteenth-century poetry affords particularly prominent evidence of the larger culture's saturation in the classics. Some of the century's major poets (Pope, Gay, Swift, Johnson, Smart, Cowper) and some distinguished writers whose work is less well known today (such as Philip Francis, Christopher Pitt, and Nicholas Rowe) devoted some of their best energies to the translation and imitation of classical verse. Many of the century's major poetic genres (pastoral, georgic, satire, ode, verse-epistle), and its poetry of scientific speculation and rural retirement, had their direct roots in classical practice. Others (burlesque, mock-heroic, the country-house poem) depended more obliquely yet no less certainly on classical precedent. Eighteenth-century literary criticism drew constant comparisons and connections between classical and English

[5] See Linda Colley, *Britons: Forging the Nation, 1707–1837* (New Haven CT, 1992), pp. 164–77.

[6] See John Summerson, 'The Classical Country House in Eighteenth-Century England', *Journal of the Royal Society of Arts*, 107 (1959), 539–87; Kenneth Woodbridge, *Landscape and Antiquity: Aspects of English Culture at Stourhead, 1718–1838* (Oxford, 1970); G. B. Clarke, ed., *Descriptions of Lord Cobham's Gardens at Stowe (1700–1750)*, Buckinghamshire Record Society, No. 26 (1990); James Turner, 'The Structure of Henry Hoare's Stourhead', *Art Bulletin*, 61 (1979), 68–77; Malcolm Kelsall, 'The Iconography of Stourhead', *Journal of the Warburg and Courtauld Institutes*, 46 (1983), 133–43.

[7] See Damie Stillman, *English Neoclassical Architecture*, 2 vols. (London, 1988).

[8] See 'Appendix IV: Sources of Mottoes', in *The Spectator*, ed. Donald F. Bond, 5 vols. (Oxford, 1965), 5. 225–32.

verse, sometimes – as in the period's numerous poems on the 'art of poetry' – imitating the form and manner, as well as echoing the concerns, of the Greek and Roman critics. Popular poetic and dramatic works such as Joseph Addison's verse-drama *Cato* (1713) took their subject matter from classical history and myth. And, as a glance at the notes in any scholarly edition will confirm, the presence of Greek and Rome history, legend, and literature is everywhere visible in eighteenth-century poetry in the form of allusion, echo, and passing reference. When providing examples for imitation by trainee poets, the poetical commonplace books of the period presented an indiscriminate juxtaposition of classical and English examples.[9]

Ubiquitous as it was, the presence of the classics in eighteenth-century English poetry – and in eighteenth-century culture more generally – was, and remains to this day, a focus of controversy. The late seventeenth- and early eighteenth-century 'Quarrel of Ancients and Moderns' (also known in England as 'The Battle of the Books') centred on whether ancient accomplishments in philosophy, science, and the arts should be regarded as absolute ideals, never to be surpassed, or whether modern writers and thinkers should strike out on their own, independent of classical precedent.[10] The more extreme Moderns cast their opponents as nostalgic reactionaries who were both insufficiently respectful of recent literature and scholarship, and inadequately attentive to the historical 'otherness' of ancient cultures. The Ancients retorted that much modern scholarship was mere pedantry or modishness, that much modern literature was incompetent, dull, and venally motivated, and that an admiration for antiquity did not necessitate slavish genuflection and inert copying. Such arguments continued as the century progressed. The earlier eighteenth-century preoccupation with the classics, its critics maintained with increasing insistence, was grounded in a belief in timeless

[9] See particularly Edward Bysshe, *The Art of English Poetry* (2 vols., London, 1702; many subsequent editions); Charles Gildon, *The Complete Art of Poetry* (2 vols., London, 1718); Edward Bysshe, *The British Parnassus* (2 vols., London, 1714).

[10] See Douglas Lane Patey, 'Ancients and Moderns', in *The Cambridge History of Literary Criticism, Vol. 4: The Eighteenth Century*, ed. H. B. Nisbet and Claude Rawson (Cambridge, 1977) pp. 32–71; Joseph M. Levine, *The Battle of the Books: History and Literature in the Augustan Age* (Ithaca NY, 1991).

human values and unchanging human nature which was inadequately attentive to cultural difference, and to the radically transforming processes of historical change. It also betrayed creative insecurity, and masked an essential lack of the 'original genius' which, some now maintained, constituted the only legitimate basis of literary greatness.

Such trends, it should be emphasized, represented only one strand in a complex web of critical opinion, and for a long time coexisted with much enduring respect for earlier poetic classicism. Works like Pope's translation of Homer's *Iliad* continued to be reprinted in popular editions, and were widely read throughout the literate population. But by the end of the nineteenth century, the eighteenth-century handling of classical literature now seemed substantially outmoded. Its reverence for classical precedent smacked of Frenchified rule-mongering. Its translations seemed decorous and 'artificial' cuttings-down of their Greek and Roman originals to the size of the Age of Elegance. The scholar Richard Bentley's celebrated reaction to Pope's *Iliad* ('A very pretty poem, Mr Pope, but you mustn't call it Homer') now seemed merely a self-evident truism.[11]

Such attitudes have remained surprisingly resilient to this day. A number of specialist studies, to be sure, have offered positive revaluations of the aesthetic foundations of eighteenth-century poetic classicism. Such work has demonstrated the sensitivity, creativity, and intelligence with which the best writers of the period engaged with the literature of Greece and Rome. It has illuminated the subtle blend of similarity and difference which the eighteenth-century poets discovered in their classical precursors – a stance far

[11] For the familiar version of Bentley's quip, see Samuel Johnson, *Works*, ed. Sir John Hawkins, 11 vols. (London, 1787), 4. 126 *n*. H. A. Mason notes that 'a more probable, and certainly a juster, account was given in *The Gentleman's Magazine*, first in October 1773 and again in June 1781, where the 'pay-off' line runs, 'Why, . . . the lines are good lines, the translation is a good translation, but you must not call it Homer, it is a good translation of Spondanus' (*To Homer through Pope* (London, 1972), p. 2). Spondanus (Jean de Sponde, 1557–95) was the author of a Latin translation of Homer, with substantial commentary (1583, many subsequent editions), on which Pope drew heavily when making his version. Spondanus's commentary contains much moralizing and allegorizing commentary on Homer's text.

removed from the naive 'essentialism' with which they have been sometimes charged.[12] But, despite such endeavours, the classicism of eighteenth-century poets remains uncongenial to many modern readers. In particular, the translations which formed such a central part of their project are nowadays mostly unread. There is, for example, no scholarly edition of the complete text of Pope's *Iliad* – a work which most eighteenth-century readers would have automatically included among the supreme poetic masterpieces of the age – currently in print.

Various cultural and educational factors seem to have conspired to produce this situation, some of which were touched on in the Introduction above, and are further explored in Chapter 11 below. The resistance to eighteenth-century classicism seems also to have a significant political and ideological dimension. In a study which is still influential a half-century after its publication, Ian Watt campaigned for the early (middle-class) novelists' emphasis on 'truth to individual experience', in the face of a supposed (élite) classicizing

[12] See, particularly, Reuben Brower, *Alexander Pope: The Poetry of Allusion* (Oxford, 1959); Howard Erskine-Hill, *The Augustan Idea in English Literature* (London, 1983); Stuart Gillespie and David Hopkins, eds., *The Oxford History of Literary Translation in English, Vol. 3: 1660–1790* (Oxford, 2005); Douglas Knight, *Pope and the Heroic Tradition: A Critical Study of his 'Iliad'* (New Haven CT, 1951); Maynard Mack, *Collected in Himself: Essays Critical, Biographical, and Bibliographical on Pope and Some of his Contemporaries* (Newark DE, 1982); H. A. Mason, *To Homer through Pope: An Introduction to Homer's 'Iliad' and Pope's Translation* (London, 1972); Fred Parker, '"Talking Scripture out of Church": Parson Adams and the Partiality of Translation', *Translation and Literature*, 14 (2005), 179–95; 'Classic Simplicity', in *Translation and the Classic: Identity and Change in the History of Culture*, ed. Alexandra Lianeri and Vanda Zajko (Oxford, 2008), pp. 227–42; Felicity Rosslyn, '"Awed by Reason": Pope on Achilles', *Cambridge Quarterly*, 9 (1980), 189–202; *Alexander Pope: A Literary Life* (London, 1990); 'Heroic Couplet Translation – A Unique Solution?', in *Translating Literature*, ed. Susan Bassnett (Cambridge, 1997), pp. 41–63; *Pope's Iliad: A Selection with Commentary* (2nd edition, London, 2002); Steven Shankman, *Pope's 'Iliad': Homer in the Age of Passion* (Princeton NJ, 1983); Robin Sowerby, 'Pope and Horace', in Charles Martindale and David Hopkins, eds., *Horace Made New* (Cambridge, 1993), pp. 159–83; 'The Augustan *Odyssey*', *Translation and Literature*, 4 (1995), 157–81; 'The Decorum of Pope's *Iliad*', *Translation and Literature*, 13 (2004), 49–79; *The Augustan Art of Poetry: Augustan Translation of the Classics* (Oxford, 2006); Frank Stack, *Pope and Horace: Studies in Imitation* (Cambridge, 1985); Charles Tomlinson, *Metamorphoses: Essays on Translation* (Manchester, 2003); Howard D. Weinbrot, *Augustus Caesar in 'Augustan' England: The Decline of a Classical Norm* (Princeton NJ, 1978).

emphasis on 'general human types' and 'general truths'.[13] And there has been a persistent tendency – no doubt reinforced by the continuing association of classical learning with educational and social privilege – to identify eighteenth-century classicism with a 'gentry' culture, fighting a rearguard action against the more 'progressive' tendencies of its age.

Some truth must be conceded to the hostile modern view of eighteenth-century classicism. The paraphernalia of classical art and learning were, indeed, sometimes used in the art and literature of the period in merely inert, conventional, and ideologically oppressive ways. Some of the classical allusions in eighteenth-century minor poetry are, to be sure, merely routine and predictable displays of learned lumber acquired in the course of a genteel education. And some of the period's translations may fairly be described as weakly derivative exercises in the Drydenian, Popeian, or Miltonic mode.[14]

But the classical engagement of the period's best poets is of an altogether different kind. In such work, the eighteenth-century poets, like their seventeenth-century predecessors who have been the subjects of earlier chapters in this book, stand in an active, dialogic relationship with their classical sources, using their encounter with a poetic peer or with styles and forms from a 'foreign' culture to nourish and revitalize the native tradition, and extending their own imaginative vision by internalizing and articulating sentiments and perceptions derived from the distant past. In recreating imaginings of their ancient predecessors, the greatest eighteenth-century poets were thus simultaneously discovering potentialities in themselves and in their own culture, and making those potentialities available to their readers. The sentiments of the late Philip Larkin (quoted in the Introduction above), the eighteenth-century classical poets would have thought, far from guaranteeing superior creative integrity, almost inevitably involve imprisoning oneself in the tunnel vision of one time, one place, one personality, and one literary tradition.

[13] Ian Watt, *The Rise of the Novel: Studies in Defoe, Richardson and Fielding* (London, 1957), pp. 9–34.

[14] See Penelope Wilson, 'Classical Poetry and the Eighteenth-Century Reader', in *Books and their Readers in Eighteenth-Century*, ed. Isabel Rivers (Leicester, 1982), pp. 69–96.

The poetic dealings of the period's greatest poet, Alexander Pope, with classical antiquity took a variety of forms, from the full-dress translation of the *Homer*, through 'imitation', to works which were more obliquely, but no less certainly, indebted to ancient styles and forms. This chapter will consider three representative examples of Pope's engagement with classical poetry, laying particular stress on the dynamically active, self-exploratory nature of his dealings with his classical forebears.

*Eloisa to Abelard*, first published in Pope's *Works* (1717), records the imagined thoughts of its heroine, writing from the convent of the Paraclete to her former tutor and lover Peter Abelard, now emasculated, and also living in monastic retirement. The main source for Pope's poem was John Hughes's English translation (1709), via the French, of the extant Latin correspondence between the two lovers,[15] but, significantly, Pope recasts this celebrated medieval love affair in the form of one of Ovid's *Heroides* – a set of fictional verse-letters from celebrated heroines of Greek mythology. This recasting can be seen to constitute both a creative reworking and an implicit critique of its classical model.[16] In his Preface to the composite Restoration translation of the *Heroides*, *Ovid's Epistles* (1680) John Dryden had drawn attention to the delicate and searching nature of Ovid's depiction of the passion of love, but had also noted the somewhat knowing and modish way in which Ovid had 'Romaniz'd his *Grecian* Dames', writing 'too pointedly for his Subject' and making 'his persons speak more Eloquently than the violence of their Passion would admit: so that he is frequently witty out of season: leaving the Imitation of Nature, and the cooler dictates of his Judgment, for the false applause of Fancy' (*Works*, 1. 114, 112). A notable feature of the *Heroides* is the way in which Ovid's deft recasting of familiar stories allows the reader a sophisticated knowingness about the heroines' emotions which goes beyond the perceptions of the women themselves. In his version of Canace's report of her incestuous

[15] For details, see *TE*, 2. 295–8.

[16] The situation is complicated by the fact that the original Latin letters show signs of having been influenced, in their turn, by Ovid's *Heroides*: see D. W. Robertson, *Abelard and Heloise* (New York, 1972), pp. 125–35, and Peter Dronke, *Women Writers of the Middle Ages* (Cambridge, 1984), pp. 107–8.

passion for her brother Macareus, quoted in Chapter 7 above, Dryden had extended this feature of Ovid's collection by adding witty strokes (conspicuously marked in his text with inverted commas) which invite the reader to speculate on Canace's feelings during the act, and to entertain a prurient superiority towards her half-regretful, half-gloating reminiscences. Dryden's knowing tone, and the neat antitheses by which it is conveyed, were immediately spotted and shrewdly parodied by the minor wit, Matthew Stevenson:

> When half denying, half contented
> We met in full, and full consented;
> Then what with joy, and what with that
> Of guilt, my heart went pitty-pat.[17]

But in *Eloisa to Abelard* Ovid's characteristic antitheses are deployed to quite different effect, to render, with absolute seriousness the tumult of Eloisa's sufferings:

> I ought to grieve, but cannot what I ought;
> I mourn the lover, not lament the fault;
> I view my crime, but kindle at the view,
> Repent old pleasures, and sollicit new:
> Now turn'd to heav'n, I weep my past offence,
> Now think of thee, and curse my innocence.
> Of all affliction taught a lover yet,
> 'Tis sure the hardest science to forget!
>
> (183–90; *TE*, 2. 335)

Eloisa's 'sad' and 'tender story', Pope makes clear in the final lines of the poem, are ones with which he feels a sense of close personal identity, and had rendered with wholehearted empathy.

During the course of the poem Eloisa attributes her woes to an irresolvable conflict between love and religious commitment. But the ultimate balance of her arguments, and of the poem as a whole, falls decidedly in favour of love. In 'Palamon and Arcite', Dryden's version of Chaucer's 'Knight's Tale', Arcite, defending himself against Palamon's charge that he has betrayed their friendship by declaring his love for Emily (with whose 'Charms' Palamon had already been

[17] [Matthew Stevenson], *The Wits Paraphrased: Or, Paraphrase upon Paraphrase. In a Burlesque of the Several Late Translations of Ovid's Epistles* (London, 1680), p. 12.

smitten), had described love as a formidably amoral force which overrides all human laws, sanctions, and obligations:

> And know'st thou not, no Law is made for Love?
> Law is to Things which to free Choice relate;
> Love is not in our Choice, but in our Fate:
> Laws are but positive: Loves Pow'r we see
> Is Natures Sanction, and her first Decree.
> Each Day we break the Bond of Humane Laws
> For Love, and vindicate the Common Cause.
> Laws for defence of Civil Rights are plac'd,
> Love throws the Fences down, and makes a general Waste:
> Maids, Widows, Wives, without distinction fall;
> The sweeping Deluge, Love, comes on, and covers all.
>
> (1. 331–6; *Works*, 7. 73)

And Dryden's translation of Lucretius' passage on love in Book 4 of *De Rerum Natura* had stressed the futility of lovers' agonized and delusory strivings to attain physical unity and satisfaction:

> For Love, and Love alone of all our joyes
> By full possession does but fan the fire,
> The more we still enjoy, the more we still desire.
>
> ('Lucretius... Concerning the Nature of Love', 50–2; *Works*, 3. 58)

Pope's Eloisa echoes the terms of both passages, but vehemently rejects their negative implications, defiantly proclaiming her unrepentantly single-minded commitment to Love's laws:

> How oft', when press'd to marriage, have I said,
> Curse on all laws but those which love has made!
> Love, free as air, at sight of human ties,
> Spreads his light wings, and in a moment flies.
> Let wealth, let honour, wait the wedded dame,
> August her deed, and sacred be her fame;
> Before true passion all those views remove,
> Fame, wealth, and honour! what are you to Love?
> The jealous God, when we profane his fires,
> Those restless passions in revenge inspires;
> And bids them make mistaken mortals groan,
> Who seek in love for ought but love alone...
> When love is liberty, and nature, law:

All then is full, possessing and possest,
No craving Void left aking in the breast:
Ev'n thought meets thought ere from the lips it part,
And each warm wish springs mutual from the heart.

(73–84; 92–6; *TE*, 2. 325–7)

Pope's rendering of Eloisa's predicament answers precisely to Dryden's description of Ovid's capacity to provoke the reader's 'concernment' with a heroine 'in the violence of her passions' (Preface to *Ovid's Epistles*; *Works*, 1. 54), while avoiding the artful 'placing' of his speakers that to more tender-hearted readers seemed like frigidly masculine condescension. As a consequence *Eloisa* was frequently applauded by early readers for its 'improvement' of the Ovidian epistle in a more passionately inward and full-blooded direction.[18] Pope's profound empathy with Eloisa, to be sure, provoked embarrassment in some pious quarters. The poet's editor, William Bowles, declared that 'The "Eloisa," alone, is sufficient to convict him of licentiousness, *gross licentiousness*'.[19] John Aikin was worried that *Eloisa* had given 'too forcible an expression to sentiments inconsistent with female purity', but finally defended the poem on the grounds that Pope 'has painted' the 'miseries' of Eloisa's plight 'with no less force than the inconsiderate raptures which led to it'.[20] Though Joseph Warton also consoled himself with the thought that Pope's ultimate intention was 'to shew the force of religion over passion at last, and to represent her as a little calm and resigned to her destiny, and way of life', he was fully alert to the 'truly poetical power' and forceful 'story painting' whereby Pope has given 'the reader a view of the various turns and tumults of passion, and the different sentiments with which Eloisa is agitated', and has created in her 'the

[18] For three modern accounts which, in different ways, endorse the eighteenth-century admiration of Pope's empathetic presentation of Eloisa, see Gillian Beer, '"Our Unnatural No-Voice": The Heroic Epistle, Pope, and Women's Gothic', *The Yearbook of English Studies*, 12 (1982), 125–51; Lawrence Lipking, *Abandoned Women and Poetic Tradition* (Chicago and London, 1988), pp. 144–52; and Susan Manning, 'Eloisa's Abandonment', *Cambridge Quarterly*, 22 (1993), 231–48.

[19] William Bowles, *Observations on the Poetical Character of Pope*, pp. 13–14, quoted in Lord Byron, *The Complete Miscellaneous Prose*, ed. Andrew Nicholson (Oxford, 1991), p. 483.

[20] John Aikin, *Letters to a Young Lady on a Course of English Poetry* (London, 1804), pp. 82–3.

genuine voice of nature and passion'. Pope, Warton believed, had previously translated Ovid's epistle of 'Sapho to Phaon' with a 'faithfulness and elegance' which 'much excels' any of the versions in the 1680 *Ovid's Epistles*. But that translation was, he believed, itself far excelled by *Eloisa*. *Eloisa*, Warton was convinced, would outlast Pope's satirical writings, since 'WIT and SATIRE are transitory and perishable, but NATURE and PASSION are eternal'.[21] Oliver Goldsmith considered 'Eloisa to Abelard' 'superior to any thing in the epistolary way'.[22] And Samuel Johnson overcame any uneasiness one might have expected him to feel at the potential blasphemy of some of Eloisa's sentiments to praise Pope's poem as 'one of the most happy productions of human wit' which has effortlessly 'excelled every composition of the same kind'.[23] Perhaps the most passionate of all the admirers of *Eloisa* was Byron, who angrily defended Pope against Bowles's charge of 'licentiousness', declaring: 'I do believe that such a subject never was – nor ever could be treated by any poet with so much delicacy mingled with at the same time with [*sic*] such true and intense passion'. 'If you search for Passion', Byron proclaimed, 'where is it to be found stronger than in the Epistle from Eloisa to Abelard?'[24]

Pope's period is still, despite the vigorous health warnings offered by several standard handbooks on the period, regularly described as the 'Augustan' age of English literature.[25] M. H. Abrams summarizes the traditional view, noting that 'the leading writers of the time . . . themselves drew the parallel to the Roman Augustans, and deliberately imitated their literary forms and subjects, their emphasis on social concerns, and their ideals of moderation, decorum, and urbanity'.[26]

[21] Joseph Warton, *An Essay on the Writings and Genius of Pope*, 2 vols. (4th edition, 1782) [Vol. 1 first published 1756], 1. 299, 305, 311, 318, 326, 329, 347.

[22] John Barnard, ed., *Pope: The Critical Heritage* (London, 1973), p. 456.

[23] Samuel Johnson, *The Lives of the Most Eminent English Poets*, ed. Roger Lonsdale, 4 vols. (Oxford, 2006), 4. 11, 72.

[24] Byron, *Complete Miscellaneous Prose*, pp. 177–8, 110–11.

[25] For the warnings, see Donald Greene, *The Age of Exuberance: Backgrounds to Eighteenth-Century English Literature* (New York, 1970), p. 91; James Sambrook, *The Eighteenth Century*, pp. 239–40.

[26] M. H. Abrams, M. H., *A Glossary of Literary Terms* (7th edition, Fort Worth TX, 1999), p. 214.

Such an account is seriously misleading in several ways. First, many of the classical poets translated, imitated and echoed in the period – Boethius, Homer, Juvenal, Lucretius, Lucan, Martial, Persius, for example – were not 'Roman Augustans' at all. (It is sometimes forgotten by students of English literature that 'classical literature' is not a time-free monolith but a body of writing from twelve and a half centuries – roughly the equivalent of the period between *Beowulf* and the present – by authors of very different types and temperaments in two different and constantly changing languages, and from a wide variety of geographical and cultural contexts.) Several of the classical poets imitated in the 'Augustan' period, moreover, are conspicuously notable for their *lack* of 'moderation, decorum, and urbanity'. Furthermore, as recent scholarship has shown, eighteenth-century English attitudes to Roman Augustanism were themselves far more complex and diverse than Abrams implies, with a Tacitean hostility to Augustus-the-tyrant coexisting with positive admiration for the emperor's achievements as peacemaker and cultural patron.[27]

Of all the Roman Augustans, Horace might be thought to be most accurately characterized by Abrams's description. But Horace was himself a controversial figure, being admired by some for his Socratic combination of familiar wit and philosophical profundity, and excoriated by others as a self-serving and ethically inconsistent flatterer.[28] Consequently Horace's complex ironies seemed to some to emanate from a poised self-awareness which undermines complacency and dogmatism, while to others they betrayed a shallow worldliness and suave sycophancy. In his *Imitations of Horace* Pope shows his awareness of both traditions, adding his own layers of irony to create a voice which is neither simply 'Pope' nor 'Horace' but the product of a complex and ever-shifting dialogue, in which the Roman

[27] For the 'Tacitean' view, see particularly Weinbrot, *Augustus Caesar in 'Augustan' England*. In *The Augustan Idea in English Literature*, Howard Erskine-Hill does full justice to the element of truth in the traditional account, while acknowledging other cross-currents, and also demonstrating that 'The Augustan Idea' is not limited to the period of English literature traditionally designated 'Augustan'. In *The Augustan Art of Poetry*, Robin Sowerby considers the term 'Augustan' specifically in relation to eighteenth-century poets' indebtedness to the artistic ideals and practice of Virgil.

[28] See Stack, *Pope and Horace*, pp. 3–17; Weinbrot, *Augustus Caesar in 'Augustan' England*, pp. 120–49.

poet is sometimes invoked as an ally, sometimes regarded at a more quizzical distance, and sometimes used as a stalking horse for highly subversive commentary on the cultural politics of Pope's own day.

Horace's first Epistle of Book 2 is a direct address to Augustus, in which the poet canvasses his emperor's support for contemporary work which, Horace maintains, surpasses that of earlier Roman poets in its refinement and elegance. Horace adopts a tone which is both genial and intimate. Extravagant eulogy is tempered and complicated with the assumption of an assertive self-confidence which emboldens Horace to offer Augustus forthright advice and to criticize aspects of the Greek literature which the emperor so loved. And Horace deploys witty self-deprecation to insinuate disarming doubts about the very modern poetry for which he is campaigning. The nuanced familiarities of Horace's tone are utterly transformed by Pope, who addresses his 'Epistle to Augustus' to King George II (George Augustus), a monarch renowned for his philistinism, and for the favours he bestowed on third-rate poets and corrupt politicians. Horace's opening praise of Augustus' military triumphs is transformed by Pope into a piece of savage sarcasm which depends on the reader's perception of how inappropriately the Horatian eulogy fits the modern monarch: the seas, Pope's readers would know, were far from 'open' at the time (English merchant ships were being regularly harassed by Spanish cruisers); and George's excursions 'in Arms abroad' were not military expeditions but prolonged, and much resented, visits to his mistress in Hanover.

> While You, great Patron of Mankind, sustain
> The balanc'd World, and open all the Main;
> Your Country, chief, in Arms abroad defend,
> At home with Morals, Arts, and Laws amend;
> How shall the Muse, from such a Monarch, steal
> An hour, and not defraud the Publick Weal?
>
> (1–6; *TE*, 4. 195)

When, later in his poem (245–7), Horace, whose text Pope prints opposite his own, explicitly praises Augustus' good literary taste, the English 'equivalent' of the Roman sentiments is clearly signalled – by an obtrusive blank space.

But Pope has not merely hijacked Horace's Epistle for the purposes of harsh Opposition satire. The central section of the poem, in which

Horace charts the evolutionary development of Roman literature from its primitive beginnings to its present refinement, is recast and extended by Pope as a retrospective review of English poetry, in which Pope deploys his Horatian persona to reflect on his own great predecessors, blending generous praise with delineations of his precursors' weaknesses so acute that they have reverberated throughout later critical discussions of those authors. His famous lines on Milton's God – still regularly cited by Milton critics – have no direct equivalent in Horace:

> Milton's strong pinion now not Heav'n can bound,
> Now serpent-like, in prose he sweeps the ground,
> In Quibbles, Angel and Archangel join,
> And God the Father turns a School-Divine.
>
> (99–102; *TE*, 4. 203)

And Horace's reflections on the spirited but rough-hewn and under-revised Roman attempts to imitate Greek tragedy are applied to more distinguished writers nearer home:

> But Otway fail'd to polish or refine,
> And fluent Shakespear scarce effac'd a line.
> Ev'n copious Dryden, wanted, or forgot,
> The last and greatest Art, the Art to blot.
>
> (277–81; *TE*, 4. 219)

In the 'Epistle to Augustus' Pope both aligns himself with Horace, seeing, and developing, modern analogies in the spirit of Horace's pocket history of Roman poetry, and simultaneously distances himself from his model, powerfully asserting the vast gulf between the opportunities afforded by ancient Rome and modern London for a poetic culture supportive of and protected by the ruling powers. Pope's use of Horace is complex. The poem complicates the binary opposition of Ancients and Moderns, speaking with the voice of an Ancient authority to assert the merits of Modern verse, while simultaneously signalling the decadence and corruption of Modern, as against Ancient, civilization. The Epistle rests, therefore, not on any simple identification of ancient and modern worlds, or on an assertion of the blanket superiority of the former over the latter, but on a subtle sense of difference-in-similarity. If Rome and London are, in some senses, very close, they are also, in others, worlds apart. Pope gains a new perspective on his own culture by partially inhabiting a vantage point outside that culture. Such a process involves a cross-cultural dialogue which Pope knows (the most exquisite irony of all) the poem's supposed addressee couldn't begin to understand.

The standard criticism of Pope's translation of the *Iliad* has been that, rather than faithfully rendering the Greek, Pope merely assimilates Homer to the 'polite' social and religious norms of eighteenth-century England and to Latinate ideals of epic decorum. Such criticisms are often illustrated by a handful of famous instances: the 'elevation' of the fly to which Menelaus is compared into a hornet (*Iliad*, 17. 642–5); the 'dignifying' of the ass with which Ajax is compared (11. 683–90); the assimilation of Homer's Zeus (1. 726–35) to Milton's God. But such examples, like the 'comic' definitions regularly quoted from Johnson's *Dictionary*, give a misleading impression of Pope's translation as a whole. For while Pope certainly modifies Homer's earthy realism and verbal directness on many occasions, to make the Greek poet more amenable to stylistic expectations derived from Virgil and Milton and commended by contemporary French critics and translators,[29] he also leaves intact the greater part of Homer's narrative, much of which, we should remember, deals with remorselessly brutal slaughter on a remote, heroic battlefield, a scenario as remote as is conceivable from any eighteenth-century drawing-room, ballroom, or library. And if Homer's Zeus is sometimes momentarily brought close to Pope's own God, there are many parts of the poem where his activities, and those of the other Olympians, are very far removed from anything conceivable within a Christian framework. Throughout his translation, Pope responds vividly to the 'animated Nature' of the epic narrative, summoning up a constant stream of English eloquence to match the 'sublime' 'fire' with which, he thinks, Homer has rendered his incidents and characters.

[29] For the sources used and methods deployed by Pope at the local level, see Felicity Rosslyn, in 'The Making of Pope's Translation of the *Iliad*' (Unpublished PhD thesis, Cambridge, 1978), which offers a full commentary on Pope's last four books. An excellent summary account of the topic is offered in the same author's 'Heroic Couplet Translation – A Unique Solution?'.

Far from merely cutting Homer down to eighteenth-century size, Pope can be seen to be mobilizing and expressing a far wider range of religious, ethical, and psychological sympathies in the act of translation than were available to him from within his own culture. He offers, for example, a remarkably uncensorious presentation of Homer's proud and irascible hero, Achilles, signalling him out, as we shall see in Chapter 11, for special admiration for the 'Air of Greatness' which he displays just before one of his most appallingly brutal acts: the slaughter of the trembling suppliant Lycaon.[30] Rendering Homer was, for Pope, both, as is abundantly and constantly clear from the Notes which accompany his translation, an exercise in scholarly and historical exploration of an alien culture, and, simultaneously and paradoxically, an encounter with 'Nature': the great unseen reality in which, Pope suggests in *An Essay on Criticism*, all human being participate, but which is normally hidden from their view, unless revealed by great art:

> First follow NATURE, and your Jugment frame
> By her just Standard, which is still the same:
> *Unerring Nature*, still divinely bright,
> One *clear, unchang'd*, and *Universal* Light,
> Life, Force, and Beauty, must to all impart,
> At once the *Source*, and *End*, and *Test* of *Art*.
> *Art* from that Fund each *just Supply* provides,
> Works *without Show*, and *without Pomp* presides:
> In some fair Body thus th' informing Soul
> With Spirits feeds, with Vigour fills the whole,
> Each Motion guides, and ev'ry Nerve sustains;
> *It self unseen*, but in th' *Effects*, remains.
>
> (68–79; *TE*, 1. 247–8)

The full glory and horror of the human condition, Pope was convinced, had been revealed more completely and variously in the Homeric epics than in any other single literary source. That fact, rather than their antiquity or fame, constituted their permanent

[30] On Pope and Achilles, see further Howard Clarke, *Homer's Readers*. Newark DE, 1981), pp. 136–40; Rosslyn, '"Awed by Reason"'; Shankman, *Pope's 'Iliad'*, pp. 3–51; Sowerby, *The Augustan Art of Poetry*, pp. 246–57.

claim on human attention. As with Virgil before him, when Pope read the *Iliad*,

> *Nature* and *Homer* were, he found, the *same*.
>
> (*An Essay on Criticism*, 135; *TE*, 1. 255)

Pope's conviction of the depth, range, and enduring validity of Homer's revelation of the human condition is nowhere more apparent than in his rendering of the passages in Book 3 of the *Iliad* depicting the plight of Helen, the Spartan queen whose abduction to Troy by Paris was the cause of the Trojan War. Near the beginning of Book 3, Helen is summoned by Iris to witness the single combat between her husband Menelaus and Paris. She is discovered at her loom:

> The golden Web her own sad Story crown'd,
> The *Trojan* Wars she weav'd (herself the Prize)
> And the dire Triumphs of her fatal Eyes.
>
> (170–2; *TE*, 7. 199)

Pope's 'fatal' (172) has multiple resonance: Helen's beauty is fat*ed* by the gods (she was given to Paris as his reward for judging Aphrodite the fairest of goddesses); it has caused many deaths on the battlefields of Troy; and it exerts a goddess-like spell over all that see her.

Iris' summons awakes Helen's 'former fires', which encompass more than merely her passion for Menelaus:

> Her Country, Parents, all that once were dear,
> Rush to her Thought, and force a tender Tear.
>
> (185–6; *TE*, 7. 200)

Pope's note on the passage conveys his sense of the compassionate understanding of Homer's depiction:

> The Reader has naturally an Aversion to this pernicious Beauty, and is apt enough to wonder at the *Greeks* for endeavouring to recover her at such an Expence. But her amiable Behaviour here, the secret Wishes that rise in favour of her rightful Lord, her Tenderness for her Parents and Relations, the Relentings of her Soul for the Mischiefs her Beauty had been the Cause of, the Confusion she appears in, the veiling her Face and dropping a Tear, are

Particulars so beautifully natural, as to make every Reader no less than *Menelaus* himself, inclin'd to forgive her at least, if not to love her.

(165*n*; *TE*, 7. 199)

'There is scarce a word' spoken by Helen, Pope affirms, 'that is not big with Repentance and Good-nature'.

The reader's feelings for Helen are confirmed by the reaction of the elders of Troy,

> Chiefs, who no more in bloody Fights engage,
> But wise thro' Time, and Narrative with Age,
> In Summer-Days like Grasshoppers rejoice,
> A bloodless Race, that send a feeble Voice.
>
> (199–202; *TE*, 7. 200–1)

These old men, who have every reason to curse Helen, find themselves marvelling at her spellbinding beauty:

> They cry'd, No wonder such Celestial Charms
> For nine long Years have set the World in Arms;
> What winning Graces! what majestick Mien!
> She moves a Goddess, and she looks a Queen!
>
> (205–8; *TE*, 7. 201)

When Helen encounters Priam on the battlements, he generously absolves her of blame for their plight:

> No Crime of thine our present Suff'rings draws,
> Not Thou, but Heav'ns disposing Will, the Cause;
> The Gods these Armies and this Force employ,
> The hostile Gods conspire the Fate of *Troy*.
>
> (215–18; *TE*, 7. 202)

But Helen cannot accept Priam's exonerating words. Her sense of guilt and shame at her betrayal of her country and 'Nuptial Bed' is so intense that she will, she says,

> mourn, 'till Grief or dire Disease
> Shall waste the Form whose Crime it was to please!
>
> (233–4; *TE*, 7. 203)

In Priam's words and Helen's reply, Pope can be seen to be responding eloquently to the 'double motivation' which, as modern scholarship has revealed, is so essential to Homer's presentation of the human lot.[31] Helen's position is, from one point of view, indeed 'fated': she had been, from the moment of Paris' arrival in Sparta, a plaything of the gods. But this does not, in her own eyes or in the reader's, exempt her from a profound sense of personal guilt. Her plight, in Pope's recreation of Homer's episode, is that of the archetypal Greek tragic protagonist, 'both an agent and once acted upon', simultaneously 'guilty and innocent'.[32]

Helen's vulnerability to Aphrodite's power is underlined later in the book, when the goddess compels her to bed with Paris, now rescued from the battlefield and returned to his chamber in Troy. Helen's 'secret Soul' is moved with passion for Paris 'unawares to herself' (497*n*). But once she recognizes the presence and working in her of the divine power, she rejects Paris, delivering a bold protest against the laws by which she must live. But, despite her courageous protest, she must obey Aphrodite's bidding. For, as the goddess makes clear to her, her survival depends on the preservation of the very beauty that has been her undoing:

> Obey the Pow'r from whom thy Glories rise:
> Should *Venus* leave thee, ev'ry Charm must fly,
> Fade from thy Cheek, and languish in thy Eye.
> Cease to provoke me, lest I make thee more
> The World's Aversion, than their Love before;
> Now the bright Prize for which Mankind engage,
> Then, the sad Victim of the Publick Rage.
>
> (514–20; *TE*, 7. 216)

Pope responds fully, in both his text and notes, to Homer's tragic conception of Helen's plight. Helen, he sees, is constrained by iron laws as binding as those which afflict the male heroes of the *Iliad*. She

[31] See Albin Lesky, 'Motivation by Gods and Men', trans. H. M. Harvey, in *Homer: Critical Assessments*, ed. Irene J. F. de Jong (4 vols., London, 1999), 2. 384–403 [first published in German, 1961]; Bernard Williams, *Shame and Necessity* (Berkeley, Los Angeles CA, London, 1993).

[32] Jean-Pierre Vernant and Pierre Vidal-Naquet, *Myth and Tragedy in Ancient Greece*, trans. Janet Lloyd (New York, 1988), p. 32.

is also endowed with a similar self-knowledge and eloquence. In his recreation of Homer's episode, Pope has moved far beyond the trivializing condescension to 'the fair sex' to be found, for example, in the pages of *The Spectator* to offer his contemporaries a deepened and extended sense of the dignity and vulnerability of female, and, by extension, all human existence.

# 11

## Pope's Trojan Geography

The first readers of Alexander Pope's translation of Homer's *Iliad*, published in instalments between 1715 and 1720, would have noticed a number of striking features which differentiated Pope's version from all that had preceded it. In addition to a substantial Preface, an 'Essay on the Life, Writings and Learning of Homer', and extensive notes on each Book commenting both on the meaning and beauties of Homer's text and on the challenges presented by the task of rendering it into English, Pope offered the reader detailed help in determining both the general physical layout of Homer's Trojan plain, and of the precise location within that terrain of each of the battles which comprise the bulk of the poem's action. In the course of his notes on the Catalogue of the Ships in Book 2, he included a fold-out map [Fig. 1] in conventional format, specially engraved by the celebrated cartographer John Senex, of 'Graecia Homerica' (comprising mainland Greece, the Aegean islands, and the west coast of Asia Minor), showing the locations from which each contingent in the Greek and Trojan armies had come. And a second map [Fig. 2] of the Trojan plain itself – an illustrated panorama of the kind frequently used in the later seventeenth century to depict contemporary battle scenes – was prefixed to 'Essay on Homer's Battels' which begins Volume 2.[1] As Robert Wood (on whom more below)

[1] I am grateful to Peter Barber and Debbie Hall of the Map Collections, British Library, for advice on Pope's maps. Both maps are omitted from Steven Shankman's otherwise excellent Penguin edition of Pope's *Iliad* (1996), and the former is even excluded from *TE* on the grounds that it would be 'illegible when reduced' – though it is reproduced, albeit in a simplified form, in the eighteenth-century octavo and duodecimo reprints of Pope's translation.

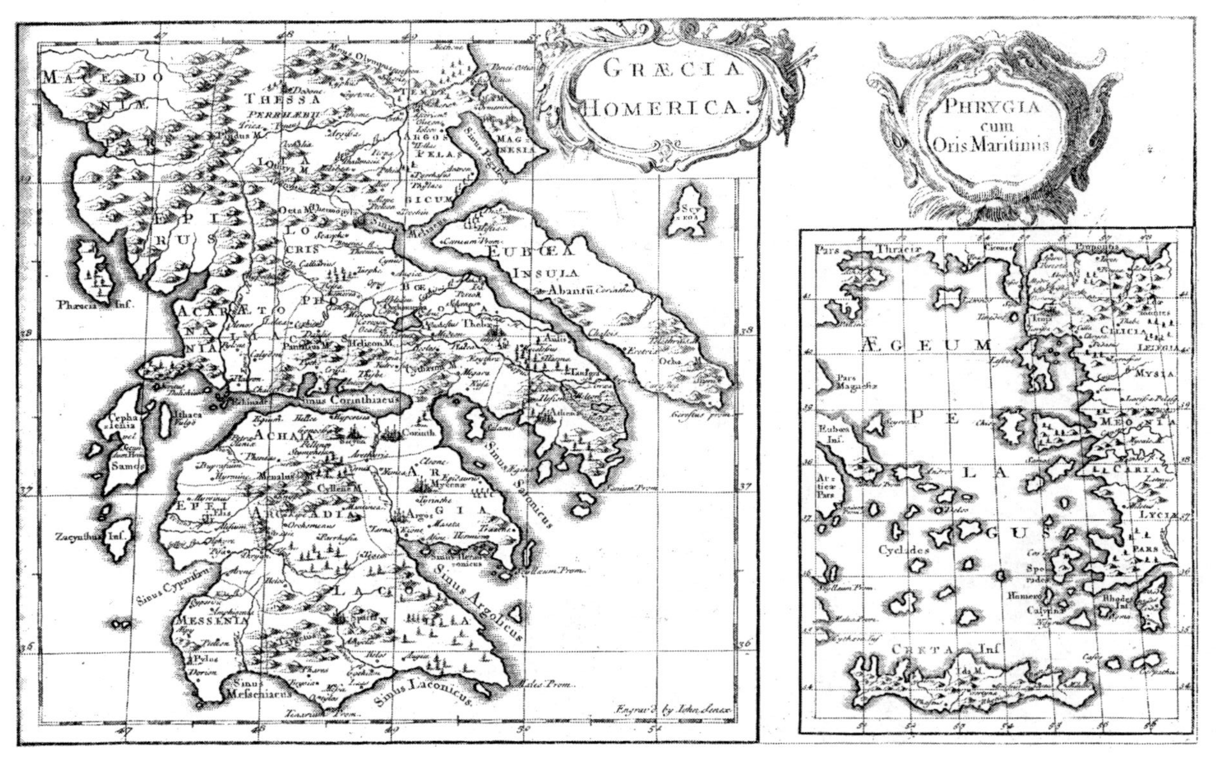


Figure 1. Pope's map of Homeric Greece (1715).

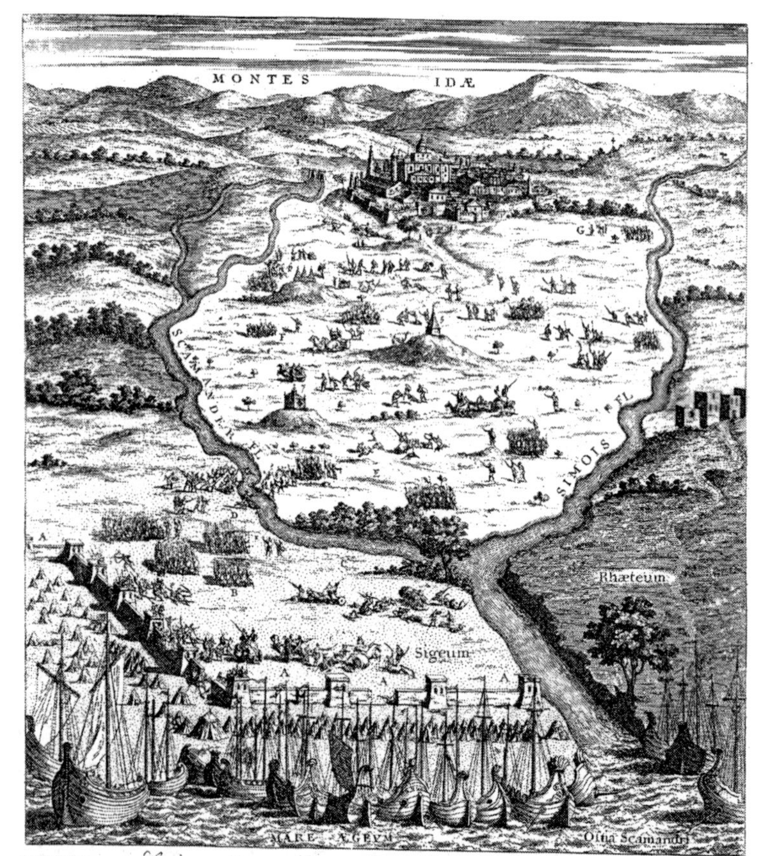


**Figure 2.** Pope's map of Troy (1716).

noted, Pope's first map was 'the only chart which has hitherto attempted to illustrate the principal scene of the action of the Iliad'. No maps had appeared in the edition of Homer by Spondanus (Jean de Sponde) or the French translation by Madame Anne Dacier, both consulted extensively by Pope while preparing his own version. Nor were there any where one might most have expected them: in the translation by John Ogilby, the work which, Pope told Joseph Spence, had provided his boyhood *entrée* to Homer, and whose author had achieved his greatest fame specifically as a compiler of maps and atlases of various kinds.[2] In addition to his maps, Pope's 'Index of Arts and Sciences' included in the last volume of his *Iliad* included a section on 'Geography': 'A TABLE *of those Places, whose Situation, Products, People, or History,* &c. *are particularized by* Homer' (*TE*, 8. 611–12).

Pope clearly took a personal interest in the preparation of his maps. On 24 August 1714, he wrote to his friend Edward Blount from Oxford, apropos of the map of 'Magna Graecia':

> I find still more reason to complain of the negligence of the Geographers in their Maps of *old Greece*, since I look'd upon two or three more noted names in the publick libraries here.

In issuing instructions to the engraver, Pope continues, he has had to modify existing maps to accommodate them to Homer's poem. This has involved the exercise of creatorly powers of the kind normally associated only with God:

> I have been forced to write to him in so high a style, that were my epistle intercepted, it would raise no small admiration in an ordinary man. There is scarce an order in it of less importance, than to remove such and such mountains, alter the course of such and such rivers, place a large city on such a coast, and raze another in another country. I have set bounds to the sea, and said to the land, *thus far shalt thou advance and no further.*[3]

Pope's map of the Trojan plain, together with his account in the 'Essay on Homer's Battels', and the 'Arguments' prefixed to each Book make it possible to reconstruct with some precision his sense of the location of Homer's action in both time and place. Pope's map views the plain of Troy from the sea. The Aegean sea is in the

[2] Robert Wood, *An Essay on the Original Genius and Writings of Homer* (London, 1775), p. 89 (henceforth *Essay*, and cited in the text). For Pope's boyhood reading of Ogilby, see Joseph Spence, *Observations, Anecdotes and Characters of Books and Men*, ed. James M. Osborn, 2 vols. (Oxford, 1966), 1. 13–14. On Ogilby's atlases, see Katharine S. Van Erde, *John Ogilby and the Taste of his Times* (Folkestone, 1976), pp. 95–143.

[3] Alexander Pope, *Correspondence*, ed. George Sherburn, 5 vols. (Oxford, 1956), 1. 246 (letter of 27 August 1714).

foreground, and into it flows the river Scamander, which has been joined by the river Simois a little distance inland. The two rivers form a figure 'Y', the arms of which enclose the bulk of the plain and the city of Troy. The Greek ships, with the tents and wall in front of them, are ranged along the shore, with the bulk of the ships on the left side of the Scamander. The Scamander itself emanates from two fountains, visible to the left of Troy, with the fig tree (mentioned by Andromache in Book 6 as the likely scene for any assault on the city) nearby. Dispersed across the plain, in front of the city, are the sepulchre of Myrinne, the monument of Ilus, and the tomb of Asietes, all landmarks that witness key events in Homer's action. The town of Callicolone (towards which Ares urges the Trojans in Book 20) is identified beyond Troy to the right. The Scaean Gate, the main gate of the city, is clearly visible facing the plain, with the beech tree, sacred to Jupiter, nearby. The mountains of Ida form a distant backdrop to the whole scene. Homer's Troy, Pope observes in the 'Essay', must have 'stood at a greater Distance from the Sea than those Ruins which have since been shewn for it' (*TE*, 7. 261) since, had the Greeks been encamped so near the city it would have been imprudent of them to have left the building of their fortifications till the tenth year of the siege. Anyway, a large space between the city and camp has to be assumed to accommodate the 'many various Adventures and Actions of war' that Homer describes.

Pope is as precise about the temporal duration of Homer's action as he is about its geographical location. The events of the *Iliad*, Pope calculates in his 'Arguments', encompass fifty-seven days *in toto*. Book 1 occupies the first twenty-two: nine days for the plague that afflicts the Greek army, one for the Greek council at which Agamemnon seizes Briseis (thereby precipitating Achilles' withdrawal from the fight), and twelve for the gods' sojourn in Ethiopia and return to Olympus. The events of Day 23, comprising the first battle between the Greek and Trojan armies and containing the *aristeia* of Diomedes, occupy Books 2–6, and conclude in Book 7, which also encompasses the truce, the funeral rites, and the building of the Greek fortifications (three further days). The second battle, in which the Greeks are driven back behind their fortifications and send an embassy to Achilles (Books 8–10), occupies Day 27. The third and fourth battles (Books 11–17), containing the Trojans' pursuit of the Greeks to their ships, and Patroclus' death at the hands of Hector, occupy Day 28. Day 29 and the ensuing night witness Hephaestus' forging of Achilles' arms. Day 30 sees Achilles' return to battle, his fight with the river, and his killing of Hector. The rest of the action (Books 23–4; Days 31–57) is taken up with the cremation and funeral games for Patroclus (three days), the lying of Hector's body in Achilles' tent (twelve days), and the truce for Hector's interment (another twelve).[4]

Each of the foregoing events is located precisely in spatial terms. The 'Scene' of Book 1, Pope writes in the 'Essay on Battels', 'lies in the Grecian Camp, then changes to Chrysa, and lastly to the Gods on Olympus' (the latter two locations being both clearly located on his map of 'Graecia Homerica'). Book 2 is set 'in the Graecian-Camp and upon the Sea-Shore; toward the end it removes to Troy'. 'It seems', Pope says, 'by the 465*th* Verse of the second Iliad',[5]

that the *Grecian* Army was drawn up under the several Leaders by the Banks of *Scamander* on that side toward the Ships: In the mean time that of *Troy* and the Auxiliaries was rang'd in Order at *Myrinne*'s Sepulchre. *Ibid.* V. 320 *of the Catal.* The Place of the *First Battel* where *Diomed* performs his Exploits, was near the joining of *Simois* and *Scamander*; for *Juno* and *Pallas* coming to him, alight at the confluence of those Rivers. *Il.* 5. V. 774. and that the *Greeks* had not yet past the Stream, but fought on that side next the Fleet, appears from V. 791 of the same Book, where *Juno* says *the* Trojans *now brave*

[4] Pope's concern for the precise duration of Homer's action was shared by René le Bossu, who computed it at forty-seven days: see *Monsieur Bossu's Treatise of the Epick Poem*, trans. W. J. (London, 1695), p. 108. Jean Racine also computed the timing of Homer's actions in his manuscript notes on the *Iliad*, altering his calculations as he worked from an initial total of forty-four days to forty-seven. Racine did not count the plague or the initial quarrel between Achilles and Agamemnon in his calculations, and his total thus tallies with Pope's, though there seem to be small discrepancies in their calculations *en route*. Racine's notes are printed in Jean Racine, *Oeuvres*, ed. P. Mesnard, 8 vols. (Paris, 1865–73), 6. 195–211. The problems connected with his revisions are discussed by Susannah Phillippo in 'The Legacy of Homer: the *Iliad* Annotations of Jean Racine,' *L'Antiquité Classique*, 65 (1996), 1–29. In his *Homeric Soundings* (Oxford, 1992), Oliver Taplin displays a similar interest in Homer's control over the timing of his action, noting that 'three quarters of the days covered by the whole poem are lumped together in blocks in the opening and closing phases', while 'there are, in fact, fourteen days of actual narrated events, and just four of them are days of battle' (p. 15).

[5] Pope specifies that his references 'are cited according to the number of lines in the Greek'.

*them at their very Ships.* But in the beginning of the sixth Book, the Place of Battel is specify'd to be between the Rivers of *Simois* and *Scamander*; so that the *Greeks* (tho' *Homer* does not particularize when, or in what manner) had then cross'd the Stream toward *Troy.*

The Engagement in the eighth Book is evidently close to the *Grecian* Fortification on the Shore. That Night *Hector* lay at *Ilus*'s Tomb in the Field, as *Dolon* tells us *Lib.* 10 V. 415. And in the eleventh Book the Battel is chiefly about *Ilus*'s Tomb.

In the twelfth, thirteenth, and fourteenth, about the Fortification of the *Greeks*, and in the fifteenth at the *Ships.*

In the sixteenth, the *Trojans* being repulsed by *Patroclus*, they engage between the Fleet, the River, and the *Grecian* Wall: See V. 396. *Patroclus* still advancing they fight at the Gates of *Troy* V. 698. In the seventeenth the Fight about the Body of *Patroclus* is under the *Trojan* Wall V. 404. His Body being carried off, *Hector* and *Aeneas* pursue the *Greeks* to the Fortification V. 760. And in the eighteenth, upon *Achilles*'s appearing, they retire and encamp without the Fortification.

In the twentieth, the Fight is still on that side next the Sea; for the *Trojans* being pursued by *Achilles*, pass over the *Scamander* as they run toward *Troy*: See the beginning of Book 21. The following Battels are either in the River itself, or between that and the City, under whose Walls *Hector* is kill'd in the twenty second Book, which puts an end to the Battels of the *Iliad.*

(*TE*, 7. 262)

However, despite such precise and extensive delineation, Pope's Homeric geography was to come increasingly under attack during the century that followed the publication of his translation. The first and most celebrated onslaught came in Robert Wood's influential *Essay on the Original Genius and Writings of Homer*, published posthumously in 1775.[6] Wood, a seasoned traveller and accomplished classical scholar, had visited the Troad with two associates in 1750, and had recorded how, delighting in 'poetic geography', they had 'spent a fortnight with great pleasure in making a map of the Scamandrian plain with Homer in our hands'. In his *Essay*, Wood admits that 'of all the languages we know, in which Homer has hitherto appeared, it is in English alone that he continues to be a Poet', and that Pope was 'the only translator who has, in a certain degree, kept alive that divine spirit of the Poet,

[6] The *Essay* was a book-length elaboration of material first contained in a letter to Wood's friend James Dawkins of *c.*1755 which had been published privately in 1767 and 1769.

which has almost expired in other hands' (*Essay*, pp. 77–8). But, though conceding the supreme poetic excellence of Pope's translation, Wood goes on to insist that it will be a disappointment to 'those, who wish to be thoroughly acquainted, either with the manners and characters of Homer's age, or the landscape and geography of his country'. Pope's 'accommodations' of Homer 'to the ideas of those, for whom he translates', Wood maintains, caused him to obscure the scrupulous accuracy, with which, Wood was convinced, Homer had described the landscapes and customs of his own day. In his rendering of the Catalogue of the Ships, Wood asserts, Pope ornamented Homer's descriptions of his locations with epithets and other poetic 'beauties' drawn inappropriately from post-Homeric sources. And Pope's map of Troy, Wood claims, is both inconsistent with the poet's own presentation of Homer's action, and with 'the real situation of the ground' – that is, the area of the Troad which Wood had himself visited. Pope, writes Wood, makes the 'capital . . . error' of 'discharging the Scamander into the Aegean sea, instead of the Hellespont'. And, in supposing 'that the Greeks had not passed the river before the beginning of the sixth book', Pope's commentary 'is inconsistent with that beautiful digression of the third book, where Priam and Helen see the Grecian leaders so distinctly from the walls of that city, as to distinguish the persons and figures of the leaders from the walls of Troy'. Being initially 'at a loss to account for so much obvious inaccuracy', in Pope's map, Wood says, he 'discovered'

> a certain method and regularity of error, which could belong to the Engraver alone, who, by a piece of negligence, not less unpardonable in the artist than fatal to Geography and Homer, has given a map, which reverses the drawing from which it was engraved, and of course changes the respective situation of all the parts, from right to left, and from left to right; so that the Sigeum stands where the Rhoeteum should be, and the Scamander runs on that side of Troy which belongs to the Simois.
>
> (*Essay*, pp. 88–9)

Wood attempted to supply Pope's deficiencies by offering his own map, drafted, as we have seen, on the Trojan plain itself. He was, in fact, modest in his own claims to have charted a scenario identifiably close to that depicted in the *Iliad*. 'The face of the country' in the Troad, he asserted, has changed considerably since Homer's day as a result of earthquakes, and close correspondences therefore could not be hoped for between the landscapes now visible and those which formed the basis of what Wood assumed were accurate depictions by Homer. 'The source of the Scamander', he noted, 'is now considerably more distant from the Hellespont, than we conceive it to have been at the time, when Homer saw it' (*Essay*, pp. 307–8). Most significantly, Wood was unable to identify the site of Troy itself, remarking that 'there are not the least remains, by which we can judge of its original position . . . : not a stone is left, to certify, where it stood' (*Essay*, pp. 338, 341).

Wood's *Essay* was very popular, particularly on the continent, where it was translated into German, French, Italian, and Spanish, and reviewed favourably by the classical scholar, Christian Gottlob Heyne, and the poet Goethe. But Wood was soon himself under attack. In the course of an exploration of the Troad in 1785, the attention of the French diplomat Jean-Baptiste Lechevalier was drawn to some springs near the village of Bunarbashi (now Pinarbashi), about ten miles from the coast of the Hellespont, to the south of the Trojan plain, which he identified with the hot and cold springs said by Homer (*Iliad*, 22. 147–56) to be the sources of the Scamander. Lechevalier concluded that Bali Dagh, the hill above Bunarbashi, must be the citadel of Troy, that the stream fed by the springs must be the Scamander, and that the river to the east of Bunarbashi was therefore not the Scamander, as Wood had supposed, but the Simois. Though the two rivers did not now meet, this could, Lechevalier thought, be explained by the fact that the stream from Bunarbashi had been diverted in post-Homeric times into the Aegean: previously, he supposed, it had met the other river, as Homer describes. Lechevalier presented his findings to the Royal Society of Edinburgh in 1791, and they were translated into English and printed in book form the same year as *Description of the Plain of Troy*. In his Preface, Lechevalier's translator, Andrew Dalzel, lamented the 'extremely unsuccessful' results of Wood's attempts to demonstrate any 'resemblance betwixt the pictures in the Iliad, and that part of a country which we may suppose [Homer] would have been careful to describe with more than ordinary precision'; The failure of Wood's endeavours, Dalzel affirmed, had 'had the effect of exciting in the mind of every elegant scholar nothing but sensations of disappointment and regret'. Lechevalier, in contrast, had found his Edinburgh audience 'highly gratified' by his revelations of 'how exactly he found the present appearance of that country still to accord with the descriptions and incidents in the Poems of Homer' (*Description*, p. vii).

In the main body of the *Description*, Lechevalier reconsiders Wood's harsh censure of Pope's map of Troy. He was, he says, at first disposed, because of the 'extraordinary mistakes' which 'appear on the face of this Map', to accept Wood's theory that it had been inadvertently reversed by Pope's engraver. But when he compared Pope's map with the landscape that he (Lechevalier) thought Homer had accurately described, he noted that Pope's 'inaccuracy' was not systematic. Pope's 'notion', for example,

> is perfectly right respecting the situation of the Greek camp betwixt the two promontories, the confluence of the two rivers at no great distance from the ships, the general shape of the plain, the course of the Simois of greater extent than that of the Scamander, the distance of the city from the sea, and the two sources of the Scamander in the neighbourhood of the city.
>
> (*Description*, pp. 69, 70)

And such inaccuracies as Pope's map does possess, Lechevalier notes, seem to square oddly with the 'most minute and complete description' of 'the different circumstances of the Trojan war' which Pope provided in his 'Essay on Homer's Battels' – a description which, Lechevalier says, complies with such 'exact conformity' to his own map of the Trojan plain that he will reprint Pope's account in full to enhance his readers' 'confidence in [his] labours'. Lechevalier offers a solution to the dilemma to which we will return later:

> Might we not suppose that this eminent author, having remarked somewhere in the Iliad, that the sources of the Scamander were to the west; and accustomed, moreover, to consider the left side of the map as the west, as is usually the case, did thus adjust every other situation, such as that of Sigéum, that of the Simois, &c. so as to agree with this fundamental principle? It is thus (if I may be allowed to suppose an eminent poet to be but an indifferent geographer) that the errors of the map in question may perhaps be accounted for, which, however, with all its imperfections, must have cost POPE an infinite deal of pains, and required on his part an uncommon power of arrangement.
>
> (*Description*, p. 71)

Lechevalier's identification of Troy with Bali Dagh was widely accepted, and commanded widespread assent for over half a century. But there were notable dissenters. Chief among them was Jacob Bryant, the quirky and cantankerous Fellow of King's College Cambridge who had edited Wood's *Essay* for publication in 1775. In 1795 Bryant published his own *Observations upon a Treatise, entitled A Description of the Plain of Troy, by Monsieur le Chevalier*, following it the next year with a longer work, *A Dissertation concerning the War of Troy, and the Expedition of the Grecians, as described by Homer; shewing that no such Expedition was ever undertaken, and that no such city of Phrygia existed.*[7] In these two works, Bryant mounts an all-out assault on Lechevalier's *Description*, arguing that Lechevalier's identifications are inaccurate and that, anyway, the whole narrative of the *Iliad* is implausible, if considered as historical fact. Bali Dagh, Bryant argues in the *Observations*, cannot be Homer's Troy, since it is positioned on a mountain eminence, rather than on the plain, as in Homer, and is, in any case, far too distant from the sea to allow the distances specified by Homer to be covered in the time he allows. Bryant notes that Lechevalier's identification of the Sigean and Rhoetean promontories (never, incidentally, mentioned by Homer) places them far too far apart for Hector's voice to be audible from one end of the Greek camp to the other (as in *Iliad*, 16. 76–8). Homer's Scamander is a much more substantial river than the stream identified by Lechevalier. The alleged monuments of the Greek warriors identified on the plain were later 'accommodations' of the terrain to the events and persons of the *Iliad*. Homer's whole story,

[7] (n.p., n.d.) Bryant's essay was, in its turn, criticized by Gilbert Wakefield in *A Letter to Jacob Bryant, Esq.* (London, 1797), and J. B. S. Morritt in *A Vindication of Homer* (York, 1798). Bryant replied to one of his reviewers in *An Expostulation, Addressed to The British Critic* (Eton, 1799), and to Morritt in *Some Observations upon The Vindication of Homer* (Eton, 1799). Later contributions to the controversy were [Thomas Falconer], *Remarks on Some Passages in Mr. Bryant's publications, respecting the War of Troy* (London, 1799), William Francklin, *Remarks and Observations on the Plain of Troy* (London, 1800), and J. B. S. Morritt, *Additional Remarks on the Topography of Troy* (London, 1800). On the controversy, see further T. J. B. Spencer, 'Robert Wood and the Problem of Troy in the Eighteenth Century', *Journal of the Warburg and Courtauld Institutes*, 20 (1957), 75–105, to which I am generally indebted in this chapter.

moreover, Bryant argues in the *Dissertation*, has self-evidently implausible elements, if regarded as historical fact. A vast Greek confederacy involving 1,186 ships (far greater than the forces later assembled by the Greek states to combat the Persians) is quite inconceivable. The Greek army would have been depleted of manpower, and its fleet decayed, by a ten-year siege. Helen, if one collates Homer's narrative with her other appearances in Greek legend, would have been 104 (by another calculation 114), and 'sufficiently old to have been Hecuba's mother' at the time of the Trojan War. The configuration of rivers in the Troad would not have allowed the combined inundation engineered (according to Homer) by Neptune and Apollo to destroy the Greek ramparts after the War. No Trojan remains are extant which square with Homer's descriptions. 'The history of Troy,' Bryant concludes, 'abounds,' in ways that were recognized in antiquity itself, 'with innumerable contradictions, and is fundamentally wrong; and utterly improbable' (*Dissertation*, p. 71). He might also have pointed out that, on at least one occasion, Lechevalier had clearly misrepresented Homer's text to make it square with his positioning of a geographical feature of the Trojan plain. Lechevalier supported his identification of the Monument of Ilus 'at a considerable distance from the city of Troy' by arguing that Priam, when journeying to the Greek camp to redeem the body of Hector, 'set out early in the afternoon' and 'did not arrive [at the monument of Ilus] till it was almost dark' (*Description*, p. 113). But Homer does not say that Priam set out early in the afternoon. Indeed, Pope, with the sharp eye for poetic verisimilitude which we have already witnessed, specifically notes that Priam 'set out in the Evening', and observed 'how exactly the Poet preserves the Unities of Time and Place, that he allots Space sufficient for the Actions which he describes, and yet does not crowd more Incidents into any Interval of Time than may be executed in as much as he allows' (*The Iliad of Homer*, 24. 427*n*; *TE*, 8. 553–4).

Despite his severe criticisms of Lechevalier, however, Bryant insists, the *fictional* scenario of Homer's Troy is imagined in remarkable detail and with remarkable consistency. Nothing he has said in the *Dissertation* about the unhistorical nature of the *Iliad*, Bryant insists in one of his replies to his critics, should be taken as designed in any way to denigrate Homer as a *poet.* The 'improbabilities' of the *Iliad,* Bryant argues,

> do not affect the Poet. On the contrary, if they are well conducted, they add to his reputation. The whole being a figment will not prove any obstacle. The Poem of the Fairy Queen is an allegory; and the history of La Mancha's Knight is a fiction. Yet did either Spencer or Cervantes suffer in their character? or was the reputation of their works diminished? Why then are we so blindly solicitous about the truth of any poetical work, if it was designed to be a fable? Many fictions serve to illustrate the subject matter and to lead to truths in disguise. If we admit nothing, but what is literally true, all tropes and metaphors must be given up: and analogy laid aside. The greatest beauties, and most useful ornaments in writing must be sacrificed. Let then the war of Troy be either real or feigned; to what does it amount? The Ilias will in all respects be the same, and its excellence unimpaired.[8]

The action of Homer's poem, Bryant insists, has its own kind of consistency and coherence. But it is the consistency and coherence of a work of fiction, not of a documentary record. Homer's power to convince us of the 'reality' of the places and events he portrays derives from the imaginative plausibility of the fictional world he has created, not from any quasi-photographic accuracy with which he has described an independently accessible action or geographical locale.

But Bryant's arguments, as we have seen, did not persuade the world to abandon belief in 'the real Troy'. Lechevalier's identification of Troy with Bali Dagh held sway until, after the archaeological excavations from the 1860s by J. G. von Hahn, Frank Calvert, and Heinrich Schliemann (later extended by Wilhelm Dörpfeld, Carl Blegen, and Manfred Korfmann), it was supplanted by Hissarlik, six miles north.[9] While most scholars still agree that Hissarlik was probably the site of the city in and around which the *Iliad* is set (whether or not there was ever an historical Trojan War), most have also been reluctant to go much further in identifying particular locations in Homer's poem with the landscapes of the region. One of the most recent editors of the *Iliad,* for example, has testified that 'except in the most general terms the epic geography of the Troad is

[8] *Some Observations on the Vindication of Homer* (Eton, 1799), p. 90.

[9] Hissarlik had been identified as Troy by the Scots journalist Charles Maclaren as early as 1822, but his findings had been generally ignored.

clearly a poetical construction'.[10] Another modern Homeric scholar has judged that 'Homer's Trojan plain is a poetic construction with its own peculiar character and order'.[11] And the author of a recent book-length study of Homer's Troy (which, incidentally, supports the Hissarlik identification) has specifically warned against any attempts

> to wander, *Iliad* in hand, through a Troy which has been reconstructed in virtual fashion on the basis of recent excavations, equating a gateway here or a bastion there with some 'counterparts' in the text, or referring to Homer to conclude that this is how Troy appeared in its heyday in about 1200 BC, that here stood Agamemnon's headquarters tent, or that there Helen pointed out to Priam the heroes of the Achaian army from the wall of Troy.[12]

Precisely such an approach, however, was adopted in 1998 by J. V. Luce in a book which marks a full-dress return to the spirit of Wood and Lechevalier.[13] In his first chapter, Luce dismisses the assumption 'that poetic creativity has absolute licence to disregard geographical fact' as the manifestation of 'a modern aesthetic' which 'is not the way to approach Homer'. 'Where landscape and locality were concerned,' Luce maintains, Homer 'aimed at fidelity to fact' (p. 10). But if Luce's general assumptions about Homer's accurate depiction of geographical realities are similar to those of Wood and Lechevalier, his specific conclusions are very different. Recent geophysical surveys of the region, he notes, have demonstrated that, as a result of long-term silting of the alluvial plain, the modern coastline of the Troad differs greatly from that of *c.*1250 BC, the putative date of the Trojan War. At that date, the geophysical evidence suggests, a substantial bay lay to the west of Hissarlik, stretching *c.*2½ miles south of the modern coastline. Previous sitings of the Greek camp near the coast, north of Troy, must, therefore, be erroneous, since such a

[10] See Bryan Hainsworth, *The Iliad: A Commentary, Vol. 3: Books 9–12* (Cambridge, 1993), on 11. 166.

[11] Agathe Thornton, *Homer's Iliad: Its Composition and the Motif of Supplication* (Göttingen, 1984), p. 150.

[12] Joachim Latacz, *Troy and Homer: Towards a Solution of an Old Mystery* (Oxford, 2004), p. 170.

[13] J. V. Luce, *Celebrating Homer's Landscapes: Troy and Ithaca Revisited* (New Haven CT, 1998). Wood is specifically cited (p. ix) as the principal inspiration behind Luce's endeavour.

camp would, at the time of the war, have been under water. The Greek camp, Luce argues, must have been situtated to the west of Hissarlik, across the bay, near the modern Kesik Tepe on the Aegean coast. The Homeric battles were thus conducted on an east–west, rather than (as has been previously assumed) a north–south axis. Luce follows through the logic of his hypothesis, attempting to identify the various landmarks mentioned by Homer – the 'swelling of the plain' (*Iliad*, 10. 161; 11. 56; 20. 3), the ford over the Scamander, the tomb of Myrine, the tomb of Aiseyetes, the tomb of Ilus, the grave of Achilles, the fort of Herakles, the Scaean Gate – with features of the modern landscape and excavations. The geophysical evidence that underpins his argument, however, presents Luce with at least one problem which, as far as I can see, he never fully acknowledges: in Homer (*Iliad*, 5. 774), the rivers Scamander and Simois meet before entering the sea. But according to the new evidence on the former positioning of the coastline, they would have entered the sea separately, both at the putative date of the Trojan War, and at the likely date of the composition of the Homeric poems. Luce, moreover, attempts to incorporate within his identification of Troy with Hissarlik Lechevalier's identification of the Bunarbashi springs with Homer's twin sources of the Scamander, arguing that Achilles pursued Hector not round the walls of Troy but in an elliptical circuit, passing the Bunarbashi springs four times. Since these lie six miles south of Hissarlik, this would involve a total pursuit of more than forty-eight miles.

Luce's account, though apparently endorsed by the broadcaster Michael Wood,[14] might seem so extreme, and to stand at such a distance from the general scholarly consensus on the historicity of Homer's Troy, that it may be wondered why I have dwelt at such length on it, and on the tradition of interpretation which it represents. I do so for two interrelated reasons. The first concerns the way in which the tradition of depreciating Pope's Homer initiated by Robert Wood has become incorporated within a larger, teleological literary-historical narrative which celebrates the supposed triumph of 'Romanticism' over the weaknesses and inadequacies of 'Neoclas-

[14] In a recorded interview appended to the DVD reissue of his TV series *In Search of the Trojan War* (BBC Worldwide, 2004).

sicism', and according to which anything apparently pre- or proto-'Romantic' in tendency is assumed to be an unquestionable 'advance' over what went before.[15] The second relates to the larger question of why readers, in many different periods and circumstances, have been drawn to identify the 'realities' (whether in terms of 'real persons', 'real events', or 'real locations') 'behind' works of fiction.

The notion that Wood's *Essay* represents an unequivocal advance on responses to Homer in the Age of Pope was most explicitly and crudely formulated over fifty years ago by Gilbert Highet:

> A decisive step towards the better comprehension of the *Iliad* and *Odyssey* was made by Wood's *Essay on the Original Genius of Homer.* The nobility and gentry of the baroque era had claimed that the Homeric epics could not be good poetry because Homeric society was in some ways less polished and precise than their own. This was a fault in their historical perspective. Wood, by describing the scenery which Homer knew, and by evoking from the life of the Near East the kind of life he described, primitive but not barbarous, simple but noble, helped to show lovers of poetry what they should really look for when they read the *Iliad.*[16]

This passage contains a number of easily demonstrable misrepresentations. Pope – who neither lived in 'the baroque era' nor was a member of the 'nobility' or 'gentry' (his father was, as Jane Austen would have said, 'in trade') emphatically did *not* 'claim that the Homeric epics could not be good poetry' because of the nature of Homeric society, or indeed for any other reason. The Preface to his *Iliad* is, in fact, a paean of praise to the poet who is, Pope says, 'universally allow'd to have had the greatest Invention of any Writer whatever' (*TE*, 7. 3). Wood, to be sure, deserves credit for an aspect of his *Essay* not hitherto mentioned in this chapter: his pioneering recognition of the oral traditions which lie behind the Homeric poems. But in many other respects his *Essay* is seriously misleading.

[15] On the importance of narrative paradigms in literary history, and on the triumphalist narrative of Romanticism in particular, see David Perkins, *Is Literary History Possible?* (Baltimore MD, 1992). Wood is specifically discussed on pp. 134–6.

[16] *The Classical Tradition* (Oxford, 1949), p. 383. More nuanced praise of Wood is to be found in Kirsti Simonsuuri, *Homer's Original Genius: Eighteenth-Century Notions of the Early Greek Epic (1688–1798)* (Cambridge, 1979), pp. 133–45, and Timothy Webb, ed., *English Romantic Hellenism, 1700–1824* (Manchester, 1982), pp. 6–9, 132–6.

Wood's attempts to draw 'parallels' between Homeric society and that of modern conditions in Asia Minor were, in fact (*pace* Highet and others), singularily *im*precise and singularly *lacking* in 'historical perspective'. In his comments on 'the manners and characters of Homer's age' (*Essay*, p. 78) he constantly blurred the 'age' *depicted* by Homer (now generally thought to be a composite of conditions drawn from the eighth century BC with memories of older traditions and institutions reaching far back to Mycenaean times)[17] with that *inhabited* by Homer – and, moreover, blurred both with conditions that Wood had observed at first hand in eighteenth-century Asia Minor. His criticisms of the supposed contradictions which result from Pope's 'embellishments' of Homer's texts, furthermore, are often based on palpable misunderstandings or misrepresentations of Pope's text. Wood alleges, for example, that Pope's description of Achilles' grief after the death of Patroclus 'contradicts itself within the compass of a few lines' when, after describing Achilles as 'stretch'd along the Shore / Where dash'd on Rocks the broken Billows roar' (23. 70–1), Pope tells how Achilles' 'languid Members fall' 'Along the Grass' (23. 74), and then, shortly afterwards, writes that, after the appearance of Patroclus' ghost, Achilles awakes, 'starting from the Sands' (23. 120). 'Should we give this sleepy Achilles to a painter', Wood comments, 'he must be strangely puzzled with the hero's rocky, grassy, sandy couch' (*Essay*, p. 85). But 'the Shore' and 'the Sands', in Pope's version, clearly indicate the region in which Achilles is lying, not the precise spot (which is on the grass *near* the shore). The 'Rocks' in Pope's description, equally clearly, are not Achilles' 'couch' but the place where the waves break on the shore, near which Achilles is lying. Similarly, when Wood alleges (in a passage quoted above) that Pope 'supposes that the Greeks had not passed the river before the beginning of the sixth book', and that this is inconsistent with the scene in Book 3 in which Priam and Helen view the Greek warriors from the walls of Troy, his remarks are straightforwardly refuted by Pope's explicit statement, in his Argument to Book 3, that the action of that Book takes place '*in the* Fields *before*

[17] For an up-to-date summary of the scholarly consensus, see Robin Osborne, in *The Cambridge Companion to Homer*, ed. Robert Fowler (Cambridge, 2004), pp. 216–18.

Troy' (a location fully endorsed by his translation of the Book's opening lines). When Pope says in the 'Essay on Homer's Battels' that the Greeks 'had not yet past the stream' at 5. 776 (Greek text), he clearly means '*at this stage in this battle*'. Wood makes much of the reversal of east and west in Pope's map of Troy, and it may indeed be, as he suggests, that Pope, or his engraver, became confused in this regard, either because the image came to be reversed in the engraving process, or because, as Lechevalier proposed, Pope mistakenly assumed that the top of his map was positioned northwards. But this slip, in fact, makes little difference to the coherence of Pope's descriptions of the fighting, since most of this takes place in a clear north–south trajectory, and it is thus of little importance that east and west are reversed on the map.

Wood's claim that 'the Iliad has new beauties on the banks of the Scamander'[18] was, interestingly, shared by Lord Byron, who rhapsodized about the difference between reading the *Iliad* 'in a snug library' and 'at Sigaeum and on the tumuli, or by the springs with Mount Ida above, and the plain and rivers and Archipelago around you',[19] and who denounced 'the blackguard Bryant' for 'impugning the veracity' of the Trojan War, declaring:

> I still venerated the grand original as the truth of *history* (in the material *facts*) and of *place*. Otherwise, it would have given me no delight.[20]

In some moods, Byron seems to have believed that 'historical places ... were sites in which direct connection with the buried subjectivity of the lived experiences associated with those places was somehow (supernaturally) possible',[21] and his conviction of the historical veracity of the *Iliad* seems to have been, at least in part, connected with such a belief – even though the 'tumuli' that he claimed made such a difference to his reading of Homer were in fact of Hellenistic date.[22]

[18] 'The Publisher to the Reader' in *The Ruins of Palmyra* (London, 1753), sig. a$^{v}$.

[19] Lord Byron, *Complete Poetical Works, Vol. 2: Childe Harold's Pilgrimage*, ed. Jerome J. McGann (Oxford, 1980), p. 310.

[20] Lord Byron, *Letters and Journals*, ed. Leslie A. Marchand, 12 vols. (London, 1973–82), 8. 22 (letter of 11 January 1821).

[21] Stephen Cheeke, *Byron and Place: History, Translation, Nostalgia* (Basingstoke, 2003), p. 13.

[22] Cheeke, *Byron and Place*, p. 65.

But Byron was also a passionate devotee of Pope's *Iliad*, and, in a letter to Leigh Hunt, defended Pope's translation of Homer's celebrated 'Moon' simile (*The Iliad of Homer*, 8. 685–708), which Wordsworth had attacked in his *Essay Supplementary to the Preface* (1815) for its supposed insensitivity to 'the phenomena of nature'. (Wordsworth had remarked that 'A blind man, in the habit of attending accurately to descriptions casually dropped from the lips of those around him, might easily depict these appearances with more truth'.) The simile, Byron affirmed,

> is no translation I know – but it is not such *false* description as asserted – I have read it on the spot – there is a burst – and a lightness – and a glow – about the night in the Troad – which makes the 'planets vivid' – & the 'pole glowing' the moon is – at least the sky is clearness itself – and I know no more appropriate expression for the expansion of such a heaven – over the scene – the plain – the sea – the sky – Ida – the Hellespont – Simois – Scamander – and the isles – than that of a 'flood of Glory.'[23]

Byron is here not so much responding to the 'buried subjectivity' of 'lived experience' preserved directly – as he supposed – in the landscapes of the Troad, as projecting on to the night sky in Asia Minor an imagining of that sky by a favourite poet who had evoked the scene so vividly that it seemed to ring true to Byron's direct experience on the spot.

A century earlier, Lady Mary Wortley Montagu had remembered or imagined herself expressing similar sentiments when writing to Pope from Adrianople, and had echoed Pope's translation in the process:[24]

> I read over your Homer here with an infinite Pleasure, and find several little passages explain'd, that I did not before entirely comprehend the Beauty of, many of the customs and much of the dress then in fashion, being yet retain'd;... It would be too tedious to you to point out all the passages that relate to the present customs, but I can assure you that the Princesses and great Ladys pass their time at their Looms embrodiering Veils and Robes, surrounded by their Maids, which are allways very numerous, in the same Manner as we find Andromache and Helen describ'd. The descrip-

[23] Byron, *Letters and Journals*, 4. 325–6 (letter of 30 October 1815).

[24] For Lady Mary's 'snowy veil', see Pope, *Iliad*, 3. 187; for Priam's counsellors 'basking in the Sun', see ibid., 197.

tion of the belt of Menelaüs exactly resembles those that are worn by the great Men, fasten'd before with broad Gold Clasps, and embrodier'd round with rich work. The Snowy Veil that Helen throws over her face is still fashionable; and I never see (as I do very often) halfe a dozen old Bashaws with their reverend Beards siting basking in the Sun, but I recollect Good King Priam and his Councellors.[25]

In a letter presented as addressed to her friend, the Abbé Antonio Conti, Lady Mary commented specifically on Homer's geography:

North of the promontory of Sigaeum we saw that of Rhoeteum, fam'd for the sepulchre of Ajax. While I view'd these celebrated Fields and Rivers, I admir'd the exact Geography of Homer, whom I had in my hand.[26]

Isobel Grundy suggests that the 'Homer' Lady Mary had in her hand was her parallel-text Greek and Latin edition,[27] but one may speculate that her impressions may also have been coloured, either at the time or retrospectively, by her memories of Pope's translation.

Pope, as we have seen, displayed a very precise sense of the landscapes of the *Iliad*, and of the locales in which its various battles take place. 'What chiefly pleases' him, he says, when commenting on Homer's description of the twin fountain-sources of the Scamander, 'is to see the exact Landskip of old *Troy*, we have a clear Idea of the Town itself, and of the Roads and Countrey about it; the River, the Fig-trees, and every part is set before our Eyes' (*TE*, 8. 463). And he also, as we have seen, admired Homer's preservation of a plausible unity of time and place. But Pope's interest in Homer's landscapes, it should be em-

[25] Lady Mary Wortley Montagu, *Complete Letters*, ed. Robert Halsband, 3 vols. (Oxford, 1965–67), 1. 332–3 (letter dated 1 April 1717). The letter is part of the 'Turkish Embassy Letters', a sequence composed later and perhaps based (how accurately is not known) on letters written at the time of the given dates. Isobel Grundy speculates that, if Lady Mary's letter is close to one actually sent to Pope, it might show that she was 'still hoping to join the circle of learned friends who helped with his Homer translations' (*Lady Mary Wortley Montagu: Comet of the Enlightenment* (Oxford, 1999), p. 145). By the time Lady Mary left for Constantinople (1 August 1716), only the first two volumes of Pope's *Iliad* (containing Books 1–8) had been published. All the details mentioned in this letter seem to refer to this portion of the poem, so, at least in that respect, the letter as we have it is compatible with Lady Mary's dating.

[26] Montagu, *Complete Letters*, 1. 420 (letter of 31 July 1718).

[27] Grundy, *Lady Mary Wortley Montagu*, p. 169.

phasized, is an interest in an *imagined time–space dimension.* Homer's scenario, he thinks, is worked out in such richly specific detail that a map can be drawn of it, and the course of his action is conceived with such precision that it can be assigned to a specified duration, in days and weeks. But, apart from the Catalogue of the Ships, which, Pope believes, is 'purely Historical, founded on the real Transactions of those Times, and by far the most valuable Piece of History and Geography left us concerning the State of *Greece* in that early Period' (*TE*, 7. 173), the precisely delineated time–space dimension of the *Iliad* is not one that can ultimately be checked off point by point against some independently verifiable scenario behind or beyond the poem. In his famous first note on Book 1 of his *Iliad*, Pope noted how Homer's commentators have been 'Voluminous in explaining those Sciences which he made but subservient to his Poetry, and sparing only upon that Art which constitutes his Character'. Such commentators, Pope says, 'were fonder of showing their Variety of Learning in all Kinds, than their single Understanding in Poetry. Hence it comes to pass that their Remarks are rather Philosophical, Historical, Geographical, Allegorical, or in short rather any thing than Critical or Poetical' (*TE*, 7. 82). On the strength of the evidence presented in this chapter, it might at first sight seem that Pope was himself guilty of precisely the same display of 'Geographical' pedantry that he here castigates. But Pope's Trojan geography, it must be emphasized, is a specifically *poetic* geography, which, whatever historical realities may lie behind the *Iliad*, or made their contribution in the process of its composition, functions in the finished poem as a device for making the narrative fully plausible to its readers and listeners. One can be confident from his general account of Homer in the Preface to his *Iliad* that Pope would have endorsed Jacob Bryant's judgement that Homer's circumstantial details, whether of place or time, are there not for their own sake, nor as a documentary record of some independent 'reality', but for the contribution they make to the poet's larger fictional scheme, and to his ability – in Pope's view unrivalled in European literature (with the possible exception of Shakespeare) – to involve the reader in his action with spellbinding intensity:

If a Council be call'd, or a Battle fought, you are not coldly inform'd of what was said or done as from a third Person; the Reader is hurry'd out of himself by the Force of the Poet's Imagination, and turns in one place to a Hearer, in another to a Spectator.

(Preface to *The Iliad of Homer*; *TE*, 7. 4).

Pope's sentiments were to be echoed over two centuries later, in very different cultural and critical circumstances, in Erich Auerbach's celebrated account of Homer's narrative art:

So long as we are reading or hearing the poems, it does not matter whether we know that all this is only legend, 'make-believe.' The oft-repeated reproach that Homer is a liar takes nothing from his effectiveness, he does not need to base his story on historical reality, his reality is powerful enough in itself; it ensnares us, weaving its web around us, and that suffices him. And this 'real' world into which we are lured, exists for itself, contains nothing but itself.[28]

Similar conclusions were also reached by G. S. Kirk, who, in the course of a searching consideration of the possible historical and geographical realities behind the *Iliad*, concluded that 'it would not matter to anyone except the historian whether the war described in the poem actually took place, so long as it is made sufficiently plausible. It merely has to be a *credible* background for the action, whether or not it was "real" in some stricter sense... [H]istorical fact and poetic description... are in the last resort separate entities.'[29] And Oliver Taplin has commented to similar effect on the amalgam of historically and geographically diverse elements that form the material world of the *Iliad*:

In matters of armour, burial, and so forth this amalgam, while historically impossible, is aesthetically coherent and convincing. What mattered to the poet was not that he should be accurate – why should that matter? – but that he should be plausible and enthralling, that he should create a past that was solidly imaginable and yet suitable for heroes.[30]

[28] Erich Auerbach, *Mimesis: The Representation of Reality in Western Literature*, trans. Willard R. Trask (1953; reprinted Princeton NJ, 1968), p. 13.

[29] G. S. Kirk, *The Iliad: A Commentary, Vol. II: Books 5–8* (Cambridge, 1990), pp. 37, 50.

[30] Oliver Taplin, 'Homer', in *The Oxford History of the Classical World*, ed. John Boardman, Jasper Griffin, and Oswyn Murray (Oxford, 1986), pp. 50–77 (p. 73).

Accordingly, Pope's recreation of Homer's simile of the moon rising above the Trojan watch fires (so passionately admired, as we have seen, by Byron) is to be remembered not merely as an accurate record of 'the sky at night' over the Aegean, or as a free-standing 'Night Piece' (though it was often quoted and anthologized as such), but for its portentous foreshadowing of the larger tragedy of Troy. It fulfils an integral function, that is, within a coherent overall narrative which – or so Pope thought – clearly manifests the hand of a single, unifying, poetic genius. Thus the 'Flames' which, with even more circumstantial precision in Pope's rendering than in Homer's original, 'lighten glimm'ring *Xanthus* with their Rays' also 'Gleam on the Walls, and tremble on the Spires' of Troy (8. 700–2; *TE*, 7. 428), ominously anticipating the city's imminent destruction.

Such was the persuasiveness of Pope's recreation of Homer's fictional 'reality' that it seems to have convinced Jean-Baptiste Lechevalier, Lord Byron, and perhaps Lady Mary Wortley Montagu, that what they 'saw' on the Troad accorded with what Pope, in his poetic recreation of Homer, had imagined – though he had, of course, never visited that region himself. The quest for 'the real Troy' – and the point can, I think, be applied *mutatis mutandis* to many similar quests for the 'reality' behind works of fiction – can surely be attributed, at least in large part, to Homer's (and, for English readers, Pope's) capacity to create an imaginative scenario and action so precise and vivid that it *must* – or so the poets' readers were convinced – accord with some independently verifiable 'reality'. But the 'reality' of Homer's Trojan geography exists ultimately in one place, and one place only: in readers' minds encountering the twenty-four books of the *Iliad*, whether in the Greek original or in its greatest English recreation, that of Alexander Pope.

# 12

## Colonization, Closure, or Creative Dialogue? The Case of Pope's *Iliad*

The second half of the twentieth century witnessed a significant revival of academic interest in the literary form that has been a central concern of the present volume: English verse translation from classical poetry which aspires to the status of English poetry in its own right. An important agent in this process was the journal *Arion*, founded at the University of Texas in 1962 and edited by a group of American and expatriate British classicists, including William Arrowsmith, D. S. Carne-Ross, C. J. Herington, and J. P. Sullivan. *Arion* was the first classical journal with an avowedly literary-critical, as opposed to historical and philological, agenda. It would, its editors hoped, perform within classics a similar role to that of *Scrutiny* or *Essays in Criticism* in English studies, and would apply to the study of classical literature the critical methods and assumptions familiar at that date in university English departments.

The founders of *Arion* were all university teachers – though D. S. Carne-Ross was a relative newcomer to the academic world, having previously worked as a producer for the BBC Third Programme –, but a crucial influence on the journal's conception and early activity came from a stridently non- (even anti-)academic source, in the form of the writings and example of the American poet, Ezra Pound. Several of the *Arion* team were passionate Poundians, and had been particularly influenced by Pound's oft-stated conviction that one of the most effective forms of literary criticism is translation, in which texts from other cultures and periods are reinterpreted and 'made new' for the modern world.[1] Consequently, an important part of *Arion*'s activity was the publication of new translations from the classics – versions which, the editors hoped, would cast as much light on their originals as the discursive analyses which occupied the rest of the journal.

One of the most distinguished and widely-discussed contributions to the early numbers of *Arion* was the essay, 'Is Juvenal a Classic?' by the British scholar H. A. Mason[2] in which central use was made of English translations and imitations of Juvenal by Ben Jonson, John Oldham, John Dryden, and Samuel Johnson to suggest a major reinterpretation of the Roman poet's satirical stance and tone. Like the *Arion* editors, Mason had long been, in his own words, a 'cranky devotee of all Pound's efforts as a translator',[3] but his study of Pound had led him not to the promotion of new translation, much of which struck him of inferior quality and insight, but to a deep immersion in the theory and practice of the earlier English translator-poets whose work has featured so centrally in the present volume.

Mason's study of these poets, pursued in a series of books and articles appearing between the late 1950s and his death in 1993,[4] convinced him of the rightness of many of their central tenets. Once translations of poetry, he believed, move beyond the level of a 'crib' – a plain prose version that makes no pretension to preserve any of the artistic quality of its original, but is merely designed to assist students in their attempts to construe the ancient text – they become answerable to a number of inexorable laws. A translation of classical poetry

[1] The claim had been made before Pound by Dante Gabriel Rossetti in his Preface to *The Early Italian Poets* (1861): see the passage quoted in note 36 to the Introduction, above.

[2] 'Is Juvenal a Classic?', in *Critical Essays on Roman Literature: Satire*, ed. J. P. Sullivan (London, 1963), pp. 93–176 [earlier version in *Arion* 1, (1962) 8–44, 51–77]. This essay is discussed in Chapter 5 above.

[3] 'Creative Translation: Ezra Pound's *Women of Trachis*', *Cambridge Quarterly*, 4 (1969) 244–72 [earlier version in *Arion*, 2 (1963), 59–81, 105–21], p. 245.

[4] See particularly, in addition to the items already cited, *Humanism and Poetry in the Early Tudor Period* (London, 1959); *To Homer through Pope: An Introduction to Homer's* Iliad *and Pope's Translation* (London, 1972); 'Horace's Ode to Pyrrha', *Cambridge Quarterly*, 7 (1976–77), 27–62; ' "Living in the Present": Is Dryden's "Horat. Ode 29 Book 3" an Example of "Creative Translation"?', *Cambridge Quarterly*, 10 (1981), 91–129.

which itself claims poetic status – one which seeks, in George Chapman's phrase, 'with Poesie to open Poesie'[5] – can only be written by a genuine poet, not a Professor of Latin or Greek *pretending* to be a poet. Since such translated verse must display, no less than any other poetry, the 'genius' famously described by Samuel Johnson as 'that power which constitutes a poet . . . that energy which collects, combines, amplifies, and animates',[6] it is fully deserving of the epithet 'creative'. It will necessarily take freedoms with the literal sense of the original, since it is impossible to render with word-for-word fidelity the full range of verbal nuance, expressive effect and verse-music in a foreign poetic text, while simultaneously preserving an 'answerable style' in the host language. An English translator, if he wishes to be readable, can no more preserve the metrical procedures and form of his original than he can retain its syntax and word-order, for verbal and artistic forms that seem natural to one language and literature will seem merely bizarre if transported mechanically into another. In all these respects, Mason was in sympathy with some of the central beliefs of Sir John Denham, John Dryden, Alexander Pope, and William Cowper, who argued, in a letter of 1794, written shortly after the completion of his own translation of Homer, that

> there are minutiae in every language, which transfused into another will spoil the version. Such extreme fidelity is in fact unfaithful; such close resemblance takes away all likeness . . . A translation of Homer so made . . . will be written in no language under heaven; – it will be English, and it will be Greek; and therefore it will be neither.[7]

For such reasons, Mason thought, it is quite inappropriate to judge verse translations by their apparent lack of fidelity at the phrase-by-phrase and line-by-line level. What should concern one is the intelligence with which the translator has engaged with the larger tone, manner, and spirit of his original. To such ends, a translator might legitimately add to or abridge the sentiments found at any particular place in his original. He might import into his rendering of a

[5] *Chapman's Homer*, ed. Allardyce Nicoll, 2 vols. (2nd edition, Princeton NJ, 1967), 1. 10.

[6] Samuel Johnson, *The Lives of the Most Eminent English Poets*, ed. Roger Lonsdale, 4 vols. (Oxford, 2006), 4. 65.

[7] Quoted in Mason, *To Homer through Pope*, pp. 185–6.

particular poem or passage sentiments found not in that passage but elsewhere in his author – or even in another poet who had been fruitfully inspired by that author. To produce a genuinely poetic rendering, moreover, a translator must engage with his source as intensely as he would engage with the raw material of his 'original' work. In this respect, Mason fully endorsed T. S. Eliot's belief, alluded to several times in the present book, that good translation is a form of self-knowledge. 'There must,' Mason wrote,

> be a degree of concern amounting to passion both on the part of the translator and of the reader before an alien body can be assimilated. The foreign book must be deeply required. Both translator and reader must come to self-expression, self-completion, self-transcendence through the act of assimilating.[8]

Translation is, on such a view, simultaneously an act of submission and surrender and of self-discovery and self-realization. It depends for its success as much on the resources and potentialities of the host language and the host poet as on the linguistic qualities and characteristics of the original. Good translation, moreover, challenges its readers by discovering 'the real needs of its age', incorporating sentiments and insights from 'foreign' cultures and periods as a challenge, complement, even rebuke, to the commonplace or superficial assumptions of the translator's own contemporaries. The translator must write in an idiom accessible and acceptable to his own age, but not in one that merely reflects the cliché wisdom or cliché expression of the present moment. Thus, when Dryden declares (in the passage quoted in Chapter 4 above) that he has tried to make an original speak as he would 'if he were living, and an *Englishman*', the claim is not merely that the original has been cut down to familiarly modish size. Dryden is, rather, affirming his conviction that a translator must find what Mason calls 'mediate terms' to negotiate between an 'alien' past and an apparently familiar modernity. 'It is . . . a claim', wrote Mason,

> that can be made for a creative translation of a Classic text that it destroys [any] false sense of approximation and reveals the classic work as at one and

[8] Mason, *To Homer through Pope*, p. 180.

the same time forever alien and yet, mysteriously, *abordable* [accessible, approachable]. It is in fact only possible to do creative translation when these two opposed orientations are simultaneously strongly felt. The translator must stand like Virgil's dead stretching out his arms *ripae ulterioris amore* [in yearning for the farther shore: *Aeneid*, 6. 316], but there must be genuine voices coming back from the further shore.[9]

Mason's 'creative translation' overlaps to a large extent with Dryden's 'Paraphrase'. But Mason's ideal also encompasses Dryden's growing conviction (discussed in Chapters 4 and 9 above) that successful translation is achieved not merely by applying a particular stylistic or compositional method but as the result of a complex, dialogic meeting of minds across the ages.

A number of developments in academic life and publishing practice over the last half-century might seem to testify to the success of Mason and the *Arion* school, and of other distinguished late twentieth-century critics – most notably George Steiner – in establishing the claims of 'creative translation' on the attention of students in both English and classics. *Arion* is itself still in business, after two phoenix-rises from the ashes. 'Translation studies' is now an established 'field' within the literary academy. And the last few decades have seen the republication of many of the most famous English translations of classical poetry, both as individual texts and in anthology form.[10] Poetic translation from the classics, moreover, as the work of Tony Harrison, Seamus Heaney, Ted Hughes, and Christopher Logue eloquently testifies, continues to be prominently practised by some of the most distinguished writers of our own day.

But there are signs that English verse translation of the particular kind admired by H. A. Mason has not taken as secure and permanent a root in academics', students', and general readers' minds as its advocates might have been hoped. Commercial pressures have, significantly,

[9] Mason, 'Creative Translation: Ezra Pound's *Women of Trachis*', p. 247.

[10] New editions of Golding's and Marlowe's Ovid, Pope's Homer, and Dryden's Virgil have been issued by Penguin Classics. Wordsworth Classics of World Literature have included Chapman's Homer, Dryden's Virgil, Garth's Ovid, and a collection of seventeenth- and eighteenth-century renderings of Ovid's amatory poems. For anthologies, see particularly *The Oxford Book of Classical Verse in Translation*, ed. Jeremy Maule and Adrian Poole (Oxford, 1995) and the volumes devoted to classical poets (Catullus, Homer, Horace, Juvenal, Ovid, Seneca, Virgil) in the Penguin Poets in Translation series.

already forced some of the new editions of the older poetic translations out of print. As was noted in the Introduction to the present volume, teachers of classics in translation and classical civilization courses in both the UK and USA, anxious about the disconcerting freedoms of 'creative translations' with the literal meaning of their originals, have tended to favour 'accurate' modern academic renderings of the classical poets over more paraphrastic versions.[11] And teachers of English literature, worried about translated verse's lack of 'originality', regularly exclude it from their consideration of the major poets, even when, as in the cases of Dryden and Pope, it is clearly central to those poets' achievement. The great translations consequently receive little or no coverage in the literary histories and anthologies most regularly consulted by undergraduates on English literature courses.

As we have seen, moreover, the kind of translation practised by the poets admired by Mason, and discussed in the present book, has recently been castigated as a species of colonization or appropriation.[12] And a similar suspicion of 'domesticating' translation has been displayed, for very different reasons, in an interesting recent study which draws on its author's experiences as a teacher of classical literature to Latin- and Greek-less students in university and adult education classes.[13] Classical literature, this book argues, should be taught not *in* but *through* translation. The essential tool for such a project is the 'glossed text', a translation that leaves key terms and concepts in the original language, thus allowing the reader access to semantic, cultural, and philosophical implications that would be obscured by a more thoroughgoing substitution of English 'equivalents'. Such glossed texts have the additional advantage of highlighting the ways in which, in the work of Homer and the Greek tragedians, key ethical and religious values and concepts are constantly debated and contested, rather than merely assumed.

[11] On this subject, see D. S. Carne-Ross, 'A Mistaken Ambition of Exactness', *Delos*, 2 (1968), 171–97.

[12] See Lawrence Venuti, *The Translator's Invisibility: A History of Translation* (London, 1995), discussed in the Introduction (above). See also the same author's 'Neoclassicism and Enlightenment', in *The Oxford Guide to Literature in English Translation*, ed. Peter France (Oxford, 2000), pp. 55–64.

[13] Jan Parker, *Dialogic Education and the Problematics of Translation in Homer and Greek Tragedy* (Lewiston, Queenston, Lampeter, 2001).

To isolate, for example, the essential terms of the Homeric heroic 'code' – *kleos, timē, geras, kudos* – is to stress the degree to which, in the unfolding narrative of the *Iliad*, such terms are unstable and fragile entities, as likely to be questioned and subverted as assented to by Homer's warriors, and by the poem's readers.[14] Moreover, it is argued, such a recognition of the radically ambiguous and polyvocal nature of ancient epic and drama encourages, at the pedagogical level, a democratic, open-ended exchange between teacher and student, in which both parties engage in a genuinely collaborative exploration of issues which were always a site of contest, and which can never be finally settled. Such a model contrasts sharply with the habits of mind encouraged by the 'assimilative' translations of such poets as Pope, which, by offering a thoroughgoing recreation of their original, effectively impose an authoritarian interpretative 'closure' on the ancient text.

Such closure has been thought to be conspicuously in evidence in Pope's treatment of the celebrated speech of Sarpedon to Glaucus in Book 12 of the *Iliad* (310–28). The speech occurs at a crucial moment in the siege of Troy. Sarpedon, a Prince of the Lycians, clients of the Trojans, turns to his companion Glaucus, exhorting him to join him in leading an attack on the Greeks, who have retreated behind their fortifications. Why, Sarpedon asks, are he and Glaucus afforded honour (*timē*) above the other Lycian chieftains, with the finest seats, food and wine at banquets, and a great domain (*temenos*) of rich farmland, if they do not fight in the forefront of the battle, thereby inspiring the admiration of their fellow Lycians? If they could live for ever, Sarpedon would neither himself enter the battle where men win *kudos*, the god-given charm that secures victory, nor would he exhort Glaucus to do likewise. But since the demons of death are standing all around them in their thousands, they should both go forward into battle, whether this results in their granting some other warrior his victory wish (*eukhos*) or his granting them theirs.

Sarpedon's speech has often been taken to define with particular force and clarity the values of the Homeric hero, and modern

[14] The contentious nature of 'the heroic code' is confirmed by Oliver Taplin, *Homeric Soundings: The Shaping of the* Iliad (Oxford, 1992), pp. 6–7.

classical scholars have stressed different details in Sarpedon's terminology and logic in an attempt to convey the precise structure of relationships and ethical convictions which they imply. In his celebrated study of Indo-European language and society, Émile Benveniste argued that the honour (*timē*) that is owing to the chieftains, and paid as a tribute (*geras*) by their people is their right, part of the life-lot afforded them by fate (*moira*) or the gods.[15] And Christopher Gill, drawing on the findings of W. Donlan, has recently suggested that Sarpedon's words should be seen as the expression of a 'generalized reciprocity', according to which the warlord is willing to take a potentially self-destructive course of action not out of a modern sense of 'altruism', or to honour an immediate contractual obligation, but in deference to a longer-term social ideal of reciprocal benefits. At the moment of delivery, Gill argues, Sarpedon's resolve to lead the assault is offered as a 'favour' (*kharis*), rather than as 'a determinate... quid pro quo for determinate privileges and status'.[16]

Here is Pope's rendering of Sarpedon's speech, first published separately in 1709, and subsequently incorporated in Pope's complete rendering of the *Iliad*:

> Why boast we, *Glaucus!* our extended Reign,
> Where *Xanthus'* Streams enrich the *Lycian* Plain,
> Our num'rous Herds that range the fruitful Field,
> And Hills where Vines their purple Harvest yield,
> Our foaming Bowls with purer Nectar crown'd,
> Our Feasts enhanc'd with Music's sprightly Sound?
> Why on those Shores are we with Joy survey'd,
> Admir'd as Heroes, and as Gods obey'd?
> Unless great Acts superior Merit prove,
> And vindicate the bount'ous Pow'rs above.
> 'Tis ours, the Dignity they give, to grace;
> The first in Valour, as the first in Place.
> That when with wond'ring Eyes our martial Bands

[15] Émile Benveniste, *Indo-European Language and Society*, trans. Elizabeth Palmer (London, 1973), pp. 341–2.

[16] Christopher Gill, 'Altruism or Reciprocity in Greek Ethical Philosophy', in *Reciprocity in Ancient Greece*, ed. Christopher Gill, Norman Postlethwaite, Richard Seaford (Oxford, 1998), pp. 303–28. For the contractual interpretation, see Bryan Hainsworth, ed. *The Iliad: A Commentary, Vol III: Books 9–12* (Cambridge, 1993), p. 352.

Behold our Deeds transcending our Commands,
Such, they may cry, deserve the sov'reign State,
Whom those that envy, dare not imitate!
Could all our Care elude the gloomy Grave,
Which claims no less the fearful than the brave,
For Lust of Fame I should not vainly dare
In fighting Fields, nor urge thy Soul to War.
But since, alas! ignoble Age must come,
Disease, and Death's inexorable Doom;
The Life which others pay, let us bestow,
And give to Fame what we to Nature owe;
Brave tho' we fall, and honour'd if we live,
Or let us Glory gain, or Glory give!

(12. 371–96; *TE*, 8. 95–6)

Since the later eighteenth century, Pope's *Iliad* has been criticized for imposing on Homer a Virgilian grandeur, rhetorical orderliness, and self-conscious philosophical abstraction and sententiousness, which are alien to the more concrete and plain-spoken original. In his lectures *On Translating Homer* (1861) Matthew Arnold famously used the example of Sarpedon's speech to support his contention that in Pope's translation 'Homer's thought has passed through a literary and rhetorical crucible, and come out highly intellectualised'.[17] And a political dimension has recently been added to such criticisms in the claim that Pope's translation of Homer 'was a strategic choice, an appropriation of the "wild" Greek text to display the refinement of his literary talents and build a readership of equally refined tastes'.[18]

In Sarpedon's speech, it has been suggested, Pope has depicted the warrior's heroic resolve in straightforwardly stirring terms, glossing over Sarpedon's fundamental reluctance to fight, affirming his conviction that his bravery will certainly be rewarded by 'Glory', and thereby imposing a false univocality on Homer's more equivocal presentation.[19] But is such a criticism entirely fair to Pope's version? It certainly cannot be denied that Pope's rendering heightens the measured shapeliness of Sarpedon's words. But what is not so often noted is the

[17] Matthew Arnold, *Complete Prose Works*, ed. R. H. Super, 11 vols. (Ann Arbor MI, 1960), 1. 109.

[18] Venuti, 'Neoclassicism and Enlightenment', p. 57.

[19] Parker, *Dialogic Education*, pp. 117–20.

English poet's searching and cogent reaching out towards the distinctive ethical structure and assumptions which he intuited to be present in the Homeric speech. In his stress on their privileges as gifts of 'the bount'ous Pow'rs above' which they owe to 'Nature', Pope can be seen not to be confusing divinely-bestowed honour with human tributes,[20] but to be observing the Homeric distinction between *timē* (honour) and *geras* (tribute), as described by Émile Benveniste. And in his portrayal of the heroes' decision to fight as an act of aristocratic magnanimity ('The Life which others pay, let us bestow'), Pope can be seen not to be merely imposing upon Homer with an 'upper-class insolence' or 'Restoration swagger',[21] but to be anticipating the modern view of Sarpedon's speech as an expression of 'generalized reciprocity' rather than narrowly contractual obligation. Sarpedon's speech, in Pope's rendering, avoids Sir John Denham's suggestion, in his version of the episode published in 1668, that the two warriors are entering the battle as an act of aristocratic self-immolation. Denham's Sarpedon addresses his speech to Glaucus

> since he did not find
> Others as great in Place, as great in Mind.

And his final resolve is that

> A thousand ways the noblest path we'll tread;
> And bravely on, till they, or we, or all,
> A common Sacrifice to Honour fall.[22]

Pope also avoids the hard-headed Whiggish contractualism of Peter Motteux's version (1707), in which Sarpedon had urged that they should fight 'for the Common good', and so that their subjects shall judge them

> Men fit to lead, and worthy to be Kings.
> No idle Monarchs, no luxurious Drones,
> The State's Disease, or Lumber of their Thrones;
> Resign'd to Sloth, and negligent of Fame.[23]

[20] *Pace* Reuben Brower, *Alexander Pope: The Poetry of Allusion* (Oxford, 1959), p. 113.

[21] Again, *pace* Brower (p. 110).

[22] *The Poetical Works of Sir John Denham*, ed. Theodore Howard Banks (2nd edition, Hamden CT, 1969), pp. 179–80.

[23] Text from *TE*, 10. 572–3; for discussion, see Julian Ferraro, 'Political Discourse in Alexander Pope's *Episode of Sarpedon*', *Modern Language Review*, 88 (1993), 15–25 (pp. 17–18).

Pope's Sarpedon, moreover, articulates a system of values far removed from the providential Christianity of the English poet's own culture.

The suggestion that Pope's version offers stirring heroic sentiments to which the poet is simple-mindedly committed also seems questionable, since Sarpedon's fundamental unwillingness to fight is signalled as clearly by Pope as in Homer's original. Indeed, it is heightened. Sarpedon's significant 'alas' of heartfelt regret ('But since, alas! ignoble Age must come') is Pope's addition, and the English poet has also subtly enhanced the loving relish with which Sarpedon remembers the 'purple' harvests, 'num'rous' herds, 'foaming' bowls, and 'purer' nectar, which he and Glaucus enjoyed in peacetime, and the 'sprightly' music which 'enhanc'd' their former feasts (all Pope's additions). And Pope's replacement of Homer's *kēres thanatoio muriai* (countless spirits of death), 'which no mortal may escape or avoid', with 'ignoble Age', 'Disease' and 'Death', can be seen not merely as the sonorous expression of a melancholy of the kind later associated with Tennyson or Housman but as a measured reminder of the inexorable conditions of life which, as in Homer's original, form the backdrop to the warriors' heroic decision. It is also doubtful whether Pope's warriors feel that they are certain to be rescued by 'Glory'. For Pope's final antithesis ('Or let us Glory gain, or Glory give!') seems not so much a confident swagger as a sober acknowledgement that, though they *may* gain 'Glory', the 'Glory' of the occasion may go not to them but to those at whose hands they will meet their death. Pope thus seems fully alive to the fragile and questionable values that Homer associates with the heroic code. And when he comes to render Homer's depiction of the death of Sarpedon in Book 16, he offers an unflinching acknowledgement of the horror and degradation of the battle which Sarpedon enters, and in which he is killed, and does not balk the 'buzzing Flies' that 'Incessant swarm' around the 'heav'nly Form' of Sarpedon's corpse 'defac'd with Dust and Gore' on the plain (*TE*, 8. 273).[24]

Pope's capacity for imaginative negotiation with the alien world of Homeric values is even more strikingly apparent in another

[24] For an excellent recent discussion of this episode, see Robin Sowerby, 'The Decorum of Pope's *Iliad*', *Translation and Literature*, 13 (2004), 49–79.

celebrated passage from his *Iliad*: the episode in Book 21 when Achilles, having returned to the fight in fury after the death of Patroclus, encounters Priam's son, Lycaon. Lycaon begs to be spared as a *xenos* (guest-friend) and suppliant, but Achilles denies his plea, and kills him brutally. Discussions of this passage in Homer's original might, it has been suggested, profitably focus on the tone of two words used by Achilles to Lycaon, 'poor fool' (*nēpios*) and 'friend' (*philos*), which are 'arguably either sarcastic or denoting a commonality between them despite their seemingly distinct status'.[25] One might speculate about Achilles' mood here ('sadistic? cold? insanely angry? philosophical? sardonic? gently sad?') and consider questions of narrative focalization. Is the episode being told from Achilles' point of view? Where do the values come from by which to judge Achilles' behaviour? One of the advantages of the 'glossed text' method of investigating such questions is that 'the reader is free to run a plurality of possibilities and hold off decisions' in a way that would not be possible when 'experiencing an interpretation in the theatre or an authoritative recreating translation'.[26] Here is how Pope renders Achilles' speech:

> Talk not of Life, or Ransom, (he replies)
> *Patroclus* dead, whoever meets me, dies:
> In vain a single *Trojan* sues for Grace;
> But least, the Sons of *Priam*'s hateful Race.
> Die then, my Friend! What boots it to deplore?
> The great, the good *Patroclus* is no more!
> He, far thy Better, was fore-doomed to die,
> 'And thou, dost thou bewail mortality?'
> See'st thou not me, whom Nature's Gifts adorn,
> Sprung from a Hero, from a Goddess born;
> The Day shall come (which nothing can avert)
> When by the Spear, the Arrow, or the Dart,
> By Night, or Day, by Force or by Design,
> Impending Death and certain Fate are mine.
> Die then!
>
> (*TE*, 8. 426)

[25] Parker, *Dialogic Education*, p. 84.
[26] Ibid. pp. 85–6, 90.

Pope does not directly translate the Homeric Achilles' address to Lycaon as *nēpie* (you poor fool), and it has been argued that he renders Homer's *philos* (friend) 'univocal' by turning Achilles into someone who 'has faced squarely the human condition and can condemn Lykaon for not doing so': 'It may be noble and brave to have looked one's own death in the face and come to terms with it, but I dare to say it is not Homeric.'[27] But such a view of the quintessentially Homeric is not universally shared.[28] In his study of Homeric influence on the epic and romance traditions, Colin Burrow has offered a powerful description of the distinctive and disturbing nature of Homeric 'sympathy' and 'pity', forms of those emotions quite different from those with which we are customarily familiar. In most post-Christian literature, Burrow argues, 'the inescapable similarity between mortal experiences' is associated with 'the desire to save, cherish, and regenerate'. But Homeric pity and sympathy, in sharp contrast, are usually associated with death:

You can kill someone through Homeric pity, not because you want to put him out of his misery, but because you accept the fact of your mortality in his death. When warriors in the *Iliad* pity a dead comrade, they rarely pause in fighting to tend their wounds. They go straight on and kill. This is usually more than revenge, or is at least an unusually complex form of revenge: it is more like an activation of mortality, a recognition that things must die, which leads to an urge to universalize that recognition . . . Sympathy of this kind, the kind that recognizes death, turns back into something which it is tempting to call ruthlessness.

On his return to the battle, Burrow argues, Achilles 'becomes Homeric sympathy militant', wishing to affirm his shared sense of mortality 'by bringing death'. Commenting specifically on the Lycaon episode, Burrow remarks:

Where sympathy ceases to be the conscious relation of particular sorrows to particular sorrows, and becomes a sense of general and universal fragility, then the mortality of another person becomes identifiable with one's own,

[27] Ibid., p. 91.

[28] As well as Colin Burrow (quoted below), see Jasper Griffin, *Homer on Life and Death* (Oxford, 1980), p. 55: '[Achilles] sees his action in the perspective of human life and death as a whole, the perspective which puts slayer and slain on a level, so that it is more than a mere colloquialism that he calls Lycaon "friend" as he kills him.'

with one's friend's, with that of any sufferer. This attitude is simultaneously a kind of universal sympathy and a form of despair, which blurs suicidal and homicidal desire into a deadly composite... The horror of [Achilles'] ruthless *aristeia* is not that it is inhumane; in a way it is so super-humane that it presses the poem's own recurrent sense of shared fragility into horror: why, if death is universal, should it not be *made* to be universal?[29]

Pope's rendering of the Lycaon episode shows him, I think, to be recreating the emotional and conceptual temper of Homer's episode in ways which strikingly anticipate Burrow's commentary, and which simultaneously cast doubt on the suggestion that Pope characteristically transforms Homer's brutal heroes into dignified 'English gentlemen'.[30] In a note on the passage, Pope expressed his distress at Achilles' implacable rejection of Lycaon's supplication:

I must confess I could have wished *Achilles* had spared him: There are so many Circumstances that speak in his Favour.

(*TE*, 8. 425)

But such qualms in no way inhibited him from rendering Achilles' final terrifying words to his victim with absolute conviction, and in a plain, unadorned diction which conveys the hero's sentiments with a measured but formidable directness. And in the same note from which I have just quoted, Pope expressed his admiration – in the old sense of the word, if not the new – of Achilles' behaviour:

There is an Air of Greatness in the Conclusion of the Speech of *Achilles*, which strikes me very much: He speaks very unconcernedly of his own death, and upbraids his Enemy for asking Life so earnestly, a life that was of so much less Importance than his own.

(*TE*, 8. 425)

Pope's translation tellingly reinforces his sense of the 'greatness' of Achilles' sentiments by imbuing his words – and marking the fact in his text by inverted commas – with an echo of Dryden's translation of the moment in Lucretius' *De Rerum Natura* (3. 1025–6) where Lucretius had himself echoed the sentiments of the Homeric Achilles to support his own haughty rejection of the fear of death:

[29] Colin Burrow, *Epic Romance: Homer to Milton* (Oxford, 1993), pp. 22–5.
[30] Venuti, 'Neoclassicism and Enlightenment', p. 57.

Mean time, when thoughts of death disturb thy head;
Consider, *Ancus* great and good is dead;
*Ancus* thy better far, was born to die,
And thou, dost thou bewail mortality?

(Dryden, *Works*, 3. 54)

Though on one level Pope's allusion might be thought to introduce into the speech a distinctly un-Homeric intertextual sophistication, his echo of the Drydenian Lucretius' scornful repetition ('And thou, dost thou') might be thought to offer an effective equivalent for the Homeric Achilles' *nēpie* (you fool) which, as we have seen, he had left untranslated at the opening of the speech.

In the foregoing discussion of the operation of 'paraphrastic' translation in two episodes from Pope's *Iliad*, I have said nothing about the alternative, 'foreignizing' tradition favoured by some recent commentators. I offer, by way of a coda, two brief comments on that subject. First, it must immediately be conceded that the 'foreignizing' mode has achieved a number of notable successes in English. The most celebrated – though it is, for several obvious reasons, a very 'special case' – is the tradition of Biblical translation from Tyndale to the Authorized Version. A more recent instance might be the Confucian Odes of Ezra Pound.[31] But the dangers of the mode surely remain those signalled by Sir John Denham and William Cowper: that the 'alien' stylistic elements preserved from the original will only be recognizable as such by those who know the source in its original language; to others they will seem merely bizarre. As had been observed, 'it is, obviously, harder to write well enough to change the norms of one's own language than it is to write competently within them, and most successful translations with greater ambitions than that of the crib have been assimilative'.[32] Secondly, there is, in practice, as we saw in Chapter 5, by no means the hard-and-fast polar opposition between 'foreignizing' and 'domesticating' translation that some commentators have suggested. Few 'foreignizing' translations are, in fact, without their local 'domesticating' elements, and vice versa. The

[31] See D. S. Carne-Ross, 'Jocasta's Divine Head: English with a Foreign Accent', *Arion*, 3rd series, 1 (1989), 106–41; Kenneth Haynes, *English Literature and Ancient Languages* (Oxford, 2003), pp. 87–8.

[32] Haynes, *English Literature and Ancient Languages*, p. 87.

translations of Dryden, for example, though broadly 'assimilative' in their method, contain, as Dryden himself acknowledged (*Works*, 5. 319–36), numerous local importations of Latin idiom, style, and diction.[33]

Pope's translation of Homer, moreover, though its general methods may place it in the 'assimilative' and 'domesticating' category, involves, as I hope my examples have shown, a much more searching and subtle imaginative dialogue with the 'otherness' of the Homeric world than such a categorizing would suggest. Pope's relationship with Homer is, I believe, far more aptly characterized by H. A. Mason's model of a translatorly stance which acknowledges ancient texts as 'forever alien, and yet, mysteriously, *abordable*', than by the alternative model of a 'familiarizing' translator confidently 'appropriating' and 'colonizing' his original. And Pope's sensitivity to the developing drama of the *Iliad*, with all its turns, reversals, and ambiguities, also casts doubt, I believe, on the suggestion that Pope has imposed on Homer a consistently monovocal interpretative 'closure'.

Pope's endeavour was to make sense of every element and every moment in Homer's narrative in ways which genuinely respond to the alien world of the Greek poem, while simultaneously effecting those 'structural substitutions' of custom and belief necessary to relate that world to modern readers' concerns.[34] Pope, moreover, sought to make every element and moment of Homer's text intelligible *in relation to every other element and moment.*[35] 'Glossed texts' of classical authors are, as has been tellingly shown, an invaluable stimulus to classroom discussion. But they can ultimately only offer *disiecta membra*: discontinuous speculations *about* a Greek text and suggestions of possibilities *within* that text, rather than a sense of the unified effect *of* the text as a whole. They can do little, that is, to provide the absorbing imaginative experience, continuously unfolding

[33] For discussion of one particularly interesting instance – Dryden's 'pause of life' (rendering the Latin 'vitai pausa') in his translation of Lucretius – see Emrys Jones, '"A Perpetual Torrent": Dryden's Lucretian Style', in *Augustan Studies: Essays in Honor of Irvin Ehrenpreis*, ed. Douglas Lane Patey and Timothy Keegan (Newark DE, 1985), pp. 47–63 (pp. 56–7).

[34] For the phrase, see Bernard Williams, *Shame and Necessity* (Berkeley, Los Angeles CA, London, 1993), pp. 18–19.

[35] See Sowerby, 'The Decorum of Pope's *Iliad*' and *The Augustan Art of Poetry: Augustan Translation of the Classics* (Oxford, 2006), Chapter 4.

in time and cumulative in its effect, that the reading (whether silent or vocal) or performance of epic and dramatic texts entails. There are undoubtedly good educational reasons for encouraging students to keep open a variety of possibilities when exploring Homer's use of his key conceptual, ethical, and religious terms. But such a luxury is simply not available to the reader of or listener to – as opposed to the participator in seminars on – classical epic and drama. In the Preface to his *Iliad*, Pope offered a vivid evocation of the experience of reading Homer:

> It is to the Strength of [his] amazing Invention we are to attribute that unequal'd Fire and Rapture, which is so forcible in *Homer*, that no Man of a true Poetical Spirit is Master of himself while he reads him. What he writes is of the most animated Nature imaginable; every thing moves, every thing lives, and is put in Action. If a Council be call'd, or a Battle fought, you are not coldly inform'd of what was said or done as from a third Person; the Reader is hurry'd out of himself by the Force of the Poet's Imagination, and turns in one place to a Hearer, in another to a Spectator.
>
> (*TE*, 7: 4)

Only a translation of Homer that constantly displays a 'Fire', 'Rapture', and 'Imagination' commensurate with those of its original can produce a readerly involvement of the kind that Pope describes. And if a translation does not produce such an effect, it is, surely, untrue to its original *in as fundamental a way as can be imagined*? For it is likely to provoke the pointed question once asked by Robert Bridges: 'If you really thought the original was like that, what can you have seen in it to make you think it was worth translating?'[36] In many obvious, important, and well-documented senses, Pope's *Iliad* is 'unfaithful' to the letter of Homer's text. Indeed, Pope himself constantly signals in the notes to his translation his conviction that it is impossible to render Homer's text with transparent and unmediated directness in the very different cultural and linguistic circumstances of a later culture.[37] But in other, equally important, ways – or so it might be

[36] Robert Bridges, *Ibant Obscuri* (Oxford, 1916), p. 40.

[37] See Introduction, above, and Michael Silk, *Homer: The Iliad* (Cambridge, 1987), pp. 46–54; Fred Parker, '"Talking Scripture out of Church": Parson Adams and the Partiality of Translation', *Translation and Literature*, 14 (2005), 179–95, and 'Classic Simplicity', in *Translation and the Classic: Identity and Change in the History of Culture*, ed. Alexandra Lianeri and Vanda Zajko (Oxford, 2008), pp. 227–42.

argued – Pope's version is by far the most radically 'faithful' rendering of Homer that we possess. If we are taking the etymological root of the term 'translation' seriously, to indicate a genuine 'bringing across' of something of the total effect of an ancient text (not merely of its construable content or discussable elements), might it not be argued that it is *only* versions which offer the fullness of imaginative and experiential participation allowed by Pope's *Iliad* that properly deserve the title 'translation' at all?

# *Bibliography*


Abrams, M. H., *A Glossary of Literary Terms* (7th edition, Fort Worth TX, 1999).

Aikin, John, *Letters to a Young Lady on a Course of English Poetry* (London, 1804).

Aldington, Richard, 'Cowley and the French Epicureans', *New Statesman*, 5 November 1921, pp. 133–4.

Allen, D. C., 'The Rehabilitation of Epicurus and his Theory of Pleasure in the Early Renaissance', *Studies in Philology*, 41 (1944), 1–15.

Amarasinghe, Upali, *Dryden and Pope in the Early Nineteenth Century* (Cambridge, 1962).

Anderson, W. S., 'The Roman Socrates: Horace and his Satires', in *Critical Essays on Roman Literature: Satire*, ed. J. P. Sullivan (London, 1963).

—— , 'Playfulness and Seriousness in Ovid's *Metamorphoses*', *Mosaic*, 12. 1–2 (1981), 192–210.

—— , *Essays on Roman Satire* (Princeton NJ, 1982).

*The Annual Miscellany: for the Year 1694* (London, 1694).

Anon, *Aesop's Fables, with Morals and Reflections... done into a Variety of English Verse* (4th edition, London, 1720).

Anon, *The War with Priestcraft* (London, 1732).

Anselment, Raymond A., 'Thomas Sprat's *The Plague of Athens*: Thucydides, Lucretius, and the "Pindaric Way" ', *Bulletin of the John Rylands University Library of Manchester*, 78 (1996), 3–20.

Arnaud, D. L., 'Aspects of Wit and Humor in Ovid's *Metamorphoses*' (Unpublished PhD dissertation, Stanford, 1968).

Arnold, Matthew, *Complete Prose Works*, ed. R. H. Super, 11 vols. (Ann Arbor MI, 1960–77).

Arthos, John, *The Language of Natural Description in Eighteenth-Century Poetry* (Ann Arbor MI, 1949).

Arwaker, Edmund, *Truth in Fiction: or Morality in Masquerade* (London, 1708).

Ashfield, Andrew and de Bolla, Peter, eds., *The Sublime: A Reader in British Eighteenth-Century Aesthetic Theory* (Cambridge, 1996).

Auerbach, Erich, *Mimesis: The Representation of Reality in Western Literature*, trans. Willard R. Trask (1953; reprinted Princeton NJ, 1968).

Ayres, Philip, *Classical Culture and the Idea of Rome in Eighteenth-Century England* (Cambridge, 1997).
Babcock, R. W., *The Genesis of Shakespeare Idolatry, 1766–1799* (Chapel Hill NC, 1931).
Bailey, C., *The Greek Atomists and Epicurus* (Oxford, 1928).
Baillet, Adrien, *Jugemens des savans sur les principaux ouvrages des auteurs*, 4 vols. (Paris, 1685–6).
Barbour, Reid, 'Between Atoms and the Spirit: Lucy Hutchinson's Translation of Lucretius', *Renaissance Papers*: 1–16 (1994).
——, 'Lucy Hutchinson, Atomism, and the Atheist Dog', in Lynette Hunter and Sarah Hutton, eds., *Women, Science, and Medicine, 1500–1700* (Stroud, 1997), pp. 122–37.
Barclay, Andrew, 'Dating Roscommon's Academy', *Restoration*, 26 (2002), 119–26.
Barnard, John, ed., *Pope: The Critical Heritage* (London, 1973).
Battegli, Anna Margaret, *Margaret Cavendish and the Exiles of the Mind* (Lexington KY, 1998).
Beard, Mary and Henderson, John, *Classics: A Very Short Introduction* (Oxford, 1995).
Beattie, James, *Poems* (London, 1760).
Beaumont, Sir John, *Bosworth-field* (London, 1629).
Beer, Gillian, '"Our Unnatural No-Voice": The Heroic Epistle, Pope, and Women's Gothic', *The Yearbook of English Studies*, 12 (1982), 125–51.
Behn, Aphra, *Works*, ed. Janet Todd, 7 vols. (London, 1992–96).
Beller, M., *Philemon und Baucis in der europäischen Literatur* (Heidelberg, 1967).
Bentley, Simon and Hammond, Paul, 'The Nativities of John and Charles Dryden', *Restoration*, 9 (1985), 56–60.
Benveniste, Émile, *Indo-European Language and Society*, trans. Elizabeth Palmer (London, 1973).
Blackburn, Simon, *Truth: A Guide for the Perplexed* (London, 2005).
Blake, William, *Complete Writings*, ed. Geoffrey Keynes (London, 1957).
Blount, Sir Thomas Pope, *De Re Poetica* (London, 1694).
Boase, Alan M., *The Fortunes of Montaigne: A History of the Essays in France, 1580–1669* (London, 1935).
Boileau-Despréaux, Nicolas, *Works* [trans. J. Ozell et al.] (London, 1711–13).
Bond, Donald F., ed. *The Spectator*, 5 vols. (Oxford, 1965).
Borgerhoff, E. B. O., *The Freedom of French Classicism* (Princeton NJ, 1950).
Bottkol, J. McG., 'Dryden's Latin Scholarship', *Modern Philology*, 40 (1943), 241–54.
Bowersock, G. S., 'The Rediscovery of Herculaneum and Pompeii', *The American Scholar*, 47 (1978), 461–70.

Bradley, A. C., *Shakespearean Tragedy* (London, 1904).
Bramble, John, 'Martial and Juvenal', in *The Cambridge History of Classical Literature, Vol. II: Latin Literature*, eds. E. J. Kenney and W. V. Clausen (Cambridge, 1982), pp. 606–9.
Branam, George C., *Eighteenth-Century Adaptations of Shakespearean Tragedy* (Berkeley and Los Angeles CA, 1956).
Bridges, Robert, *Ibant Obscuri* (Oxford, 1916).
Brink, C. O., *On Reading a Horatian Satire: An Interpretation of Sermones II. 6* (Sydney, 1965).
Broderson, G. L., 'Seventeenth-Century Translations of Juvenal', *Phoenix*, 7 (1953), 57–76.
Brody, Jules, *Boileau and Longinus* (Geneva, 1958).
Brooks, Harold F., 'The "Imitation" in English Poetry, especially in Formal Verse Satire, before the Age of Pope', *Review of English Studies*, 25 (1949), 124–40.
Brower, Reuben, *Alexander Pope: The Poetry of Allusion* (Oxford, 1959).
Brown, A. D. J., 'The Little Fellow Has Done Wonders', *Cambridge Quarterly*, 21 (1992), 120–49.
Brown, Joseph Epes, ed. *The Critical Opinions of Samuel Johnson* (Princeton NJ, 1926).
Bryant, Jacob, *An Expostulation, Addressed to The British Critic* (Eton, 1799).
—— , *Some Observations upon The Vindication of Homer* (Eton, 1799).
Buckingham, George Villiers, Duke of, *Plays, Poems, and Miscellaneous Writings Associated with George Villiers, Duke of Buckingham*, eds. Robert D. Hume and Harold Love, 2 vols. (Oxford, 2007).
Bulstrode, Whitelocke, *An Essay of Transmigration* (2nd edition, London, 1693).
[Burnet, Gilbert], *Utopia: Written in Latin by Sir Thomas More, Chancellor of England: Translated into English* (London, 1684).
—— , *History of his Own Time, with Notes by the Earls of Dartmouth and Hardwicke, Speaker Onslow, and Dean Swift*, 6 vols. (2nd edition, London, 1833).
Burrow, Colin, *Epic Romance: Homer to Milton* (Oxford, 1993).
Byron, Lord, *Letters and Journals*, ed. Leslie A. Marchand, 12 vols. (London, 1973–82).
—— , *Complete Poetical Works, Vol. 2: Childe Harold's Pilgrimage*, ed. Jerome J. McGann (Oxford, 1980).
—— , *Complete Miscellaneous Prose*, ed. Andrew Nicholson (Oxford, 1991).
Bysshe, Edward, *The Art of English Poetry*, 2 vols. (London, 1702).
—— , *The British Parnassus*, 2 vols. (London, 1714).

Bywaters, David, *Dryden in Revolutionary England* (Berkeley and Los Angeles CA, 1991).

Cameron, William J., ed., *Poems on Affairs of State: Augustan Satirical Verse, 1660–1714, Vol. V: 1688–1697* (New Haven CT and London, 1971).

Campbell, Oscar James, ed., *A Shakespeare Encyclopedia* (London, 1966).

Carew, Thomas, *Poems*, ed. Rhodes Dunlap (Oxford, 1949).

Carne-Ross, D. S., 'A Mistaken Ambition of Exactness', *Delos*, 2 (1968), 171–97.

—— , 'Jocasta's Divine Head: English with a Foreign Accent', *Arion*, 3rd series, 1 (1989), 106–41.

Chapman, George, *Chapman's Homer*, ed. Allardyce Nicoll, 2 vols. (2nd edition, Princeton NJ, 1967).

Charleton, Walter, *Epicurus' Morals, Collected and Faithfully Englished*, ed. F. Manning (London, 1926).

Charron, Pierre, *Of Wisdom*, trans. George Stanhope, 3 vols. (2nd edition, London, 1707).

Cheeke, Stephen, *Byron and Place: History, Translation, Nostalgia* (Basingstoke, 2003).

Chetwood, Knightly, 'A Short Account of Some Passages of the Life & Death of Wentworth, late Earle of Roscommon', ed. Greg Clingham, *Restoration*, 25 (2001), 117–28.

Clapp, Sarah Lewis Carol, ed., *Jacob Tonson in Ten Letters by and about him* (Austin TX, 1948).

Clarke, G. B., ed., *Descriptions of Lord Cobham's Gardens at Stowe (1700–1750)*, Buckinghamshire Record Society, No. 26 (1990).

Clarke, Howard, *Homer's Readers: An Historical Introduction to the* Iliad *and the* Odyssey (Newark DE, 1981).

Clingham, Greg, 'Another and the Same: Johnson's Dryden', in *Literary Transmission and Authority: Dryden and Other Writers*, ed. Earl Miner and Jennifer Brady (Cambridge, 1993), pp. 149–50.

—— , 'Roscommon's "Academy", Chetwood's "Life of Roscommon", and Dryden's Translation Project', *Restoration*, 26 (2002), 15–26.

Coleman, R., 'Structure and Intention in the *Metamorphoses*', *Classical Quarterly*, 21 (1971), 461–77.

Colley, Linda, *Britons: Forging the Nation, 1707–1837* (New Haven CT, 1992).

Collingwood, R. G., *An Autobiography* (Oxford, 1939).

Combe, Kirk, 'Clandestine Protest against William III in Dryden's Translations of Juvenal and Persius', *Modern Philology*, 87 (1989), 36–50.

Comes, Natalis, *Mythologiae* (Venice, 1567).

Congreve, William, *The Mourning Bride, etc.*, ed. B. Dobrée (Oxford, 1928).

Cowley, Abraham, *Poems*, ed. A. R. Waller (Cambridge, 1905).

——, *Essays, Plays and Sundry Verses*, ed. A. R. Waller (Cambridge, 1906).

Crump, M. M., *The Epyllion from Theocritus to Ovid* (London, 1931).

Cruttwell, Patrick, *The Shakespearean Moment and its Place in the Poetry of the Seventeenth Century* (London, 1954).

Danchin, Pierre, ed., *The Prologues and Epilogues of the Restoration*, 6 vols. (Nancy, 1981–88).

Denham, Sir John, *Poetical Works*, ed. Theodore Howard Banks (2nd edition, Hamden CT, 1969).

Dennis, John, *Critical Works*, ed. E. N. Hooker, 2 vols. (Baltimore MD, 1939–43).

de Quehen, Hugh, 'Ease and Flow in Lucy Hutchinson's Lucretius', *Studies in Philology*, 93 (1996), 288–303.

Detienne, Marcel, *The Gardens of Adonis: Spices in Greek Mythology* (1972), trans. Janet Lloyd (Hassocks, 1977).

Dillon, Wentworth, fourth Earl of Roscommon, *An Essay on Translated Verse* (2nd edition, London, 1685).

Dobson, Michael, *The Making of the National Poet: Shakespeare, Adaptation, and Authorship, 1660–1769* (Oxford, 1992).

Donno, Elizabeth Story, ed., *Elizabethan Minor Epics* (London, 1963).

Dover, K. J., 'Translation: The Speakable and the Unspeakable', *Essays in Criticism*, 30 (1980), 1–8.

Downie, J. A., *To Settle the Succession of the State: Literature and Politics, 1678–1750* (London, 1994).

Dronke, Peter, *Women Writers of the Middle Ages* (Cambridge, 1984).

Dryden, John, *Letters*, ed. Charles E. Ward (Durham NC, 1942).

——, *The California Edition of the Works of John Dryden*, ed. E. N. Hooker, H. T. Swedenberg Jr. et al., 20 vols. (Berkeley, Los Angeles CA, London, 1956–2000).

——, *The Poems*, ed. Paul Hammond and David Hopkins, Longman Annotated English Poets, 5 vols. (London, 1995–2005).

Due, O. S., *Changing Forms: Studies in the Metamorphoses of Ovid*, Classica et Mediaevalia: Dissertations x (Copenhagen, 1974).

Eliot, T. S., ed., *The Selected Poems of Ezra Pound* (London, 1948).

——, *Selected Essays*, (2nd edition, London, 1934).

Empson, William, 'Mine Eyes Dazzle', *Essays in Criticism*, 14 (1964), 80–6.

Erskine-Hill, Howard, *The Augustan Idea in English Literature* (London, 1983).

Fabian, Bernard, 'Pope and Lucretius: Observations on *An Essay on Man*', *Modern Language Review*, 74 (1979), 524–37.

[Falconer, Thomas], *Remarks on Some Passages in Mr. Bryant's Publications, respecting the War of Troy* (London, 1799).

Fanshawe, Sir Richard, *Selected Parts of Horace* (London, 1652).
—— , *The Poems and Translations*, ed. Peter Davidson, 2 vols. (Oxford, 1997–99).
Fantham, E., 'Ovid's Ceyx and Alcyone', *Phoenix*, 33 (1979), 330–45.
Fara, Patricia and Money, David, 'Issac Newton and Augustan Anglo-Latin Poetry', *Studies in the History and Philosophy of Science*, 34 (2004), 549–71.
Ferraro, Julian, 'Political Discourse in Alexander Pope's *Episode of Sarpedon*', *Modern Language Review*, 88 (1993), 15–25.
Fish, Stanley, *Is there a Text in this Class? The Authority of Interpretive Communities* (Cambridge MA, 1980).
Flatman, Thomas, *Poems and Songs*, (3rd edition, London, 1682).
Fowler, Robert, ed., *The Cambridge Companion to Homer* (Cambridge, 2004).
Francklin, William, *Remarks and Observations on the Plain of Troy* (London, 1800).
Fränkel, H., *Ovid: A Poet Between Two Worlds* (Berkeley and Los Angeles CA, 1956).
Frécaut, J.-M., *L'Esprit et l'humour chez Ovide* (Grenoble, 1972).
Frost, William, *John Dryden: Dramatist, Satirist, Translator* (New York, 1988).
Galinsky, G. K., *Ovid's 'Metamorphoses': An Introduction to the Basic Aspects* (Oxford, 1975).
Garrison, James D., 'The Universe of Dryden's *Fables*', *Studies in English Literature*, 21 (1981), 409–23.
Gildon, Charles, *The Complete Art of Poetry*, 2 vols. (London, 1718).
Gill, Christopher, 'Altruism or Reciprocity in Greek Ethical Philosophy', in *Reciprocity in Ancient Greece*, ed. Christopher Gill, Norman Postlethwaite, Richard Seaford (Oxford, 1998), pp. 303–28.
Gillespie, Stuart, 'Dryden's Sylvae' (Unpublished PhD thesis, Cambridge, 1987).
—— , and Hopkins, David, eds., *The Dryden-Tonson Miscellanies, 1684–1709*, Cultural Transformations: The Eighteenth Century, 6 vols. (London and Toyko, 2008).
—— —— , eds., *The Oxford History of Literary Translation in English, Vol. 3: 1660–1790* (Oxford, 2005).
Glanvill, John, *Poems* (London, 1725).
Goldhill, Simon, *Love, Sex, and Tragedy: How the Ancient World Shapes our Lives* (London, 2004).
—— , 'Cultural History and Aesthetics: Why Kant is No Place to Start Reception Studies', in *Theorizing Performance: Greek Drama, Cultural History, and Critical Practice*, ed. Edith Hall and Stephe Harrop (forthcoming, London, 2010).

Goldie, Mark, 'The Roots of True Whiggism: 1688–94', *History of Political Thought*, 1 (1980), 195–236.

Gordon, Cosmo Alexander, *A Bibliography of Lucretius* (London, 1962).

Greene, Donald, *The Age of Exuberance: Backgrounds to Eighteenth-Century English Literature* (New York, 1970).

Gregory, Olinthus, *Memoirs of the Life, Writings, and Character, Literary, Professional and Religious, of the Late John Mason Good, M. D.* (London, 1828).

Gresham, James, *The Picture of Incest. Lively Portraicted in the Historie of Cinyras and Myrrha* (London, 1626).

Griffin, Dustin, 'Venting Spleen', *Essays in Criticism*, 40 (1990), 124–35.

Griffin, Jasper, *Homer on Life and Death* (Oxford, 1980).

Grundy, Isobel, *Lady Mary Wortley Montagu: Comet of the Enlightenment* (Oxford, 1999).

Guthrie, W. K. C., *The Sophists* (Cambridge, 1971).

Hainsworth, Bryan, *The Iliad: A Commentary, Vol III: Books 9–12* (Cambridge, 1993).

Hale, John K., *Milton's Languages: The Impact of Multilingualism on Style* (Cambridge, 1997).

Hammond, Paul, 'The Integrity of Dryden's Lucretius', *Modern Language Review*, 78 (1983), 1–23.

—— , 'Dryden's Philosophy of Fortune', *Modern Language Review*, 80 (1985), 769–85.

—— , 'John Dryden: The Classicist as Sceptic', *The Seventeenth Century*, 4 (1989), 165–87.

—— , *Dryden and the Traces of Classical Rome* (Oxford, 1999).

—— , 'Dryden, Milton, and Lucretius'. *The Seventeenth Century* 16 (2001), 158–76.

—— , 'The Janus Poet: Dryden's Critique of Shakespeare', in Claude Rawson and Aaron Santesso, eds., *John Dryden (1631–1700): His Politics, his Plays, and his Poets* (Newark NJ and London, 2004), pp. 158–79.

Hardie, Philip, 'The Presence of Lucretius in *Paradise Lost*', *Milton Quarterly*, 29 (1995), 13–24.

—— Barchiesi, Alessandro, and Hinds, Stephen, eds., *Ovidian Transformations: Essays on Ovid's 'Metamorphoses' and its Reception*, Proceedings of the Cambridge Philological Society, Supplementary Volume No. 23 (Cambridge, 1999).

Hardwick, Lorna, *Reception Studies*, Greece and Rome New Surveys in the Classics, No. 33 (Oxford, 2003).

—— and Stray, Christopher, eds., *A Companion to Classical Receptions* (Oxford, 2008).

Harris, Tim, *London Crowds in the Reign of Charles II* (Cambridge, 1987).

—— , *Politics under the Later Stuarts: Party Conflict in a Divided Society, 1660–1715* (London, 1993).

Harrison, C. T., 'The Ancient Atomists and English Literature in the Seventeenth Century', *Harvard Studies in Classical Philology*, 45 (1934), 1–79.

Haskell, Francis and Penny, Nicholas, *Taste and the Antique: The Lure of Classical Sculpture, 1500–1900* (New Haven CT, 1981).

Haynes, Kenneth, *English Literature and Ancient Languages* (Oxford, 2003).

Heninger, Jr., S. K., *Touches of Sweet Harmony: Pythagorean Cosmology and Renaissance Poetics* (San Marino CA, 1974).

Highet, Gilbert, *The Classical Tradition* (Oxford, 1949).

Homer, *Homeri Quae Extant Omnia*, ed. J. Spondanus [Jean de Sponde] (Basel, 1583).

—— *The Iliad of Homer, Translated by Alexander Pope: A New Edition*, ed. Gilbert Wakefield, 4 vols. (London, 1806) [1st edition, 1796].

—— *The Iliad*, trans. Alexander Pope, ed. Steven Shankman (Harmondsworth, 1996).

Hooker, Helen M., 'Dryden's *Georgics* and English Predecessors', *Huntington Library Quarterly*, 9 (1946), 273–310.

Hopkins, Charles, *Epistolary Poems: On Several Occasions* (London, 1694).

Hopkins, David, 'Two Hitherto Unrecorded Sources for Dryden's Ovid Translations', *Notes and Queries*, 219 (1974), 419–20.

—— , 'Dryden's Cave of Sleep and Garth's *Dispensary*', *Notes and Queries*, 221 (1976), 243–5.

—— , 'Dryden and the Two Editions of Sandys's Ovid', *Notes and Queries*, 221 (1976), 552–4.

—— , *John Dryden* (Cambridge, 1986).

—— , 'Dryden and the Garth-Tonson *Metamorphoses*', *Review of English Studies*, 39 (1988), 64–74.

—— , 'Dryden, John Harvey and the Tenth Satire of Juvenal', *Notes and Queries*, 240 (1995), 54–6.

—— , 'Charles Montague, George Stepney, and Dryden's *Metamorphoses*,' *Review of English Studies*, 51 (2000), 83–9.

—— Review of *John Evelyn's Translation of Titus Lucretius Carus* De Rerum Natura, ed. Michael M. Repetzki, *Translation and Literature*, 11 (2002), 114–18.

—— , *Writers and their Work: John Dryden* (Tavistock, 2004).

Horace, *His Art of Poetry, Pistles and Satyrs Englished* [trans. Thomas Drant] (London, 1567).

—— , *Poems* [ed. Alexander Brome] (London, 1666).

—— , *Odes, Satyrs, and Epistles of Horace. Done into English* [trans. Thomas Creech] (London, 1684).

——, *A Poetical Translation of the Works of Horace* [trans. Philip Francis], 2 vols. (3rd edition, London, 1749).
——, *The Works of Horace in English Verse. By Several Hands. Collected and Published by Mr. Duncombe*, 2 vols. (London, 1757–59).
——, *Works*, ed. E. C. Wickham, 2 vols. (Oxford, 1891).
——, *Les oeuvres d'Horace: Satires*, ed. P. Lejay (Paris, 1911).
——, *Satires*, ed. F. Villeneuve (Paris 1932).
[Howard, Sir Robert], 'Of Natures Changes from Lucretius, Book the 5th. by a Person of Quality', in *Sylvae: or the Second Part of Poetical Miscellanies* (London, 1685), pp. 406–17.
Howe, Elizabeth, *The First English Actresses: Women and Drama, 1660–1700* (Cambridge, 1992).
Hume, David, *An Enquiry Concerning Human Understanding*, ed. Tom L. Beauchamp (Oxford, 1999).
Hunter, Michael, 'John Evelyn in the 1650s: A Virtuoso in Quest of a Role', in *Science and the Shape of Orthodoxy: Intellectual Change in Late Seventeenth-Century Britain* (Woodbridge, 1995), pp. 67–98.
Hunter, William B., 'Lucretius', in William B. Hunter, ed., *A Milton Encyclopedia*, 5 vols. (Lewisburg PA, 1978–83).
Hutchinson, G. O., *Latin Literature from Seneca to Juvenal: A Critical Study* (Oxford, 1983).
Hutchinson, Lucy, *Order and Disorder*, ed. David Norbrook (Oxford, 2001).
Jeffares, A. Norman, *W. B. Yeats: Man and Poet*, (2nd edition, London, 1962).
Jenkyns, Richard, 'Juvenal the Poet', in *Three Classical Poets: Sappho, Catullus and Juvenal* (London, 1982), pp. 151–221.
Johnson, Samuel, *Works*, ed. Sir John Hawkins, 11 vols. (London, 1787).
Johnson, Samuel, *Samuel Johnson On Shakespeare*, ed. H. R. Woudhuysen (Harmondsworth, 1989).
——, *The Lives of the Most Eminent English Poets*, ed. Roger Lonsdale, 4 vols. (Oxford, 2006).
Jones, Emrys, ' "A Perpetual Torrent": Dryden's Lucretian Style', in *Augustan Studies: Essays in Honor of Irvin Ehrenpreis*, ed. Douglas Lane Patey and Timothy Keegan (Newark DE, 1985).
Jones, Howard, *The Epicurean Tradition* (London, 1989).
Joy, L. S., *Gassendi the Atomist* (Cambridge, 1987).
Jungkuntz, R. P., 'Christian Approval of Epicureanism', *Church History*, 31 (1962), 279–93.
Juvenal, *Sixteen Satyrs, or A Survey of the Manners and Actions of Mankind* [trans. Sir Robert Stapylton] (London, 1647).
——, *Decimus Junius Juvenalis and Aulus Persius Flaccus Translated and Illustrated... by Barten Holyday* (Oxford, 1673).

Juvenal, *A Modern Essay on the Thirteenth Satyr of Juvenal* [trans. Henry Higden] (London, 1686).

——, *A Modern Essay on the Tenth Satyr of Juvenal* [trans. Henry Higden] (London, 1687).

——, *The Tenth Satyr... Done into English Verse. By J[ohn] H[arvey], Esq.* (London, [1693]).

Kallendorf, Craig W., ed., *A Companion to the Classical Tradition* (Oxford, 2007).

Kargon, R. H., *Atomism in England from Hariot to Newton* (Oxford, 1966).

Kelsall, Malcolm, 'The Iconography of Stourhead', *Journal of the Warburg and Courtauld Institutes*, 46 (1983), 133–43.

Kenyon, J. P., *Revolution Principles: The Politics of Party, 1689–1720* (2nd edition, Cambridge, 1990).

——, *Stuart England* (Harmondsworth, 1978).

Kewes, Paulina, 'Shakespeare and New Drama', in David Womersley, ed., *A Companion to Literature from Milton to Blake* (Oxford, 2000), pp. 575–88.

Kirk, G. S., *The Iliad: A Commentary, Vol. II: Books 5–8* (Cambridge, 1990).

Knight, Douglas, *Pope and the Heroic Tradition: A Critical Study of his 'Iliad'* (New Haven CT, 1951).

Kupersmith, William, *Roman Satirists in Seventeenth-Century England* (Lincoln NB, 1985).

Lafaye, G., *Les Métamorphoses d'Ovide et leurs modèles grecs* (Paris, 1904).

La Fontaine, Jean de, 'Philémon et Baucis', in *Fables, Contes et Nouvelles*, ed. René Groos and Jacques Schiffrin (Paris, 1954).

[La Mothe Le Vayer, François] 'Orasius Tubero', *Quatre dialogues faits à l'imitation des anciens* (Frankfurt, '1506' [in fact 1632–33]).

Larkin, Philip, *Further Requirements: Interviews, Broadcasts, Statements, and Book Reviews, 1952–85* (London, 2001).

Latacz, Joachim, *Troy and Homer: Towards a Solution of an Old Mystery* (Oxford, 2004).

Leavis, F. R., *Nor Shall My Sword: Discourses on Pluralism Compassion, and Social Hope* (London, 1972).

Le Bossu, René, *Treatise of the Epick Poem*, transl. W. J. (London, 1695).

Leonard, J., 'Milton, Lucretius, and "the Void Profound of Unessential Light"', in *Living Texts: Interpreting Milton*, ed. K. A. Pruitt and C. W. Durham (Selinsgrove PA, 2000), pp. 198–207.

Leranbaum, Miriam, *Alexander Pope's 'Opus Magnum', 1729–1744* (Oxford, 1977).

Lesky, Albin, 'Motivation by Gods and Men', trans. H. M. Harvey, in *Homer: Critical Assessments*, ed. Irene J. F. de Jong, 4 vols. (London, 1999), 2. 384–403.

Levine, Joseph M., *The Battle of the Books: History and Literature in the Augustan Age* (Ithaca NY, 1991).

Lewalski, Barbara Kiefer, Paradise Lost *and the Rhetoric of Literary Forms* (Princeton NJ, 1985).

Lewis, C. S., *A Preface to 'Paradise Lost'* (Oxford, 1942).

Liebeschuetz, J. H. W. G., *Continuity and Change in Roman Religion* (Oxford, 1979).

Lindsay, Alexander, 'Dryden and Juvenal' (Unpublished PhD thesis, Trinity College, Dublin, 1982).

Lipking, Lawrence, *Abandoned Women and Poetic Tradition* (Chicago and London, 1988).

Lloyd, William, *A Chronological Account of the Life of Pythagoras* (London, 1699).

Loiseau, Jean, *Abraham Cowley's Reputation in England* (Paris, 1931).

Longinus, *A Treatise of the Loftiness or Elegancy of Speech, Written Originally in Greek by Longin; and now Translated out of French by Mr. J[ohn] P[ulteney]* (London, 1680).

—— , *An Essay upon Sublime. Translated from the Greek of Dionysius Longinus Cassius, the Rhetorician. Compar'd with the French of the Sieur Despreaux Boileau* (Oxford, 1698).

—— , *The Works of Dionysius Longinus, On the Sublime; or, a Treatise Concerning the Sovereign Perfection of Writing* [trans. Leonard Welsted] (London, 1712).

—— , *On the Sublime: Translated from the Greek, with Notes and Observations... by William Smith* (London, 1739).

Løsnes, Arvid, 'Dryden's *Aeneis* and the Delphin *Virgil*', in Maren-Sophie Røstvig et al., *The Hidden Sense and Other Essays* (Oslo, 1963), pp. 113–57.

Lounsbury, T. R., *Shakespeare as a Dramatic Artist, with an Account of his Reputation at Various Periods* (London and New York, 1902).

Luce, J. V., *Celebrating Homer's Landscapes: Troy and Ithaca Revisited* (New Haven CT, 1998).

Lucretius, *An Essay on the First Book of T. Lucretius Carus De Rerum Natura, Interpreted and Made English Verse* [trans. John Evelyn] (London, 1656).

—— , *T. Lucretius Carus the Epicurean Philosopher, His Six Books* De Natura Rerum *Done into English Verse, with Notes* [trans. Thomas Creech] (Oxford, 1682).

—— , *T. Lucretius Carus. The Epicurean Philosopher, His Six Books* De Natura Rerum *Done into English Verse, with Notes. The Second Edition, Corrected and Enlarged* [trans. Thomas Creech] (Oxford, 1683).

—— , *The Nature of Things: A Didactic Poem. Translated from the Latin of Titus Lucretius Carus* [trans. John Mason Good] 2 vols. (London, 1805).

Lucretius, *De Rerum Natura, Book III*, ed. E. J. Kenney (Cambridge, 1971).

—— , *Lucy Hutchinson's Translation of Lucretius:* De Rerum Natura, ed. Hugh de Quehen (Ann Arbor MI, 1996).

—— , *John Evelyn's Translation of Titus Lucretius Carus De Rerum Natura: An Old-Spelling Critical Edition*, ed. Michael M. Repetzki (Frankfurt, 2000).

Macaulay, Lord, *History of England*, ed. C. H. Firth, 6 vols. (London, 1914).

Mack, Maynard, *Collected in Himself: Essays Critical, Biographical, and Bibliographical on Pope and Some of his Contemporaries* (Newark DE, 1982).

—— , ed., *The Last and Greatest Art: Some Unpublished Poetic Manuscripts of Alexander Pope* (Newark DE, 1984).

Maguiness, W. S., 'The Eclecticism of Horace', *Hermathena*, 27 (1938), 27–46.

Manning, Susan, 'Eloisa's Abandonment', *Cambridge Quarterly*, 22 (1993), 231–48.

Marsden, Jean I., *The Re-Imagined Text: Shakespeare, Adaptation, and Eighteenth-Century Literary Theory* (Lexington KY, 1995).

Martindale, Charles, *John Milton and the Transformation of Ancient Epic* (London, 1986).

—— , *Redeeming the Text: Latin Poetry and the Hermeneutics of Reception* (Cambridge, 1993).

—— , *Latin Poetry and the Judgement of Taste: An Essay in Aesthetics* (Oxford, 2005).

—— , 'Dryden's Ovid: Aesthetic Translation', in *Translation and the Classic: Identity as Change in the History of Culture*, ed. Alexandra Lianeri and Vanda Zajko (Oxford, 2008), pp. 83–109.

—— , 'Performance, Reception, Aesthetics: Or Why Reception Studies Need Kant', in *Theorizing Performance: Greek Drama, Cultural History, and Critical Practice*, ed. Edith Hall and Stephe Harrop (forthcoming, London, 2010).

—— and Thomas, Richard F., eds., *Classics and the Uses of Reception* (Oxford, 2006).

Mason, H. A., *Humanism and Poetry in the Early Tudor Period* (London, 1959).

—— , 'Is Juvenal a Classic?', in *Critical Essays on Roman Literature: Satire*, ed. J. P. Sullivan (London, 1963), pp. 93–176 [earlier version in *Arion*, 1 (1962) 8–44, 51–77].

—— , 'Creative Translation: Ezra Pound's *Women of Trachis*', *Cambridge Quarterly*, 4 (1969) 244–72 [earlier version in *Arion*, 2 (1963), 59–81, 105–21].

—— , *To Homer through Pope: An Introduction to Homer's* Iliad *and Pope's Translation* (London, 1972).
—— , 'Horace's Ode to Pyrrha', *Cambridge Quarterly*, 7 (1976–7), 27–62.
—— , 'Sir Thomas Wyatt and the Birds of Fortune', *Cambridge Quarterly*, 7 (1977), 281–96.
—— , '"Living in the Present": Is Dryden's "Horat. Ode 29 Book 3" an Example of "Creative Translation"?' *Cambridge Quarterly*, 10 (1981), 91–129.
—— , ed., *Sir Thomas Wyatt: A Literary Portrait* (Bristol, 1986).
—— , 'Clique Puffery in Roscommon's *Essay on Translated Verse*', *Notes and Queries*, 235 (1990), 296.
Mason, Tom, 'Dryden's Chaucer' (Unpublished PhD thesis, Cambridge, 1977).
—— , 'Cowley and the Wisdom of Anacreon', *Cambridge Quarterly*, 19 (1990), 103–37.
—— , 'Is There a Classical Tradition in English Poetry?', *Translation and Literature*, 5 (1996), 203–19.
—— , '"Et Versos Digitos Habet": Dryden, Montaigne, Lucretius, Virgil and Boccaccio in Praise of Venus', *Translation and Literature*, 10 (2001), 89–109.
Maule, Jeremy and Poole, Adrian, eds., *The Oxford Book of Classical Verse in Translation*, (Oxford, 1995).
Mayo, T. F., *Epicurus in England (1650–1725)* (Dallas TX, 1934).
McCabe, Richard, *Incest, Drama, and Nature's Law* (Cambridge, 1993).
Michael, Fred S. and Emily, 'A Note on Gassendi in England', *Notes and Queries*, 235 (1990), 297–9.
Miller, John, 'The Glorious Revolution: "Contract" and "Abdication" Reconsidered', *Historical Journal*, 25 (1982), 541–55.
Miller, Rachel, '"Physic for the Great": Dryden's Satiric Translations of Juvenal, Persius and Boccaccio', *Philological Quarterly*, 68 (1989), 53–75.
Milton John, *Paradise Lost*, ed. Alastair Fowler (2nd edition, London, 1998).
—— , *Paradise Lost*, ed. T. Newton, 2 vols. (London, 1749).
Miner, Earl, *Dryden's Poetry* (Bloomington IN, 1967).
—— , ed., *Poems on the Reign of William III* (Los Angeles CA, 1974).
Monod, Paul Kléber, *Jacobitism and the English People: 1688–1788* (Cambridge, 1989).
Montagu, Lady Mary Wortley, *Complete Letters*, ed. Robert Halsband, 3 vols. (Oxford, 1965–7).
Morritt, J. B. S., *A Vindication of Homer* (York, 1798).
—— , *Additional Remarks on the Topography of Troy* (London, 1800).
Morton, Richard, *Examining Changes in the Eighteenth-Century French Translations of Homer's* Iliad *by Anne Dacier and Houdar de la Motte* (Lewiston, Queenston, Lampeter, 2003).

Munro, J., ed., *The Shakespeare Allusion Book: A Collection of Allusions to Shakespeare from 1591 to 1700* (1909), with new Preface by E. K. Chambers, 2 vols. (Oxford, 1932).

Murray, Barbara A., *Restoration Shakespeare: Viewing the Voice* (Madison WI and London, 2001).

Myers, William, *Dryden* (London, 1973).

Nethercot, A. H., 'The Reputation of Abraham Cowley', *PMLA*, 38 (1923), 588–641.

—— , 'Abraham Cowley's Essays', *Journal of English and Germanic Philology*, 29 (1930), 114–30.

Nicholas, Barry, *An Introduction to Roman Law* (1962; reprinted Oxford, 1975).

Norbrook, David, 'Margaret Cavendish and Lucy Hutchinson: Identity, Ideology and Politics', *In-Between: Essays and Studies in Literary Criticism*, 9 (2000), 179–203.

Ogg, David, *England in the Reign of Charles II* (2nd edition, Oxford, 1956).

Ogilby, John, *The Fables of Aesop, Paraphras'd in Verse* (2nd edition, London, 1668).

Oldham, John, *Poems*, ed. Harold F. Brooks, with Raman Selden (Oxford, 1987).

O'Sullivan Jr, Maurice, 'Running Division on the Groundwork: Dryden's Theory of Translation', *Neophilologus*, 64 (1980), 144–59.

Otis, Brooks, *Ovid as an Epic Poet* (2nd edition, Cambridge, 1970).

*Ouvrages de prose et de poésie des sieurs de Maucrois et de La Fontaine* (Paris, 1685).

Ovid, *Ovids Metamorphosis Englished, Mythologiz'd, and Represented in Figures* [trans. George Sandys] (Oxford, 1632).

—— , *Les Métamorphoses... avec quinze discours contenant l'explication morale des fables*, ed. N. Renouard (Paris, 1640).

—— , *Opera*, ed. Borchard Cnipping, 3 vols. (Amsterdam, 1670).

—— , *Les Métamorphoses... avec de nouvelles explications historiques, morales et politiques sur toutes les fables*, ed. P. Du-Ryer (Brussels, 1677).

—— , *Two Essays, The Former Ovid de Arte Amandi...* [trans. Thomas Hoy] (London, 1682).

—— , *Ovid's Elegies* [trans. Anon] (London, 1683).

—— , *Opera*, ed. Daniel Crispinus, 4 vols. (Lyon, 1689).

—— , *Metamorphoses, in Fifteen Books. Translated by the most Eminent Hands* [ed. Sir Samuel Garth] (London, 1717).

—— , *Opera, e textu Burmanni*, 5 vols. (Oxford 1826).

—— , *Shakespeare's Ovid: Being Arthur Golding's Translation of the Metamorphoses*, ed. W. H. D. Rouse (London, 1904).

——, *Metamorphoseon Liber XII*, ed. R. S. Lang (Oxford, 1927).

——, *Les Métamorphoses*, ed. G. Lafaye, 3 vols. (Paris, 1928–30).

——, *Metamorphoses: Books 6–10*, ed. W. S. Anderson (Norman OK, 1971).

——, *Metamorphoses, Book 11*, ed. G. M. Murphy (Oxford, 1972).

——, *Metamorphoses Books 12–13*, ed. Franz Bömer (Heidelberg, 1982).

Owen, Susan J., *Restoration Theatre and Crisis* (Oxford, 1996).

Panichas, G., *Epicurus* (New York, 1967).

Parker, Fred, 'Foul Disproportion: Rymer on *Othello*', *Cambridge Quarterly*, 17 (1988), 17–27.

——, *Scepticism and Literature: An Essay on Pope, Hume, Sterne, and Johnson* (Oxford, 2003).

——, '"Talking Scripture out of Church": Parson Adams and the Partiality of Translation', *Translation and Literature*, 14 (2005), 179–95.

——, 'Classic Simplicity', in *Translation and the Classic: Identity as Change in the History of Culture*, ed. Alexandra Lianeri and Vanda Zajko (Oxford, 2008), pp. 227–42.

Parker, Jan, *Dialogic Education and the Problematics of Translation in Homer and Greek Tragedy* (Lewiston, Queenston, Lampeter, 2001).

Patey, Douglas Lane, 'Ancients and Moderns', in *The Cambridge History of Literary Criticism, Vol. 4: The Eighteenth Century*, ed. H. B. Nisbet and Claude Rawson (Cambridge, 1977), pp. 32–71.

Peacock, M. L., ed., *The Critical Opinions of William Wordsworth* (Baltimore MD, 1950).

Pepys, Samuel, *The Diary*, ed. Robert Latham and William Matthews, 11 vols. (London, 1970–83).

Perkin, M. R., *Abraham Cowley: A Bibliography* (Folkestone, 1977).

Perkins, David, *Is Literary History Possible?* (Baltimore MD, 1992).

Philips, Katherine, *The Collected Works*, ed. Patrick Thomas, G. Greer, and R. Little, 3 vols. (Stump Cross, 1990–93).

Phillippo, Susannah, 'The Legacy of Homer: the *Iliad* Annotations of Jean Racine,' *L'Antiquité Classique*, 65 (1996), 1–29.

Pintard, René, *La Mothe Le Vayer – Gassendi – Guy Patin: Études de bibliographie et de critique suivies de textes inédits de Guy Patin*, Publications de l'Université de Poitiers, Série des sciences de l'homme, 5 (Paris, 1943).

Pocock, J. G. A., 'The Varieties of Whiggism from Exclusion to Reform: A History of Ideology and Discourse', in *Virtue, Commerce and History: Essays on Political Thought and History, Chiefly in the Eighteenth Century* (Cambridge, 1985), pp. 215–310.

*Poetical Miscellanies: the Fifth Part* (London 1704).

Pope, Alexander, *The Iliad of Homer: A New Edition, with Additional Notes, Critical and Illustrative*, ed. Gilbert Wakefield, 6 vols. (London, 1806) [1st edition, 1796].

—— , *Prose Works*, ed. Norman Ault and Rosemary Cowler, 2 vols. (Oxford 1936–86).

—— , *The Twickenham Edition of the Poems of Alexander Pope*, ed. John Butt et al., 11 vols. (London, 1939–69).

—— , *Correspondence*, ed. George Sherburn, 5 vols. (Oxford, 1956).

—— , *Selected Prose*, ed. Paul Hammond (Cambridge, 1987).

Pound, Ezra, *Literary Essays*, ed. T. S. Eliot (London, 1954).

—— , *Selected Letters, 1907–1941*, ed. D. D. Paige (London, 1971).

Powell, Jocelyn, *Restoration Theatre Production* (London. 1984).

Price, Curtis, *Music in the Restoration Theatre* (Ann Arbor MI, 1979).

Prior, Matthew, *Literary Works*, eds. H. Bunker Wright and Monroe K. Spears, 2 vols. (2nd edition, Oxford, 1971).

Quint, David, 'Fear of Falling: Icarus, Phaethon, and Lucretius in *Paradise Lost*', *Renaissance Quarterly*, 57 (2004), 847–81.

Quintilian, *Institutio Oratoria*, ed. Donald A. Russell, 5 vols. (Cambridge MA and London, 2001).

Racine, Jean, *Oeuvres*, ed. P. Mesnard, 8 vols. (Paris, 1865–73).

Ramsey, Laurence, *The Practise of the Diuell* (London, ?1577).

Rapin, René, *Reflections on Aristotle's Treatise of Poesie*, trans. Thomas Rymer (London, 1674).

Real, Hermann Josef, *Untersuchungen zur Lukrez-Übersetzung von Thomas Creech* (Bad Homburg, 1970).

Rees, Emma L. E., '"Sweet Honey of the Muses": Lucretian Resonance in *Poems and Fancies*', *In-Between: Essays and Studies in Literary Criticism*, 9 (2000), 3–16.

Reverand II, Cedric D., *Dryden's Final Poetic Mode: The* Fables (Philadelphia PA, 1988).

Rist, J. M., *Epicurus: An Introduction* (Cambridge 1972).

Robertson, D. W., *Abelard and Heloise* (New York, 1972).

Robinson, Douglas, ed., *Western Translation Theory, from Herodotus to Nietzsche* (Manchester, 1997).

Ross, Alexander, *Mystagogus Poeticus* (2nd edition, London, 1648).

Rossetti, Dante Gabriel, *The Early Italian Poets from Ciullo D'Alcamo to Dante Gabriel Rossetti* (London, 1861).

—— *Works*, ed. W. M. Rossetti (Revised and enlarged edition, London, 1911).

Rosslyn, Felicity, 'The Making of Pope's Translation of the *Iliad*' (Unpublished PhD thesis, Cambridge, 1978).

Rosslyn, Felicity, '"Awed by Reason": Pope on Achilles', *Cambridge Quarterly*, 9 (1980), 189–202.

——, *Alexander Pope: A Literary Life* (London, 1990).

——, 'Heroic Couplet Translation – A Unique Solution?' in *Translating Literature*, ed. Susan Bassnett (Cambridge, 1997), pp. 41–63.

——, *Pope's Iliad: A Selection with Commentary* (2nd edition, London, 2002).

Røstvig, Maren-Sophie, *The Happy Man: Studies in the Metamorphosis of a Classical Ideal: Vol. 1: 1600–1700* (2nd edition, Oslo, 1962).

Rothstein, E., 'Jonathan Swift as Jupiter: "Baucis and Philemon"', in *The Augustan Milieu: Essays Presented to Louis A. Landa*, ed. H. K. Miller, E. Rothstein, and G. S. Rousseau (Oxford, 1970), pp. 205–24.

Rudd, Niall, *The Satires of Horace* (Cambridge, 1966).

—— *Themes in Roman Satire* (London, 1986).

Russell, D. A. and Winterbottom, M., eds., *Ancient Literary Criticism: The Principal Texts in New Translations* (Oxford, 1972).

Saintsbury, George, ed., *Minor Poets of the Caroline Period*, 3 vols. (Oxford, 1905).

Sambrook, James, *The Eighteenth Century: The Intellectual and Cultural Context of English Literature, 1700–1789* (2nd edition, London, 1993).

Scott, Jonathan, *The Pleasures of Antiquity: British Collectors of Greece and Rome* (New Haven CT, 2003).

Segal, C. P., 'Myth and Philosophy in the *Metamorphoses*: Ovid's Augustanism and the Augustan Conclusion of Book XV', *American Journal of Philology*, 90 (1969), 257–90.

Selden, Raman, 'Juvenal and Restoration Modes of Translation', *Modern Language Review*, 68 (1973), 481–93.

——, *English Verse Satire, 1590–1795* (London, 1978).

Sellar, W. W., *Roman Poets of the Augustan Age: Horace and the Elegiac Poets* (Oxford, 1892).

Seneca the Elder, *Declamations*, ed. M. Winterbottom, 2 vols. (Cambridge MA and London, 1974).

Seneca the Younger, *Naturales Quaestiones*, ed. T. H. Corcoran, 2 vols. (Cambridge MA and London, 1971–2).

Shadwell, Thomas, *The Tenth Satyr of Juvenal, English and Latin* (London, 1687).

——, *Complete Works*, ed. Montague Summers, 5 vols. (London, 1927).

Shankman, Steven, *Pope's 'Iliad': Homer in the Age of Passion* (Princeton NJ, 1983).

Sharp, L., 'Walter Charleton's Early Life, 1620–59, and Relationship to Natural Philosophy in Mid-Seventeenth Century England', *Annals of Science*, 30 (1973), 311–40.

Shelley, Percy Bysshe, *Prose*, ed. David Lee Clark (Albuquerque NM, 1954).

Sherbo, Arthur, 'Dryden's Translation of Virgil's *Eclogues* and the Tradition', *Studies in Bibliography*, 39 (1985), 262–76.

Sherbo, Arthur, 'Dryden and the Fourth Earl of Lauderdale', *Studies in Bibliography*, 39 (1986), 199–210.

Sherburne, Sir Edward, *Poems and Translations... Excluding Seneca and Manilius*, ed. F. J. Van Beeck, S.J. (Assen, 1961).

Silk, Michael, *Homer: The Iliad* (Cambridge, 1987).

Simonsuuri, Kirsti, *Homer's Original Genius: Eighteenth-Century Notions of the Early Greek Epic (1688–1798)* (Cambridge, 1979).

Slaughter, Thomas P., '"Abdicate" and "Contract" in the Glorious Revolution', *Historical Journal*, 24 (1981), 323–37.

Sloman, Judith, 'An Interpretation of Dryden's *Fables*', *Eighteenth-Century Studies*, 4 (1970–71), 199–211.

—— , *Dryden: The Poetics of Translation* (Toronto, 1985).

Smallwood, Philip, 'Pope's "Short Excursions" and Dryden: An Unrecorded Borrowing', *Notes and Queries*, 26 (1979), 243–5.

—— , 'Shakespeare: Johnson's Poet of Nature', in Greg Clingham, ed., *The Cambridge Companion to Samuel Johnson* (Cambridge, 1997), pp. 143–60.

Smart, Christopher, *Poetical Works, V: The Works of Horace Translated into Verse*, ed. Karina Williamson (Oxford, 1996).

Smith, David Nichol, *John Dryden* (Cambridge, 1950).

Solodow, Joseph, *The World of Ovid's 'Metamorphoses'* (Chapel Hill NC, 1988).

Sowerby, Robin, 'Chapman's Discovery of Homer', *Translation and Literature*, 1 (1992), 26–51.

—— , 'Pope and Horace', in Charles Martindale and David Hopkins, eds., *Horace Made New* (Cambridge, 1993), pp. 159–83.

—— , 'The Augustan *Odyssey*', *Translation and Literature*, 4 (1995), 157–81.

—— , 'The Decorum of Pope's *Iliad*', *Translation and Literature*, 13 (2004), 49–79.

—— , *The Augustan Art of Poetry: Augustan Translation of the Classics* (Oxford, 2006).

Spence, Joseph, *Observations, Anecdotes, and Characters of Books and Men*, ed. James M. Osborn, 2 vols. (Oxford, 1966).

Spencer, Hazelton, *Shakespeare Improved* (Cambridge MA, 1927).

Spencer, T. J. B., *Fair Greece, Sad Relic: Literary Philhellenism from Shakespeare to Byron* (London, 1954).

—— , 'Robert Wood and the Problem of Troy in the Eighteenth Century', *Journal of the Warburg and Courtauld Institutes*, 20 (1957), 75–105.

—— , 'Lucretius and the Scientific Poem in English', in D. R. Dudley, ed., *Lucretius* (London, 1975), pp. 131–64.

Spingarn, J. E., ed., *Critical Essays of the Seventeenth Century*, 3 vols. (Oxford, 1908).

Sprat, Thomas, *The Plague of Athens* (London, 1659).

Spufford, Margaret, *Small Books and Pleasant Histories: Popular Fiction and its Readership in Seventeenth-Century England* (London, 1981).

Stack, Frank, *Pope and Horace: Studies in Imitation* (Cambridge, 1985).

Stanley, Thomas, *The History of Philosophy* (3rd edition, London, 1700).

Stechow, Wolfgang, 'The Myth of Philemon and Baucis in Art', *Journal of the Warburg and Courtauld Institutes*, 4 (1941), 103–13.

Steiner, George, 'A Reading Against Shakespeare', in *No Passion Spent* (London, 1996), pp. 108–27.

Steiner, T. R., 'Precursors to Dryden: English and French Theories of Translation in the Seventeenth Century', *Comparative Literature Studies*, 7 (1970), 50–81.

—— , *English Translation Theory, 1650–1800* (Assen, 1975).

[Stevenson, Matthew], *The Wits Paraphrased: Or, Paraphrase upon Paraphrase. In a Burlesque of the Several Late Translations of Ovid's Epistles* (London, 1680).

Stillman, Damie, *English Neoclassical Architecture*, 2 vols. (London, 1988).

Summerson, John, 'The Classical Country House in Eighteenth-Century England', *Journal of the Royal Society of Arts*, 107 (1959), 539–87.

*Sylvae: or the Second Part of Poetical Miscellanies* (London, 1685).

Taplin, Oliver, 'Homer', in *The Oxford History of the Classical World*, ed. John Boardman, Jasper Griffin, and Oswyn Murray (Oxford, 1986), pp. 50–77.

—— , *Homeric Soundings: The Shaping of The* Iliad (Oxford, 1992).

Taylor, Gary, *Re-Inventing Shakespeare: A Cultural History from the Restoration to the Present* (London, 1990).

Terry, Richard, *Poetry and the Making of the English Literary Past, 1660–1781* (Oxford, 2001).

Thomson, James, *The Seasons*, ed. James Sambrook (Oxford, 1981).

Thornton, Agathe, *Homer's Iliad: Its Composition and the Motif of Supplication* (Göttingen, 1984).

Tissol, Garth, *The Face of Nature: Wit, Narrative, and Cosmic Origin in Ovid's* Metamorphoses (Princeton NJ, 1997).

—— , 'Dryden's Additions and the Interpretive Reception of Ovid', *Translation and Literature*, 13 (2004), 181–93.

Tomlinson, Charles, *Metamorphoses: Essays on Translation* (Manchester, 2003).

Turner, James, 'The Structure of Henry Hoare's Stourhead', *Art Bulletin*, 61 (1979), 68–77.

Underwood, Dale, *Etherege and the Comedy of Manners* (New Haven CT, 1957).

Van Doren, Mark, *John Dryden: A Study of his Poetry*, (Revised edition, Bloomington IN, 1963).

Van Erde, Katharine S., *John Ogilby and the Taste of his Times* (Folkestone, 1976).

Venuti, Lawrence, 'The Destruction of Troy: Translation and Royalist Cultural Politics in the Interregnum', *Journal of Medieval and Renaissance Studies*, 23 (1993), 197–219.

—— , *The Translator's Invisibility: A History of Translation* (London, 1995; 2nd edition, 2008).

—— , 'Neoclassicism and Enlightenment', in *The Oxford Guide to Literature in English Translation*, ed. Peter France (Oxford, 2000), pp. 55–64.

Vernant, Jean-Pierre and Vidal-Naquet, Pierre, *Myth and Tragedy in Ancient Greece*, trans. Janet Lloyd (New York, 1988).

Vickers, Brian, ed., *Shakespeare: The Critical Heritage*, 6 vols. (London, 1974–81).

—— , ed., *English Science: Bacon to Newton* (Cambridge, 1987).

Virgil, *Aeneid, Book 2*, ed. R. G. Austin (Oxford 1964).

Wakefield, Gilbert, *A Letter to Jacob Bryant, Esq.* (London, 1797).

Waller, Edmund, *The Second Part of Mr. Waller's Poems* (London, 1690).

Walton, G., *Metaphysical to Augustan: Studies in Tone and Sensibility in the Seventeenth Century* (London, 1955).

Warton, Joseph, *An Essay on the Genius and Writings of Pope*, 2 vols. (4th edition, Oxford, 1782).

Watson, Gerard, 'The Natural Law and Stoicism', in *Problems in Stoicism*, ed. A. A. Long (London, 1971), pp. 216–38.

Watt, Ian, *The Rise of the Novel: Studies in Defoe, Richardson and Fielding* (London, 1957).

Webb, Timothy, *The Violet and the Crucible: Shelley and Translation* (Oxford, 1976).

—— , ed., *English Romantic Hellenism, 1700–1824* (Manchester, 1982).

Weinbrot, Howard D., *Augustus Caesar in 'Augustan' England: The Decline of a Classical Norm* (Princeton NJ, 1978).

West, David, 'Of Mice and Men', in T. Woodman and D. West, eds., *Quality and Pleasure in Latin Poetry* (Cambridge, 1974), pp. 67–80.

West, Michael, 'Dryden's Ambivalence as a Translator of Heroic Themes', *Huntington Library Quarterly*, 36 (1972–3), 17–38.

White, R. S., *Natural Law in English Renaissance Literature* (Cambridge, 1996).

Wilding, Michael, 'Dryden and Satire: "Mac Flecknoe, Absalom and Achitophel, The Medall", and Juvenal', in *Writers and their Background: John Dryden*, ed. Earl Miner (London, 1972), pp. 191–233.

Wilkinson, L. P., *Ovid Recalled* (Cambridge, 1955).
Williams, Bernard, *Shame and Necessity* (Berkeley, Los Angeles CA, London, 1993).
Williamson, G., *The Proper Wit of Poetry* (London, 1951).
Wilmot, John, Earl of Rochester, *Works*, ed. Harold Love (Oxford, 1999).
[Wilson, John], *Specimens of the British Critics, by Christopher North*, introd. David Hopkins (Delmar NY, 1979).
Wilson, Penelope, 'Classical Poetry and the Eighteenth-Century Reader', in *Books and their Readers in Eighteenth-Century*, ed. Isabel Rivers (Leicester, 1982), pp. 69–96.
Winn, James Anderson, *John Dryden and his World* (New Haven CT and London, 1987).
——, '"Complying with the Times": Dryden's Satires of Juvenal and Persius (1693)', *Eighteenth-Century Life*, 12 (1988), 76–87.
Wood, Robert, *The Ruins of Palmyra* (London, 1753).
——, *An Essay on the Original Genius and Writings of Homer* (London, 1775).
Woodbridge, Kenneth, *Landscape and Antiquity: Aspects of English Culture at Stourhead, 1718–1838* (Oxford, 1970).
Woodhead, Abraham [as R. H.], *A Compendious Discourse on the Eucharist* (Oxford, 1688).
Wycherley, William, *Posthumous Works* (London, 1718).
Zwicker, Steven N., *Politics and Language in Dryden's Poetry: The Arts of Disguise* (Princeton NJ, 1974).

# *Acknowledgements*

Earlier versions of the chapters in this book first appeared in the following places, and I am grateful to the various editors and presses for permission to reprint:

Chapter 1: '"The English Homer": Shakespeare, Longinus, and English "Neo-Classicism"': from *Shakespeare and the Classics*, ed. Charles Martindale and A. B. Taylor (Cambridge: Cambridge University Press, 2004).

Chapter 2: 'Cowley's Horatian Mice': from *Horace Made New: Horatian Influences on British Writing from the Renaissance to the Twentieth Century*, ed. Charles Martindale and David Hopkins (Cambridge: Cambridge University Press, 1993).

Chapter 3: 'The English Voices of Lucretius from Lucy Hutchinson to John Mason Good': from *The Cambridge Companion to Lucretius*, ed. Stuart Gillespie and Philip Hardie (Cambridge: Cambridge University Press, 2007).

Chapter 4: '"If he were living, and an *Englishman*": Translation Theory in the Age of Dryden': from *The Oxford History of Literary Translation in English, Vol. III: 1660–1790*, ed. Stuart Gillespie and David Hopkins (Oxford: Oxford University Press, 2005) and *The Dryden-Tonson Miscellanies, 1684–1709*, ed. Stuart Gillespie and David Hopkins (London: Routledge; Tokyo: Edition Synapse, 2008).

Chapter 5: 'Dryden and the Tenth Satire of Juvenal': from *Translation and Literature*, 4 (1995), 31–60.

Chapter 6: 'Dryden's "Baucis and Philemon"': from *Comparative Literature*, 28 (1976), 135–43.

Chapter 7: 'Nature's Laws and Man's: The Story of Cinyras and Myrrha in Ovid and Dryden': from *The Modern Language Review*, 80 (1985), 786–801.

Chapter 8: 'Dryden and Ovid's "Wit out of Season" ': from *Ovid Renewed: Ovidian Influences on Literature and Art from the Middle Ages to the Twentieth Century*, ed. Charles Martindale (Cambridge: Cambridge University Press, 1988).

Chapter 9: 'Translation, Metempsychosis, and the Flux of Nature: "Of the Pythagorean Philosophy" ': from *Dryden and the World of Neoclassicism*, ed. Wolfgang Görtschacher and Holger Klein (Tübingen: Stauffenburg Verlag, 2001).

Chapter 10: 'Varieties of Pope's Classicism': from *A Companion to Eighteenth-Century Poetry*, ed. Christine Gerrard (Oxford: Blackwell Publishing, 2006) (as 'The Classical Inheritance').

Chapter 11: 'Pope's Trojan Geography': from *Translation, Trauma, Tradition: The Classic and the Modern*, ed. Jan Parker and Timothy Mathews (Oxford: Oxford University Press, forthcoming).

Chapter 12: 'Colonization, Closure, or Creative Dialogue: The Case of Pope's *Iliad*': from *A Companion to Classical Receptions*, ed. Lorna Hardwick and Christopher Stray (Oxford: Blackwell Publishing, 2008).

# Index


Abrams, M. H.,
*Glossary of Critical Terms*, 260–1
Addison, Joseph, 41
*Cato*, 54, 252
Aikin, John,
*Letters to a Young Lady*, 259
Akenside, Mark,
*Pleasures of the Imagination*, 104
Alexander the Great, 136, 148, 152–3
Anacreon, 122
Apollodorus,
*Library*, 180
*Arion*, 293–4, 297
Aristophanes, 184
Aristotle, 39
*Historia Animalium*, 185
*Rhetoric*, 183
Arnold, Matthew,
'Falkland', 5
*On Translating Homer*, 14, 301
Arrowsmith, William, 293
Atterbury, Francis,
Preface to *The Second Part of Mr Waller's Poems*, 119–20
Auerbach, Erich,
*Mimesis*, 291
Auden, W. H., 1
Augustus, 208, 262
Austen, Jane, 285

Bacon, Francis,
'Of Vicissitudes of Things', 244
Baillet, Adrien,
*Jugemens des Savans*, 204
Baker, Henry,
*Medulla Poetarum Latinorum*, 103–4
Battle of the Books, 252
Beattie, James,
Translation from Lucretius, 95
Beaumont, Francis,
*Salmacis and Hermaphroditus*, 82
Beaumont, Sir John,
Translation of Horace, *Sermones*, 2. 6, 79
Behn, Aphra,
'Essay on Translated Prose', 116
Bentley, Richard, 253
Benveniste, Émile,
*Indo-European Language and Society*, 300, 302
*Beowulf*, 261
Blackburn, Simon,
*Truth*, 31–3
Blackmore, Sir Richard,
*Creation*, 105–6, 111
Blackwall, Anthony,
*The Sacred Classics Defended*, 52
Blake, William,
*Milton*, 2
Blegen, Carl, 282
Blount, Edward, 273
Blount, Sir Thomas Pope,
*De Re Poetica*, 113
Boccaccio, Giovanni,
*Decameron*, 164
Boethius, 261
Boileau-Despréaux, Nicolas, 123
*Satires*, 118
*Traité du sublime*, 38, 46–51
Bolingbroke, Henry St John, Viscount, 109
Bowles, William,
*Observations on the Poetical Character of Pope*, 259
Boyle, Robert, 248
Bradley, A. C.,
*Shakespearean Tragedy*, 45
Bridges, Robert,
*Ibant Obscuri*, 309
Brody, Jules,
*Boileau and Longinus*, 46–7

Brome, Alexander, 90
  *Poems of Horace*, 57
Brown, A. D. J.,
  On Pope's Shakespeare, 44
Bryant, Jacob,
  writings on Troy, 280–2, 287, 290
Bulstrode, Whitelocke,
  *Essay of Transmigration*, 241–2
Burnet, Gilbert,
  *History of his Own Time*, 139
  *Pastoral Letter*, 246
  translation of More's *Utopia*, 123
Burrow, Colin,
  *Epic Romance: Homer to Milton*, 305–6
Byron, Lord,
  *Childe Harold's Pilgrimage*, 357
  *Letters and Journals*, 288, 292
  *Observations* on Bowles, 260
Bysshe, Edward,
  *Art of English Poetry*, 103
  *British Parnassus*, 104

Calvert, Frank, 282
Camerarius, Joachim,
  translation of Homer, 19
Canning, George,
  *Anti-Lucretius*, 105, 111
Carew, Thomas,
  'An Elegie upon the Death of the Deane of St Pauls', 2
  'To Saxham', 79
Carne-Ross, D. S., 293
Casaubon, Meric, 91
Certon, Salomon,
  translation of Homer, 19
Chapman, George,
  translation of Homer, 19, 21, 22, 24, 25–8, 122, 240, 295
Charleton, Walter,
  *Epicurus' Morals*, 65–7, 75, 77
Charron, Pierre,
  *De la sagesse*, 232–4, 237
Chaucer, Geoffrey, 16, 164, 205, 239–40, 247
  *Knight's Tale*, 205–6, 257–8
Cicero, 143, 250
  *Pro Cluentio*, 182–3, 185, 194
Claudius, 187
Cnipping, Borchard,
  edition of Ovid, 270
Collingwood, R. G.,
  *Autobiography*, 32–3
Condillac, Émile Bonnot, abbé de, 93
Congreve, William,
  Dedication to *The Dramatick Works of John Dryden*, 163
  *The Old Batchelor*, 55
  'To Mr Dryden', 240
Conti, Abbé Antonio, 289
Cotton, Charles, 24
Corneille, Pierre,
  *Pompée*, 118
Cowley, Abraham, 10, 11, 115, 118
  *Anacreontiques*, 72, 86
  'The Country Mouse', 55–87, 118
  *Essays, in Verse and Prose*, 57, 59–60, 73
  'The Garden', 67–8
  Imitation of Horace, *Odes* 1. 5, 118
  'Of Liberty', 59–60
  Preface to *Pindarique Odes*, 117
  *Verses upon Several Occasions*, 57
Cowper, William, 252
  on Cowley, 59
  on translating Homer, 295, 307
Crashaw, Richard, 24
Creech, Thomas,
  edition of Lucretius, 92
  translation of Horace, 73
  translation of Lucretius, 91–2, 98–9, 104, 122, 123
  translation of Theocritus, 122
Crispinus, Daniel,
  Delphin edition of Ovid, 170, 172, 188
Crowne, John,
  Shakespeare adaptations, 43
Cynics, 184
Cyrenaics, 65–6, 69, 72

Dacier, Anne,
  translation of Homer, 272–3
Dalzel, Andrew, 278
Davenant, Sir William, 121
  *Law Against Lovers*, 42
  *Macbeth*, 41

Democritus, 139, 144–5, 147, 248
Demosthenes, 136–7, 143–4, 250
Denham, Sir John, 115, 117, 121, 295, 307
Preface to *The Destruction of Troy*, 116–7, 240
'Sarpedon's Speech to Glaucus', 302
'To Sir Richard Fanshaw', 116
Dennis, John,
adaptations of Shakespeare, 41
Divus, Andreas,
translation of Homer, 19
Donlan, W., 300
Donne, John, 1, 58
Dörpfeld, Wilhelm, 282
Dover, K. J.,
on translation, 15
Drant, Thomas,
translation of Horace, *Sermones*, 2. 6, 79
Dryden, John, 10, 11, 40, 88, 113–29, 295, 298
*Absalom and Achitophel*, 23
'Account of the Ensuing Poem', prefixed to *Annus Mirabilis*, 204–5
Aeneis *of Virgil*, 3, 156
*Aureng-Zebe*, 197, 199–201
'Authors Apology for Heroique Poetry', 48, 58
'Baucis and Philemon', 163–76
'Canace to Macareus', 197, 199, 256–7
'Ceyx and Alcyone', 207, 222–37
'Cinyras and Myrrha', 177–201
Dedication to *Amphitryon*, 147
Dedication to *Aureng-Zebe*, 95
Dedication to *Don Sebastian* 147, 161–2
Dedication to *Examen Poeticum*, 113, 127, 238, 245
Dediction to *The* Aeneis *of Virgil*, 113, 129
'Discourse Concerning... Satire', 113, 127–8, 134, 136, 145, 149–50
*Don Sebastian*, 197, 245
*Essay of Dramatick Poesie*, 46
'The First Book of Homer's *Ilias*', 18–31, 166, 170, 175, 239
'The First Book of Ovid's *Metamorphoses*', 22
'The Flower and the Leaf', 164
'The Fourth Book of the *Georgics*', 22
'The Grounds of Criticism in Tragedy', 48–9
Horace, translations of, 75–6, 125, 147, 148, 154, 161
Juvenal, translations of, 127, 294
*Love Triumphant*, 197–8, 200
Lucretius, translations of, 72, 95–6, 100–3, 109, 110, 125–6, 148–9, 221, 258, 306–7
'Meleager and Atalanta', 22
'Of the Pythagorean Philosophy', 11, 221–2, 238–49
(with Nathaniel Lee) *Oedipus*, 197
'Palamon and Arcite', 168, 357–8
Preface to *Fables*, 15–16, 18, 20, 113, 129, 164, 168–9, 195, 205–6, 233, 239, 241, 243
Preface to *Ovid's Epistles*, 113, 115–16, 118, 119, 123, 130, 205, 238, 256, 259
Preface to *Sylvae*, 15, 96, 113, 124, 125–7, 149, 241, 296
'The Sixteenth Satyr of Juvenal', 132
'The Sixth Pastoral of Virgil', 25
'The Seventh Book of the *Aeneis*', 22
'The Tenth Satyr of Juvenal', 11, 130–62
'The Third Satyr of Juvenal', 132–3
'To My Ingenious Friend, Mr Henry Higden', 146, 149
'To the Earl of Roscommon', 124
(with Sir William Soame) Translation of Boileau's *L'Art poétique*, 120–1, 123, 176
'The Twelfth Book of Ovid his *Metamorphoses*', 206–7, 208–21
Dunkin, William,
translation of Horace, *Sermones*, 2. 6, 74, 76, 80
Du-Ryer, P.,
translation of Ovid, 179
Du Souhait, S.
translation of Homer, 19

Eliot, T. S., 135
Introduction to *The Selected Poems of Ezra Pound*, 33, 87, 144, 371

Eliot, T. S (*cont.*)
'Tradition and the Individual Talent', 8, 37–8
Empson, William, 5
Eobanus Hessus, Helius,
translation of Homer, 19
Epicureanism, 11, 64–70, 88–112 *passim*, 161
Erasmus, Desiderius, 34
Euripides, 2, 178
Evelyn, John,
translation of Lucretius, 90–1, 98, 102–3
Exclusion Crisis, 138

Fairfax, Edward, 121
Fanshawe, Sir Richard, 91
translation of Guarini's *Il Pastor Fido*, 115
translation of Horace, *Sermones*, 2. 6, 79
Fawkes, Francis,
translation of Horace, *Sermones*, 2. 6, 61, 73
Flatman, Thomas,
translation of Lucretius, 95, 104
Fletcher, John, 40
Florio, John, 240
Fontenelle, Bernard Le Bovier de,
*Entretiens sur la pluralité des mondes*, 116
Francis, Philip, 252
Freud, Sigmund,
*Introductory Lectures on Psychoanalysis*, 189–90, 194

Gadamer, Hans Georg, 7
Garth, Sir Samuel,
Preface to *Ovid's Metamorphoses*, 163, 246
Garrison, James D.,
on Dryden's *Fables*, 165
Gassendi, Pierre, 65, 75
Gay, John, 251
*Genesis*, 172–3
George II, King, 262–4
Gildon, Charles,
*Complete Art of Poetry*, 103
Gill, Christopher,
on altruism and reciprocity, 300
Glanvill, John,
translation of Lucretius, 95
Goethe, Johan Wolfgang, 278
Goldhill, Simon,
on Kantian aesthetics, 9
Golding, Arthur,
translation of Ovid's *Metamorphoses*, 122, 169–70, 171, 179, 186, 242
Goldsmith, Oliver,
on *Eloisa to Abelard*, 260
Good, John Mason,
translation of Lucretius, 92–3, 99
Grand Tour, 250
Grantham, Thomas,
translation of Homer, 19
Gray, Thomas,
'Elegy written in a Country Churchyard', 72, 104
Great Seal, 246
Gresham, James
*Picture of Incest*, 186
Groto, Luigi,
translation of Homer 19, 24
Grundy, Isobel,
on Lady Mary Wortley Montagu, 289

Hainsworth, Bryan,
on the Troad, 282–3
Hahn, J. G. von, 282
Hammond, Paul,
on 'invention', 53
Harrison, Tony, 297
Haynes, Kenneth,
on 'foreignizing' translation, 307
Heaney, Seamus, 297
Henninus, Henricus Christianus,
edition of Juvenal, 152
Herculaneum, 250
Herington, C. J., 293
Heyne, Christian Gottlob, 278
Higden, Henry,
translations of Juvenal, 146, 150–5
Highet, Gilbert,
on Robert Wood and Homer, 285
Hobbes, Thomas, 43
translation of Homer, 19, 24

Holyday, Barten,
translation of Juvenal, 122, 127, 128, 145
Homer, 10, 46–54, 111, 208, 239, 261
*Iliad*, 17–31, 81, 220, 264–9, 298–310
*Odyssey*, 72
Homeric Hymns, 2
Hopkins, Charles,
*Epistolary Poems*, 186, 223–4, 236
Horace, 10, 39, 60, 126, 146–7, 261
*Ars Poetica*, 20
*Epode* 2, 62
*Epistles*, 72, 161
*Odes*, 69–70, 75–6
*Sermones*, 2. 6, 55–87
Howard, Sir Robert,
'Of Nature's Changes', 94
Hughes, John,
*Letters of Abelard and Eloisa*, 256
Hughes, Ted, 297
*Tales from Ovid*, 3
Hume, David, 31–3
Hunt, Leigh, 288
Huygens, Christian, 93
Hutchinson, Lucy,
*Order and Disorder*, 90
translation of Lucretius, 89–90, 97–8, 101–2
Hyginus,
*Fabulae*, 180

Iser, Wolfgang, 7

James II, King, 141, 143, 245
Jauss, Hans Robert, 7
Johnson, Samuel, 251
*Dictionary*, 264
imitations of Juvenal, 131, 294
*Lives of the Poets*, 1, 16–17, 59, 112, 115, 196, 220–1, 260, 295
*Preface to Shakespeare*, 53–4, 237
Jonson, Ben, 40
*Sejanus*, 294
'To Penshurst', 79
translation of Horace's *Ars Poetica*, 115–16
Juvenal, 10, 111, 261, 294
Codex Pithoeanus, 152
Tenth Satire, 11, 130–62

Kant, Immanuel,
*Critique of Judgement*, 8–9, 12
Kennett, White,
translation of Erasmus' *Encomium Moriae*, 122
Kenney, E. J.,
edition of Lucretius, 97, 102
Kenyon, J. P.,
*Stuart England*, 140–1
Killigrew, Anne, 240
Kirk, G. S.,
edition of Homer's *Iliad*, 292
Kneller, Sir Godfrey, 246
Korfmann, Manfred, 352

Lafaye, Georges, 282
La Fontaine, Jean de,
'Philémon et Baucis', 167, 175
La Mothe le Vayer, François de,
'Le Banquet sceptique', 191–3
La Motte, Antoine Houdar de,
translation of Homer, 17
Larkin, Philip,
*Further Requirements*, 1, 2, 255
Latacz, Joachim,
*Troy and Homer*, 283
Leavis, F. R.,
*Nor Shall my Sword*, 12–13, 28
Lechevalier, Jean-Baptiste,
*Description of the Plain of Troy*, 278–9, 284, 287, 292
Lesky, Albin,
'Motivation by Gods and Men', 268
Lewis, C. S.,
*Preface to* Paradise Lost, 162
Logue, Christopher,
versions of Homer, 297
Loyd, William,
*Chronological Account of the Life of Pythagoras*, 242
Locke, John, 93
'Longinus',
*On the Sublime*, 38–54
Loredano, G. F.,
burlesque version of Homer, 19
Lucan, 261

Luce, J. V.,
*Celebrating Homer's Landscapes*, 283–4
Lucian, 173
Lucretius, 10, 11, 88–112, 125–6, 146, 149, 248, 261

MacNeice, Louis, 1
Maecenas, 60–1, 208
Marolles, Michel de,
translation of Lucretius, 90
Marsden, Jean I.,
*The Re-Imagined Text*, 41
Martial, 60, 261
Martindale, Charles, 31
*Redeeming the Text*, 4–7
*Latin Poetry and the Judgement of Taste*, 8–10
Marvell, Andrew,
'An Horatian Ode', 244
Mary Magdalene, 220
Mary, Queen, 180
Mason, H. A., 294–7, 298, 308
'Is Juvenal a Classic?', 131, 134–5, 158, 294
*To Homer through Pope*, 29–30,
'Wyatt's Birds of Fortune', 33–6
Maynwaring, Arthur,
translation of Homer, 19
Melchior de Polignac, Cardinal,
*Anti-Lucretius*, 105, 111
Meres, Francis, 46
Messalina, 148, 158–60
Milton, John, 19, 58, 264
'Lycidas', 2
'Naturam non pati senium', 106
*Paradise Lost*, 22, 23, 28, 99, 106–8, 171–2, 209, 173, 210–11, 213–14, 223, 244, 263
Miner, Earl,
*Dryden's Poetry*, 164–5
Molière, Jean-Baptiste Poquelin,
*Amphitryon*, 173
Montagu, Charles, 18
Montagu, Lady Mary Wortley, 288–9, 292
Montaigne, Michel Eyquem de, 60, 193–4
*Apologie de Raymond Sebonde*, 190
Montgomery, Sir James, 143
Morgan, Matthew,
prefatory poem to *The Praise of Folly*, 122–3
Motteux, Peter,
'The Speech of Sarpedon to Glaucus', 302
Murphy, G. M.,
edition of Ovid, 207, 232, 233, 235

Nepos, Cornelius, 122
Nero, 138
Newton, Sir Isaac, 93, 105
'North, Christopher' (see Wilson, John)

Obsopoeus, V.,
translation of Homer, 19
Ogilby, John,
*Fables of Aesop*, 79–80
translation of Homer, 19, 23, 273
Oldham, John, 122,
imitation of Horace, *Ars Poetica*, 119
imitation of Juvenal, 294
Ovid, 10, 19, 82, 111
*Fasti*, 217
*Heroides*, 197, 199, 201, 256–60
*Metamorphoses*, 11, 163–76, 177–249

Parker, Fred,
on Rymer and *Othello*, 44
*Scepticism and Literature*, 111
Parker, Jan,
*Dialogic Education*, 298–9, 304
Pepys, Samuel, 82
Perrot D'Ablancourt, Nicolas,
on translation, 114, 240
Persius, 240, 261
Philips, Katherine,
on translation, 118
Pitt, Christopher, 251
Plato, 2
Plutarch, 34
Pompeii, 250
Pompey, 142
Pope, Alexander, 10, 40, 58, 252, 295, 298
*Correspondence*, 15, 163
'Eloisa to Abelard', 256–60
*Essay on Criticism*, 7, 121, 265–6

*Essay on Man*, 89, 108–12
'The First Epistle of the Second Book of Horace', 121, 262–4
'The First Satire of the Second Book of Horace', 75
(and Jonathan Swift) 'The Sixth Satire of the Second Book of Horace Imitated', 80–1, 82–5
*Iliad of Homer*, 3, 11, 17–18, 25–31, 50–3, 169, 253, 264–9, 270–92, 299–310
*Imitations of Horace*, 261–2
Preface to *The Iliad of Homer*, 16, 25–6, 50–1, 309
*Works of Shakespear*, 44–5, 50, 52
Pound, Ezra, 135, 293–4
*Confucian Odes*, 384
*Literary Essays*, 3, 14
*Selected Letters*, 31
Prateus, Ludovicus,
edition of Juvenal, 133, 152
Prior, Matthew,
'Hymn to Venus, upon a Marriage', 104
'The Ladle', 173
Prologue to *The Late Revolution*, 245
Pulcharelius, Constantinus, 19
Pythagoreanism, 62, 241–9

Quarrel of Ancients and Moderns, 252, 263
Quintilian, 203–4

Rapin, René,
*Reflections on Aristotle's Treatise of Poesie*, 201
Racine, Jean, 178
Ravenscroft, Edward,
*Titus Andronicus*, 43
Reverand II, Cedric D.,
*Dryden's Final Poetic Mode*, 165, 243
Rochester, John Wilmot, Earl of, 122
'An Allusion to Horace', 118
'Love and Life', 244
'A Satyre against Reason and Mankind', 119
'Timon', 119
translations from Lucretius, 94
Roscommon, Wentworth Dillon, Earl of,
*Essay on Translated Verse*, 123–5, 240–1
Rossetti, Dante Gabriel,
*The Early Italian Poets*, 14
Rosslyn, Felicity, 30
Rowe, Nicholas, 252
Rymer, Thomas,
*Short View of Tragedy*, 44

Salel, Hughes,
translation of Homer, 19
Saltonstall, Wye,
*Country Mouse and the City Mouse*, 77
Sambrook, James,
edition of Thomson's *The Seasons*, 105
Sandys, George,
translation of Ovid's *Metamorphoses*, 169–70, 171, 172, 179, 181, 224–5, 235, 242–3
Schliemann, Heinrich, 282
Schrevelius, Cornelius,
edition of Juvenal 152
Scudamore, James,
burlesque version of Homer, 19, 22–3, 25
Seneca the Elder,
*Controversiae*, 202–3
Seneca the Younger, 60
*Naturales Quaestiones*, 203–4
Senex, John, 270
Servius,
commentary on Virgil, 189
Shadwell, Thomas, 132
adaptation of *Timon of Athens* 42, 44, 157
*Tenth Satyr of Juvenal*, 127–8
Shakespeare, William, 19, 37–54, 58
*Coriolanus*, 41
*Julius Caesar*, 49
*King Henry VI*, Parts 1–2, 43
*King Lear*, 41, 42, 44, 49
*King Richard II*, 49
*King Richard III*, 50
*Macbeth*, 23, 41, 50, 232
*Measure for Measure*, 42, 44
*Othello*, 44, 53
*Romeo and Juliet*, 83

Shakespeare (*cont.*)
*The Tempest*, 43, 231
*Timon of Athens*, 42, 44
*Titus Andronicus*, 43
*Troilus and Cressida*, 48–9
Shelley, Percy Bysshe,
translations from the classics, 2
*Defence of Poetry*, 5
Sherburne, Sir Edward,
translation of Lucretius, 93–4
Sloman, Judith,
on Dryden's *Fables*, 165
Smart, Christopher,
translation of Horace, *Sermones*, 2. 6, 74, 76
Smith, William,
translation of Longinus, 49–50, 54
Soame, Sir William,
translation of Boileau's *L'Art poétique*, 120–1
Sophists, 184
Southey, Robert, 121–2
Sowerby, Robin,
on Dryden's and Pope's Homer, 30
*Spectator, The*, 269
Spence, Joseph, 58, 109, 273
Spencer, Hazleton,
*Shakespeare Improved*, 41, 44
Spenser, Edmund, 24, 58, 121, 239, 240
Spondanus (Jean de la Sponde),
edition of Homer, 19, 21, 24, 272
Sprat, Thomas,
'Account of the Life and Writings of Mr Abraham Cowley', 117
*Plague of Athens*, 93
translation of Horace, *Sermones*, 2. 6, 57
Stanley, Thomas,
*History of Philosophy*, 65
Stapylton, Sir Robert,
translation of Juvenal, 127, 139, 142, 145
Steiner, George,
on Shakespeare, 45
on translation, 297
Stevenson, Matthew,
*The Wits Paraphras'd*, 257
Stoicism, 161–2, 183–4
Sullivan, J. P., 293
Swift, Jonathan, 251
'Baucis and Philemon', 173–4

Tacitus,
*Annals*, 158–9
Taplin, Oliver,
on Homer, 291
Tate, Nahum,
poem to Creech, 92
adaptations of Shakespeare, 41, 42
Taylor, Jeremy, 91
Terence, 33
Thomson, James,
*The Seasons*, 104–5
Tiberius, 139, 154
Tonson, Jacob, 125, 166
poem on Creech's Lucretius, 122
Tyndale, William, 307

Valla, Lorenzo,
translation of Homer, 19
Valerie, Abbé de la,
translation of Homer, 19, 21
Venuti, Lawrence,
on translation, 9–10, 31, 301, 306
Vernant, Jean-Pierre and Vidal-Naquet, Pierre,
on Greek tragic heroes, 268
Vickers, Brian,
on neoclassical criticism of Shakespeare, 38–9, 40
Virgil, 60, 112, 208, 264, 266
*Georgics*, 62, 74
*Aeneid*, 116, 219, 227, 240

Wakefield, Gilbert,
edition of Pope's Homer, 51
edition of Lucretius, 92
Waller, Edmund, 119–21
poem on Evelyn's Lucretius, 91
translation of Corneille, 118
Warton, Joseph,
*Essay on the Genius and Writings of Pope*, 163, 259–60
Watt, Ian,
*The Rise of the Novel*, 254–5

Welsted, Leonard,
translation of Longinus, 49–50
Whitmarsh, Tim,
on reception, 13
William III, King, 139–40, 142, 143, 243, 244
Williams, Bernard,
*Shame and Necessity*, 7
Wilson, John ('Christopher North'),
on Dryden's *Fables*, 164
Wittgenstein, Ludwig,
on Shakespeare, 45
Wood, Michael, 284
Wood, Robert,
*Essay on the Original Genius and Writings of Homer*, 271, 276–9, 284, 285–7
Wordsworth, William,
*Essay Supplementary to the Preface* (1815), 288
on Cowley, 59
Wyatt, Sir Thomas,
'Luck, my fair falcon', 33–6
Wycherley, William, 163

Xerxes, 136

Yeats, W. B.,
on Dryden's Lucretius, 103